THE MIEGUNYAH PRESS

The general series of the
Miegunyah Volumes
was made possible by the
Miegunyah Fund
established by bequests
under the wills of
Sir Russell and Lady Grimwade.

'Miegunyah' was the home of
Mab and Russell Grimwade
from 1911 to 1955.

FIRST
PRINCIPLES

THE MELBOURNE LAW SCHOOL 1857–2007

JOHN WAUGH

THE
MIEGUNYAH
PRESS

THE MIEGUNYAH PRESS
An imprint of Melbourne University Publishing Ltd
187 Grattan Street, Carlton, Victoria 3053, Australia
mup-info@unimelb.edu.au
www.mup.com.au

First published 2007
Text © John Waugh 2007
Design and typography © Melbourne University Publishing Ltd 2007

Edited by Averil Lewis
Text designed by Phil Campbell
Cover designed by Catherine Nolan-Biondic
Typeset in Bembo by J&M Typesetting
Printed in Australia by Griffin Press

National Library of Australia Cataloguing-in-Publication entry

Waugh, John, 1962– .
First principles : the Melbourne Law School 1857–2007.

Bibliography.
Includes index.
ISBN 9780522854480 (hbk.).

1. University of Melbourne. Law School – History.
2. University of Melbourne. Law School. 3. Law schools –
Victoria – Melbourne – History. I. Title.

340.07119451

TABLE OF CONTENTS

CURRENCY AND QUOTATIONS

Before the introduction of decimal currency in 1966, Australian currency was denominated in pounds, shillings and pennies. Twelve pennies (d) made a shilling (s), twenty shillings made a pound (£) and twenty-one shillings made a guinea. In 1966, one pound was worth two dollars.
All quotations have retained their original spelling and punctuation.

FORMER DEANS AND PROFESSORS

Tables of former deans and professors will be found with information about the Melbourne Law School's history at www.law.unimelb.edu.au.

LIST OF ILLUSTRATIONS

PREFACE

In 1937, Kenneth Bailey, dean of the Melbourne Law School and professor of public law, was off to Britain and the United States. Overseas travel in the 1930s was still slow and expensive enough for his visit to be a special event. It was funded by the Carnegie Foundation, and its purpose was not Bailey's usual research on constitutional law and international relations, but something rather different: the teaching of law.

Bailey was in the midst of a long struggle over the kind of education the university should give its law students, and it was partly to collect information for the fight that he went overseas. His antagonist was the Law Institute of Victoria, the organisation that represented the state's solicitors. It wanted practical training for its future members, and scorned the university's preference for history, Roman law and jurisprudence over useful subjects such as taxation and company law; Bailey and his colleagues wanted to teach law as a social science, and believed that the best preparation for legal practice was an understanding of fundamentals rather than technical knowledge. 'Clearly a University course in Law cannot possibly include a survey of all the branches of law which are in current professional use', Bailey wrote; 'it must concentrate its attention on the inculcation of first principles'.[1]

Writing about his trip, Bailey saw Victoria's unusual legal profession through a visitor's eyes. He remarked on the way Victorian law fused barristers and solicitors, admitting all practitioners as both, though in practice the two callings were still sharply separated. He catalogued some of the many differences between American and Australian law schools. And he noted something about the University of Melbourne's law course that few of its American counterparts shared. In Victoria, as elsewhere in Australia, law graduates faced no separate bar exam, but only practical training under articles of clerkship before they were admitted to practise. The university's exams were recognised by the rules controlling entry to the profession as a sufficient test of their legal knowledge. The Americans had a name for this freedom from a separate admission exam: they called it 'diploma privilege'.[2]

The idea of legal education as something more than technical training, and the link with entry to the profession, were defining characteristics of the Melbourne Law School from the start. The first was nothing unusual in university law schools, but its combination with the second was uncommon, later shared with other Australian law schools but not often found elsewhere. Diploma privilege brought students to the law course and guaranteed its survival; the course's symbiosis with admission to practise became even stronger when recognition turned into compulsion, and all would-be lawyers were forced to study at university, a step taken remarkably early in Victoria. It placed the law school at the centre of debates over the nature of legal education that reached their height in the fourteen-year war with the Law Institute.

This book tells the story of the law school, its students and its staff, in this distinctive setting. It is, in a sense, an authorised biography. The initiative came from the dean, Michael Crommelin, and I was a member of the law school's staff while I wrote the book. But one of the main aims of the project from the beginning was to make this history as independent as it could be, given these constraints. It was never intended to be, as many institutional histories are, a chronicle of achievement, though achievements of many kinds are to be found in it. Nor could it be a comprehensive record of people and events, over such a long period. Instead, it aims to interpret the history of the law school in its two, sometimes conflicting, roles of preparing students to be lawyers and teaching them about the law as an academic discipline.

As in any history, the book's aims have imposed some limitations. It is less biographical than Ruth Campbell's pioneering history of the law school, published in 1977. It has drawn on questionnaire responses sent by graduates of all ages, and from interviews with former staff and students, but it had space for only some of this wealth of material. The questionnaire replies were glimpses of the law school in the lives of its students, and they ranged widely, from happy tributes and reminiscences to frustrations and regrets. Some will find that their memories are not reflected here, or that people who loomed large for them are not mentioned, though I have tried to capture, in summary at least, the most common responses.

Because the book marks the 150th anniversary of the start of teaching, it covers the whole of the law school's history, up to the present day. As a result, the last chapter is even more provisional than most history. Future historians will have both a different range of sources and a different perspective from which to write about the last two decades. What stood out for me from this period was not so much the day-to-day life of the law school (increasingly complex and diverse though it was), or what it was like to be there, but its responses to the changing university and, beyond it, the system of higher education, as successive waves of reform made their influence more insistent than ever before. From a distance, they shaped the experiences of students and staff, culminating in plans for a transformation that was both a new departure and a revival of ideas with deep roots in the law school's past.

1

A SCHOOL OF LAW

1857–88

In the 1850s, when the University of Melbourne started teaching law, most lawyers in the common-law world had never been to university. In England and its colonies, and in the United States, studying contemporary law at university was the path to legal practice for only a small minority. The rules that controlled admission to the profession did not require or, in many cases, even recognise university study as part of training for legal practice. The most common form of training was apprenticeship or spending time in a practitioner's office, but even this was often not compulsory; many, probably most, received no legal education at all.

Law in one form or another had been studied at European universities for hundreds of years, and in many places on the Continent a university education in law became obligatory not only for practitioners, but also for government officials. In England, the rise of the distinctive common law, different from the Roman law that dominated other European countries, led to altogether different forms of legal education. Law had been taught in English universities, certainly, but not to most would-be lawyers; universities taught the Roman-based civil law, not the home-grown common law. The law faculty at

Oxford trained students for the few English courts that followed civil law procedure, such as the ecclesiastical courts and the courts of admiralty. It also provided general education (linking civil law with the study of philosophy), and training for the church. But by the end of the eighteenth century, even this had suffered in a general decay of teaching and examining.[1]

When William Blackstone began his famous lectures on the common law at Oxford in 1753, he was thus taking the university into a new field. But the lectures were independent of examinations and degrees; there were still no degrees or systematic exams in the common law at Oxford in 1846. Although Blackstone advocated making 'academical education', including the rudiments of the law, a prerequisite for legal practice, his lectures had more to do with a different ideal, the broad education of people who would never practise as lawyers: 'a competent knowledge of the laws of that society, in which we live, is the proper accomplishment of every gentleman and scholar; an highly useful, I had almost said essential, part of liberal and polite education'.[2]

Oxford established a school, or separate examination, in law and modern history in 1850, as part of the reform movement that was reviving the university's moribund teaching. Law, in the form of a final honour school of jurisprudence (for the degree of Bachelor of Arts), separated from modern history in 1872. Even then, students mainly studied Roman law, jurisprudence and international law, and learned only of the history of English law, not the law of their own times. In the words of the Oxford law school's historian, 'anything less like a professional law school could hardly be imagined'. The separate Bachelor of Civil Law exam had few students.[3]

At Cambridge, there were exams for the degree of Bachelor of Laws from 1816 to 1857, but their subject-matter was civil law, not the common law, and lectures were held only intermittently. Jurisprudence and history were part of a new moral sciences tripos, or exam leading to the degree of Bachelor of Arts, that was established in 1848, and a board of studies for law and an LLB (Hons) degree were established in 1854. But, as two historians of legal education have put it, 'these reforms were driven largely by internal university politics rather than by a broader vision of legal education'. The law tripos (again leading to the degree of BA) was established in 1858; it was dominated by Roman law.[4]

The teaching of English law was stronger in London, closer to the courts and the centres of the profession. Lectures in English law and jurisprudence began at the new University of London in 1828, delivered by John Austin and Andrew Amos; Austin's fame as a legal philosopher grew only after his death, and his dry and inaudible classes drove students away. Yet none of these various university courses were comprehensive or, most significantly, connected with admission to practise, except that graduates in arts or law could be admitted more quickly to the bar. A parliamentary select committee could still declare in 1846: 'no Legal Education, of a public nature, worthy of the name, is at this moment to be had', in either England or Ireland. Things were little different in Scotland, where training in the separate, Roman-based legal system was based on apprenticeship, when any training was provided at all. Scottish universities awarded no law degrees other than honorary ones down to 1862.[5]

In England, the most important steps to remedy this situation, however slowly, were taken by practising lawyers themselves. The Inns of Court, the societies of barristers and judges that came to control admission to practise in the advocates' branch of the profession, had evolved by the fifteenth century a system of legal education so extensive that they were sometimes collectively described as a university. Over time, the system fell into decline, and by the early nineteenth century, admission to practise as a barrister involved no test of legal knowledge at all, but only the minor ritual of eating a prescribed number of dinners at one of the Inns, often coupled with pupillage with one of their members. Fees and the need for testimonials, however, filtered entrants, and barristers retained a higher social status than attorneys and solicitors (once separate callings, but effectively a joint profession by 1800), who were trained through apprenticeship under articles of clerkship.[6]

The powerful law-reform movement that turned a searching gaze on the iniquities of the English legal system in the nineteenth century encouraged a revival of legal education by the profession, underpinned by the economic benefits of raising barriers to entry, and belief in the social usefulness of better-trained lawyers. In London, the solicitors' Law Society provided lectures from 1833 and cooperated with written exams from 1836. In 1846 the Inns of Court established readerships in English law and made attendance at two courses a prerequisite for admission to the bar. The Inns of Court established the Council of Legal Education in 1852 to supervise the training of barristers, and agreed that a voluntary exam would be an alternative to attendance at lectures as a prerequisite for admission.[7]

Although England was the most influential reference-point for Australian lawyers, providing features either to emulate or avoid, a significant number of early Victorian lawyers came from Ireland. Among them were William Stawell, chief justice of the Supreme Court from 1857 and founding member of the University of Melbourne's council, and Redmond Barry, Supreme Court judge and the university's first chancellor. In their home country, a movement for reform of legal education had been gathering recruits since the late 1830s. The English parliamentary select committee of 1846 originated as an inquiry into Irish legal education, its scope later broadened to include both jurisdictions, and by 1850 two professorships of law had been established in Dublin and attendance at lectures made compulsory for admission to the bar. Direct references to the Irish precedent are scarce (though it figured in the reform of law teaching at Melbourne in 1873), but Stawell and Barry were probably well aware of the reform movement there.[8]

North America was another source of ideas, although more often called on in Australian constitutional debates than in other branches of law. In Canada, university training in law was strongest in the French-based system of Quebec, where a law school had been established at McGill University in 1848. Elsewhere, apprenticeship and (in Ontario) highly developed training by the profession were the foundations of admission to practise, even after the first common-law school opened, at Dalhousie University, Nova Scotia, in 1883.[9]

The range and variety of legal education across the many jurisdictions of the United States in the nineteenth century defy easy summary, but admission standards imposed during the colonial period were commonly weakened or abandoned, and entry to practice usually depended on nothing more than personal recommendation. Among university law schools, the example of Harvard (whose LLB course began in 1817) acquired almost mesmeric force, as the teaching methods and pattern of graduate study it developed in the late nineteenth century became a model for other universities. But the universities competed with a large number of independent law schools run for profit, and only a minority of states recognised law degrees for admission to practise. The spread of university law study as a preliminary to a separate bar admission exam was a trend mainly of the twentieth century, as entrance standards rose and universities came to dominate American legal education.[10]

In Australia, legal training, such as it was, depended on apprenticeship and self-education. Until lectures began at Melbourne in 1857, there was no systematic teaching of law. In New South Wales, of which Victoria was a part until 1851, the early, fused legal profession was formally divided in 1834, after which solicitors who had not already been admitted in Britain or Ireland were admitted to practise after serving as articled clerks or clerks of court, and (from 1838) passing written exams administered by the Supreme Court's board of examiners. Admission in England or Ireland was the only route to practice for barristers until 1849. From then on, in New South Wales and later in Victoria, would-be barristers could pass local admission exams, but they had to teach themselves or find private tutors.[11]

The University of Sydney, founded in 1851, showed an early interest in teaching law. Its senate passed a by-law in 1855 stating that there would be a faculty of law in the university, and in 1858 another by-law facilitated the establishment of a board of examiners in the subject. Yet the implementation of these good intentions was long delayed, and no members were appointed to bring the faculty by-law into operation. Lecturing in law did not begin until 1859, and there was no board of examiners until the mid-1860s; the first student graduated, with an LLD, in 1866. Law lectures ceased altogether in the 1870s, and although they were revived in the 1880s it was not until 1890 that the appointment of William Pitt Cobbett as Challis professor of law, and other, part-time staff, allowed teaching to begin in a comprehensive law course.[12]

The early lectures at Sydney were conceived as part of a general education, not training for legal practice, and the early degrees earned by reading and examination were grades of distinction in legal knowledge rather than steps towards becoming a lawyer. Without would-be practitioners as prospective students, the establishment of a law school looked to the university like an unwelcome drain on its funds rather than a rich source of fees. Why this recognition was delayed so long is largely a matter of conjecture, but one important influence was scepticism, in the university and in the profession, about the very idea of academic training for lawyers. Sydney's first reader in jurisprudence, John Hargrave, himself doubted the value of academic legal education, and preferred training by the profession itself.[13]

The most important reason for the long delays and false starts in the establishment of the Sydney Law School was the relationship between the university's examinations and admission to practise. The university's great difficulty in teaching law was that until the 1890s its law examinations were not recognised by the boards that controlled admission, and the qualifications it offered were therefore of no direct assistance in becoming a barrister or solicitor (although arts graduates did not have to sit the humanities sections of the admission exams, and served a shorter term under articles to become solicitors).[14]

At the University of Melbourne, law was likewise missing from the first lecture courses when teaching began in 1855. But after the university's second year of classes, student numbers were so alarmingly low that teaching in law and medicine was proposed as a means of boosting them. Adding law to its courses had practical advantages for the new university. It could be taught more cheaply than sciences that required expensive equipment, and it could attract a useful number of students.[15] The pattern was distantly repeated in the establishment of new Australian law schools in the 1990s: law was cheap to offer, it was prestigious, and plenty of students were willing to pay to study it.

The study of law for its own sake was all very well, but to attract significant numbers of students the university needed to offer a course that, unlike those at English universities, counted towards admission to practise. The judges of the Supreme Court made the admission rules, so by happy accident Redmond Barry was in the right place to further the interests of the university, though institutional favouritism was far from the judges' only motivation in adapting the rules to suit the law course. University training also served the profession's own purposes, by taking up the recommendations for systematic legal education circulating in Britain and responding to concerns about the poor quality of Melbourne's gold-era lawyers. The new admission rules were in place before the start of first term, 1857, and exempted successful students at the university from the Supreme Court's law exams. They created a fundamental difference in law teaching between the universities of Melbourne and Sydney that lasted until the 1890s.[16]

In Victoria, then, would-be lawyers had a choice between tackling the court's exams without any guidance, and doing the university's law course. With this assistance, Barry's strategy to lift numbers worked like a charm: the thirty-three law students of 1857 more than doubled the university's enrolments, helping to take the total to fifty-four from only fifteen the year before. Law continued to make up more than half the university's enrolments into the 1860s, when other courses (notably medicine, from 1862) expanded their share.[17]

Initially, as a way of maximising enrolments, the university offered only a certificate that would satisfy the court's requirements, rather than a longer degree course; the university's engineering school followed the same pattern, although in its case the university's act of parliament withheld the power to grant degrees. Staffing in Law was accordingly modest. A single 'Reader or Lecturer'—the council was initially unable to make up its mind about the title—would teach the whole course, but would be paid enough to make the part-time position an attractive one: £100 for each of the three terms, with the right to receive the fees of the non-matriculated students, who made up most of the class, as an extra incentive. They paid £4 for each term, twice the fee of the students who had passed the university's matriculation exam, which went to the university rather than the lecturer. By 1860, the students' fees more than doubled the official salary.[18]

The council appointed the law teachers, after the first, as readers; Barry liked the grander title, which had been used at the Inns of Court in London, and the incumbents (there were now two) agreed when he asked them in 1870. The university's calendar, however, ignored their preference, continuing to list the law staff as lecturers, like their counterparts elsewhere in the university. When the course was reorganised and new teachers appointed in 1873, the title of reader disappeared, until its revival by the university in 1954.[19]

⇒•⇐

For its first lecturer in law, the university chose a learned, versatile, well-qualified and, it soon emerged, altogether unsuitable candidate. Richard Clarke Sewell was an Englishman, one of twelve children of a solicitor and local worthy from the Isle of Wight. The family were high achievers, and no fewer than five of them appear in the *Oxford Dictionary of National Biography*. Richard's sister Elizabeth was a novelist, brother James was the long-serving head of New College, Oxford, Henry became the first prime minister of New Zealand (although his time in office was even shorter than Richard's brief period as a law lecturer), and William's fissiparous creativity fuelled a prominent, if somewhat erratic, career as university teacher, college administrator, religious polemicist and Anglican clergyman.

Richard shared the energy and drive of his notable siblings, and the family was affluent enough to put him on the track to a university education. From public school (Winchester), he went to Oxford, where he became a fellow of Magdalen College and ultimately graduated with a doctorate in civil law (though this was merely a formality at the time). His earliest publication was the poem with which he won the Newdigate prize in 1825. Like others, he combined his Oxford fellowship with outside work, and he became a barrister. Through the 1830s and 1840s, he published a string of books and shorter monographs on a remarkable range of topics, including common law procedure, local government law, ecclesiastical courts, electoral law and university politics. History was among his varied interests, and he edited a collection of documents of the reign of the medieval English king Stephen.

The book for which he was best known in Australia was a treatise on the law of coroners, published in London in 1843. How Sewell became interested in this branch of the law is now unknown, but the work was much more than a legal text. To provide a comprehensive manual for coroners, he not only wrote about questions of jurisdiction, procedure and criminal law, but delved into forensic pathology, outlining the indications of the causes of death in cases of hanging, strangling, smothering, drowning, starving, burning, poisoning and even spontaneous human combustion. These he gathered from books on medical jurisprudence, and from two friends who were prison surgeons.

Why this able and well-established academic lawyer came to Victoria in his fifties, in 1855, is hard to gauge. His decision was probably influenced, as his biographer guesses, by the protracted financial troubles that engulfed the family after his father died heavily in debt, but thirteen years elapsed between his father's death and his departure for Melbourne. None of his Australian obituarists mentioned a reason for his emigration; maybe the attraction of Victoria's gold-rush prosperity was taken for granted. Whatever the circumstances, once in Melbourne he was promptly admitted to the bar, on the strength of his admission in London, and he quickly developed a prominent practice in criminal law.

Sewell defended in some cases, but prosecuted in two that attracted enormous attention in 1856–57: the trial of the bushranger 'Captain' Melville and eight other convicts for the murder of a warder, and that of some of the convicts who killed John Price, the inspector-general of penal establishments. He drew on all the resources of Victorian pathos when addressing the jury in the case of one defendant who faced the death penalty:

> To die—Do you know what death is? … Pass in imagination from the Court to the Condemned Cell: Picture the last few hours of life … Fancy him taken thence into the horrid chamber of Death—with all its ghastly details—then comes the last pang of mortal anguish—the last struggle of expiring life—and the soul of a sinner stands naked and trembling before his God. That is the fate, Gentlemen, which hangs on your lips …[20]

In a less histrionic vein, he used his knowledge of electoral law in an appearance before the Legislative Assembly's elections and qualifications committee, after the 1856 elections.[21] Publishing continued to attract him, and he edited Victoria's first, short-lived legal journal, the *Victoria Law Times*, which reported Supreme Court decisions before the advent of official law reports. In his editorials, Sewell argued for higher professional morality (enforced by a professional association, an inn of court along English lines), and against amalgamation of the two branches of the profession. The burden of editing the weekly publication must have been heavy, and Sewell lasted only three months; three other editors followed in succession before the journal folded, after surviving for less than a year.

Such an applicant, with his Oxford doctorate and fellowship, his extensive record of publications and his rapidly acquired prominence at the Melbourne bar, would have been hard to pass over when the university advertised for a lecturer in law, and Sewell was a natural choice. The other applicants included his fellow barrister, James Wilberforce Stephen, MA of Cambridge and fellow of St John's

College. Sewell used his Oxford degree to get an automatic, *ad eundem* doctorate in laws from the University of Melbourne, the first law degree awarded by the university.

Sewell made a good start, delivering an accomplished inaugural lecture that placed his intentions for the course firmly in the tradition of gentlemanly legal education. Blackstone was evidently his hero: the lecture echoed Blackstone's 'Discourse on the Study of the Law' in outlining the value of the study of law for varied groups of people, it cited his *Commentaries on the Laws of England* throughout, and Sewell announced that he would use them as his textbook. The value of legal study for practitioners was, naturally enough, one of the purposes he highlighted. He described the narrow-minded, avaricious, dishonest lawyers of fiction and real life; the law school's founders, he said, aimed 'to rescue the profession from obloquy such as this, to save it from bitter contumely and scorn'.[22]

This, however, was not the only, or even the first, purpose of legal education as Sewell saw it. It was just as beneficial to non-lawyers, to jury-members and magistrates (most of whom had no legal training), to coroners and clergymen, to people in business, to land owners, and to just about anyone. A high moral purpose was explicit in all this. Sewell paid fulsome tribute to the recently retired chief justice of the Supreme Court, Sir William à Beckett, who warned against the moral dangers of social dislocation in the gold rush, and whose Tory Anglicanism chimed with Sewell's. 'None but rash and unthinking visionaries or selfish and unprincipled egotists are the advocates of a wide-sweeping destruction of time-honoured ordinances and customs', Sewell wrote in defence of the segregated profession in the *Victoria Law Times*, although in other issues he argued for reforms in procedure and practice.[23]

There were some discordant notes in his otherwise impressive debut at the university. The value of law for a broad education was all very well, but the Melbourne course was, in its conception and through its vital link with the rules for admission to practise, essentially one for would-be lawyers rather than a means to furnish the minds of the gentlemen of Victoria, as Sewell seemed to hope. He began with modest acknowledgements of his weighty task and the importance of his responsibility, but took this rhetorical device so far, with such self-deprecation and doubt, that his audience must have wondered whether he was equal to the job.

> And then arises a natural anxiety on my own part, lest I should have rashly taken upon myself a burden which I am unable worthily to bear,—to my own bitter humiliation; to the equally bitter disappointment of those to whose kindness, and, I fear, too favourable an estimate of my qualifications, I owe the distinguished honour of addressing this audience as Reader in Law to the University of Melbourne ... And thus, amidst hopes and fears, while I stand, as it were, at the vestibule of the Temple of Justice, my faltering step seems to refuse to enter the hallowed precincts. And yet an attempt must be made. To recede would be even more disgraceful than to fail. Success no man can command—to shrink from duty serves only to stamp him as a coward.[24]

Despite his learning, there was something inept about Sewell. As a fellow of Magdalen, he played a part in the highly charged college politics of the 1840s, in which adversaries took sides according to their positions in the theological controversies swirling around John Henry Newman and the high-church Oxford Movement, which was dividing the Church of England. A candidate Sewell opposed (a supposed sympathiser of Newman) came up for election to a fellowship. The anti-Newman forces had the numbers and were about to win, when one of the other fellows was so disgusted by something Sewell said that he switched his vote at the last minute, defeating Sewell's candidate and handing the fellowship to his opponents.[25]

In court, too, Sewell seemed sometimes to make his own bad luck. In one of the sensational trials in which he appeared, the Stephen (Exhibition) Street brothel murder, a prosecution witness gave evidence that the defendants were at the scene of the crime, and described their clothes, including patent-leather boots. Sewell, appearing for one of the defendants, repeatedly ridiculed the idea that they had ever worn such boots in their lives, when a voice from the gallery called out, 'One of them has a pair on now!' The defendants were convicted.[26]

As reader in law, Sewell was unable to fulfil the promise of his inaugural lecture. His second lecture, on 'the nature of laws in general', also survives, but it was a very different production from his first, with none of its polish and oratorical flourishes. An introduction to the branches of the law, forms of government, and statutory interpretation, it was blandly expository, and reads now like a miscellany of information Sewell believed the students should know, but had no gift for explaining.[27]

It was not so much the quality of his lectures that put an end to Sewell's teaching career, as his difficulty in getting to the university to deliver them. Like many of the barrister–lecturers who followed him, he sometimes found his commitments in court made it impossible for him to get to class, and his poor health kept him away at other times. How many lectures he cancelled was itself a point of contention between Sewell and his students, but they were frequent enough for the council to ask him about them within a couple of months of the start of the course. His explanation was judged satisfactory for the time being, but the controversy went on. Nor were his absences the only problem. 'I might here object to several of his lectures', one student wrote to the *Herald*, complaining about the cancellations, 'but I would rather drop the subject'.[28]

Sewell was defensive, and angry that the students took their complaint to the *Herald* rather than to him, but their discontent led to a public meeting and a petition to the council: 'the continuity of your memorialists' studies has been destroyed and their task rendered irksome and dispiriting beyond measure', they wrote. As corroboration, they pointed to a sharp drop in attendance. The university's plentiful new source of enrolments threatened to dry up almost as soon as it had begun, but Sewell resigned. His stated reason, ill-health, sounded like a pretext, given the demands of his practice and the protests of the students, but it was probably at least part of the truth. He continued in practice at the bar, but was said to have been in failing health for a considerable time when he died in 1864.[29]

The outline of the new course was not settled until after Sewell was appointed, and he may have had some of the responsibility for its design, although Barry, looming large as the prime mover of the plan to teach law, must also have been involved. The course was divided, not into subjects, but into terms and years, and began with an encyclopaedic introduction. In their first term alone, the students were to cover: the study of law; the nature of laws in general; written law and rules for interpretation; the laws of England; constitutional law; private rights; rights and duties of husband and wife; parent and child; guardian and ward; master and servant; and corporations. The main texts were volumes one and three of Blackstone's *Commentaries*. Volumes of Blackstone were prescribed for four of the six terms of the course.[30]

In second term, the students dashed onwards to real property (not yet including the Torrens system, still to be adopted in Victoria). Third term's lectures covered personal property and the law of wills (Chitty on contract was prescribed), and the first term of the second year turned to common law pleading, evidence and practice. Criminal law pleading, evidence and practice occupied second term, while third term covered equity pleading, evidence and practice, and the ecclesiastical and insolvency practice of the Supreme Court.

The course was heavily weighted towards pleading, evidence and practice, which took up nearly half the lectures. The doctrinal subjects that became the core of the course from 1873—tort, property, contract and so on—were confined to the first year (with the exception of criminal law). The orientation towards practice, and particularly practice in the higher courts, reflected the purposes and market for the course, but it also showed the prominence of procedural law before the abolition of the forms of action strengthened the distinction between it and substantive law.

For all this, the approach of Sewell and his successors was not purely vocational. 'The object of these lectures', the second reader, Henry Chapman, announced to his class in 1861, 'is to induce students to adopt such a course of study as will *elevate their views* above the mere practice of the law as a trade. Hence they are invited without neglect of practice to make themselves familiar with the principles of the law and also with its historical development.' But Chapman tempered this ideal with awareness of who was actually turning up to his classes. 'I presume that by far the greater number of those who attend the law lectures do so with the intention of adopting the law as their profession', he told his students, 'but I am not without a hope that some will so attend as a necessary part of the education of a gentleman'. The largely technical course would have meant most to future practitioners. Chapman intended to give 'much more ample development to the used than to the unused parts of law, so as to render these lectures a practical introduction to the business that comes most frequently before our courts'.[31]

The Supreme Court's new admission rules of 1857 looked ahead by covering both graduates who took a bachelor's degree in law, and students who attended lectures and passed the university's law exams without taking a degree. They also applied to both barristers and solicitors. Three years after the law classes began, the university fulfilled the expectation in the rules and created an LLB course, whose first graduates received their degrees in 1865. The sparse records of this important change provide few clues to its genesis or motivation. The university's basic mode of teaching was lecturing and examining for the award of degrees, so it probably appeared a natural extension of the plan for the certificate course. It also added a more academic strain to the law course, one that probably fitted the professors' ideas of the university better than the purely professional training course so far offered in law. Sending the proposed LLB regulation to the council, the chairman of the professorial board declared that 'a University Degree should mark somewhat more than a technical education', and the board ensured that LLB students would do two years of compulsory and optional arts subjects before turning to the study of legal doctrine in their final two years.[32]

To suit the requirements of the degree course, the teaching was rearranged and divided for the first time into four distinct subjects, although they still merged such a wide range of topics that they were called simply Law, parts I to IV. The shape of the original course could be detected in the outline of the new subjects. Part I, like the old first-year lectures, covered the 'Rights of Persons' and personal property, but added contracts and torts under their own names for the first time. Real property also remained in the first year of law lectures, in part II, along with wills, conveyancing and intestacy, while practice and pro-cedure again dominated the final-year classes. Part III covered pleading, evidence, procedure, 'Crown law' (that is, civil proceedings involving the Crown) and criminal proceedings; part IV was a jurisdictional miscellany consisting of equity, insolvency, admiralty, and courts of inferior jurisdiction.

To honour the professors' intentions for something more than a merely technical education, LLB students also had to pass Greek, Latin, the two parts of the combined subject English and Logic, Ancient History, and Constitutional History parts I and II, along with seven other arts subjects that they could choose for themselves. This covered so much of the BA course that when, in 1882, a BA became a precon-dition for entry to the LLB course, the faculty and the university's governing bodies adopted the new regulation with little or no debate. So untroubled were they that they left no record of their reasons for taking such a seemingly momentous step. Probably the new regulation was prompted by changes in the BA course that were made at around the same time, and lower enrolments for the degree (as against the certificate) limited the numbers likely to object. LLB students now faced an extra year of study, spending three years on the BA before covering their law subjects in two years.[33]

The rules governing admission to practise shaped the law course and the choices of the students who undertook it. They also controlled the openness, or otherwise, of the profession, and the relationship between barristers and solicitors. The Supreme Court's first rules concerning admission to practise, made in 1852, preserved the division of the profession already established by the Supreme Court of New South Wales before the separation of Victoria. The 1852 rules created a separate board of examiners for each of the two branches, its membership reflecting the professional hierarchy. The judges were members of both boards. Barristers had the privilege of electing two representatives for theirs, and the attorney-general's notional status as the leader of the bar, though generally little more than a nod to English tradition in Victoria, earned him a place. Solicitors (or attorneys, as the rules generally called them) had representatives chosen for them by the judges. Barry liked to think that the advocates' board was something like the self-regulating benchers of the Inns of Court in London, likewise made up of senior judges and barristers.[34]

The boards themselves examined candidates for admission; in the absence of a university or professional organisations (the university did not begin teaching until 1855, and even then not in law), there was no one else. For the rest of the nineteenth century, the judges treated their responsibility for admission to practise as including examination as well as prescription of standards, at least for solicitors.

The judges designed an examination that cast prospective barristers as gentlemen with a broad education, much as the university's LLB course later did. Their five prescribed law subjects (real property; common law pleading and practice; equity and insolvency; criminal law; and evidence and contracts) were matched by five others: Greek and Latin; mathematics and algebra; ancient history; English history; and 'universal history'. Solicitors, on the other hand, had no need for these refinements, and the judges demanded only that they sit three examinations, in real property, the practice of the Supreme Court, and criminal law. Barristers paid thirty guineas into the court's library fund as their admission fee (unless they had previously been admitted elsewhere), while a slightly less genteel twenty-five guineas were demanded from solicitors. The first barrister to be admitted after passing the local exams was a law reporter for the *Argus*, John Morris Travers McDonogh, in 1853.[35]

The distinction between barristers and solicitors, and the barriers to admission to the bar, were strengthened when the admission rules changed in 1853. The judges did not explain their reasons, but the upheavals of the gold rush provide clues. 'A great wave of barristers set out from England and Ireland', in the words of the bar's historian, Arthur Dean, and admissions of new immigrants to the bar rose from two in 1851 to twenty-three in 1853 (from a starting-point of six or seven barristers in practice in 1851).[36] Among the more conservative lawyers, such as Sewell and Fellows, the influx later caused concern about the maintenance of ethical standards; anxiety about competition was not explicit, but its existence is a safe guess. Such thinking about the preservation of the best traditions of the bar probably lay behind the tighter admission rules of 1853, and if they had the effect of protecting existing practitioners as well, that would not have been an argument against them in the eyes of the judges. The population had been increasing so rapidly, and the threats to the social order were so patent to old colonists such as Stawell's predecessor as chief justice, Sir William à Beckett, that legal standards must have seemed to need defending against erosion by a long tail of less able barristers who lacked the skill and professional acculturation of their better-known colleagues (the early lecturers among them).

The new admission rules of 1853 were strikingly protective of the existing bar. Aspiring barristers who had not been admitted elsewhere had to live in Victoria for three years without engaging in a trade or business. How such people were to survive for three years when most sources of income were closed to them was not the concern of the judges. The rule had an English precedent, on which Barry later relied, but in Victoria it was both rigid and strictly applied, and it became a serious obstacle.[37]

In practice, teaching, journalism and (initially) the civil service were not regarded as coming within the description of 'trade or business', leaving these opportunities for would-be barristers to support themselves until they were admitted. In 1864, however, the Supreme Court decided that work in the civil service was a trade or business under the rules, although being a member of parliament outside business hours (parliament did not sit during the day) was all right, and school teaching kept its unbusinesslike status. Barristers already admitted in Great Britain or Ireland who sought to practise in Victoria faced the lesser barrier of satisfying the examiners about the appropriateness of their employment since ceasing to practise in Britain, and providing references from 'two or more respectable housekeepers' for good measure, as evidence of their good character.[38]

The judges guarded the professional standards of solicitors less jealously. They demanded residence in Victoria for only one year, although the period that future solicitors had to serve under articles, locally or in Britain, remained five years. Admission fees also protected the bar's numbers, if not its standards; in the 1853 rules, partly reflecting the inflation of prices during the gold rush, they rose to fifty guineas for barristers not previously admitted elsewhere, and forty guineas for solicitors.

The new rules treated local applicants for the bar particularly harshly; fees for admission of practitioners who had already been admitted elsewhere were much lower (ten guineas for barristers, and five for solicitors). The cost, time and trouble of travelling to Australia were themselves a barrier to entry by British lawyers, and the judges were content to rely on admission requirements in the United Kingdom without putting migrants through the indignity of exams in Victoria.

The bar's exclusivity roused opponents in parliament. Wilson Gray, barrister and president of the quasi-parliamentary Land Convention that propelled free selection of Crown land for small farms to the top of the Victorian political agenda in the late 1850s, proposed legislation to abolish the three-year rule on trade or business, and to allow solicitors to apply for admission as barristers. The admission rules offended the sense of freedom of opportunity that found expression in his land policy. He even linked the question explicitly with the democratisation of the parliament, which had abolished property requirements for voting and for membership: under the three-year rule, he maintained, 'a property qualification might as well be required from every aspirant to the bar', such was the advantage it gave to those with private means.[39]

Prominent barristers in parliament were unperturbed. The existing rules preserved the dignity and honour of practitioners, and the well-being of the community, said Butler Cole Aspinall. The bill was offered 'as a sop to democracy', said Richard Ireland; it was American, and had had bad effects in the United States; it would allow the admission of 'sweeps and shoe-blacks' as barristers. But Gray's opponents found their safest and ultimately most successful argument in a procedural point. Parliament had given the power to make the admission rules to the judges, and parliament should not interfere with the rules without checking with the judges first. Until the judges were consulted, the bill should not be passed. The reformers had the numbers in the lower house, but in the Legislative Council, barrister Thomas Fellows had the bill sent off to languish in a select committee, so that the judges could be consulted. The committee never reported, and the bill died at the end of the session.[40]

The judges themselves abandoned the three-year rule in 1865.[41] Once it had gone, it was easier to become a barrister than a solicitor. Only intending solicitors had to spend time working as articled clerks before admission; not only was their work usually unpaid, but they generally had to pay their principals a substantial fee, or premium, in order to be taken on as clerks. Someone intending to become a barrister, on the other hand, could hold a paying job while studying, although not as a solicitor or law clerk.

As a royal commission on law reform pointed out in 1899, after the system had changed, the old rules allowed the admission of some of Melbourne's ablest lawyers, 'who were able by their own exertions to defray the expense of their University course, but who would have been quite unable to pay a large sum for their articles, and spend three years in a lawyer's office without pay, and without liberty to engage in other occupations'. Henry Higgins, who chaired the royal commission, had good reason to know the truth of this: he became a barrister by working his way through university in the 1870s as a teacher and private tutor. Other law students who supported themselves by working as teachers or in government jobs before going to the bar included Alfred Deakin, Edward Carlile (later Victorian parliamentary draftsman), and future judges George Webb, William Irvine, Isaac Isaacs and Frank Gavan Duffy. The *Summons* corroborated the truth of the commission's summary. In parliament, businessman Donald Melville complained that the payment of large premiums for articles might even be called blackmail.[42]

The higher barriers to entry for barristers had implications for the debate about amalgamation of the two branches of the profession that grew in the 1860s and 1870s. Many solicitors opposed fusion or practice across the division between the branches, fearing competition from junior barristers if advocates could deal directly with clients. It was the poaching of solicitors' work by barristers, rather than court advocacy by solicitors, that many foresaw as the most significant outcome of amalgamation.

When an amalgamation act was finally passed in 1891, the solicitors' Law Institute formally resolved to give the new law a fair trial, but leading solicitors accepted a boycott imposed by senior barristers, effectively joining forces against the less successful barristers who had less to lose from the end of the monopoly on advocacy in the Supreme Court and more to gain from working directly with clients. The Bar Association froze out 'amalgams' who combined both kinds of practice, and reduced most of the intended results of amalgamation to nothing.[43]

There were limits to the accessibility of the bar. From 1865, barristers, like solicitors, had to matriculate, a requirement that excluded the bulk of students, who never reached secondary school. Prospects for a career as a barrister depended on more than just hard work, and the club-like atmosphere of the bar in colonial Melbourne made the task of working-class aspirants doubly difficult. One of the few who succeeded was John Mackey, who was said to have taught himself to read and write, and supported himself through university in the 1880s with work in the public service and as a private tutor. Even he, though, made his career more as a member of parliament, government minister and lecturer (he lectured in equity for more than twenty years) than as a barrister. As an MP, he introduced the bill that enabled women to be admitted to practise as lawyers in Victoria.[44]

In 1863, there were just over 300 solicitors in practice in Victoria, most of them (about 58 per cent) in Melbourne. Forty-five barristers listed themselves in the comprehensive local directory, a fair indication of the number in private practice in the city. By 1891, the number of solicitors had risen to something over 450, now (like the general population) more concentrated in Melbourne, which accounted for two-thirds. The directory listed 113 Melbourne barristers.[45]

The rate of growth seems to have been much faster for barristers than solicitors, although the figures are so approximate that calculations are only rough guesses. If true, the pattern would bear out the royal commission's story of easier access to the bar. A more definite trend is that the profession was growing more slowly than the population, which doubled between 1861 and 1891. The growth of any profession is hastened or slowed by many things, but one obvious suspect is the admission rules: the educational requirements may have been making legal practice more difficult to enter.

※

As the debate about barriers to entry continued, a parallel process changed the requirements for admission to practise. It gave the university an even more privileged place in legal education, and accentuated the differences between Victoria, the rest of Australia and most common-law jurisdictions overseas. The judges' first rules recognising the law course (Barry's probable favour to the struggling university in

1857) gave the students who completed it full exemption from further examination in law subjects, whichever branch of the profession they intended to enter. This largesse was short-lived, at least for would-be solicitors. Soon the judges reasserted their right to re-examine the products of the law school, but at the same time they took a significant step, and for the first time in Australia made an instalment of university study compulsory for admission to this branch of the profession. From 1863, would-be solicitors had to matriculate and pass two exams from the first two years of the LLB course, before tackling the court's own exam.[46]

For aspiring barristers, university study was initially merely an alternative, albeit an attractive one, to self-teaching and examination under the admission rules. From 1865, it shortened the period they had to serve as students-at-law, during which they were notionally enrolled at the Supreme Court and, more importantly, unable to work as solicitors, law clerks or clerks of court. The full LLB course reduced the studentship to one year; arts graduates and students who passed four law exams from the LLB course (omitting the arts component of the degree course) did two years; others did four years, and then sat the court's exam.[47]

Then in 1872 the judges extended their unusually early enthusiasm for university training, taking it a step further for barristers than for solicitors by requiring all students heading for admission to the bar, and not already admitted elsewhere, to graduate with a full bachelor's degree in law from the University of Melbourne, or some other university recognised by it. At the same time, they allowed graduates in law or arts to serve a shorter period under articles—three years instead of the usual five—before becoming solicitors. Alfred Deakin, the future prime minister, was one of the last to enrol as a student-at-law before the new rules came into force, and thus one of the last to be admitted as a barrister without an LLB. He was only sixteen when he gave the necessary notice to commence his studentship in 1872; he completed the law subjects at the university, but not the full degree course.[48]

With these changes, the court made at least some university study compulsory for all locally trained candidates for admission as barristers or solicitors, and abandoned its role as an examining body for barristers, handing responsibility for their assessment entirely to the university. The step was so unusual for the time that it requires some explanation. In New South Wales, university study was not compulsory for admission until 1966, and even then only in the sense that the University of Sydney hosted teaching (by a separate lecturing staff) for the admission board examinations that were an alternative to obtaining a university degree. As late as 1927, not a single state of the United States required attendance at law school as a prerequisite for admission to practise. In England and Wales, the professional organisations of barristers and solicitors dominated legal training. Even in 2007, while a university degree (not necessarily a law degree) was required for most would-be solicitors in England, their compulsory academic legal training could be obtained at a range of institutions, including universities and the College of Law originally established by the solicitors' Law Society (though now independent).[49]

It would be easy to guess that Barry's solicitude for the university to which he devoted such energy was a reason for the court's indirect support of the law course, which gained students from the court's insistence that study there would be, not merely a helpful option, but compulsory. The university also had a friend in Sir William Stawell, the chief justice, who was involved, like Barry, in the gestation of the plan to expand the teaching staff and establish the law faculty, implemented just six months after the judges made their new rules. Personal links were crucial when a similar step was taken in South Australia a decade later. The country's third university, Adelaide, refused to open a law school unless enrolments were guaranteed by making university study a condition of admission to practise. Its vice-chancellor was in the right place to change the admission rules: he was the chief justice. The new law school opened in 1883, and all aspiring lawyers had to attend its classes.[50]

Yet a favour for the university and its planned law faculty is unlikely to have been the whole story, in Melbourne or Adelaide. In England, advocates of reform in legal education had been arguing for compulsory study before admission for more than twenty years, and it was in 1872 that passing an exam became a prerequisite for admission to the bar in London. The teaching that prepared candidates for this exam was provided by the Inns of Court, not by a university, just as the solicitors' Law Society had run lectures and compulsory exams for articled clerks since the 1830s.[51] Nevertheless, the trend was unmistakeably towards increasing requirements for study and examination. To the extent that the Victorian judges caught this trend, the teaching needed to implement it could be provided, not by the small local profession, but only by the university. A spirit of reform to provide better training, the local conditions that made the university the only viable law teaching institution, and the personal connections of two of the judges combined to produce the happy side-effect, for the university, of guaranteeing the enrolments of its law school.

The lecture notes of Henry Chapman, the second reader, give the first detailed impressions of what the early lectures were like, what they covered and how a teacher approached them. The appointment of Chapman was Barry's initiative, to fill the gap left by Sewell's resignation part-way through the year. He was another barrister, but different from Sewell in background and temperament, and better suited to his task. He did not have his predecessor's deep scholarship, but he was more gregarious and widely connected, working not only in the law but in journalism, politics and business. His international, or intercolonial, career traversed widely scattered parts of the British Empire, along networks linking business, lobbying and appointments in the British colonial service.[52]

Born in England, Chapman spent eleven years as a merchant in Canada, where he became increasingly involved in liberal–radical politics, established a newspaper, and studied law, in the civil law system of Quebec. He returned to London as an agent and lobbyist for the liberal members of the legislature of Lower Canada. The establishment of self-government there in the 1840s, which Chapman advocated, was repeated in the eastern colonies of Australia in the 1850s. He drew on his experience of the system in a monograph on responsible government in 1854.

The roots of his teaching lay not in academic research, as Sewell's had, but in wide experience and in fluent and knowledgeable journalism. He published extensively on politics and economics as a journalist and pamphlet-writer in the 1830s, and was called to the bar in London in 1840. Plans for the colonisation of New Zealand became a special interest of his, promoted in a new journal he established. This connection led to his appointment as a judge of the Supreme Court in Wellington in 1843, from where he moved to another colonial appointment, as colonial secretary of Van Diemen's Land, in 1852. After his dismissal for opposing convict transportation, he established himself as a barrister in Melbourne.

He seemed to have a finger in every pie. He was soon elected to the Legislative Council, where he did the drafting and provided much of the debating muscle for the introduction of the secret ballot. He was the intermediary for the formation of a new government in 1858, and could have become premier himself, but chose instead to be attorney-general for a second time. His electoral support was chancy, and his broken parliamentary career included several defeats at the polls, where he was supported by 'the advocates of a liberal and progressive system of government'.[53]

His work as a barrister continued (he was prosecuting when Sewell so embarrassingly failed to notice the defendant's patent-leather boots) and was involved in a range of local businesses, from banking to coal-mining. His appointment as attorney-general forced his resignation as reader in law in 1858, but he returned two years later, only to resign again to become an acting judge in 1862. His third, brief period as reader, from October 1863 to March 1864, ended when he returned to New Zealand, where he served as a judge of the Supreme Court.

Chapman's surviving notes date from 1860 onwards, and cover many topics of the first year of the course, including contracts, personal property, the court system and an introduction to constitutional law. His lecture notes on contract had nothing to say about the general principles of formation and content that loomed large for later teachers, but centred on particular kinds of contracts and the varied grounds of incapacity and illegality. His coverage of personal property was likewise taxonomic rather than analytic, cataloguing forms of property and ways of acquiring title.

He came into his own when introducing the students to constitutional law, a topic closer to his own interests and experience. His outline of the constitution of England—'the country of our birth', as he described it to his students—was set in the context of a wider view of constitutional principles. It included an extended discussion of the constitutional law of the United States, including its state constitutions. Chapman was lecturing on the American constitution on 12 April 1861, the day fighting began in the American civil war (but long before that news would reach Melbourne). Commenting on the rhetoric of freedom and equality in the Declaration of Independence, he told his students that between 150 000 and 200 000 Americans were born slaves every year.

His New Zealand background, too, emerged in his lectures. It made him alert to questions of sovereignty in the acquisition of colonies that most Australian lawyers of the period ignored or took for granted. He delivered a lecture to his Melbourne students on the 'Status of Native races considered in relation to the Sovereignty', in which he affirmed that discovery and occupation (rather than the Treaty of Waitangi) were the basis of British sovereignty over New Zealand, and maintained that Indigenous laws and customs inconsistent with Christian morality were void. He nevertheless argued, as some judges of Australian courts had argued in the 1830s and early 1840s, that Indigenous people retained a limited sovereignty among themselves, until they relinquished it by treaty.[54]

Chapman's second-term exam in 1861 asked students to explain the foundation of the Queen's title-paramount to the territory of New South Wales and Victoria, and (perhaps prompted by John Batman's attempted purchase of land around Port Phillip from the

Wurundjeri, the original inhabitants of the area, in 1835) questioned them about the effect of a purchase of land from Aboriginal tribes. Such issues did not re-emerge in the Property course (at least with such prominence) until the 1970s, after the first extended analysis of Aboriginal land rights in an Australian court, in *Milirrpum v. Nabalco Pty Ltd*.[55]

<hr/>

Chapman was less equipped for the practice and procedure taught in the second year than for the substantive topics of the first, and he must have found the demands of the encyclopaedic certificate course more than any one person could handle. At the end of 1857, on Barry's initiative, the council agreed to the appointment of a second reader, to take charge of the second year of the course.[56] The job went to Richard Billing, in whom the university found, at last, a law teacher who could stay for longer than a few years. He remained on the staff until 1882, when he was appointed as a County Court judge, only to die soon afterwards.

Like all the early lecturers, Billing was a barrister, but his education had been in Ireland, where he studied law and was called to the bar after emigrating from Scotland. He came to Victoria in his early forties, ostensibly for the sake of his health, and perhaps, like most of the Irish barristers who began practice in Melbourne in 1856–57 (six in all), also to take advantage of better opportunities in the growing colony. The number of Melbourne barristers with a record of publications as well as practice was small indeed, and Billing was not one of them. Bar tradition remembered him as 'an able all-round lawyer', 'able without being brilliant', with a taste for the good life, for literature and music; he was a member of the Melbourne Club, and built the mansion later known as Labassa, now owned by the National Trust. He was generous to his students, presenting a gold medal to the best of them each year until the reorganisation of the course in 1873. They reciprocated his goodwill. The silver-mounted emu eggshell cup was a popular showpiece for silversmiths in the second half of the nineteenth century, and Australia's earliest surviving example was given to Billing by his students in 1859.[57]

Chapman's place as first-year lecturer was taken in 1858 by James Wilberforce Stephen, whose extended family included Sir James Stephen, powerful permanent under-secretary of the Colonial Office from 1836 to 1847, Sir Alfred Stephen, chief justice of New South Wales, and a string of other judges and lawyers. James Wilberforce, a graduate in arts from Cambridge and a former fellow of St John's College, continued the Oxbridge connection established with Sewell. He had come to Victoria with his parents and wife after a few years' practice as a barrister in London, and became the acknowledged leader of the equity bar. His time as a lecturer, however, was brief, and ill-health caused his resignation in February 1860. Chapman, out of office as attorney-general, took over from him, but not before the students protested to Barry at finding themselves without a lecturer at the start of term.[58]

When the demands of higher office again took Chapman away in 1862, the council chose, for the first time, one of the law school's former students as a lecturer. An emigrant from England for the sake of his health, George Webb studied law while working as the government shorthand writer, winning the exhibition offered by the chancellor to the best student in the first-year law exams, and completing the certificate course with the second group of students to do so. He became one of the first barristers to have been trained through the university law course, admitted in 1860. Ostensibly because of Webb's lack of experience in practice, Chief Justice Stawell and other members called a council meeting to rescind his appointment to the vacant readership, upon which he resigned, saying that he would not have 'the moral support or the sympathy of the Council as a whole'.[59]

Webb certainly lacked legal experience, but criticism of his appointment also had a political angle. The *Argus* alleged it was a piece of patronage, and part of a complicated scheme said to include Chapman's appointment as temporary judge. Which council members were supposed to have been part of this plot was left unsaid (Webb's appointment had been proposed by Alexander Morison and Godfrey Howitt, neither of them politicians), and the *Argus* seemed to assume that the university was just another branch of the civil service, where selection on personal and political grounds was commonplace. At least one element of the conspiracy theory was wrong: Webb was not going to keep his government job, as the newspaper had alleged. His resignation had been a condition of his university appointment. He failed in another application for the readership in 1864, but later became a QC and Victoria's first locally trained Supreme Court judge.[60]

Webb's resignation left the way clear for the appointment of John Atkins, an Irish barrister like Billing, briefly editor of the *Victoria Law Times* in 1856, and Barry's choice for the position. Atkins, though, was forced to resign when another man's wife sued him for maintenance of her child, claiming he was the father. Publicly acknowledged adultery (Atkins admitted the relationship, while denying paternity) was too much for the council in 1863, although what happened in private was another matter. The university tolerated Barry's long relationship with Louisa Barrow, whose husband was still alive when he became chancellor.[61] Time rehabilitated Atkins, and the council chose him for one of the new lectureships created in 1873.

<hr />

The person who came to personify the early law school for later generations was not one of the early law lecturers, but the professor of history and political economy, William Hearn. Although he had been involved with the university's law teaching from the start, it was initially just one of his phenomenally wide range of interests. It was only gradually that this polymath settled on law as his disciplinary base in the university, and he also figures in the genealogies of the study of history, economics, sociology and political science at Melbourne.[62]

Hearn was Irish, and retained 'just a hint of a brogue', but he was not part of Catholic Ireland; his ancestors were English, and his father was an Anglican clergyman. His education was in Dublin, at Trinity College, where he studied classics, philosophy and law with great success before becoming professor of Greek at the newly established Queen's College, Galway. While teaching there, he was admitted to practise as a barrister in Dublin.[63]

A professorship at the newly established University of Melbourne must have been an attractive prospect for Hearn, still in his late twenties and supporting a wife and children on an income of about £150 a year in a country he regarded as 'the weakness, the sting, and the disgrace of Britain'. In its first flush of prosperity, paying high salaries to attract teachers from the United Kingdom, Melbourne offered £1000 and free accommodation to its foundation professors. Hearn became an omnibus professor of modern history and literature, political economy and logic. Although the formal scope of his responsibilities was soon reduced to history and political economy, in practice he seemed to occupy an encyclopaedic chair of the humanities and social sciences. His training in Greek and Latin equipped him to stand in for the absent professor of classics during two periods, and when he became seriously ill in 1875, classes in no fewer than seven subjects had to be cancelled or suspended: History of the British Empire, Jurisprudence, Ancient History, Roman Law, International Law, Constitutional Law, and Political Economy.[64]

He served as an examiner for the law course in 1857, and later delivered some of Chapman's lectures for him. Once the degree course began, he regularly lectured to the LLB students in their compulsory subjects of Ancient History and Constitutional History. The classroom brought out an engaging side that was too often invisible in Hearn's public persona. In his 'most palpable' wig, and a gown that faded over the years, he charmed the students with lectures that would stray into anecdotes, poetry, history and etymology. He was so knowledgeable and enthusiastic that the detours seem to have enhanced rather than dampened his undoubted popularity. On his home ground of history, economics and law, he was 'the most interesting & stimulating teacher we had', Henry Higgins wrote. To another former student, his classes were 'the green oases in the arid wilderness of law lectures'; 'the Doctor's lectures were enjoyable, while most of other law lectures were regarded as so much necessary drudgery to be got through somehow and anyhow'.[65]

He also involved his students in the classes as few law teachers did, then or for years afterwards. 'He would, soon after lectures began for the year, sort out from his class a troupe who formed the *dramatis personae* in his little drama of "Legal Duties and Rights"', an arts student remembered. The cast included a 'perpetual plaintiff' who was the victim successively of a burglar with homicidal tendencies, a usurious moneylender and other predators. 'Cases have even been known of men taking up Jurisprudence as an extra subject, merely because "it was such a pleasant way of spending a morning hour."' Forty years after Hearn's death, this sort of thing was so rare that he was still remembered for putting problems to his students and asking for their opinions.[66] Teaching like this was enough to give Hearn a prominent place in the small university, but it was merely the complement to other work that reached outside the classroom and the campus. Here the charm was less evident, the fixed gaze on his own aims and plans more distancing.

Hearn's concentration and singleness of purpose were most fruitful in his writing, and he produced four major books, the first three of which attracted attention in Britain and America. His text on political economy, *Plutology* (he hoped to popularise a new name for the discipline, borrowed from an earlier French writer), was praised by the English economists William Jevons, Alfred Marshall and Francis Edgeworth. *The Government of England*, Hearn's book of constitutional law and history, drew flattering notice from A. V. Dicey, who acknowledged its influence in his classic *Introduction to the Study of the Law of the Constitution*. Its flowing, lucid style shows the gift for exposition that Hearn displayed in his lectures, though without the characteristic asides and diversions that took up much of his time in class. It was a book of synthesis rather than original research, and its characteristic sources were the classic authorities on British parliamentary history and practice, Edward Coke, Edmund Burke, Thomas Macaulay, Henry Hallam and Thomas Erskine May. *The Aryan Household*, perhaps best described as a work of historical sociology, was unlucky in the grim connotations twentieth-century history attached to the first word in its title, but it, too, was reviewed 'with considerable respect' in England and America. Although historians debate Hearn's originality as an economist, the profile of his books among academic audiences far from his new home was remarkable, and a source of pride for the university.[67]

In his writing, he espoused his 'unbounded belief in English institutions and in English men', and articulated a conceptual framework for *laissez-faire* policies, competition, free trade and small government. 'Our mission', he said in a public lecture, 'is to spread the British language, the British religion, the British laws, the British institutions, over this remote portion of the globe'. He aimed to vindicate the freedom guaranteed by 'the unwritten traditions of our political systems' against 'the ingenious inventors of paper constitutions', the rationalist constitution-writers of the eighteenth century (France and the United States, though unnamed, fitted his description).[68]

Hearn, the Irishman who had migrated from one British colony to another, articulated a system of government based on English history and tradition, representative but not democratic, answerable to parliament and giving each rank and locality its place but rejecting mere weight of numbers. 'Whatever may be its merits', Hearn wrote, 'democracy has no place in English law'.[69] First published in 1867, at a time of intense debate about democracy in Victoria (centring on protracted deadlocks between the two houses of parliament) and in Britain (where the parliamentary franchise was being extended for the first time in thirty-five years), *The Government of England* had a staunchly conservative message.

Merely spreading these ideas, no matter how wide the audience within and beyond the colony, was not enough. Hearn wanted to implement them, to get into positions of leadership and power. The university was one field for these ambitions, and he became an active and sometimes abrasive member of its council, president of its academic board, warden of its senate, and, briefly, chancellor, as well as being a member of the council of its first residential college, Trinity. Yet even this exhausting work could not contain him. He was a journalist, an influential member of the Anglican church in Melbourne, and chairman of the Australian Freehold Banking Corporation, though fortunately for him he did not live to see it collapse in the depression of the 1890s.[70]

Most of all, parliament drew him like a magnet, even though his greatest gifts were for expounding its law and history, not for mastering its politics. He was not a powerful public speaker, and although in this he was far from alone among MPs, it was a poor start in an age when public meetings were to electoral campaigning what media appearances became in more recent times. 'A certain weakness of voice, if not of delivery, caused him to stop short of any claim to commanding oratory', one of his contemporaries remembered. 'He never was able to take his stand upon a platform and sway the multitudes by impassioned harangues'.[71]

Even a Hearn with greater skills as a platform speaker might have found a parliamentary career difficult. Contemporaries attested to his charm, but also to an intellectual zeal and determination in pursuit of his own aims that created alienation and distrust. His friend and former student, the journalist and teacher Alexander Sutherland, brought to life in his obituary the humour and enthusiasm of Hearn's lectures, but knew some thought the professor 'was wanting in sympathy, that in him the intellectual faculties dominated so completely that the humanising influences were imperceptible'.[72] Some clever, bookish lawyers did succeed in the nineteenth-century Victorian parliament— George Higinbotham, Alfred Deakin, Henry Higgins and Isaac Isaacs are examples—but the tough elections and shifting alignments of the populist lower house were an unlikely environment for a learned professor.

To make matters worse, Hearn was a supporter of free trade, at a time when protection of local industry was becoming a major fault-line in Australian politics, and mass support in Victoria was swinging towards higher tariffs. He ran unsuccessfully for the Legislative Assembly in 1859, 1874 and 1877, before finding a seat in the very different atmosphere of the upper house, the Legislative Council. There, a small electorate, who qualified to vote mainly on grounds of wealth, chose members consisting largely of imperturbable conservatives whose job was to contain the tempestuous democracy of the lower house.

Hearn's opinions were better received in the Council, his legal skills were more highly valued, and he made for himself a role as unofficial leader of the house, not in the sense of a party leader chosen as the general of a parliamentary army, but as an expert who would inform and guide the independent-minded members in their response to legislation. Drawing on his knowledge of British precedent, he brought scholarly firepower to a fight with the lower house over the Council's composition and powers in 1878, and drafted a long and tendentious memorandum setting out the upper house's side of the case when the government appealed for British intervention. Its straight-faced argument that the constitutional clashes of the last fifteen years were entirely the Assembly's fault strained credibility.[73]

He had a surer touch in the classroom and in print than in his other interests, whether in the running of the university or the affairs of government. A lasting blot on his record was his role in the drafting of a new land act in 1862. As a barrister, admitted to practise in Victoria in 1860 on the strength of his admission in Ireland, he occasionally took on legal work, including cases concerning disputed parliamentary elections and constitutional, land and mining law. When he was briefed to draft the land act, he accepted a heavy responsibility. Whether pastoral runs should be broken up to allow selection of Crown land for small farms was one of the most bitterly contested issues of the day, and the cause of seemingly endless fighting in parliament. That the lands minister in charge of the bill was Charles Gavan Duffy, Irish nationalist, advocate of land reform for Ireland and (as a Roman Catholic) target for Victoria's vituperative sectarian antagonism, only made the task more sensitive. For reasons that remain a matter of speculation, Hearn fluffed the drafting. Pastoralists and speculators exploited loopholes in the provisions for selection, defeating the act's purpose. Haste and inexperience apparently undermined Hearn's work, although whether most blame attaches to him or his political masters is still debated.[74]

Despite this debacle, parliamentary drafting became a notable part of Hearn's career. He helped attorney-general George Higinbotham with the first consolidation of Victoria's legislation in 1864–65, drawing together scattered enactments and amendments into accessible, re-enacted statutes, and he produced a consolidated local government bill in 1879. Clarifying the law and making it readily available became the great task of the last years of his life, when he conceived and led a mammoth project for the codification of Victorian law. Working on a scale that would have daunted almost anyone else, he proposed to reduce not only the colony's statute-law, but English and local case-law as well, to a clarified and restated form, in a General Code enacted by parliament and embodying 'the whole General Substantive Law of Victoria'.[75] Hearn shared some of the reforming zeal of the 'inventors of paper constitutions' he once derided, though in his case only for restating, not changing, the law.

Visionary in the Australian context, Hearn's idea had precedents not only in the French *Code Napoléon*, but in codification movements in India, Britain and the United States. Although he mustered a team of eminent lawyers, and with them produced draft codes that were considered by the parliament, the degree of comprehensiveness and accuracy needed to restate the law was almost impossible to achieve, and it was doubly difficult to reassure uncertain politicians that the codes were sufficiently reliable. Despite declining health, Hearn pressed on with the work, but the code remained unenacted when he died, at the age of sixty-two, in 1888. Without his personal drive the project soon ended, replaced by a second consolidation of Victoria's statutes.[76]

In the background of this public career was a private sorrow. Hearn had married Rose (or Rosalie) Le Fanu in Ireland, and she travelled to Melbourne with their children to join him at the university. But by 1877 they were living apart, William at the university, Rosalie by herself in St Kilda. Three of their children had died in

1860–62, but whether their marriage was unable to withstand these bereavements, or other causes were at work, is now impossible to say. All that remains of Rosalie's last years is the record of the inquest into her death in 1877. Her daughters visited her regularly, and Hearn had seen her about a fortnight earlier, but she died alone, 'of intemperate habits', evidently an alcoholic. Of the reaction of Hearn and his surviving children, there is only silence. He said that in some ways his was a hard life; perhaps he had this small tragedy in mind.[77] He later remarried, his second wife joining him in his apartment in the quadrangle.

The voters' lack of enthusiasm was not the only obstacle Hearn had to surmount to get into parliament. His candidacy in 1859 set off a reaction at the university, whose chancellor, Barry, thought that professors should stay out of politics. The council adopted a new statute barring professors from membership, not only of parliament, but of political associations as well. The professors protested and petitioned the governor to block the new statute (as he had power to do, under the act that set up the university), but to no avail.[78] Hearn's parliamentary ambitions were put on hold, until a separate development coincidentally revived them: the establishment of a faculty of law.

Until 1873, law teaching at the university was governed directly by the council and the professorial board; there was no board or committee with special responsibility for law, and no head or administrator to manage law teaching, beyond the lecturers and the officials of the university. It was the council that decided the details of the courses and dealt with the students' complaints about such things as Sewell's absences and the location of lectures. Other disciplines were in the same position. Not just in law, but elsewhere in the university, there were no faculties to take charge of particular fields of study.

The university was so small—still only 134 students in 1872, of whom 53 were studying law—that such an arrangement had been both viable and sensible, but some, Hearn among them, thought the situation was ripe for change by the early 1870s. A council committee investigated the possibility of expanding the law teaching by establishing more subjects and lectureships, and at the same time creating a new body, the faculty, to oversee them. While the committee's long and fitful deliberations were continuing, Barry broadened the debate by proposing faculties of arts and medicine as well. His concern was management of the growing number of part-time lecturers, and regularisation of the administration of the various schools, but a power shift was involved as well, since the establishment of faculties would hand greater responsibility to academic staff, albeit still under the supervision of the council. Watching with interest and some concern were the professors (there were none on the committee or the council), whose influence, with the exception of Hearn, had been undermined by the profession's weight in the university's law teaching.[79]

The council committee referred to this change as the establishment of a school of law, and 'law school' and 'law faculty' have been sometimes interchangeable, and sometimes confusing, terms ever since. The university called its law classes the 'School of Law' within a few months of their commencement in 1857, and it has referred to teachers and students in particular disciplines as schools throughout its history. Occasionally it used the word in other ways, and its early calendars also referred to schools in the Oxford sense of disciplines in honours exams, rather than academic departments. Despite the ambiguous terminology, what the council had in mind in 1872–73 was the creation of the faculty and the attendant reorganisation of the teaching.[80]

The convenor of the council committee was George Mackay, barrister, MP and doctor of laws of the universities of Dublin and Melbourne. Its members showed little interest in their task, and they came so infrequently to meetings that Mackay had to write the report by himself, submitting it in draft to the council as his personal opinion and the best the committee could do. He took 'the modern Law Schools' of London and Dublin as his models, and urged the use of examiners other than the lecturers.[81] The report itself has not survived, and its contents can only be guessed from Mackay's covering letter and the resulting statute, which adopted most of its recommendations.

Hearn put the views of the law teaching staff to Barry. They liked the plan to establish a faculty, and no wonder: it would give a body dominated by the dean and the lecturers powers that until now had been in the hands of the council. If they had had their way, faculty membership would have been limited cosily to the teaching staff. Hearn's status as dean-in-waiting was clear in the list of subjects they said the dean should be responsible for, since they were the ones he already taught. The course they proposed consisted of the dean's subjects (Constitutional Law, Roman Law, International Law and General Jurisprudence) and the four existing 'technical law' subjects.[82]

Barry suggested to Hearn that he should add the work of the dean to his existing appointment as professor of history and political economy, but Hearn would not play along. He had several good reasons, most of which he explained to the chancellor. History and political economy were 'something quite different' from the subjects the dean would teach, and only Hearn's wide interests had combined knowledge of all of them in one professor, an accident not likely to be repeated in future. Barry was effectively asking him to add the work of a second chair (in the shape of the law teaching) to his existing chair, along with the work of the dean, without any additional pay. Whatever the compensation, Hearn's health would not permit it, and even if he had been well enough, he would not do it. It was a different story, however, if the deanship could be separated from Hearn's chair. Then he would be willing to take the new post, an arrangement that would have the advantage of leaving the university in need only of a teacher of history and political economy, easier to find, Hearn thought, than a teacher of jurisprudence, Roman law and international law.[83]

This was all true enough, but it was also disingenuous. The office of dean offered Hearn an advantage that he failed to mention to Barry. The statute for the faculty had yet to be drafted, and its details were uncertain, but Hearn was talking about becoming a dean instead of a professor, and if he was no longer a professor, he would no longer be disqualified from membership of parliament. And so it turned out. As adopted a few months later, the new statute provided for Hearn's situation, doubtless with him in mind. A professor could give up a chair to become dean with no loss of tenure or pay, and without losing a seat on the professorial board (the dean was automatically a member). The council duly appointed Hearn as dean, and he resigned from his chair.[84] The two new lectureships went to John Atkins, now deemed sufficiently respectable, and equity barrister Thomas à Beckett, nephew of the former chief justice and one of the many part-time law lecturers who later became judges.

It did not take Hearn long to make use of this dispensation. He ran again for parliament in 1874, and was again unsuccessful. It was apparently only now that Barry realised this implication of the new statute, but when he protested to Hearn, the dean replied that the ban on professors in parliament no longer applied to him. Soon the other professors were asking for the privilege to be extended to them too, but to no avail.[85] Liberation from the university's ban may have been, for Hearn, a happy by-product of the move to create a faculty, but the way he took advantage of it hinted at a degree of cunning that did little for his reputation or, indeed, that of the university.

One of the lecturers in the medical school, James Robertson, told his friend John Castieau, governor of the Melbourne gaol, about the 'dodge' that had allowed Hearn to stand, as Castieau recorded in his diary: 'Professor Hearn's friends were siezed [sic] with a brilliant idea & made him a Dean with all the privileges & responsibilities of a Professor; the change of name had this advantage that Deans were not prohibited from interfering in politics & so Mr Hearn's candidature'. Hearn remained a professor in substance though not in name. As a later chancellor, Brownless, put it when Hearn died, 'though he was not called a Professor, he virtually occupied the position of one, as he had the same salary and the same tenure, though he was not subject to the same restrictions'.[86]

Under the new statute, the Faculty of Law consisted of the dean, the lecturers (as yet all part-time), and all the lawyers on the university council (whether judges, barristers or solicitors). Like its later professional counterpart, the Faculty of Medicine, it was never composed only of the teaching staff, although they generally dominated its meetings; its work was linked to the profession through the membership of important outsiders. The new body was to advise the council on 'all questions relating to the Studies, Lectures, and Examinations for Degrees in Laws', and on the selection of lecturers and external examiners. The dean would 'subject to the control of the Faculty exercise a general superintendence over the administrative business connected with the Faculty'. Whatever the professorial board might have hoped, its influence was, if anything, weakened by the direct channel of advice to the council from a faculty dominated by the profession.[87]

What this structure meant in practice varied with changing personnel and the dynamics of university politics. From the start, the curriculum was at the core of the faculty's work, although its control was far from absolute. Its proposals were second-guessed, and often amended in detail, by the council and the senate. Another constant in the faculty's agendas until the 1960s was the appointment of academic staff below the level of professor, although here, too, the faculty made recommendations and the council made the decisions. Meetings were usually brief and formal. Convened when needed, they averaged less than two per year in the faculty's first twenty years; in 1875, it took five attempts, and most of the year, before the dean could even muster a quorum. Meetings came to life in the 1880s and 1890s when there were disagreements about course changes, and again in the middle years of the twentieth century, when the faculty served as a joint committee of staff and influential outsiders, but much of the time it was merely the place to endorse decisions that had already been made elsewhere.

For all the rhetoric of law as part of a gentlemanly education, the structure of the certificate course suited students who were already employed, rather than those who studied full-time. Their varied backgrounds and destinations show that the course was undertaken by more than young students on their way to becoming lawyers, although they made up the bulk of the classes. Among the first group to be awarded law certificates by the university, in April 1859, George Bartrop became a clerk of court, a barrister and a long-serving police magistrate in Melbourne. Edmund FitzGibbon, already the town clerk of Melbourne, was one of the second group of students, who received their certificates in May 1860. He was admitted to practise as a barrister, but law was only an interest or an additional qualification for him, and he stayed in public administration, remaining town clerk for more than thirty years before working for another fourteen years as the first chairman of the Melbourne and Metropolitan Board of Works.[88]

Enrolments trended slowly upwards, reaching fifty for the first time in 1860 and one hundred in 1891, before dipping again in response to hard times and changes in the admission rules. Most of the students came from Melbourne, but a few came from other parts of Australia, to take advantage of the law course before an equivalent was available to them at home. These included a small group of notable Queenslanders, who made the long journey to Melbourne before the University of Sydney began offering a comparable course in 1890 and the University of Queensland's law school opened in 1936.[89]

A string of scholarships brought Thomas Byrnes from Bowen Primary School in northern Queensland to Melbourne; he was briefly premier of Queensland before his early death in 1898. Littleton Groom, another Melbourne graduate from Queensland, became a federal politician. The most notable of the Queenslanders among the nineteenth-century graduates was Thomas Joseph Ryan, who gained his LLB in 1899, as an external student, after moving north from Victoria, where he had grown up. Premier in 1915–19, he was a key figure in Queensland political history, and when he moved to federal politics he became a potential leader of the Australian Labor Party; premature death cut short his career in 1921.[90]

Law teaching began in the university's original, and at that time only, building. Known later as the quadrangle, even before it gained its fourth side, it consisted of three wings in Tudor gothic style around a courtyard, and housed not only classrooms, offices and the embryonic library, but also the professors, who lived there with their families. The law lectures were initially delivered three days a week at 6 p.m., and attendance was a prerequisite for sitting the exam. For those who worked in the city, trudging a couple of kilometres to the university in winter for the evening lectures, through muddy, unlit streets, was a trial, one that made Sewell's absences all the more irritating. Almost as soon as the lectures began, students asked for them to be moved to 'some more central location'. The council refused, but did suggest that the lectures be held at an earlier time in winter.[91]

Despite the protests of students unhappy at having to drag themselves to the campus after work, classes remained at the university, with the exception of some held in the chambers of one barrister–lecturer because of his bad health. But in 1880 the opening of the new court complex in William Street provided a new potential venue, and when twenty-four Property students petitioned the council in 1884 asking for all evening lectures to be delivered at the new courts, they found a more receptive audience. With Hearn's backing, the council decided that most lectures would be delivered at the new courts for the remainder of the term, that they would be held only between 4.15 and 6.15 p.m., and that the rolls would be 'regularly called and kept'. The results of the experiment were favourable enough for the faculty to recommend that lectures should continue in the city, and the council agreed.[92]

The move highlighted the divisions between part-time and full-time students, certificate and degree students, and would-be barristers and solicitors. For the minority who were full-time students, moving to the city weakened university spirit: five students sent a counter-petition, protesting against the move to the city and invoking 'the unity of the University'. In the 1890s, the student union echoed their complaint, lamenting the 'disastrous effect on the social life of the students' caused by holding lectures outside the university.[93] On the other hand, the city venue suited the part-time lecturers, who consistently supported it in faculty meetings.

The ethos of the course was not the only drawback. The rooms at the law courts, in the library building, were uncomfortable, the acoustics were bad, and they had little furniture and no heating (the fireplaces were left empty). 'Our sympathy, we confess, lies with those who for two hours have to sit in cold, bare rooms,' the *University Review* reported in 1884, 'straining their ears to catch the reverberant echoes of the lecturer's voice'. The chairs and tables in the lecture rooms were cast-offs from nearby offices, and wear and tear soon reduced them to a 'disgraceful condition', so bad that the university provided its own chairs.[94]

Nor could the increasing number of students fit in the available space. Property students complained in 1893 that a class of about one hundred had to fit into a room furnished with a single table that seated twenty at most. With such crowding, 'the atmosphere, towards the end of a lecture, becomes unwholesome in the extreme'. Conditions back at the university were not much better. 'As regards the University buildings', education minister (and former lecturer) Charles Pearson wrote in 1886, 'there can be little doubt that they are bad in every way, unsafe and ill-adapted for their purposes. The lecture rooms are probably some of the worst in the world for accommodation and acoustic properties.'[95]

The council was caught in the middle of a battle of petitions for and against city lectures. When one group of students complained about the lack of space, chairs and air, the council's response was predictable: 'The Students to be informed that the lectures are held at the Law Courts for their convenience—if the accommodation provided there is inadequate it will be provided at the University'. Some classes moved first one way, then the other: International Law headed into the city in 1888, at the students' request, but another petition asked for Jurisprudence to move in the opposite direction when Hearn's successor was appointed, and the council agreed. Both subjects returned to the university under the new dean, Edward Jenks.[96]

The Property students were the most vocal, or suffered the most, and petitions from them led the council to decide to move all the lectures back to the university in 1893. But other students, and the faculty, were not happy. The number of students in Property was unusually high, the council was told, because a change in the course regulations had brought enrolments forward. The courts were a more convenient location for the lecturers and most of the students, who were working in the city.[97] The protests first delayed, and then defeated the move back to the campus.

Ultimately the needs of the courts ended the judges' hospitality, as they took over the available space for other purposes. The law classes were gradually squeezed into even less suitable accommodation, and then out of the court precinct altogether. In 1898, the university lost the use of a room in the library building where lectures had been held, and had to move upstairs, to one of the 'small and ill-ventilated' rooms in the dome where juries slept during long trials. In 1913, when the lectures were using two of the dome rooms, the dean reported that the rooms were 'filled to their utmost capacity & a good deal beyond the limits of comfort', but the influx of students after World War I created even worse problems. 'You are aware of the unsatisfactory character of the accommodation we have had at the Law Courts', he wrote to the registrar, 'but as we were there by courtesy we could not grumble'.[98]

The law school grabbed other spaces in the court complex when it could, but the solutions were always temporary. In 1919, it gained the use of two rooms in a building at the back of what were then the Crown law offices (now the Court of Appeal), behind the Supreme Court, and paid for their refurbishment, but conditions there were little better.[99] The secretary of the students' representative council, John Foster, later, as the university's registrar, all too familiar with the difficulties of finding space for teaching, described the situation in one of the rooms. It doubled as the Licensing Court during the day:

Students have to find seats where they can—on the steps of the dais, at the clerks' table immediately beneath the lecturer, or on the judicial bench at his side—but even then up to a dozen of them have to sit in the adjacent room around the door at the back of the Licensing Court, trying vainly to catch the accents of the lecturer which permeate through the partition.[100]

The dean did not find conditions quite so bad when he went to have a look for himself, but the building's days were numbered, and the opening of the arts and education building (now Old Arts) provided more lecture rooms on the campus.[101] The federal government's plans for its own court building, fronting Little Bourke Street and used by the High Court and later the Federal Court, required the demolition of the rooms used for the law lectures. Construction of the new courts began in 1926, and the law lectures returned to the university, where they settled permanently.

For the forty years during which they were held largely at the law courts, the location of the law lectures linked the course to the profession even more strongly than did the preponderance of barristers among the lecturers. Once they completed their arts subjects, the degree students spent most of their class time at the courts; articled clerks spent an even higher proportion of their time as students away from the university. It was the court building, not the campus, that formed the backdrop for their group photograph in 1915. By coincidence, the move back to the university prefigured a renewed emphasis on the academic, rather than the vocational, side of the law course.

2

CINDERELLA

1889–1927

Hearn's death in 1888 opened the way for a reappraisal of the curious arrangement that had made him dean but no longer a professor. The university council decided to fill his place by appointing a dean who would be professor of law in name and not merely in substance. It looked for a man who could teach the same subjects: jurisprudence, Roman law, constitutional law and international law.[1] Hearn's influence lingered after his death in this division of teaching, which also suited the university. Part-time lecturers were more easily found for other, more doctrinal subjects.

The post was not only the university's, but Australia's, first chair of law, though other universities soon followed. At Sydney, the Challis bequest funded the appointment of Pitt Cobbett as the university's first professor of law in 1890, while Adelaide's full-time law lecturer, Frederick Pennefather, was promoted to professor in the same year. William Jethro Brown became the first lecturer in law at the University of Tasmania three years later, and was promoted to professor in 1896.[2]

There could hardly be an established career path to such a tiny group of positions, and the backgrounds of the people who held them varied widely. Pennefather had a BA and an LLM from Cambridge; he was briefly a barrister in England, then a governor's private secretary in South Australia and New Zealand, and a lawyer in Wellington. His predecessor as full-time lecturer at Adelaide, Walter Phillips, was another barrister and Cambridge graduate, appointed at the age of twenty-eight.[3] Cobbett had a doctorate in civil law from Oxford, had been called to the bar in London, and worked as a private tutor and author before he came to Sydney.

At Melbourne, the council specified that the new professor should be not much under thirty and not much over forty. The job was one for an intelligent, presentable young man with English qualifications and plenty of promise; it was not until 1947 that the university appointed a law professor who was over thirty years old or who had completed a doctorate, and not until 1951 that it appointed one who did not have an English university degree.[4]

The university advertised the new post in Australia and Britain. A few years before, the council had experimented with advertising overseas only if chairs were not filled by local applicants, but in 1885 it had given up this Australia-first policy, and revived its London chair committees.[5] In the case of the chair of law, the Council of Legal Education, which oversaw the training of barristers in London, provided a committee to select a shortlist, and Victoria's agent-general interviewed the top three candidates. Pitt Cobbett applied from London; John Salmond (later professor at Adelaide, and solicitor-general and judge in New Zealand, but best known for his writing, including *The Law of Torts*) applied from New Zealand. One of the law school's graduates, now a part-time lecturer, Casimir Woinarski, was also an applicant.

Edward Jenks' record, at the age of twenty-eight, seemed ideal: first-class honours in law and history at Cambridge, with the chancellor's medal for law, followed by the prize for the best student in the admission exam of the Inns of Court in 1887, a teaching post at Jesus College, Cambridge, and then a fellowship at King's College. The son of a London furniture dealer, he had left school and was working as an articled clerk when a legacy from his mother's estate enabled him to go to Cambridge. Even so, his was no knock-out application. The London committee had difficulty choosing between him and barrister Albert Carter, whom Jenks edged out thanks to his greater teaching experience. When the university council came to make the appointment, Martin Irving, the vice-chancellor (an unpaid deputy to the chancellor, not yet a university chief executive along modern lines), pleaded Carter's case, despite the London recommendation, but Jenks was appointed by a majority.[6]

Jenks' energy in his new job was impressive. In the midst of his other tasks, he was an indefatigable speaker and organiser of the far-flung adult education classes that went under the name of university extension.[7] Back on the campus, he delivered and published an introductory lecture, setting out his ideas about legal study, giving advice to the students and commenting on the exams he had marked. It was an engaging performance, good-humoured and to the point. Some of the students had found him a hard marker, he said:

> as I have in certain quarters been represented somewhat in the light of an ogre, crunching with relish the bones of innocent victims, I should like to say that I freely acknowledge the general existence of one very admirable feature in the examination answers. They showed undoubted evidence of hard work; and I should be the last to deny the supreme importance of this quality. But it is not possible by any expenditure of mere muscular exertion to become a good lawyer. Other qualities necessarily have a place in the composition, and it was the absence of these qualities that struck me very painfully.[8]

He commented on the differences between school and university, where his job was not to do students' work for them, or to compel them to do it, but to guide, advise, explain, plan and encourage. His advice about taking notes in lectures was often repeated in different ways by later teachers (and just as often students had other ideas).

Remember that you are not taking down a mass of evidence which will disappear if not committed to writing; but you are trying to catch ideas, to glean hints, and pick up information … the plan I invariably followed as a student was to devote my energy to taking in rather than to taking down.[9]

In order to teach Victorian constitutional law, Jenks himself had much to learn, as he acknowledged. The experience of having to teach himself part of the subject brought home to him the students' difficulties: 'I could find no text-book which would give me even an outline idea of the subject. The only authorities prescribed by the Faculty were the Acts of Parliament for the time being in force in Victoria on various branches of it.'[10] His response was to write the book himself, gleaning his material from original sources in the Melbourne public library. To do this in two years (the book appeared in 1891), and on a topic of which he had, as he said, no special knowledge, was prodigious.

The work was notable, not only as the first textbook of Australian constitutional law, but also for meshing law with history and politics. The history courses taught by Hearn and his successor Elkington were dominated by England and Rome; in his constitutional history lectures, Jenks became the university's first teacher of Australian history, and he used this material in his book.[11] Its first half was historical, covering both the changing form of government and some of the general history of Victoria. Unusually for the time, it focused not only on parliament and the governor, but on police, public officials, local government and the courts. Although some of what he wrote was inevitably compromised by lack of time and the difficulties of his sources, the book was a model of a broad conception of constitutional law. Jenks maintained his interest in Australian history, and later published a history of Australia and New Zealand that went through three editions. Nor, while he was in Melbourne, was this all; before he left, he wrote a second book, on the history of the doctrine of consideration, which won Cambridge's Yorke prize for an essay on a legal subject.

Despite all these great virtues, Jenks' relations with some of his colleagues were disastrous, with consequences that outgrew their often trivial causes and overshadowed everything else about his time at the university. Soon after his arrival, he became embroiled in a quarrel with the registrar, Edward à Beckett (son of the former chief justice, and himself briefly a barrister before he became registrar). Jenks came to Melbourne in the middle of a campaign by the professors against à Beckett's proposal for the appointment of a principal, with general authority to manage the university, including its teaching. The plan mutated into one for a paid vice-chancellor, before the professors, joined energetically by Jenks, successfully fought it off as a threat to their own powers. Now Jenks had à Beckett excluded from meetings of the professorial board, complaining that its confidential proceedings had been leaked in the past.[12] The imputation about à Beckett's trust-worthiness could only have been offensive.

Relations were already bad, then, when Jenks gave the registrar's office a notice convening a meeting of the faculty, only to find that it went out under the registrar's name rather than his. The dean thought it was obvious that the notice should go out in his name, as the university's statutes implied, but in pointing this out to the registrar, he added an acid (and uncalled-for) warning about the dangers of changing signatures on documents. À Beckett buttoned his lip and merely replied that he had followed the usual custom, but he relieved his feelings in a draft letter to Jenks left in his office file: 'If you claim a superior knowledge and experience of the theory and practice of forgery and have only given me a friendly hint I beg to thank you for it'.[13]

The sad irony was that the hint was needed, although neither man knew it at the time; if à Beckett's knowledge of forgery had been better, he might have detected the embezzlements by the university's accountant, Frederick Dickson, that were already secretly depleting its funds. They were not revealed until 1901, when the scandal and loss of money developed into a full-scale disaster. After another letter from Jenks, à Beckett complained to the council, but whatever it thought of Jenks' tone, it decided that the registrar need not sign the notices.[14]

More was at stake for Jenks in these battles than just the affairs of the law school. He had a keen eye for the way the university was run, who controlled it and, in that sense, what sort of university it was. His ideal was self-government by the teachers. In the same way as he had opposed control by a salaried vice-chancellor, he attacked the interference of poorly qualified council members in academic affairs they were not competent to administer, reminded them of the purposes of the university, and added that it was known overseas, not by their insignificant reputations, but by those of its more famous teachers. He published these reflections during the fight over the vice-chancellorship: 'powerful and important advice but woundingly made', in Selleck's words.[15]

A dispute over the content of the law course triggered the final breach between Jenks and the university, although the substance of the disagreement was once again out of all proportion to the intensity of the battle that erupted. It was not in the council, the target of Jenks' public criticism, but in the senate, the gathering of the university's masters and doctoral graduates, that the trouble started. The law course had been under review since Hearn's death presented an opportunity to reorganise the curriculum. The faculty, on Jenks' motion, proposed to expand the teaching of constitutional law and legal history, turning the subject Constitutional Law into a larger one, Constitutional and Legal History (which, despite its name, would still include constitutional law, merging law and history much as Jenks' book later did). Equity would be united awkwardly in one subject with procedure.

Something had to be cut to make space for the extra teaching, so public international law would disappear from the course, leaving only private international law, under the title of the Conflict of Laws. Jenks scorned international law. 'Misled by the name', he told the *Argus*, 'many people are not aware that "international law" bears only the faintest analogy to law usually so termed. Simply, it is diplomatic history, and a school of history is the place for it.' While he thought it 'an almost essential element in a modern liberal education', he believed it did not belong in the law course, and told his students as much in his introductory lecture. He found support among the practitioners on the faculty, which voted to delete International Law.[16]

The council at first went along with the course changes, but the necessary alterations in the university regulations also had to be approved by the senate. Jenks, not a Melbourne graduate, was not a member, but he attended to put his case, and made the nationalists of the senate bristle with a reference to Australia's colonial status. In the words of the *Argus*: "'We are not a nation,'" observed Professor Jenks placidly, "and therefore we don't require to study public international law.'"[17]

In the senate, to Jenks' annoyance, public international law found defenders, including two barristers and future lecturers, Casimir Woinarski and John Mackey. They lined up against advocates for the faculty, the professor and the new course, among them barristers Leo Cussen and Henry Higgins. The leading defender of the status quo was Thomas McInerney, barrister, LLD graduate of the university, and external examiner in Roman Law. International Law should stay in the course, he said:

> The mere liking or disliking of the professor for the subject of international law had nothing to do with the case. The only reason that had been offered for the exclusion of the subject was one which was an insult to every Australian, namely, that Australia was not a nation, and therefore did not require international law.[18]

This misrepresented Jenks' argument, which had more to do with the status of international law than with the status of Australia, but the underlying point was a good one. The academic reasons he gave for removing the subject were weak: its standing as a branch of legal study was unarguable as a matter of both history and practice, and in one form or another, it was compulsory in all Australian law schools until World War I. Although Australia had no independent international legal personality, the colonies were affected by international law as part of the British Empire—as when the visit of the confederate war-ship *Shenandoah* entangled Victoria in the tail end of the American civil war in 1865—and the colonial governments dealt with foreign states through local consuls and in the negotiation of postal treaties.[19]

If it had been possible to make the subject optional, as it later became, much of the difficulty might have been avoided, but staffing, the requirements of admission to practise, and the relatively short length of the course did not allow the inclusion of any optional law subjects, as distinct from arts subjects, until the second professor was appointed in 1931 (when Public International Law became the first such option). Back in Jenks' time, it had to be compulsory, or else be deleted altogether. This suited his dislike of the subject, but it forced both sides in the debate to extremes. Nor did the way the issue reached the senate allow it to consider what, for Jenks, should have been the main question: whether legal history or international law should be in the course, when he was not willing or able to teach both.

The senate and, ultimately, the council, agreed that International Law should be retained, but Jenks took such offence at McInerney's comments that he refused to speak to him.[20] Unfortunately the pair had to agree on the exam paper for Roman Law. Like a character in a bad comedy, Jenks would not address McInerney directly, but com-municated only in the third person, through the registrar: 'Will you have the goodness to inform Dr McInerney ...' McInerney, for his part, refused to include the registrar in the correspondence, and insisted on writing direct to Jenks. The dean committed himself ever more deeply, unable to compromise, unable to retreat. It took a special meeting of the council and a thinly veiled threat of dismissal to get him to meet McInerney to discuss the Roman Law paper in 1890; somehow, they managed to produce a paper, but several days late.

Jenks was still addressing his colleague in the third person a year later, when the two again feuded over the questions the poor Roman Law students should be asked. McInerney recorded the dispute in numbing detail, to which Jenks responded in kind, standing on invisible points of principle and justifying himself with almost obsessive stubbornness. Finally the council appointed a third examiner, at McInerney's request, and the three produced a paper.

Retaining public international law was an issue of real substance (not least because council and senate now expected both it and legal history to be squeezed into the curriculum), but another, apparently trivial, aspect of the course plan also led to trouble. John Gregory, the lecturer in Property, revived in the senate a minor proposal that had failed to find support in the faculty meeting: the Law of Obligations should stay in the first year of the course and not move to second year, as the faculty wanted. Jenks tried to head him off. The change would force students to do Constitutional and Legal History as one of their arts subjects, in order to avoid an overload in first year law. The new subject was unsuitable for arts students, he objected, and he was not competent to teach it 'from an Arts standpoint'. When a senate committee adopted Gregory's scheme, Jenks fought on. An additional lecturer would now be needed, he said; in a sign both of the level to which relations had sunk and of questionable legal judgement, he began to call on the terms of his contract of employment, saying it would be breached if he had to teach legal history.[21]

The senate's meddling with the course plan was exasperating, especially when it approved the addition of legal history without allowing anything to be dropped to make room for it, but the problem of teaching both legal history and international law was out of all proportion to the scale of the battle Jenks now waged. His unhappiness in Victoria and in a state university run along Melbourne lines, evident in his private letters, probably made him fight even more stubbornly, heedless of the weakness of his position. The law faculty had unanimously agreed to the inclusion of constitutional law in the arts course when the BA was reviewed the previous year, and the combined subject of Constitutional and Legal History, which he now refused to teach, had been proposed by Jenks in the first place. When this was pointed out, he replied that he had only offered to teach it if public international law was dropped.[22]

He took his case to the governor, who, as visitor to the university, was the tribunal of last resort in appeals against its decisions, and had to approve the amendments now being made to the course details in the regulations. But all Jenks had to fall back on was his argument about contract, which Henry Higgins comprehensively disposed of in a formal response drafted for the council. No professor could claim a contract that prevented the university changing its statutes, and no such contract existed here. If Jenks thought otherwise, he could sue. Armed with this, and with advice from the attorney-general, the governor approved the new statutes, but Jenks refused to cooperate. Students who came to classes in Constitutional and Legal History found that the professor would lecture only on constitutional law. When the chancellor, alerted by the students, asked what was going on, Jenks told him that he was sticking to his contract.[23]

Jenks' intransigence on self-perceived points of principle, and the breakdown of his relations with many in the university, made his job increasingly difficult. Private sorrow also blighted his last year in Melbourne, and must have contributed to his decision to leave. His wife died in May 1891; they had been married for nearly a year, and she had just given birth to their son. Although he liked some of the other professors, and privately tried to make the best of the knowledge and 'all-round capacity' he gained in his work, he disliked Victoria from the start, was quick to see its obvious faults, and was slow to value the things it did offer him, such as a prominence and seniority that he would have had to wait years for in England. His sense of being out of place in the university and the city contrasted oddly with his energy for outreach in the university extension lectures, and with his enthusiasm for work on Victoria's history and constitution. After another spat with the council over Constitutional and Legal History (Jenks said he would act as examiner only if paid extra), he resigned in November 1891.[24]

He returned to England, but only briefly to Cambridge. He had resigned his paid fellowship at King's during an earlier crisis over whether he would stay on in Melbourne, at the start of 1890.[25] The involvement in the wider community that he sought in his university extension work, and his strong interest in legal education, soon drew him away from the older universities, despite his nostalgia for them while he was in Australia. He moved to another civic university, or rather university college, at Liverpool, and then spent seven years at Balliol College, Oxford, but for the bulk of his remaining career he was director of legal studies for the Law Society (which was responsible for the training of solicitors), before becoming a professor at the University of London. The multi-volume *Digest of English Civil Law*, which he edited, systematised the common law for readers from other legal systems.

To Tony Honoré, Jenks was 'the person most responsible for raising the professional and academic standing of teachers of law in the early part of the twentieth century, for making English private law accessible to continental lawyers of that period, and for ensuring that the education of solicitors was less narrowly technical than, left to itself, the profession would have chosen'.[26] Happily, in his home country he found causes that were better served by his tenacity.

The cumbersome machinery of the London committee was set in motion again, only three years after the chair of law had last been vacant. The committee thought that the post should be offered to Carter, previously their second choice, without advertisement, but the university had already advertised the position in Australia, and by the time applications closed, Carter had declined. Perhaps he was now better settled in London; maybe he was put off by the propaganda of the disgruntled Jenks, who was writing vigorously to English journals, to warn prospective applicants about the many failings of the University of Melbourne. Jenks' attack was aimed mainly at the council, which, forewarned by Jenks himself, anticipated it by sending to London a large dossier of original correspondence about his quarrels in Melbourne.[27]

The council's strategy was well judged. Jenks' general criticisms of an ill-qualified and interfering council had much truth in them, particularly when applied to the fractious university of the 1880s, but in the documents selected by the council he appeared at his worst. The sense of duty and the efforts to make the best of things that appeared in his private letters were nowhere to be seen. Instead, his correspondence with the university portrayed him as peevish, ready to go to extremes over seeming trivialities, and obsessed with disagreements that, from the other side of the world, must have looked ridiculous.

On the council's instructions, the agent-general made the dossier available for anyone interested to read, but published none of it, thus washing no more dirty laundry in public and avoiding contradiction by the university's English critics. If any of the London applicants worked their way through them, Jenks' own letters probably took away much of the force of his attack on the university. At any rate, the field was again a strong one. John Salmond and Jethro Brown applied for a second time (Pitt Cobbett was now in Sydney, and out of contention). Charles Maturin, a barrister and graduate of Trinity College, Dublin, impressed the London committee with his barrow-load of prizes, but it was the young William Harrison Moore whom they ranked first. He accepted the appointment, and began work early in 1893.[28]

At the age of just twenty-five, Moore appealed to the committee because of his outstanding examination record, his personality, and the promise of good things to come, coupled with a little teaching experience. Like Jenks, he had gone into the workforce when he left school: in Moore's case, as a newspaper reporter, following in his father's footsteps (he continued to use shorthand in later life). He began to read for the bar, enrolled in the LLB course at the University of London, and sat for the admission exams administered by the Council of Legal Education. Once he got going, the prizes he won helped pay his way, and a scholarship took him to Cambridge, where he capped his career as a student with the unusual distinction of first place in both the first and second parts of the law examination, or tripos (at that time part of the BA course).

He had done some supervising, or tutoring, of law students at Cambridge, and taught law students privately in London, but at his age, it could only be a start. 'He does not appear to have had much experience in lecturing or teaching', Victoria's agent-general reported after interviewing him. Frederic Maitland, already eminent, rapidly emerging as one of England's greatest legal historians, and with the even rarer distinction of being, by repute, the only man in Cambridge able to change Edward Jenks' mind, was one of Moore's referees: 'Of all the men who have taken a law degree at Cambridge during the last five years, I think that he is the one most likely to make a good teacher of Law'. The agent-general described him as 'an active, intelligent young man … he looks even younger than he is'.[29]

Kenneth Bailey, Moore's successor as professor, looked back at the end of his own life, and left an eloquent description of his teacher and friend. 'He was not big or robust physically', Bailey said; 'quite on the contrary, he was small, small-boned, very quiet, mild in demeanour and in speech, hesitant in speech, extremely lucid in thought … kind and considerate, good-humoured, good tempered, humorous, really, though not a great joker'.[30]

> He was extraordinarily kind to colleagues and friends and particularly to the young, whom he brought out and guided without the slightest trace of either condescension or direction. He was simply your friend and he would discuss anything with you and give his advice when you asked and never proffer it … Learned, philosophical, lucid, speculative, enquiring, intellectually very courageous, he made a tremendous impression on the University.[31]

The other staff members of the law school consisted, as they had since 1873, of the four part-time lecturers. A professor of law at Melbourne was, until Bailey's appointment in 1927, an import, a gifted graduate from overseas. The early lecturers, too, had been immigrants, but the pattern changed as locally trained practitioners grew in number after 1860. Of the teachers at the time of Moore's arrival, Frank Dobson was one of the older generation of lecturer-barristers who had studied elsewhere. He was appointed in 1864, and remained on the staff until his death thirty-one years later. Son of a lawyer and brother of a judge, he travelled from his birthplace in Van Diemen's Land to England, and studied at Cambridge, eventually earning a doctorate in law. After admission to the bar in London, he returned to Australia, and practised as a barrister in Melbourne, becoming a Queen's counsel. His work as a lecturer was just part of his wide-ranging activities as member of parliament, royal commissioner, trustee of the Public Library and National Gallery, and active member of the Church of England.[32]

John Rogers was an Englishman who had studied at Oxford and came to Australia in 1855, to take the job of solicitor-general of Van Diemen's Land. After self-government made the post a political one, he moved to Melbourne, serving as a County Court judge. His dismissal in the Black Wednesday government purge of 1878 was followed by his reinstatement and then resignation, in protest at cabinet's refusal to give County Court judges the same security of tenure as their colleagues on the Supreme Court. He became a QC, and, like Dobson, made lecturing part of a wide range of public duties. As a member of the university council in the 1860s and 1870s, he annoyed the vice-chancellor and the registrar with his great loquacity and with his support for their opponents.[33]

The other two lecturers at the time of Moore's arrival illustrated the generational shift towards appointment of highly ranked graduates of the law school who had gone on to practise as barristers. Leo Cussen was one of a long line of Melbourne graduates who lectured while they built up successful practices at the bar, and later went on to become judges: among the others were two chief justices of the High Court (Duffy and Latham), three other High Court judges (Fullagar, Menzies and Aickin), and a string of Supreme Court judges. The job was a useful adjunct to specialisation in practice, and gave those with a taste for teaching and research a foothold in the university.

Cussen had returned to study at the age of twenty-five, after training as an engineer, and completed degrees in law and arts; his reputation as a barrister was only eclipsed by his standing as one of the most highly regarded judges to have sat on the Supreme Court. His extraordinary labours accounted for most of the work involved in two consolidations of the whole of Victorian statute law, and the compiling of the Imperial Acts Application Act 1922, to which Moore also contributed. He taught International Law and the Law of Obligations until, like many of his successors, he found the demands of practice made his work at the university impossible to sustain. Again like others after him, he remained a member of the faculty.[34]

The fourth lecturer had a similar background, but his career had a very different trajectory. John Burslem Gregory was one of the university's earliest LLB graduates, the second to get first-class honours (he was the top student when he graduated in 1866). He became a barrister, and when he applied for one of the new lectureships in 1873, he was professional and parliamentary assistant to the Crown law officers. He taught Property; his colleague Dobson noted his 'eagle's eye for technicalities'.[35]

A mild-mannered man, he had trouble keeping order in class. 'It appears that very great latitude has been allowed to the students—in playing pranks and practical jokes during the lecture-hour—by their inoffensive lecturer, Mr. Gregory', the *Melbourne University Review* reported. 'This conduct of the students is primarily indefensible, but it should never have been permitted, and it would have been well had the first breach of discipline been met with instant reprimand, or other punishment, instead of allowing the disturbances to grow in audacity and number.' When one of the students blocked the door of the lecture room with a chair, to stop Gregory coming in, he had to force the door and break the chair in half. The professorial board threatened to cancel the lectures for the rest of the term, and the students promised to behave, but a week later Gregory was back at the board with a complaint of impertinence against one of the students, who promised that he meant no disrespect.[36]

Gregory had to take over Hearn's jurisprudence class during the dean's illness early in 1888, and by April the added strain had proved too much for his state of mind. Whether he showed earlier signs of mental trouble is unknown, but he was now admitted to the

Metropolitan Lunatic Asylum. He was suffering from 'the effects of over brain-work', his wife said; his doctor diagnosed '"Brain fag" with symptoms of general excitement & debility'.[37]

After seven months in the asylum, he was discharged cured, and returned to work. As he went on to fight against Jenks over the curriculum, losing in the faculty and then rallying support in the senate, did his colleagues think or say where he had recently been? The supposed cure worked in the asylum did not last, and in 1896 he was again unable to work, suffering from delusions and suspecting his wife of tampering with his food and his papers.[38] When he forced her out of their house, he was taken to the asylum again, but turned to the courts to get himself out. Battling the asylum authorities with points of law, he was able at length to engage a solicitor and take out a writ of habeas corpus, representing himself in the Supreme Court. The *Herald* was fascinated:

> Behold the scene. Three judges on the bench, Mr Coldham with voluminous briefs and piles of reference books at the barristers' table, the Crown Solicitor at hand to give him assistance, a handful of spectators, and in the centre of all, occupying also a seat at the barristers' table, the venerable-looking man, whom half a dozen doctors allege to be a lunatic, and who yet argued and worried out legal problems with the easy confidence and convincing manner of a master mind. Surely this was no uncommon lunatic who time after time confounded those opposed to him, and in the end beat them all at their own pastime of technicality.[39]

He succeeded in convincing the appeal judges that the certificates under which he was detained lacked information required by statute, but they declined to release him. The court ordered a fresh assessment of his condition by a single judge, during which the asylum's barrister questioned him at length in the witness box about his delusions. Backed by a fresh opinion from two doctors, the court concluded that he should be sent back to the asylum. There he remained until, in 1901, he took advantage of the privilege he had been given of walking in the grounds without an escort, and escaped. He made his way to California, where he died in 1910.[40]

The records of the faculty maintained a discreet and impartial silence about the troubles of its Property lecturer. When he returned to work in 1889, five of his students asked that Frank Gavan Duffy should mark their papers, since he had given the lectures, but the council refused.[41] Beyond that, the consequences of his illness were recorded only in requests for leave while he was in the asylum, which the university granted. His paranoia seems to have left his legal powers unimpaired.

Thanks to their professional standing and the fact that their main work was outside the university, the law lecturers had a degree of autonomy that set them apart from many of their counterparts in other disciplines. Moore explained to a royal commission on the university in 1902:

> The lecturers in the Law School are what we call independent lecturers. They are not responsible to me. The Lecturer in Classics is responsible to the Professor in Classics; the Lecturer in Mathematics is responsible to the Professor in Mathematics; the several demonstrators are responsible to the men in whose departments they are, but in the faculty of law the individual lecturer is the ruler of his work in the same way as the Professor is the ruler of those subjects he takes charge of.[42]

Independent lecturers were also appointed in other faculties.[43] The title lasted for some part-time Law staff into the 1990s, still designating practitioners and even the occasional judge who combined teaching with their main work in the profession, much as their predecessors had done in the nineteenth century.

These teachers were the active core of the faculty, but they were not its only members. From the start, the faculty could never be equated just with the teaching staff, in the American sense. The legal members of the university council (judges and others who had been admitted to practise, whether graduates of the law school or not) had always joined the professor and lecturers on the law faculty, but their main involvement in the university was elsewhere, and their attendance at faculty meetings tended to be patchy. From 1903, in a general expansion of the composition of the faculties that coincided with the creation of the faculties of arts and science, and that perhaps showed a calculated appreciation of the value of co-opted outsiders as the university weathered the storm that followed the Dickson frauds, the council could appoint additional members. The number was unlimited until 1921, when the statutes imposed a limit of three.[44]

The law faculty was slow to take up the opportunity, probably because the independent lecturers, the legal members of the council, and Moore's own excellent connections provided sufficient links with the profession and the wider community, or at least with the influential people who mattered most to the law school. In 1920, seven of the eleven members of the faculty were legal members of the council, including two judges (Henry Higgins and Leo Cussen), the chairman of the *Herald* newspaper group (Theodore Fink, who had headed two royal commissions on education, including the inquiry into the university after the Dickson frauds), the chairman of the National Bank (Sir John Grice, who was also the university's vice-chancellor), a member of parliament (Agar Wynne), and the speaker of the Legislative Assembly, John Mackey, who was also the lecturer in Equity. The list shows the weight of outsiders in the faculty and the significant number of lawyers on the council—and, incidentally, some of the varied destinations of the law school's students, since all had studied law at Melbourne. After Latham resigned from the teaching staff in 1920, he became the first faculty member appointed by the council, not to build a new link outside the university but to maintain an old one.[45]

The next outside appointment, in 1921, employed talent closer to home, and made a rare direct link between the working of the faculty and the university's colleges. John Behan had been an outstandingly successful law student at Melbourne and Oxford. He graduated with first-class honours and the Supreme Court prize in 1904, and became Victoria's first Rhodes scholar, in the face of controversy about his very modest sporting record, which some thought failed to meet Rhodes' criteria. He entered the history of the Oxford law school by winning, in the same year, first class honours in both the jurisprudence final honour school and the Bachelor of Civil Law exam, together with the Vinerian and Eldon scholarships. Two of the papers were scheduled at the same time; Behan spent half the time on one, then turned to the other. He was a young man in too obvious a hurry for some at Oxford, which changed the rules to make his feat impossible in future, and he attracted disapproval when, as a lecturer at University College, he sold lecture notes for all the examination subjects. Nevertheless, in the *History of the University of Oxford* published ninety years after he was a student, he was still 'the prodigy J.C.V. Behan'.[46]

Admission to the bar, teaching, and wartime work in government occupied him in London until he became warden of Melbourne's Trinity College in 1918. Although he never joined the law school's teaching staff, aside from some temporary lecturing, he took on significant responsibilities as a faculty member. When Moore went on leave to travel overseas in 1923, Behan was his choice to act in his place, and the faculty even elected him as dean.[47] If the election had been valid, Behan would have been the faculty's only external dean, but under the university's statutes, a professor had to fill the position. After a few months, awareness of this percolated into the faculty's minutes, which gave up calling Behan the dean, and said instead that he was merely acting.

Behan acted again as dean after Moore's departure in 1927, and briefly in the absence of Paton and Bailey in the summer of 1937–38. For the faculty to go outside the teaching staff for this choice may

seem strange, but the conditions of the time make it more understandable. In 1923, the four independent lecturers were all fully occupied elsewhere: John Gregory, Wilfred Fullagar and Walter Sproule
(Latham's successor in Contract and Personal Property) were barristers, while Mackey (now Sir John), the elderly lecturer in Equity,
could not be both dean and speaker of the Legislative Assembly. Behan
had authority, and he was on the campus rather than working in the
city, an important consideration at a time when much of the dean's
work was in the day-to-day tasks of enrolling students and handling
their inquiries.

Despite his close involvement as acting dean, and the scholarly
effort he put into the thesis on property law for which he was awarded
the LLD in 1923, Trinity absorbed most of Behan's energies. He published little after his thesis appeared as a book, but when the chair of
jurisprudence became vacant in 1930, his often difficult relations with
the unruly Trinity students were deteriorating, and he let the chancellor know that he would like to be considered confidentially for the
appointment, without submitting a formal application. The chair committee preferred George Paton, and Behan remained at Trinity until
his retirement in 1946, reconciled with the students but feuding with
his counterpart at Trinity's offshoot for women students, Janet Clarke
Hall. His association with Moore continued, as the former dean joined
the council at Trinity after his retirement in 1927.[48]

The barriers to becoming a student in Moore's time would seem slight
to later generations, when entry to the law school was a competition
and admission a prize. There was no quota, no ranking of applications,
no high score to reach in order to get in. Yet the barriers were real, and
they filtered the students just as much as later selection schemes, albeit
in different ways. There were two main obstacles: matriculation, and
fees. Matriculation was the entrance exam administered by the university itself. LLB students and, from 1863, articled clerks too, had to pass
it, with Latin as a compulsory subject.

The matriculation failure rate was high, but for most of the population, even sitting the exam was unreachable, because of the lack of secondary schooling. Until Victoria's first government secondary school, now Melbourne High School, opened in 1905, students had to find their secondary education at so-called public schools affiliated with churches, at others run as profit-making businesses, or through the extra subjects that some state primary schools offered after hours. All, including the extra subjects at state schools, required payment of fees, except from the winners of the few available scholarships (like the one that took the young Robert Menzies to secondary school). As late as 1939, 70 per cent of new law graduates from the university had come from private schools, and even this figure was low compared with Medicine, where barely one graduate in ten came from a state school.[49]

Those who passed the matriculation exam (or its successors—from 1905, the senior public, and, from 1913, the school leaving) still had to be able to pay the university's fees. In 1891, articled clerks paid fees of about £15 15s 0d a year, depending on their choice of subjects, while LLB students paid £25 4s 0d a year, or roughly 30 per cent of average annual earnings in a manufacturing job. Again, a few scholarships lowered the barrier for high achievers: the university awarded one scholarship in law each year in the early 1890s, and there were twenty-five state government exhibitions for university study in 1912, when Menzies received one. From 1919, the state government funded a university student loan scheme. Most students, though, had to pay. Many got the money from their families, while others earned their fees in outside jobs.[50]

The largest single group who worked to pay their way were the articled clerks, or at least the sub-group of clerks who received wages (many went unpaid for at least part of their clerkships). School teaching and private coaching were other occupations that students managed to fit in around their university commitments. Maurice Blackburn, the future Labor parliamentarian and supporter of civil liberties, worked as a teacher and librarian while he studied (he graduated in law in 1909).[51] John Latham and Charles Lowe, both later judges and chancellors of the university, also taught their way through the law course, in Latham's case as a college tutor. Alfred Deakin was another teacher–student.

But the achievements of these gifted people were exceptional. When the university surveyed its students in 1919, just over 30 per cent were paying their university expenses partly or wholly from their past or present earnings. About a quarter were in paid employment (the figure for law, if it had been calculated separately, would have been higher, thanks to the presence of the articled clerks). Some 17 per cent—who had returned from the armed forces—had assistance from the Commonwealth government, and another 22 per cent had all or some of their fees paid by scholarships, bursaries or exhibitions, or had free places funded by the state education department.[52] In all, the university, the state or the Commonwealth helped nearly 40 per cent of the university's students to pay their fees, although post-war help for returned service-people swelled this figure, and many must have supplemented their awards from paid employment or family help. The rest had to find the money for themselves, from family, private sponsors, or their own exertions.

The exclusion of women from the university as a whole ended in 1880, but informal barriers and, most importantly, discouragement from entry to the profession, deterred women from enrolling in law for another seventeen years, although there was nothing in the university's statutes or the council's resolutions to stop them. They joined the male law students in their compulsory arts subjects long before then; Louisa Wilson, one of the early residents of the Trinity College women's hostel (later Janet Clarke Hall), was one of the students who petitioned for lectures in jurisprudence, at that time an arts subject, to be held at the university in 1888.[53]

Family encouragement was a crucial adjunct to personal determination for many of the women who took the new, open rules of the university at their word, and enrolled in its courses. The first woman to enrol in the law course, Flos Greig, followed two sisters to university (they had graduated in medicine), and another sister graduated in law after her. Anna Brennan, who graduated in 1909, came from a farming family at Emu Creek, near Bendigo, whose members supported each other's education in turn.[54]

When Greig enrolled in 1897, the university had long settled the question of women's right to be students, but whether the law continued to bar them from practice as barristers and solicitors was yet to be determined. The other students revived many of the arguments and instinctive reactions heard during the long debate about admission of women to the university, but with an additional element centring on legal practice. Women depicted as emotional, unintelligent and flighty could not make good lawyers: 'The first alarming feature of the innovation would be the substitution of emotion for pure reason, as the groundwork of all legal argument. What chance could the less favoured male counsel have despite all his erudition against an adversary with smiles and tears, and blushes at her command?' These common assumptions and familiar jokes reassured and bonded male lawyers against the threat of change, but they were far from universally held. In 1897, doubtless in response to Greig's arrival, the all-male Law Students' Society debated whether women should be admitted to practise, and decided in favour by sixteen votes to ten.[55]

On Greig's graduation in 1903, second in her class and with third-class honours, whether a woman would be admitted to practise became a pressing question. In many other common law jurisdictions—the United States, Canada, South Africa and Western Australia among them—women turned to litigation, to discover whether the courts would resolve ambiguity in the law of legal practice in favour of their admission. In Victoria, too, the question could have been treated as one of statutory interpretation. The legislation and rules of court governing admission used masculine pronouns, but without expressly excluding women, and in such a case general principles of interpretation dictated that the provisions should apply equally to both genders.[56]

Yet litigation, expensive and uncertain, turned out to be unnecessary. There was sufficient political support for any doubt about the status of women applicants to be resolved in their favour by a special act of parliament, which was passed in 1903. The process was much slower in New South Wales. The first woman to graduate from an Australian law school was Ada Evans, at the University of Sydney in 1902, but, despite her persistent efforts, the law did not allow her admission to practise until legislation was enacted in 1918.[57]

The ease with which the Victorian bill passed is surprising, when it is compared with the parliament's record on the key issue for women's rights at the time, the extension of the right to vote. Victoria was the last jurisdiction in Australia to give women the vote, in 1908, after the failure of some nineteen previous bills.[58] The upper house, still elected on a restrictive franchise and dominated by conservatives much as it was in Hearn's time, had been a stronghold of resistance to women's voting rights, but it accepted the admission of women as lawyers with little dissent.

Greig's own activism is probably one reason for this outcome. She was an effective and articulate advocate for the admission of women, as she showed in an extended article she wrote on the topic in 1909. The role of John Mackey, who introduced the bill for the admission of women, is also significant. One of Greig's lecturers, he was a new member of the lower house, but he rapidly gained authority, and became a minister in 1904. His bill, pitched as moderate and logical, found general support in parliament and managed not to rouse the opposition that defeated a similar measure nine years earlier. In comparable jurisdictions, the goal of entry to the profession was sometimes kept separate from wider aims for equality, partly as a tactic to placate wavering male politicians, and partly as a response by women lawyers who did not see themselves as part of a wider movement.[59]

The students found admission of women to the profession less troubling than their admission to the LSS itself. The all-male members debated this question in 1913, and the leading advocates on each side then put their cases in the *Melbourne University Magazine*. 'Equity' (who chose a surprising pen-name, but presumably saw exclusion of women as equity for men) argued that the presence of women would change the atmosphere of the students' gatherings, taking away the freedom men enjoyed in an all-male social group: 'Members will be extremely careful to let nothing escape their lips which were better unsaid in the circumstances'. Apart from the constraints of propriety in the presence of women, who had to be protected from the men's grosser natures, there was the problem of nerves for younger members who spoke in the society's moots. 'A man doesn't mind very much if he makes a fool of himself in front of men; but no man cares to risk it before women.'[60]

'Quo Vadit', who supported the admission of women as members, put forward a case based on rights, equality, and higher authority. Women were admitted to the university and to the profession, he said, so the LSS should not exclude them. He unknowingly took up a theme from many common-law jurisdictions, where women's assimilation to professional culture and acceptance of dominant ideas in the profession were features of the process of gaining admission, when he reassured his opponents that a woman lawyer would have to act like a man: 'she will have to regard herself as one of those with whom most of her work will be done, and amongst whom most of her time will be spent. In other words, when at Rome, she will have to do as they do in Rome.'[61]

'Quo Vadit' and his supporters had the better of the debate. The meeting voted by a majority of one to allow women to become members, but the minority threatened to counterattack and reverse the decision. In the absence of LSS minutes for the period, later events are hard to trace, but women appear not to have become active in the society until the 1920s. The number of women in the law course remained so small—still only 8 per cent in 1950—that the LSS remained largely a male preserve (though with notable exceptions, particularly during World War II).[62]

It was one thing for a woman to be admitted to practise (Greig became the first in Australia), but another for her to find a career as a lawyer. Greig worked as a solicitor, initially as a sole practitioner, but apparently business did not prosper; during World War I, she was employed at two solicitors' firms in Melbourne, standing in for men who had left for the armed services. At the end of the war, she wrote to her friend John Latham about the dilemma posed by their imminent return, which would leave her without a job:

> I have no desire to commence practice afresh myself, I can't profess to particularly like the routine or the mixed lots & varied assortments of the work of a solicitor's office.
>
> What I really would enjoy & could still put a good deal of enthusiasm & hard work into would be more specialized Law—But except for a few Government appointments there is very little work of the sort to be had & I do not know how to set about finding such positions as there are.
>
> It has occurred to me from various articles in magazines & so forth that after the war is over there are going to be tremendous changes within the British Empire itself such as reconstructing the government of Eastern Dominions & particularly of the Pacific Islands such as Fiji & others.
>
> I am sure there are few people who love the moist tropical outskirts of the Empire as I do & it struck me that there are sure to be various positions for lawyers on some of the Administrative staffs—of course I realize that women never have got such positions, but the war has made such a changed outlook & women doctors are getting appointments all over the world.[63]

She became a frequent visitor to Asia, but as a traveller, not as a lawyer, and in the 1930s worked as an employee in a solicitor's office in country Victoria. Among the other early women law students, Anna Brennan, the second woman admitted to practise in Victoria, had a long career as a solicitor and in community organisations; Christian

Jollie Smith (LLB 1911) became a solicitor, but in 1918 was reportedly Melbourne's first woman taxi-driver, and then became a founding committee-member of the Communist Party of Australia and a successful labour lawyer in Sydney. Joan Lazarus (later Rosanove), who completed the articled clerks' course in 1917, became the first woman to sign the Victorian bar roll, and the first to become a Victorian Queen's counsel. Like their male counterparts, some moved in and out of the profession or found their work elsewhere. Gladys Hain (LLB 1910) was successively a solicitor, a journalist and then a barrister; Lesbia Keogh (later Harford), LLB 1916, is best known as a poet and left-wing activist; and Alice Hoy (LLB 1927) became principal of the secondary teacher training centre at the University of Melbourne.[64]

One small group of students had experiences of the law school unlike those of their colleagues: the blind and those with impaired vision. The success of some lawyers who had lost their sight showed the appeal of law as a career for the blind. Of these, the best known in the Victorian profession was George Maxwell, who was already well-established as a barrister when he became blind in the 1920s; both Arthur Dean, judge and historian of the Victorian bar, and Robert Menzies, barrister and prime minister, described him as the greatest criminal advocate they had encountered.[65]

The first of the law school's blind students appears to have been Charles Chase, who studied arts and law in the 1870s and 1880s. He passed the matriculation exam in 1873, and enrolled in the articled clerks' course four years later, after an unsuccessful attempt at the BA. When he narrowly failed Property in February 1889, his lecturer, John Rogers, discovered that he was blind only after marking his exam. (Presumably Chase did not attend lectures—nothing unusual when many country articled clerks never came to class—and, like later blind students, had lecture notes read to him and dictated his exam answers.) Rogers asked for the faculty's permission to change the result to a pass, 'considering the great disabilities under which Mr Chase had to labour in communicating his knowledge of the subject by a written Examination'.

But Rogers' colleagues disagreed. The faculty regretted that 'having regard to the Regulations of the University, it cannot suggest anything that can be done to meet Mr Chase's wishes'. What Chase himself thought about this is, like so much of his university career, unknown. It may have been an appeal from Chase that led Rogers to reconsider the result, but many blind students rejected any suggestion of adjusting standards to suit them: 'it is inappropriate to take a person's disability into account in assessing the quality of his or her work', as a blind law student of the 1990s put it. Chase was not deterred, and he completed the remaining subjects of the articled clerks' course in October 1889.[66]

Of later blind students, one of the best known was Dudley Tregent, who lost his sight fighting in France in World War I. He received the help needed to make the printed sources of the course available to him from the residents of his local community at Carrum, near Melbourne, who paid to support his studies in braille. He graduated LLB in 1925, and became a solicitor; as agent for a Northern Territory colleague, he acted for the appellant in the successful appeal to the High Court in *Tuckiar v. The King*, the first reported High Court decision in which an Aboriginal person was a party to the proceedings.[67]

After World War II, the faculty and the Law Students' Society became more involved in supporting blind students, although through the efforts of individuals rather than under a systematic program. The professor of jurisprudence, David Derham, organised assistance, in much the same way as he became known as the man to go to for help in getting articles. He explained the background to a blind student at the University of Adelaide, who asked for advice in 1962:

> Since the war there have been only two blind law students who have graduated and proceeded to articles and admission in Victoria. In each case I made special arrangements for their

articled clerkship, and of course there had to be secretarial assistance provided for them which created financial problems ...
there is no established method of providing that necessary financial assistance. In each of the two cases I mentioned special
arrangements were made, in one case depending upon the generosity of private individuals in Melbourne ... No system for the
articling of blind students has been established in Victoria. Each
case has been dealt with as a separate problem.[68]

Arrangements for assessment and lectures were made separately
for each student. Where copies of acts of parliament were allowed in
exams, the faculty decided in 1941 that the examination supervisor
could read extracts to a blind examinee. When Lawrence McCredie
was a student in the 1950s, he used a tape-recorder in lectures and
dictated his exam answers to an amanuensis. Decisions about the use
of braille machines and tape-recorders in class were still left to individual lecturers in the early 1970s, and the university provided a writer
and a special venue for examinations. The LSS also helped in organising teams of readers for blind students, as some lecturers had in the
1950s.[69]

Attempts to form a law students' society, to help their studies, bring
them together socially, and represent their interests, began at the same
time as the law lectures themselves. Sewell mentioned in his inaugural
lecture that the students had already established a legal debating society,
and when he was forced to cancel lectures, he tried to notify students
through its secretary. But its life was short, and a fresh and more elaborate attempt was made in 1860, when the students formed the
University Forensic (that is, Legal) Society. Establishing a pattern that
lasted for a hundred years, they brought in outsiders to hold some of
the society's offices, for help and patronage. The first president was Sir
Redmond Barry, who favoured the society with one of his set-
piece public addresses, full of windy rhetoric and classical allusions,

published in the newspaper and as a pamphlet. The teaching staff became vice-presidents.[70]

The society held meetings and debates on legal questions at the Fitzroy courthouse, the County Court and the Carlton Inn (across the road from the site where the law building would be constructed 140 years later), but reports of its activities petered out after 1864, and it seems to have faded away. The same fate befell the Melbourne Forensic Society, established by a later group of law students in 1871 under Hearn's presidency. After nearly two years, it too succumbed to lack of interest.[71]

The articled clerks' co-workers, the law clerks who made their careers as employees in solicitors' offices (rather than serving under articles and becoming practitioners), formed their own society in 1878. In contrast with the law students' clubs, the Victorian United Law Clerks' Society did not bother with debating, but brought members together in social gatherings, helped them find employment, and represented their interests in dealings with the profession and the judges. It met to discuss the effect of new rules of court in 1884, and later lobbied, unsuccessfully, for the admission to practise of managing clerks with ten years' experience. Its annual cricket match became something of an institution. When it was held at the Melbourne Cricket Ground in 1880, the members ate lunch in a pavilion put up for the purpose, while a band provided music. Most of all, though, it was a benefit society and charity, collecting funds for members suffering hardship. Before the existence of state-sponsored social security, support from such organisations was often the only income for the sick, bereaved or unemployed.[72]

The Law Clerks' Society lasted into the 1890s or later, but law students, with their distinct interests, moved again to create a society of their own. A fresh attempt in 1887 managed, for the first time, to survive beyond the brief organisational lifespan of a single generation of members. The new club began as the Articled Clerks' Law Debating Society. Its name and constitution captured the social division between clerks and degree students: LLB students were initially excluded, although links with the profession were entrenched by a requirement for the president and vice-presidents to be practising solicitors.

Its meetings ranged from moots on tort, property, contract, succession and other branches of private law, to debates on questions of current affairs, such as abolition of trial by jury and capital punishment; two profitable 'smoke night concerts' brought in revenue in 1889. For a few years in the early 1890s, meetings debated wider questions. One meeting at the depth of the financial crisis of 1893, when Melbourne's banks were collapsing in the crash that followed the boom of the 1890s, began with news from the treasurer that he had rescued most of the society's funds from its bank before it folded; members went on to discuss the problem of the power to prosecute for crimes committed by the managers of the bubble companies during the boom and the bust (Isaac Isaacs, former law student and future chief justice and governor-general, resigned as solicitor-general on the day of the society's meeting, in protest at cabinet's refusal to prosecute one of the most notorious land boomers). As if to confirm the gloomy tone, members then debated the question, 'Is suicide in any case justifiable?' At least they decided that the answer was 'no'.[73]

Attempts to get the university student union to provide accommodation for the society failed, and it met in the city: in a company boardroom provided by a sponsor, in the Law Institute's council room at the law courts (where the Institute was based from 1883 to 1924), and then in city cafés. The society successfully affiliated itself with the United Law Students' Society of London, and lobbied for the creation of prizes for articled clerks (a campaign that succeeded when the Supreme Court donated funds for the purpose in 1891).[74]

From 1892, degree students were allowed to join, and the society changed its name accordingly, to the Law Students' Society. This widening of the membership base, along with a jump in enrolments as students tried to beat the start of new admission rules in 1891, tided the society through the depression of the 1890s. The LSS not only survived, but branched out. From 1891, it published its own journal, the *Summons*, containing articles on legal subjects ranging from the learned to the topical. Members organised football matches against the medical students, a boat race, and a theatre night, along with regular moots, and claimed credit for getting the government to introduce an act of parliament to clarify a section of the Legal Profession Practice Act 1891.[75]

Despite these successes, a lingering problem with the society's membership and purpose grew and finally precipitated a crisis. To maintain links with the profession—a theme of the society for much of its history—practitioners could become members, but on an honorary basis, without paying fees. By the end of 1900, attendances at meetings had fallen, and solicitors dominated the membership. 'It has now virtually come to be merely a monthly meeting of Junior Members of the Legal Profession,' the committee reported. This was not the aim of the society, nor was a club composed mainly of honorary members viable. 'It consisted so largely of men of wide legal experience, comparatively speaking, that mere beginners were swamped out', three students (John Latham among them) told the members.[76]

A new committee took over in 1901, halved the membership fee, and made solicitors pay equally with students. Sadly, it also cut the *Summons* loose, putting it under a separate management committee, who were to run it 'independently of the Society'. Despite its quality, it had long been a financial burden, and without the society's support, the magazine's remaining life was short. Moore, the long-serving LSS president, prompted the election of a recent graduate to succeed him in 1901; Henry Christian Winneke won the vote, and Moore agreed to stay on as vice-president for a year, to ease the transition.[77] The plan to revive the society succeeded, at the cost of the *Summons*, which ceased publication two years later. New members became involved, and attendances rose.

———— ⤜●⤛ ————

The job of the law school's teachers was lecturing, and lecture they did, maintaining the expository monologue as not just the mainstay, but almost the exclusive method of teaching. It was not for want of ideas about other ways of doing things. Back in 1857, the council had reported that the course would combine lectures with 'the Tutorial system of teaching', and Sewell said in his inaugural lecture that he would prepare questions on each lecture, for students to answer in writing for themselves, and orally to him. If anything came of these early good intentions, it has left no trace, other than Hearn's engaging discussions and hypotheticals, but both Jenks and Moore, who had experienced the close contact with teachers provided by Cambridge's supervision system, were aware of the benefits greater interaction could bring. Jenks held a 'conversation class' once a fortnight at his home, at which students read papers, followed by informal discussion.[78]

Moore's interest in the techniques and problems of legal education was conscientious rather than a central focus of his work. They did not engage his curiosity and imagination as they did those of Jenks ('father of the Society of Public Teachers of Law', after his return to Britain) or Bailey, who was preoccupied with the curriculum for years, partly because of the campaign waged by the Law Institute against his ideas.[79] Nor did Moore write about legal education with the originality or vigour of his contemporary Jethro Brown, who taught successively at Hobart, Sydney, London and Aberystwyth, and was professor at Adelaide for ten years while Moore was at Melbourne.

Nevertheless, Moore joined Brown in an important innovation: a turn towards the United States for ideas about legal education. Brown described the American law schools he visited in 1904 as a wonderland. He marvelled at the 'extraordinary perfection' of their buildings and the zeal of their teachers and students, and perceptively observed their styles of teaching. He anticipated the reaction of many Australian visitors to the best American law schools for years afterwards: 'their general excellence is almost calculated to arouse in one a feeling of despair'.[80]

Moore was the first of Melbourne's law professors to visit American law schools and find out about their teaching. Even before this, it was to the United States, not Britain, that he looked for models of legal education: 'What we have to learn we have to learn from

America', he declared to the university royal commission in 1902. He spent about four weeks at Columbia and Harvard in 1911, and wrote about his experience and the implications he saw for Melbourne. His attention naturally centred on the case method, 'the exclusive teaching of law through discussion in class of decided cases', using casebooks (extracts from the raw material of judicial decisions), rather than text-books that presented summaries and drew conclusions. The kind of Socratic interrogation that characterised the case method in many American law schools was already well-established. 'Sometimes the professor will heckle a single student for ten minutes or more', Moore observed, 'before he passes on to some one else'.[81]

He saw both the merits and the disadvantages of this sort of teaching. It encouraged familiarity with legal method and the process of legal development, students gained confidence and 'a critical habit of mind', and the contest with other students and the teacher was stimulating. But there were problems that became familiar to later generations of Melbourne students and lecturers. In large classes (Moore visited none that had fewer than a hundred members), only a few students could take part in the discussion, and the same few appeared prominently in different classes. The course of the debate might be illuminating or might not; Moore himself sometimes left the class unsure of the law on the topic. Some professors combined the case method with expository lectures for this reason.[82]

The use of the case method at Columbia and Harvard depended on certain preconditions, Moore found. It needed 'a certain maturity on the part of students'—provided by graduate entry—and a large academic staff, allowing branches of the law to be broken down into smaller subjects for teaching purposes. The law of contract and personal property was one subject at Melbourne; at Harvard, its various subdivisions occupied eight. With a small staff, undergraduate entry and no casebooks, Melbourne enjoyed none of these advantages. Nor did Adelaide, where Brown's use of class discussions and alternatives to exams ended after his departure in 1916 to become president of the state Industrial Court.[83]

Moore thought students could get the benefit of the case method if it was used fully in just one or two subjects, while the rest of the course fell back on textbooks and expository lectures. But he also had more searching, if speculative, philosophical reservations about its use in America, hinting at some of the criticisms later voiced by legal realists. Relying exclusively on the study of cases overemphasised the logic, form, consistency and harmony of the law, perhaps with wider social effects: 'the law may become less and less an instrument for accomplishing present social ends, and more an institution to the needs of which social ends themselves must be adapted'.[84]

After his return, Moore made 'tentative experiments' with the case method. But conditions made its use almost impossible, he told the council: 'the absence of "case-books" & the consequent necessity for resort by a whole class to the one set of Law Reports in the Library, offer difficulties which prevent any considerable use of the system here, while the demands which it makes upon time present a further difficulty as the year passes'.[85]

He encouraged students to tackle sources for themselves in the library, although success brought its own difficulties. 'The use of the Library by law students has increased in recent years in a way which is gratifying but embarrassing', he reported in 1913.

> It is gratifying because it indicates a better appreciation of right methods of legal study—the student is not seeking to substitute his lecture note book for a first hand study of the reports & statutes. On the other hand, it is a principal factor in the overcrowding of the Library.[86]

If the case method could not be used effectively in lectures, tutorials could help students engage with the material, especially in the more practical and technical branches of the course. When the university was appraising its current and future needs in 1919, Moore recommended the appointment of two tutors,

> to follow the courses of lectures particularly in Property, Procedure, Equity and Contracts by classes for going through and explaining the principal forms of documents in common use in the various departments of legal business, both litigious, and other, e.g., Conveyances, settlements, mercantile instruments, pleadings and judgments. This is provided in the University of Sydney ...[87]

But the teaching staff, perhaps influenced by parsimony, perhaps by caution at such innovations, thought that an extra class each week in Property, combined with the issuing of printed notes for students in the relevant subjects, would do the job, and the faculty agreed.[88]

Tutors were appointed to help returned servicemen at the end of World War I, but they finished their work in 1919. Once they had gone, tutors were employed only for a different purpose, teaching by correspondence. Students who enrolled in the articled clerks' course while working in solicitors' offices outside Melbourne had long struggled with the problem of being in two places at one time: in their offices in Bendigo, Ballarat, or other centres, and at lectures in Melbourne. Most got by, using lecture notes that they bought or borrowed, but from time to time they mobilised for better conditions. A group of Ballarat law students proposed to establish their own, self-funded branch law lectureship in 1861, but were put off by the chancellor, and the Geelong Law Students' Society supported local students in the 1890s.[89]

The university, reluctant to take any steps towards teaching by correspondence, offered few concessions, but in 1919 the state government took an interest in the students' welfare, and the premier negotiated with the university to provide more help. Two tutors for country students were appointed in March 1920. They and their successors operated a tutorial system by correspondence for country students throughout the 1920s and 1930s, sending out exercises and receiving answers. The Wimmera Law Association, one of several regional practitioners' groups, paid for an additional three-year tutorship for country students in 1948, and offered students summer employment.[90]

The objective was laudable, but the correspondence course created as many pedagogical problems as it solved. The students laboured under great disadvantages, not least in getting access to books, and many failed or dropped out. In 1922, the professorial board, wary of correspondence courses and students who spent little time on the campus, urged Arts and Law to fall into line with other faculties and require 'substantial attendance' at the university for their courses. But the faculty thought compulsory attendance at lectures might drive students away from the degree course and into the articled clerks' course, which the university did not control (although it provided the teaching). After two pages of careful equivocation, it recommended no change in the rules concerning attendance at lectures, but conceded that vigilance was needed, in case absentee students became a problem in the future. The correspondence system continued, but its shortcomings and the heavy burden it placed on the staff became a preoccupation of the faculty in the 1950s. Enrolment was progressively restricted to smaller categories of students until it was abolished altogether in 1962.[91]

Lecture outlines supplied by the teachers could help country and city students alike. Jenks produced an outline of his constitutional law lectures in 1889, as a first step to make up for the lack of a textbook, but the process was cumbersome and, doubtless, expensive; at a time when typewriters were only just becoming available, the only practical way to make the outline available was to have it typeset and printed.[92]

Not everyone agreed about the merits of printed notes. Even if money had been available, most of the lecturers opposed giving outlines to students, on pedagogical grounds. In 1906, the council asked for faculties' opinions about the possibility of printing lecture notes, in order to reduce attendance at overcrowded classes, but the response from law was not enthusiastic. 'Text-books (& even printed lectures) can only give information upon the subject: they can not teach it', Casimir Woinarski, the independent lecturer in Wrongs and Procedure, told the dean. Moore summarised the faculty's objections for the council: the course varied from year to year, there were already textbooks, and the students needed to learn how to take notes. The reference to note-taking was a telling sign of what most of the staff expected of their students. The standard lecturing style, little better than dictation, gave 'no scope of any kind to inquire or to be taught', one student told the royal commission in 1902. 'It is simply a statement of the law which he takes down, and then goes away to learn.'[93]

Moore was less sceptical than his colleagues, and began experimenting with typed lecture notes for his students in 1907. It became his usual practice to give students a 'very full synopsis'; soon the university had machinery for 'multiplying' them, as Moore put it, or duplicating them without having to have them typeset and printed. To expand the system of typed outlines, Moore recommended the appointment of a shorthand writer–typist. Esme May took over this position in 1924, when she answered the university's advertisement for a 'Lady typist' with knowledge of duplicating and legal terminology, to act as secretary to the law school. She had learned shorthand at the Methodist Ladies' College business school, and picked up legal language while working for two years at a city law firm.[94]

Moore's outlines were extensive (examples survive in his papers), but they did not provide the connected narrative offered by full lecture notes. Officially, the only way to get these was for students to come to lectures and write them for themselves. This could be difficult, not only for those who lived outside Melbourne, but also for many who worked their way through university with the help of paid jobs elsewhere. Sets of lecture notes circulated among the students, handed on as favours or in return for cash. This caught the attention of an entrepreneur in 1922: a 'scrivener' turned up in Moore's jurisprudence class and started taking shorthand notes, in order to write them up for sale. But he soon disappeared, Moore said, 'owing apparently to the technicalities of the lectures'. The following year, a former student, now an articled clerk and so barred from other employment, got permission to earn an income outside office hours by typing up and selling her own lecture notes, updated with help from current students.[95]

The university in the 1860s

Law school staff and students in the 1870s

Flos Greig

After a lecture, 1953

Private International Law, 1954

Design for a new law building, 1953

Law library, 2001

Melbourne Law School, 2007

At the end of Moore's time, the law school recouped some of the cost of the duplicated outlines by charging for them, despite the objections of some of the students. A few lecturers chose to go further: Philip (P. D.) Phillips circulated a full set of his lecture notes in Modern Political Institutions and lectured from them in 1929.[96] The pedagogical debate about notes and attendance at lectures recurred as it became easier for teachers to give students the substance of their classes without publishing books, and later as computers allowed staff and students alike to work from a distance. By the end of the century, the university was uneasily balancing its commitment to the exciting modernity of information technology against its insistence, like that of the professorial board of 1922, on campus-based education as a mark of the kind of institution it wanted to be.

———◆———

When fighting ended between Jenks, the council and the senate, the course retained the basic structure it had had since the introduction of the graduate LLB in 1882. Degree students and articled clerks did the same law subjects, but LLB candidates had to complete the BA course first, making sure they included Jurisprudence and Constitutional and Legal History (both arts subjects). Their law studies then took two years, during which they tackled Roman Law, Property, Obligations, International Law, Wrongs (which included criminal law), and Equity and Procedure.

Beyond the faculty itself, the most important influences on the shape of the course were the university's council and senate, and the judges of the Supreme Court. For most of the law school's history, parliament and government had little direct effect on its curriculum, important though they were in establishing the legislative framework for the university and the profession, and in providing funding. The way lawyers should be trained was treated as a matter primarily for the judges, who had retained authority over admission to practise since the establishment of the Supreme Court of Victoria in 1852.

In amalgamating the two branches of the profession in 1891, parliament made one of its rare direct interventions in the structure of legal education, with unintended but important consequences for the law school. After thirty years of repeated attempts in parliament to weaken or remove the division of the profession between barristers and solicitors, a bill was passed that not merely allowed the members of one branch to practise in the other, as the earliest, unsuccessful amalgamation bills had aimed to do, but fused the two branches completely.

The significance for the law school was not so much in the perennial debates about economy and efficiency, experience and specialisation, and self-interest and the public good that dominated the long contest over fusion, but in its effect on legal training. A boycott by the Bar Association (which had been formed to defend the separation of the advocates' branch) nullified most of the intended effects of fusion, with the result that the two branches of the profession remained separate in practice although not in law, each with its own professional organisation. The framework for training and admission to practise, however, did change, and has treated intending barristers and solicitors alike ever since, although the Bar Association later imposed its own, additional requirements for membership.

The act that fused the profession, the Legal Profession Practice Act 1891, modelled the new admission rules on the existing requirements for solicitors rather than barristers. Instead of the LLB and the one-year studentship prescribed for barristers since 1872, the act opted for the university law exams (effectively the LLB without its arts prerequisite), three years of articles, and the court-controlled final exam. Matriculation remained compulsory. This spared practitioners the time and expense of taking out the LLB; as a graduate degree, it would have been an unacceptably high hurdle for all new lawyers to jump, especially in the depression years of the early 1890s. But there was a catch: for the first time since the university started teaching law, every new practitioner, whether intending to practise as a barrister or a solicitor, and whether a graduate or not, had to pass the court's final exams, which, since 1863, had been mandatory only for solicitors.

The new framework for admission to the fused profession brought mixed benefits and disadvantages for the university. On the one hand, by increasing the number of university law subjects prescribed for those who would formerly have been admitted as solicitors, it brought increased enrolments. It also brought forward the enrolments of intending barristers who found it was no longer in their interests to enrol in arts before doing law. 'The immediate result of this', in the words of the *Summons*, 'was that everyone who would under the old system have become an articled clerk and practically everyone who would have taken up the Arts course with the intention of becoming a barrister entered at once for the Law subjects', tripling the attendance at most lectures.[97]

On the other hand, the act presented a serious problem for the LLB. The graduate degree course had effectively served only one branch of the profession: most students who intended to practise as solicitors could qualify more quickly through the articled clerks' course, although they had the option of doing the LLB. If the degree course had been prescribed as the single route to admission, as in an earlier fusion bill, it would have taken over, but the 1891 act rejected this option, with the result that merger of the two branches deprived the LLB of its main function. No longer compulsory for barristers, the degree course now had little attraction for anyone whose aim in studying law was to be admitted to practise as quickly and easily as possible.[98]

Fusion bills had been debated for so many years that the likely effect on the law school had long been foreseen. Barrister John Box warned in 1885:

An unforeseen result of the proposed amalgamation of the two branches of the legal profession will undoubtedly be the ruin of our Law School. No one will be found ready to enter on a severe course of study for the degree of LL.B. when the object for which such training would be necessary is taken away by the fusion of the profession. The course of study at present prescribed for the solicitors' branch is a much easier and more elementary one than that which is required from barristers. This course would be the one that all lawyers of the future would pursue, to the great and lasting detriment of legal education, and the death, by inanition and want of students, of the Law School.[99]

The university council agreed, and threw its support behind the opponents of amalgamation. Whatever the bill's merits as a matter of public policy, it was clearly against the university's self-interest to have one of its degrees strangled, and it petitioned parliament in opposition. For less obvious reasons, the articled clerks, too, lobbied against amalgamation, voting strongly against it in a meeting of their society, and sending their own petition to parliament. Their public reasons were all matters of high-minded principle, casting doubt on the ability of each branch to do the other's work, and foreseeing 'degeneration and confusion in legal matters'.[100] Any mention of the likely effects on the incomes of different groups of practitioners was conspicuous by its absence, although they must have been in the minds of the articled clerks and junior solicitors who made up the society and faced losing business to newly versatile junior barristers if the bill went through.

Hopes of greater efficiency and lower legal costs, supported by business groups, outweighed these objections in parliament, which passed the bill. Once it came into force, the gloomy predictions for the LLB came true. Most students saw no advantage in the long degree course, since the shorter articled clerks' course covered the same law subjects and prepared them equally well for the admission exams. What was happening was 'the practical extinction of the LL.B. degree', as Moore put it.[101]

Help for the moribund course came, just as the greatest threat had, from parliament. Having nearly killed the degree, the government revived it by introducing an amendment to the 1891 act, which reduced the length of articles for LLB graduates from three years to two and explicitly recognised the degree, while still preserving the final admission exam. A group of law students urged the university council to support the bill, saying it would be an inducement to take the LLB degree and raise the educational standard of future barristers (they assumed that intending solicitors would not bother with the degree course). It would also reverse the indirect damage done to the arts course when it lost the students who used to enrol in the BA as a prerequisite for the LLB.[102]

The incentive of shorter articles was a boost, but the graduate LLB course was unsustainable in these circumstances. The faculty proposed to rescue it by uncoupling it from the BA, re-integrating arts subjects into the early years of the LLB, and cutting the overall time until graduation to four years. In short, it would return to something like the course that had been taught in Hearn's time.[103]

This meant throwing open the whole curriculum for debate. John Gregory again put forward his ideas for subject changes, and the dean responded with his own. Moore's most important proposal was outside the university's control: the Supreme Court's final admission examination should be reduced in scope, though not abolished. His ideas for the subjects of the degree course were easier to implement. Now that the admission exams were compulsory for all practitioners, the law school could reduce its teaching in one of the subjects they covered, Procedure, which articled clerks could pick up in their offices. Roman Law and Jurisprudence could become one subject, to be taught in Law rather than Arts; the Jurisprudence papers of the arts students, ill-prepared for the more technical legal aspects of the course, had been 'enough to make one despair'. Moore also wanted students to write four essays over their last two years (they could substitute reports of cases they attended at the law courts for two essays, if they chose).[104]

The faculty adopted most of Moore's ideas, although he lost out on the narrower title and content for Procedure. The council agreed (it faced losing the LLB course if it tried to retain graduate entry), but came back with a money-saving idea of its own. The merger of Roman Law and Jurisprudence was going to save Moore three hours' teaching a week. So surely he could take over one of the other subjects, and allow the university to dispense with one of the independent lecturers? The faculty resisted, but had to sacrifice something to save money. After some fencing between the faculty and the council, the senate, officious as ever, took up the faculty's offer to jettison Moore's proposed essays and reports, and vetoed the merger of Roman Law and Jurisprudence. The LLB became, once more, an undergraduate degree, and the four independent lecturers kept their jobs, but the new kinds of assessment sank without trace, victims of the university's poverty and the senate's interference.[105]

The act that amalgamated the profession had another unintended side-effect: it eventually killed off the Supreme Court's final admission examination, Victoria's closest approach to a separate bar exam. The amateurish and sometimes eccentric papers set by the board of examiners were badly suited to their important role, and the controversies that resulted left them with few defenders when the framework for admission was revised, for other reasons, in the early 1900s. The final exams were bizarre, even by nineteenth-century standards. They were set without teaching of any kind, and initially without giving candidates any guidance as to what was in them, beyond the titles of the subjects. When the failure rate reached 80 per cent in 1891, the law students complained to the judges about the 'petty catch questions' set by the examiners ('What is the penalty for shooting a house dove?' was one example), the lack of information about the exams, and the absence of prescribed texts.[106]

> At present the startled candidate may, after spending weary months in wandering through the mazes of common and statute law, be confronted with a question like this—'How is distance measured for the purposes of any Act passed after the Acts Interpretation Act 1890?' and he will feel hurt, after wasting his precious half-hour vainly composing an elaborate answer, to discover that the answer is simply, 'In a straight line.'[107]

The judges, wiser than their board of examiners, agreed with the students' objections, but rejected their challenge to the results, since the exams were consistent with the loosely drawn rules of court. At least they forced the reluctant board to prescribe textbooks and to publish past papers for the students' guidance. Yet the examiners' ideas about assessment seemed to be beyond reform, and continuing problems provoked more complaints in 1900, about questions that went beyond the scope of the subjects and were too long to answer in the time available. The judges responded by holding an additional exam, and two members of the board of examiners resigned. As Sir John Latham wrote long afterwards, 'how could anybody set "Common Law" simpliciter as a subject for an examination?' He judged that the exam was still incompetent when he sat it in 1904; he must have seen through its weaknesses very thoroughly, since he won the prize for the best student.[108]

These shortcomings prepared the ground for the abolition of the admission exam, although it was a side-effect of amalgamation that precipitated the change. The 1891 amalgamation act disrupted the local admission of practitioners who had already qualified elsewhere in Australia, or in other parts of the British Empire, by recognising only qualifications that were of equal value to those required in Victoria. The standard was hard to satisfy, thanks to the stringency of the local combination of university study, articles and final exam, and the Supreme Court raised the barrier still further by giving the equivalence test the strictest possible interpretation.[109]

After an unsuccessful attempt in 1895 left the problem unsolved, a legislative remedy was found eight years later, as the result of evidence about legal education given to the royal commission on the university. The rigid statutory test for recognition was dropped, and replaced with flexible rules based on reciprocal rights of admission. Rather than hand the responsibility of administering the system and making the admission rules back to the Supreme Court, parliament gave it to a new, broader-based entity, a Council of Legal Education, composed of the judges, the attorney-general, the solicitor-general, the dean of the law faculty, and representatives of the university council, the bar and the Law Institute.[110]

The new council, which controlled admission to the profession for the rest of the twentieth century, was thus a by-product of a by-product, the end result of a chain of consequences starting with amalgamation. With its creation, parliament gave up its experiment, dating from the act of 1891, in prescribing the details of the qualifications for admission to practise. The practical difficulties of framing statutory admission rules were too great, and parliament handed the responsibility back to the lawyers, content to leave judges, profession and university to sort out the rules for themselves.

The Council's rules, made in 1905, preserved two paths to admission, and so kept some of the lines of the segregated rules for the divided profession before 1891. Would-be lawyers could either take the LLB degree and then serve as articled clerks for a year (much as barristers had once served as students–at–law) or, like solicitors of old, sign on for a longer period of articles (now four years) and undertake a shorter course at the university at the same time. The content of the shorter articled clerks' course, unlike the LLB, was prescribed by the Council. On the other hand, as the university royal commission had recommended, the court's admission exams disappeared, with the consequence recorded by Harrison Moore: 'In all cases the Final Examination has been abolished, so that all the examinations in law are now in the hands of the University'.[111]

The decision confirmed the divergence between Victoria and New South Wales, where university study remained only one path to legal practice, and the exams of the admission boards trained more students for practice until the 1960s. This relative ease of entry to the profession helped boost the number of practitioners: New South Wales consistently had more lawyers in proportion to population than Victoria through the twentieth century. Other factors, including the size and structure of the economy, were also involved: Queensland, which also had an admission board system alongside university training until 1970, had fewer lawyers in proportion to population than Victoria.[112]

Handing sole responsibility for admission assessment to the university was, like the changes that made university study compulsory for all would-be lawyers by 1872, partly a result of reformist ideas about legal education, but largely due to local conditions and accidental side-effects. The university replaced the court's examiners, supplanting the separate admission exams that were, and would remain, the final hurdle to practice in the United States and Britain. Not only would all lawyers have to study at the university, but it would be the sole judge of their academic fitness to practise. This monopoly would be both a source of influence and a lightning-rod for contention in the years to come.

———※◦※———

Federation in 1901 affected the law school in significant, if indirect, ways. Moore naturally took a close interest in its progress, as Jenks had before him, and found in it the subject of his major published work, *The Constitution of the Commonwealth of Australia*. Moore's book, Quick and Garran's *Annotated Constitution of the Australian Commonwealth* and Inglis Clark's *Studies in Australian Constitutional Law* were, in George Winterton's words, the 'three celebrated works on the new Constitution' that greeted the inauguration of the Commonwealth. Moore's students—chief justice Sir Owen Dixon prominent among them—kept his name alive, and even now the High Court continues to cite Moore's book and some of his other publications. They are used both as a record of federation-era thinking and as a source of ideas and authority in current controversies, outliving even Hearn's works as texts of more than merely historical interest.[113]

Federation also impinged on the content of the course. Once all the colonies (except the reluctant Western Australia, which joined with only six months to spare) had voted to federate, and the constitution had gone to London for enactment, Moore put forward a plan for more teaching in constitutional law. 'The establishment of the Commonwealth of Australia with an intricate Constitution', he wrote with pardonable exaggeration, 'is bound to give to Constitutional Law an importance such as it has in the United States and Canada, where an intimate knowledge of the constitution is necessary to every practising lawyer'. After informal consultation with the faculty, the planned teaching in constitutional law and history sprawled across three subjects, merging with public international law. Private international law would cohabit uncomfortably with administrative law, and the union of Jurisprudence and Roman Law, agreed to by the faculty five years earlier, would finally take place.[114]

That Constitutional History and Law parts I, II and III took up so much of the students' time would have seemed a provocation in later years, when the Law Institute acted as watchdog over the university's tendencies to intellectual abstraction. The separation between the law course and the admission exams, which lasted only a few more years, until 1905, made it easier for Moore to expand the more theoretical subjects and leave some of the more practical material to the Supreme Court's examiners.

The new admission rules of 1905 presented a further opportunity, when they left Jurisprudence out of the list of subjects prescribed for articled clerks. Moore welcomed the opportunity to teach a more academic course when the clerks were absent:

> in the case of one subject—Jurisprudence (including Roman Law)—I am satisfied that we shall be able to secure a keener interest & a higher standard of work now that the subject is practically confined to students who are proceeding to the Degree of LL.B.; this class of student is able to relate the work done to work which he has done in other departments, notably History and Philosophy.[115]

But this was a matter of teaching practice rather than curriculum changes. The heavy weighting of subject titles towards constitutional law lasted until 1917, when the real content of the three constitutional law and history subjects was more accurately reflected in new names. They became Modern Political Institutions, Sources and History of

English and Australian Law, and Constitution of the Commonwealth of Australia.[116]

Modern Political Institutions was a catch-all introduction to the course that, despite its name, reached deep into English constitutional history. Its outline promised details of 'principles involved in the assemblies of 1295, 1305 &c', along with more recent constitutional history, public international law, and imperial relations. The subject became a millstone around Moore's neck, 'the heaviest subject which the Professor of Law looks after'. A growing number of arts students enrolled, making up nearly half the class (it was available in the arts course, just as its predecessor, Constitutional and Legal History, had been, continuing the close affiliation, established by Hearn, with the university's teaching of history and political economy). 'Gradually, the historical, the political, and comparative aspects of the subject predominated over the legal', Moore wrote. 'It has become the nearest approach that we have to a course in Political Science'.[117]

The subject's new emphases followed Moore's own interests. Although his text on the constitution (unlike Jenks') stuck generally to legal doctrine, he had an instinct for the political setting of constitutional principles that harmonised with his work as a government adviser. He reported to the council in 1907:

> During the year we have made a beginning in systematically providing books on Political Science for the University Library, & I hope that before long we shall have at any rate a fair working students' library in that department, which is so closely connected with the work of the Faculty.[118]

He had earlier urged the council to provide for the systematic teaching of political science, and prepared a memorandum proposing courses on the history of political thought, and the functions and structure of the modern state.[119]

World War I, more distant and less immediately threatening, affected the law school less severely than World War II. In the absence of conscription, vetoed in the referendums of 1916 and 1917, the machinery for mobilisation of civilians for the war effort was much less intrusive than it became in the early 1940s. Nevertheless, student numbers fell sharply, from 160 in 1914, to 83 in both 1917 and 1918. In 1917, Moore's largest final-year class had thirteen students, compared with thirty only four years earlier. Many new graduates went into the armed forces rather than the profession; at least six out of the eighteen who finished the course in 1914 joined up soon afterwards, and others followed over the next few years.[120]

Among the staff, two friends had very different wars. John Latham, independent lecturer in Contracts and Personal Property, temporarily left his practice at the bar to become head of naval intelligence, and joined the Australian delegations to the imperial war conference of 1918 and the Paris peace conference of the following year. His friend Robert Gregory, barrister and independent lecturer in Property, was thirty-eight when he enlisted in the Australian Imperial Force in 1917, as one of the Sportsmen's Thousand, under the slogan, 'Join together, train together, embark together, fight together ... show the enemy what Australian sporting men can do'. He had already served in the militia (the part-time citizen reserve) for two years, and now went overseas, to France, where he ended up in the army education service. 'I expect to have quite a fair amount of time for lecturing', he wrote to Latham, as the war was ending and the education service began to fill the time the soldiers had on their hands.[121]

Moore, an Empire loyalist and moderate supporter of conscription, thought highly of Gregory's patriotism, and got the council to welcome him back when he was discharged from the army in 1919.

> For a middle-aged man, with a practice just large enough to make it a very real risk to leave it, a family, and serious family responsibilities, to enlist as a private with the drawbacks & uncongenialities of a private's life, as well as the meagre pay,

was a very big sacrifice which calls I think for some exceptional recognition.[122]

Gregory went on lecturing until illness incapacitated him in 1931. He was a member of the committees that chose Moore's successor and reorganised the law school on his retirement, he represented the university on the Council of Legal Education, and he played host to faculty meetings in his chambers (as his father had before him). But his wartime experience may have left its mark; at least he seems to have put his service revolver to a new use. John Foster, a law student in the early 1920s, later recounted that Gregory 'had some difficulty in preserving order'.

> One day he produced a revolver in class at the beginning of a lecture and sweeping with the muzzle round the class he remarked that he had had difficulty in preserving order but he proposed to deal with the first offender today. He had a reputation for eccentricity already and he lectured for an hour in deadly silence.[123]

That a gun-toting lecturer would share in the task of choosing the next dean now seems so unlikely that a lingering doubt hangs over the story. Perhaps it grew in the telling (although it was confirmed by others); possibly the Gregory involved was not Robert, but his father John, who certainly had trouble with his students, and whose revolver figured in his Supreme Court case. But John ceased lecturing some twenty-five years before Foster came to the university. More likely, Robert shared some of his father's problems with students, and the margin for eccentric behaviour by lecturers was wider in the 1920s than it later became.

In another anticipation of what happened on a larger scale after 1945, the law school had to cope with an influx from the armed forces at the end of the war. Those who had already graduated were allowed to attend law lectures for short periods without paying fees, 'with a view to "brushing up" their work'. Moore and the lecturers prepared summaries of legal developments since 1914 to help them.[124] Others returned to study, or came to the university for the first time.

Most of the students who returned from military service arrived during first term in 1919. Three tutors were appointed to help them catch up with the work they had missed in the first few weeks, and they continued to look after the returned servicemen until the end of the year. One of the tutors was Robert Menzies, who had served in the part-time militia but did not enlist for overseas service. The fact that prominent students stayed at home (Menzies was president of the Students' Representative Council and editor of the *Melbourne University Magazine*) drew criticism during the war, and political opponents would taunt him with his record long afterwards.[125] The returning students themselves, however, seem to have been more tolerant.

Student numbers rose across the university, not merely catching up with delayed demand from those who had postponed courses during the war, but growing faster still, as rising population and prosperity increased the tiny proportion of people who undertook higher education. In the law school, enrolments reached 200 for the first time in 1919, and exceeded 300 in 1920. As student numbers increased, the government grant to the university, which provided about a quarter of its income in 1922, failed to keep pace. The grant dropped from £26 per student in 1901 to £15 in 1921. At the University of Sydney in 1921 it was £21, and at Adelaide it was £35.[126]

The law school's aspirations for money and resources were modest, partly out of a sense that little was needed for its work, and partly, no doubt, because the chances of receiving more were slim. In 1878, the faculty responded to the council's request for a statement of its needs by saying its only requirement was for more books (admittedly it asked for a substantial sum to pay for them, £500).[127] The new staff appointed when the faculty was created five years earlier had probably met all Hearn's needs for the time being, but the culture of needing little and making do persisted into the 1920s, in strong contrast with some of the university's more importunate faculties, whose requirements for staff and equipment were far greater.

When the council summarised the university's requirements in 1912, and again when it set out its needs as part of a campaign for additional support from the state government in 1919, Law was the only faculty for which no new resources of any kind were requested. Moore was equally cautious in 1927, when he answered another request from the council to state the law school's needs with a brief handwritten note to the registrar. The report from the dean of Medicine, by contrast, was an elaborate typeset document filling six closely printed pages.[128]

The university library's collection of law books (there was no separate law library) suffered from the prevailing parsimony. Jenks found that the library had no complete set of English statutes, although this was soon remedied, at his suggestion. He did his research on the Victorian constitution and its history at the Public Library, in the city, and found the sources for his prize-winning monograph on the history of the doctrine of consideration in the Supreme Court library. By 1914, the librarian rated the university's holdings of English reports as 'fairly complete', but (showing their lesser importance as sources of authority in the law school's teaching) acknowledged that this could not be said of the Australian law reports. As for monographs, he could only say, with tactful understatement, that 'the Theory of Law is not fully represented'. As late as 1947, the only Australian state reports in the library came from Victoria and New South Wales, although others were added from then on.[129]

The money provided for law books was miserably inadequate. In 1919, the law collection was getting an annual allotment of £15 to £20 from the library vote, 'plus about £22 for subscriptions to Law Reports and Periodicals'. Law was not singled out, and funding for other disciplines was as bad or worse; the library spent an average of £20 a year on history books and periodicals in 1911–13. But the amount would pay for only the most basic acquisitions, and it was considerably less than the fee that just one student paid the university to do the law course. Special grants helped from time to time (they paid for a set of Halsbury's *Laws of England* in 1913, and two French legal journals in 1919), but Moore had to buy books for himself and lend them to students.[130]

Donations and exchanges supplemented this small change. Moore gave over a hundred volumes to the library around the time of his retirement, presumably including those he had bought to supplement the library's meagre stocks. In 1929, the Law Institute decided to give the library the journals it received in exchange for the *Law Institute Journal*, and from 1935, the Law Students' Society journal *Res Judicatae* brought in copies of other periodicals: 'the magazine as a medium of exchange, secures for the library a harvest of periodicals from overseas', Paton recorded happily. The library also received £350, raised by the legal profession to honour Moore on his retirement, the income from which was to be used to buy new editions of textbooks.[131]

The library's one complete set of law reports and statutes made things increasingly difficult for the growing number of students. Not only were essential references in short supply. The library was open for only a few hours each day—from 10 a.m. to 1 p.m. and from 2 p.m. to 5 p.m. during the week in 1898, with another two hours on Saturday morning—and students were not allowed to use ink, or to borrow books without their lecturers' permission. Opening hours were extended slightly the following year, and the installation of gas lighting allowed the library to open in the evenings in 1905, but Moore's mild observation in 1913 must have drawn a veil over many irritations and frustrations: 'much inconvenience arises from the number of people desiring to consult the same works about the same time'.[132]

The faculty asked the council for a grant for the purchase of additional law reports in 1918. Two years later, it was still saying that the purchase of at least one additional set was essential, but also that there was nowhere to put them: 'it is impossible to provide accommodation for such additional Reports and Statutes and facilities for their use in the present Library'. The duplicate sets of the *Victorian Law Reports* and the *Commonwealth Law Reports* finally arrived in 1930, along with duplicates of all the other law reports.[133]

It was almost as hard to find space to put the books as it was to find money to buy them. Moore told the council in 1919:

> The matter of Library accommodation is of peculiar concern to this School, seeing that a Library to the Law students should be something like the Laboratory to the Science students. At present the conditions discourage this most important part of the work. It is useless to provide books unless they can be placed where they are immediately accessible.[134]

'The admission of new books has become an almost insuperable difficulty', the librarian said around the same time.[135]

When the university at last authorised the purchase of a duplicate set of English law reports, there was no room for them on the shelves, as Behan, the acting dean, pointed out. He added his voice to the long lament, echoed in other faculties:

> the Library is sadly lacking in multitudinous standard authorities which it would be quite impossible for a student to procure for himself. These facts seem to point to the conclusion that it will be impracticable to carry on the work of the Law School in the manner in which one would, for the credit of the University, hope to see it carried on, unless accommodation for a separate Law Library can be provided at the University, and a considerable sum of money allocated to the purchase of books.[136]

One of the most exasperating things about this situation was that it made nonsense of the lecturers' exhortations to the students to read cases and statutes for themselves, rather than rely on notes and textbooks. Moore told the council:

> While we are insisting that students must carry on their reading in a Library and must learn there to use their materials, and while notes are compiled for the purpose of facilitating and compelling this mode of study, the actual conditions in the University itself

make it impracticable for the students as a whole to carry out this advice. Men grow tired of going to the Library and finding themselves unable to get books or space for reading them. Some students go to the Public Library; but many others tend simply to fall back upon their notes of lectures, and seek with this material supplemented by a minimum of text book reading to pass their examinations. This sorry state of things must last until it is realised that a school in which there are 155 Degree students cannot be efficient on the provision that would not be adequate for half their number.[137]

The only immediate prospect of improvement came from the chance to expand the university library, after the opening of the new arts and education building (later Old Arts) in 1924 freed up space in the quadrangle. When the north side of the quadrangle was gutted to make the new general library, Moore hoped to turn its old home, upstairs in the northern extension, into a separate law library, but the new Faculty of Commerce got the space instead. The university put this down to its inability to meet the increased cost of supervision that the separate law library would entail. Moore himself had urged the creation of Commerce, but now it blocked his hopes for better accommodation for the law books.[138]

After the move of the general library, the law section, such as it was, occupied shelves at its western end. Law students used two tables nearby; later-year students monopolised one of them, which became known as the High Court. In his early years in the law course, Geoffrey Sawer used to ask one of the friendliest senior students, Douglas Menzies, for help:

I remember often coming along to Douglas at the High Court and asking him to explain the rule in Shelley's case or the doctrine of implied immunity of instrumentalities or some such thing, and how he would always push aside whatever he was working on and help me with this.[139]

Later Menzies sat on the real High Court. The custom of appropriating tables for senior students lasted until the late 1950s, when Mary Hiscock encountered it: 'I sat down in my first week at what I thought was a very pleasant table in the sun, to be informed coldly that this was reserved for final-year students, and would I kindly remove myself'.[140]

Squeezed into the quadrangle along with the library, other departments and the university's small central administration, law school staff shared the problems of overcrowding and poor accommodation. When Jenks arrived in 1889, he had to ask twice before he was given any office space at all. He ended up in a small room shared with the lecturer in mining; 'the room is also used,' he protested, 'for domestic purposes, by the recently appointed Lecturer in Classics and Philology'. Whatever the unspecified domestic purposes were, they were obviously not conducive to the work of the professor of law. Teaching space was equally hard to find. Jenks used Hearn's lecture room (which was too small), and also held classes on the dais of Wilson Hall.[141]

When space could be found, it was often in poor condition, exacerbated by the university's periodic bouts of cost-cutting. The royal commission of 1902–04 found that under the economies made since the depression of the 1890s, repairs had been postponed and the main building had been 'wholly neglected'; architects reported that the quadrangle was not particularly well built in the first place, and the stonework had become decayed and dangerous. In 1935, as the state and the university slowly recovered from another depression, the law school's administrative office, on the ground floor on the western side of the quadrangle, was in a dismal condition. 'The room badly needs redecorating', Bailey complained. 'It is very far from being a good example to the crowds of people who go into it. It is also very depressing to work in.' There was a hand-basin, particularly needed by staff who worked the duplicating equipment, but it had no drain; they had to carry the water outside in a bucket.[142]

Things were not much improved five years later, when the university accountant asked the chair of the council's finance committee about requests for new carpet and linoleum in what he called the inquiry office of the law school. These requests had been put off 'while there was a possibility of moving the School upstairs', but now no change was likely in the near future: 'Would you approve of the expenditure of about £15 for these additions? The room is very shabby and the present carpet is threadbare.'[143]

Some of the lawyers came to see themselves as Cinderellas, a metaphor that came, apparently spontaneously, to writers about the law school decades apart. An anonymous graduate wrote in 1927:

> there is just a possibility that for too long the Law School has been the Cinderella of the University. It has occupied that position, and been content to occupy it, because it has suffered from an inferiority complex.[144]

Other faculties, the former student wrote, asked long and loudly for resources, and usually got something. The same tag occurred to Zelman Cowen when he tried, in his turn, to rouse support for the law school, thirty years later.[145] In the recurring financial hardships of the 1890s, the Dickson frauds and the aftermath of World War I, the university consisted largely of Cinderellas, with few favoured sisters, but Law found itself towards the bottom of an impoverished hierarchy. Teaching cheaply in its borrowed classrooms at the courts, it was easily overlooked.

As student numbers grew and the law school otherwise remained much as it had been for twenty years and longer, Moore developed other outlets for his considerable energies. Most notable was his growing involvement as a government adviser. Hearn had been a political player through his parliamentary career and his codification campaign, while Jenks had been a close observer rather than a participant, relishing his privileged access to the participants in the 1890 federal conference and becoming an 'affectionate and admiring friend' of chief justice George Higinbotham.[146] With Moore, the dean became a constitutional adviser to state and federal governments, establishing a pattern that continued under Bailey. The local field of constitutional experts was very small, and Moore had a prominent place thanks to his book, but, even so, the authority he acquired was remarkable.

As a barrister, he had retainers at different times from the state and federal governments, and appeared in several leading cases from 1905 onwards, among them *Huddart Parker v. Moorehead*, an early contest about the scope of the Commonwealth parliament's power over corporations. He shared chambers in the city until the early 1920s, and held faculty meetings there. It was as an adviser, though, that he made a distinctive role for himself, coming into his own as World War I generated questions that ideally suited his interests in constitutional and international law. For the first six months of the war, he was spending all the time he could spare on advice for the Commonwealth government on points of international law raised by the conflict. He took part in the discussions that led to the abandonment of a referendum on amendment of the constitution in 1915, and worked on the Imperial Acts Application Act 1922, the Victorian act that rationalised, for the first time, the ragbag of English statute law received as part of local law through the process of colonisation. He also went to London as a federal government adviser for the 1926 imperial conference.[147]

Most remarkably, he became a personal adviser to the governor and the governor-general on the exercise of some of their powers; one of the first academics to become an adviser to the monarch's representatives in Australia, he entered a select group made up until then of judges and politicians. When the defeat of a second referendum on conscription caused a crisis in 1917 (prime minister Billy Hughes had promised to resign if the referendum was defeated, but had no obvious successor and predictably wanted to keep the job), Moore was one of the few consulted by the governor-general. This was only one of the most sensitive of the several occasions on which he provided advice, becoming the governor's go-to man for difficult constitutional questions where research and special knowledge were needed.[148]

Moore's knowledge of the constitution and his independence obviously appealed to those in power, along with his capacity to investigate the more hidden recesses of law and constitutional practice. Both Labor and conservative governments sought him out, but his social position placed him as the right sort of person for confidential work for the Anglophile upper crust: a member of the exclusive Melbourne Club, he had married into the à Beckett family, whose web of connections through Melbourne society was fictionalised in Martin Boyd's novels. Calm, discreet and judicious, he must have found rewards of his own in the trust placed in him and the questions he became involved in, but what he felt about his work has left little trace.

Moore's successor, Kenneth Bailey, inherited some of these tasks: 'they'd got used in Victoria to the services of the Professor of Law at the University for matters that involved unusual researches and the like', he later said. Bailey's more conspicuous services for the state included writing a long memorandum on the charter of legislative independence for the British dominions, the Statute of Westminster 1931, advising the government on disputes between the Legislative Assembly and the Legislative Council, and representing Victoria in the High Court in one of the transport regulation cases of the 1930s.[149]

Moore never shirked his obligations to the law school and the university, but the more mundane work of teaching became irksome to him, and its burden was one of the reasons for his early retirement in 1927 (at sixty instead of the more usual sixty-five). He was unhappy, too, with the way the university was being run, controlled by a rigid oligarchy under the chancellor, Sir John MacFarland, from which Moore was excluded.[150] It was outwards from the university, towards his involvement in constitutional affairs and, increasingly, international relations, that his energy and imagination turned, and it became the focus of his very active retirement.

3

LIBERAL AND CULTURED

1928–45

Moore's retirement in 1927 set off a long-meditated reorganisa-tion of the law school. The range of subjects Moore taught was impressive but unsustainable, and the growth in student numbers after World War I had made the need for another full-time teacher increas-ingly obvious. Moore reported to the council in 1919:

> It is not possible for one man to do justice to Jurisprudence, Roman Law, Legal History, Constitutional History, Constitutional Law (English and Australian), Public International Law, Private International Law, and Administrative Law.[1]

Quite apart from the breadth of subject-matter, he had too many students. In 1900, there were sixty-seven law students, though this figure was inflated by would-be arts graduates who enrolled in law for their first two years (the courses were much the same) before transfer-ring, to avoid compulsory Greek in the BA. Twenty years later, there were 313. Numbers stayed above three hundred throughout the 1920s, except in 1923, when there was a temporary drop after the post-war bulge worked its way through the course.[2]

A committee of two judges (Sir Leo Cussen and Charles Lowe) and the independent lecturer Robert Gregory reported on plans for the law school post-Moore. They observed that the part-time correspondence tutors for country students had been the only additional members of the academic staff appointed in the thirty-five years since Moore became dean; they could have added that, apart from the tutors, the teaching staff had consisted of one professor and four independent lecturers ever since the faculty was created in 1873. A second professor was obviously needed, and the committee adopted Moore's idea that the two chairs should have new designations, one for jurisprudence and one for public law.[3] The council agreed, but it was unable for the moment to do more than rename Moore's chair as the chair of jurisprudence, leaving its intended public-law partner to be created when funds were available.

Moore's successor combined Melbourne affiliations with Oxford experience. Kenneth Bailey was the first former student of the university appointed to a chair in the faculty—a former student, but not yet a graduate of Melbourne, since he interrupted his course after first year to join the army in 1918, and then went to Oxford on a Rhodes scholarship after only one year back in Australia. Scholarships had been his path to Wesley College and then to the university. At Oxford, his first interest was history, but disappointing results led him to revive an earlier plan to do law and then the bar admission exams. Even at that stage, he had an academic career in mind.[4]

After his return to Melbourne, he became vice-master of Queen's College at the university, tutored in the law school, and lectured in history. He applied unsuccessfully for the chair of law at the University of Western Australia in 1927 (the Perth selection committee preferred Frank Beasley, who became another early leader of legal academia in Australia), and was being considered as a possible master of Queen's when his appointment to follow Moore in the chair of jurisprudence supervened. He had just turned twenty-nine when the council appointed him at the end of 1927, young enough to repeat Moore's experience of being mistaken for one of the students (at the registrar's office, Bailey was told to go and enrol downstairs). Perhaps influenced by strong evangelical links in his mother's family, he was a leading member of Christian groups on the campus. He was already popular at the university, and to older heads he had that ill-defined but powerful assurance of social and intellectual reliability summed up in the word 'sound', as Moore recorded: 'there are few young men I know whom I regard as at once so stimulating and so sound as he is'.[5]

In the words of one of his students, Jack Richardson (later his biographer), Bailey 'had an aura of intellectual isolation which created a gulf which few students could bridge, yet he attracted their respect'. Geoffrey Sawer, another student, later a colleague with his own prominent place in the history of Australian legal education, described his teaching:

> Ken Bailey was not, I think, a very good lecturer to large, undergraduate, doughy students. He was too hesitant in his conclusions; he would say something and then qualify it and qualify the qualification, and the students were apt to look for something more definite that they could swot up and dish back to him in examinations. But as a teacher of honours students and as a tutor of small groups he was absolutely admirable, because he was so careful, not pedantic in the bad sense of the word at all, just careful about ideas and about statements and events and so forth, and I certainly owed a great deal to him in first of all, for the first time discovering the meaning of rigorous thought, of really pursuing a thing to its conclusion and seeing all the difficulties along the way. And finally perhaps deciding that if that is the conclusion to this line of thought, then we've got to chuck it away and start afresh. He was quite admirable in that respect.

'Professor Bailey's style was baroque', James Lemaire, another student, recalled. 'I remember him saying ... "Whenever the writer uses the word dicta instead of dictum my miserable teeth chatter."'[6]

Bailey's hesitations and qualifications upon qualifications were baroque indeed. In the words of Geoffrey Lindell, who knew him much later in Canberra, he had the two-handed disease: when he gave his opinion, it was always 'on the one hand ... on the other hand ...' Bailey deliberated with exaggerated care on the question of whose office he should use while he was standing in for the vice-chancellor in 1938. He would have preferred his own room, he wrote, but on the other hand, there were countervailing considerations; and 'on the other hand, yet again', were even more factors to be taken into account. Still hovering, he devised a complicated timetable for dividing his time between the two rooms each week.[7]

Yet Bailey's policy for the law school was the antithesis of wavering between alternatives. He was determined to increase the full-time staff and build on Moore's work, believing, like him, that 'Law was best studied as one of the social sciences against a social science background'. Reforming the course was one focus of this plan, but the first priority was to appoint another professor, as the Cussen committee had recommended and as the Sydney Law School had done in 1920. Here, help came from what might seem an unlikely source. Since the 1850s, when the Supreme Court began admitting local practitioners, the fees it had charged for the privilege had been paid into the court's library fund. The fees were heavy, and concerns about their effect, coupled with a suspicion that they protected practitioners from competition, led parliament to reduce and cap them in 1895. But the Law Students' Society complained that they remained 'most burdensome', and despite the demands of acquisitions for the court's fine library, a substantial balance accumulated.[8]

Somehow, the university and the court agreed in 1930 that the work of the law school was a fitting purpose for the fund. Exactly how this happened is obscure. Bailey, newly-appointed, probably lacked the seniority to approach the rather Olympian judges and suggest that they spend their money on the law school. Perhaps an interest in legal education on the part of the chief justice, Sir William Irvine, played a part; as premier and attorney-general in 1903, he presided over the creation of the Council of Legal Education, although the impetus had come from Fink's university royal commission. Proposing the grant from the library fund, Irvine 'referred to the need for maintaining the standard and extending the scope of legal education', which he and the judges had discussed with 'the proper authorities' at the university. 'This need was recognised by such authorities, but they entirely lacked the money to supply it.'[9] Possibly, too, the judges feared that the government might have its eye on the library fund for its own purposes, as money became increasingly scarce in the intensifying depression. And the court already had a record of helping the law school, by providing prizes for top students and venues for lectures.

The outcome was a remarkable donation of £30 000, to create a second chair in the law school, designated as the chair of public law. The subjects to be taught by the new professor suited Bailey's interests: 'My first Chair was Chair of Jurisprudence and I had no training in philosophy. My personal interests were rather more in the sphere of public law, that is constitutional and international law, than in the philosophy of law. I was also interested a good deal in constitutional and legal history.' So he indicated an interest in taking the new chair, adding some information about his experience in public law, to reassure the university about appointing a professor of public law who had so recently become a professor of jurisprudence. The university was receptive, and Bailey changed his title (and got a pay rise: the professor of public law was paid more than his colleague, a premium that was still attached to the chair in the 1950s).[10]

Bailey's translation to the new chair left the university looking for a professor of jurisprudence. It chose what was becoming a recognisable type: a young man with little professional or teaching experience, but an outstanding academic record, promise for the future, and a reassuring social background. George Paton was the son of a moderator of the Presbyterian Church, a Melbourne graduate in arts, and an athlete and Rhodes scholar like Bailey. At Oxford, he won first-class honours in his undergraduate degree, and in 1929, the year before he applied for the chair, completed his BCL and was called to the bar in London.

He was an assistant lecturer in law at the London School of Economics; he had published nothing. Nine of the thirteen applicants for the chair were under thirty, and Paton was only twenty-seven when he applied.[11]

***

The new professor shared Bailey's ideas about the importance of a broad education for law students, and an aversion to technical professional training. Paton's approach was sociological, as Zelman Cowen, one of his students, remembered: 'he taught that law had a distinctively social function and was judged by its effectiveness as an instrument of social engineering'.[12] Doubling the full-time academic staff (even if only by increasing it from one to two) greatly increased the scope for teaching the so-called liberal or cultural subjects, and the two professors quickly made the most of the opportunity.

Within a few months of Paton's arrival, the faculty adopted a new plan for the degree course. The introductory subjects that students had been able to choose from anywhere in the arts course disappeared, replaced by more focused preparation for legal study: economics, British history (Bailey wanted political science, but the faculty traditionalists prevailed), and French, Latin or psychology. Legal history and Roman law were pulled out of larger subjects and became compulsory in their own right. Later-year students supplemented the familiar doctrinal subjects with one of five pairs of options, including logic, political science, economics, and international relations (in which public international law appeared as a separate subject for the first time). Bailey and Paton even had discussions with the Council of Legal Education about abolishing the articled clerks' course, the logical conclusion of their insistence on a broad, academic education, but without success.[13]

Bailey and Paton's course was more jurisprudential, less professional and vocational, and directed more towards the social and theoretical context of law. The core doctrinal subjects remained, but the defined options and the new compulsory subjects reshaped their

setting. The course aimed 'to teach the technical rules of law in a setting of social studies' and 'to maintain the liberal and cultured tradition
of the profession'. As Bailey put it, 'we systematized and extended the
social science background of the course as a whole'; the changes were
an attempt 'to use Law itself more fully as a medium of education and
culture'. He estimated that, as a result, the degree students spent 42 per
cent of their time on private law, 10 per cent on public law, 28 per
cent on the social sciences and 20 per cent on the history and theory
of the law.[14]

Bailey foresaw conflict between the aims of the university and the
profession in implementing these ideas, and waved a red rag at the
Law Institute in one of his first public statements as dean. 'In any clash
between these interests, those of the University must be considered
paramount,' he told the Law Students' Society a few months after
becoming professor. This was not only because the law faculty was
part of the university, he said, but so that law would remain a learned
profession, 'and that its members might be better fitted to be leaders of
the community'.[15]

The Law Institute had been advocating change in the law course
for several years. Its journal supported the law school, welcomed the
appointment of the second professor, and recognised the value of the
'cultural studies' in the course, but it wanted to bring the training of
lawyers 'more into line with the requirements of practice'. It had been
trying since at least 1928 to have accounting made a prerequisite for
the LLB or for admission. Most of all, it wanted the law school to
expand the teaching of subjects it neglected, notably company law,
bankruptcy and conveyancing. The practical slant of the Institute's
program sounded progressive, compared with traditional lectures. 'The
student, under the present system, simply becomes a diligent note-
taker', one anonymous graduate complained, 'with no training in the
practical analysis of legal problems'; there should be more reasoning
aloud, and practice in dealing with problems.[16]

As the conflict developed, the Institute felt its weakness in the
faculty, made up of the professors and lecturers, the legal members of

the council, and three others chosen by the faculty itself: Behan, Frederic Eggleston (former state minister and university council member) and P. D. Phillips. Completely excluded from the curriculum debates of 1931–32, the Institute asked for representation; the faculty allowed it to choose a nominee to fill an existing vacancy, and later, in 1941, gave it a designated place.[17]

Changes to the degree course were primarily a matter for the faculty, since the admission rules recognised the course as a whole, without saying anything specific about its contents. But they had consequences for the articled clerks' course, which shared most of its subjects. To maintain a degree of consistency between the two courses and avoid a flight of students away from a longer degree course, Bailey and Paton proposed to extend the clerks' course as well. That meant changing the rules of the Council of Legal Education, so they prepared the way by caucusing with its members, and made the proposal more palatable to the Law Institute by agreeing to an extension of the period of articles for graduates to two years. The Institute went along with this, although it refused to swallow Roman law for articled clerks, which was left out of the so-called office course as a result, and the Council blocked the extension to articles.[18]

All this, however, was mere skirmishing. The Institute's most effective criticism of the course was that it ignored areas of law that were increasingly important in practice. A faculty committee chaired by Bailey took the first steps on the long road towards meeting this demand when, in 1934, it recommended adding teaching in company law and bankruptcy; the lectures were squeezed into Equity, which gradually became a catch-all subject for the study of business structures of all kinds.[19]

The reform campaign was soon resumed with redoubled energy. As the Institute saw it, the trouble started with the amalgamation of the profession in 1891, when the requirements for the training of solicitors had been reduced to match those for barristers:

> Ultimately articles were reduced to one year, new cultural subjects were included in the University course, the Supreme Court

examination, which older practitioners look back to as having given them the most valuable part of their qualification, was abolished, and the present most unfortunate state of affairs came into being.

The result was a neglect of training in matters that solicitors needed to be able to deal with: 'four-fifths of the time formerly given to practical training in an office has gone, for the sake of book reading in Roman law, the history of the law and other topics rarely heard of in Collins Street'.[20] Company law was not given its due weight, and taxation was not taught at all. The Institute wanted degree students to do three years of articles, one of them concurrent with the final year of the degree course; the articled clerks' course should take six years. All students should have to pass a set of exams in practical subjects before they could be admitted to practise.

The councillors of the Law Institute believed in the value of practical training, and daily saw in their own offices the importance of subjects that the law school did not teach, but other influences were also at work. Only a minority of Victorian solicitors were members of the Institute, and their composition was changing. After parliament gave corporate status to the Institute in 1917, it gained a hegemony over the independent regional law associations that had flourished outside Melbourne. Country members joined the Institute in increasing numbers, to such an extent that they changed the balance of power in its council in 1932. Coupled with the effects of a protracted fight within the Institute over the introduction of compulsory audits and fidelity insurance, this transformed the organisation; as legal historian Rob McQueen observed, 'from being a largely city-based Institute it had become an almost exclusively rural club in the late 1930s'.[21]

Cultural divides ran through the debate, separating barristers and solicitors, graduates and articled clerks, and sometimes city and country. 'The right education and training of solicitors is of much greater importance to the community than that of barristers,' the Institute said, 'both because of the far greater number of solicitors, and because of the nature of the services they can render to clients'. Disdain for over-educated theoreticians without practical skills resurfaced in the contest over the introduction of an entrance quota in 1960. Some of the dislike was reciprocated, although Paton, in particular, was conciliatory throughout, in spite of strong provocation. Frederic Eggleston deplored the scorn of 'eminent law teachers' for both their students and 'the average efficiency of the Solicitors' branch of the profession'. The fact that neither Bailey nor Paton had practised law in Australia diminished the weight that their views carried with the Law Institute.[22] Nor had either worked as an articled clerk.

In the background, less often articulated, were economic motives, sharpened by the slow recovery from the economic depression of the 1930s. Bailey and the Law Institute alike warned of the dangers of over-supply in the profession. As the Institute's president put it,

> candidates are entering the legal profession at an alarming rate. There is not sufficient work for all ... It may not be proper to make admission unduly difficult merely for the purpose of protecting the interests of those already admitted but I suggest we might examine the matter carefully to see whether in many ways admission is not now unduly easy and we may regard it as a duty we owe the community to prevent unwholesome overcrowding.

How alarming the Institute's figures were depended on your point of view: of the 1132 practising barristers and solicitors in 1938, about a quarter, or 276, had been admitted in the past four years. But neither the university's nor the profession's proposals for the law course were a strong response to over-supply. The Institute's urging for an extra year or two of articles (partly at the expense of full-time study) would have raised the barrier to entry, but not to anything like the extent of the reforms advocated by professional organisations in the United States in the same period. There, requirements for legal training and for pre-legal study grew during the 1930s, partly in response to a

concerted campaign to reduce competition in the overcrowded profession. In Victoria, the university already had a monopoly over legal
education, and broad pre-legal studies already made up the first year of
the course for those aiming for a degree, although not for articled
clerks.[23]

A longer period of articles would have expanded the pool of
cheap workers available for solicitors, since articled clerks received low
wages, and often none at all. Many paid their employers a substantial
fee, or premium, for taking them on. Harold Ford was lucky that the
firm who employed him in 1937 waived a premium, 'which was most
unusual'; it could be anything from £50 to £1000. After his first
eighteen months, they also paid him ten shillings a week. Russell
Boughton's premium was 100 guineas (£105) in the early 1930s, but
at least he was paid £1 a week. When Geoffrey Sawer was looking for
articles around the same time, he found a solicitor willing to make a
bet with him: if he won the Supreme Court prize, he would be paid
thirty shillings a week; if not, he would be paid nothing, but would be
charged no premium. He won the prize, and a salary. By 1953, payment of wages had become usual, although the rates were still low.
Clerks who got articles through the university's appointments board
were paid between £3 and £8 a week; the average was about £5.
Once they were admitted to practise, male solicitors could expect to
be paid £12 to £15 a week in their first year, or around the minimum
legal wage for men.[24]

Melbourne solicitors were less explicit about their need for these
willing workers than their counterparts in New Zealand—or perhaps
the labour of articled clerks was less important to them. In New
Zealand in the 1950s, solicitors openly acknowledged the need for the
cheap labour of students to maintain their businesses (although there,
since the abolition of articles in the nineteenth century, the students'
presence was not required for admission to practise, but the result of a
waning custom under which most law students studied only part-
time). In Victoria, it was the general opinion of articled clerks, the Law
Students' Society said, 'that use is eagerly made of their services in the

performance of routine duties to avoid the employment of salaried clerks'. The economic value of a one-year articled clerk would often have been low, but clerks who served for longer periods would have been worth more to their employers.[25]

Bailey did his best to hold the line against the encroaching trade school and defend the practical studies already included in the course. 'Under the general title of "Equity"', he wrote, 'the Melbourne student spends almost as much class time on company law, bankruptcy, administration and probate as the student taking the Final Examination of the Law Society in London'. But the argument for including branches of the law that were growing in importance was hard to answer. As early as 1937, Paton thought that the course should be rearranged to give 'greater satisfaction to the solicitors' branch of the profession'.[26] Bailey may have been happy to go along, if it was not that it meant squeezing his favourite cultural subjects out of the course, as the Law Institute well knew.

In 1936 the Institute took the fight to the Council of Legal Education, which asked the law school to respond with proposals of its own. These emerged at the glacial pace that characterised many of the law school's curriculum reviews, but a definite plan was ready by 1940, after more discussions with the Institute. The faculty was willing to add more practical subjects, such as commercial law, company law, evidence, drafting, taxation, domestic relations and industrial law, but it wanted a fifth year of the course in which to teach them. It took the call for more practical training and, adopting an old idea of Bailey's, used it for its own purposes, turning it into a plan for tutorials that would do a better job of practical training than could be hoped for from longer articles.[27] Few in articles received systematic training, an old grievance of the clerks.

Money would be needed to pay for the extra teaching. The call for new subjects had the backing of the Council of Legal Education, which was dominated by the judges (and chaired by the chief justice); with remarkable generosity, they put their money where their mouths were, and made another large donation of £25 000 from their library

fund, to employ new part-time lecturers and tutors. The two donations were still supplementing the law school's income nearly fifty
years later.[28]

After 1939, the intensifying war overseas led to an uneasy truce in
the hostilities closer to home. The Institute's president in 1939–40,
Alan Moir, supported the expansion of university training and even
the abolition of the articled clerks' course, though he was in a minority.
The Council of Legal Education backed the faculty's plan to add a
year to the course, but the victory counted for little, since implementation had to be postponed for the duration of the war. The Council
asked the faculty to do what it could to squeeze the additional practical subjects into the existing course, as a temporary measure. In the
meantime, teaching in procedure and commercial law was extended,
practitioners began taking drafting tutorials in conveyancing, and there
was a general reorganisation of subjects.[29]

The Law Institute regrouped. Blocked by the faculty, it now
attacked the university's monopoly over legal education. For the law
school, this was a grave development, although hardly surprising. The
Institute had long used the English system of solicitors' training as a
model, one that gave universities only a minor role. Although the
Institute made no use of the example, in many provinces of Canada,
too, the profession had monopolised legal education, though its hold
was weakening. The establishment of a second route to legal practice
threatened the law school with a substantial drop in student numbers,
to say nothing of its implications for the kind of training received by
Victorian lawyers.

The Institute's new strategy included adding taxation and accounts
to the requirements for admission to practise. It resolved on direct
action: it started teaching the courses itself in April 1944, without
waiting for anyone's approval, as a first step towards taking back control over the training of solicitors. 'We wish you to have no control
whatever of the teaching of subjects which we are quite qualified to
undertake', the Institute's president told Paton. The small number of
practising solicitors on the faculty and the Council of Legal Education

was a gnawing grievance: 'solicitors' education is mutilated in the interests of the degree course at the University and in the interests of the training of barristers', the Institute complained. Getting the upper hand in the Council became one of its aims.[30]

Despite the prevailing antagonism, the battle lines were not clearly drawn between the Institute and the law school. There were minor differences of opinion among the teaching staff, but they presented a united front, and divisions never reached the level that caused the separation of the Department of Jurisprudence and International Law within Sydney's law faculty in 1947. The fight at Melbourne was nevertheless one within the faculty as well as outside, since the Institute and the supporters of more practical training had their representatives there. Personal connections at the top of the city's small legal community were strong. No one better embodies these cross-currents than Edmund Piesse, solicitor, long-serving editor of the *Law Institute Journal*, and fiery general of the Institute's forces as its president from 1942 to 1944.

The presidency of the Law Institute was a surprising close to Piesse's remarkable career. A graduate in both science and law from the University of Tasmania, as a young man he was part of the successful campaign for the permanent adoption of proportional representation for the state parliament, and then moved into intelligence work, rising to the post of director of military intelligence during World War I. The close study of Australia's international relations in the Pacific that this entailed became a lifelong interest and the focus of his work in the prime minister's department after the war. Marginalised under prime minister Billy Hughes, not least because he opposed Hughes' discrimination against Japan in immigration and trade, Piesse left the government and took up practice as a solicitor, although he continued to write on defence and foreign affairs, and remained an active member of groups concerned with Australia's international relations.[31]

His second, legal, career overlapped with his first. His classic book, *The Elements of Drafting*, earned a glowing review in the *Law Quarterly*

Review from no less an authority than Robert Megarry, the future vice-chancellor of the Supreme Court of England and Wales, and has run to ten editions, remaining in print for sixty years. Piesse himself became a teacher as a result of the Institute's campaign, taking on much of the burden of the drafting tutorials that began in 1941, and delivering lectures on taxation for the Institute. The outlines he issued to the students make a small, if very dry, textbook, running to more than a hundred pages.[32]

As the Institute's representative, he became a member of the faculty. Paton could quite sincerely thank him for his great help, and the faculty recorded its 'deep debt for his public service' when he died in 1947, but this gratitude must have been sorely tested at times. The aggression of the Institute's pronouncements owed much to Piesse, as he blazed away at the academic irrelevancies of the degree course. 'At present the University wallows in antiquities wherever it can find them', he declared. He wrote to Paton, who had taken over as dean: 'we are not interested in discussing any difficulty that might cause you to object either to two years' articles or to wish to lengthen the course to over five years. It is for you to put up a scheme within the limits we want.'[33] The Law of Property was one of his favourite targets; it spent too much time on the English background, and not enough on the Torrens system of land titles that dominated dealings in Victoria.

Extended apprenticeship and control by the Institute might have had regressive overtones, but Piesse adroitly neutralised them: his program had a forward-looking, nationalist appeal, as hopes for post-war reconstruction dawned.

> Let us make a new start with things as they are now, ignore past history as far as we can ... and rewrite the lecture courses so that what is now the law in Australia becomes the backbone of the teaching and what happened in earlier centuries on the other side of the world does not absorb time that is urgently wanted for instruction in the things we have to do every day.

The course should be one 'in the modern, living, law which lawyers apply in practice'.[34]

Piesse was no barbarian at the gates. He was not only a friend of Bailey, but his personal solicitor, and a colleague in internationalist groups including the Round Table. His background in government and his involvement in international relations made him very different from many of the solicitors he was championing. The contradictions of his stance were obvious to Latham, although he was mistaken in assuming that Piesse had an arts degree: 'I doubt whether he realises how much of his intellectual equipment is due to his University training in the Faculty of Arts', Latham wrote to the chancellor. Like many others, Piesse was the subject of vice-chancellor John Medley's satirical verse, but the satire was friendly, part of a gentle ribbing of members of the Boobooks dining club at its 400th meeting:

> My name is Piesse but I wage war
> Against the Faculty of Law.
> And nothing my excitement stirs
> Like sliding down the Barristers.[35]

After Piesse retired as president, the Institute's tone remained belligerent, although its agreement on one year of articles for degree students was a conciliatory gesture. For his part, Paton toyed with letting the Institute do some teaching (but under the faculty's supervision) and thought of ditching Roman law, always an irritant to the pragmatic solicitors, in favour of taxation. 'This is a retrograde step, but perhaps a polite compromise in the circumstances', he wrote; in the end, Roman law clung on as an option until 1946.[36]

The faculty also looked into ways of accommodating the divide between the practical solicitor and the intellectual barrister by differentiating the pass and honours courses, although it was not until after the war that these changes materialised. In another interim step, it made cuts to fit evidence into the degree course, and implemented the concession Paton had proffered, by integrating the Institute's classes in taxation, accounts and professional conduct into the lecture program, as subjects to be taken during articles from 1945. Bailey, now based in Canberra and on the fringes of the debate, warned against tinkering: only an agreed general settlement with the Institute would satisfy the pressure for a 'legal tradesman's' course:

> On the whole matter however I have been bothered by the feeling that we are in danger of moving towards a narrowly technical concept of legal education, at the very moment when other comparable communities are moving steadily towards the more liberal conception of which hitherto we have always been something like pioneers.[37]

He called on the traditions of the law school, going back to Hearn, which he feared were slipping away.

Behind the scenes, the retiring chief justice, Sir Frederick Mann (who chaired the Council of Legal Education), advocated splitting the training of solicitors and barristers. His successor, Sir Edmund Herring, suggested a shorter LLB course with two years of articles, differentiated from an honours or LLM course with no articles at all. P. D. Phillips unsuccessfully urged this scheme within the faculty. Sir John Latham had advice about tactics:

> The Law Institute has, I think, an entirely exaggerated view of the value of articles. I should rather like to see the faculty carry the war into the opposing camp by urging that the present five year period of articles required from articled clerks should be reduced by at least one year.

He also vetted the faculty's language, frowning on the word 'trepidation': 'I do not like to see so feminine a word in a report of the Faculty of Law'.[38]

In order to keep its pre-war monopoly, the faculty tried to give the Institute what it wanted, but within the confines of the articled clerks' course; it argued against the creation of a second training school ('Piesse's Coaching College', one faculty member called it), for which the state lacked both the staff and the finance. The articled clerks' course would take on all the new, practical subjects, some of which would be taught by the Institute. The fact that this left the articled clerks hopelessly overloaded was a problem for another day. As for the degree students, the faculty reluctantly gave up its plan for a five-year course, packing some, but not all, of the extra subjects into the four-year course instead. Succession, company law and taxation were added to the final year.[39]

When the dust settled, much of Bailey's course of 1932 had changed. Instead of his structured studies in political science, international relations, economics, public administration or philosophy, degree students chose a smaller number of arts subjects for themselves, making room in the course for the new subjects in mercantile law, evidence, succession, company law and taxation. New admission rules completed the modernisation of training, by requiring passes in procedure, accounts and professional conduct before students could begin practice. The Council of Legal Education again rejected the Institute's bid for a longer period of articles, but the Institute itself rejected Piesse's plans for greater supervision to improve the education of articled clerks.[40] Training for admission to practise had been reasserted among the sometimes conflicting purposes of the degree, and in future the broad education long valued by the professors would be found in other ways: in the few arts subjects in the law course, in the wider perspectives brought by teachers to their own law subjects (particularly as optional subjects grew in number from the late 1960s), in the increasing popularity of combined degrees, and in revival of the idea of graduate entry to the law course.

———※◆※———

Bailey turned the war with the Law Institute to advantage wherever he could. As well as using it to try to extend tutorials and the length of the course, he relied on the looming introduction of new subjects to propose the appointment of another member of the full-time teaching staff, the first below the level of professor. Medley acknowledged in 1939: 'the University has long known that the Law School has been seriously undermanned'.[41] With his backing, the appointment was made the following year, while the argument over course changes continued.

The new senior lecturer (for so the new teacher was described) was Geoffrey Sawer, a popular, gregarious and left-wing graduate of the law school, which he had reached via Scotch College on scholarships for war orphans, his father having died of illness contracted while serving in World War I and his mother soon afterwards. The terms of his university scholarship would not allow him to study arts, so he turned to law, but without losing sight of his first choice; he completed an arts course after World War II, while a staff member. His self-description as a 'professional swot' made him sound like a bookworm, but it really meant that he had developed the skill of packing a remarkable amount of work into a short time, leaving ample opportunity to write for *Farrago* and join the campus Labour Club, where he gravitated away from the communists and toward the social democrats.[42] He won the Supreme Court prize, giving him, if not exactly a guarantee of a job at the law school, at least a good chance.

His early working years had kept his professional options open but showed a leaning towards academia. He worked as a law clerk and then a barrister, and taught as a private coach, a tutor at Ormond College and a casual lecturer in the law school, taking over Constitutional Law I in Bailey's absences. He followed Moore and Bailey into the Round Table, the influential discussion group concerned with the British Commonwealth and international affairs, as a result of an effort to bring 'young men of left-wing views' into the generally conservative membership. Bailey regarded him as a 'professed Marxist' in his early days at the university, 'but quite apart from what you might call the Socialist trend in his thinking, there was a freshness and an originality, a directness and an unconventionality about his assessments and his generalisations that were immensely stimulating to teachers and his fellow students'. He was 'simply a born teacher'.[43]

It was in this period that Sawer took over what was effectively the law school's first course in media law, organised at the request of newspaper proprietors. A meeting of the staff made the arrangements:

> they all turned and stared at me as Mr. Junior, so to speak, and said 'Well, apparently these characters need a course in the law affecting journalism. Of course you, Sawer, will be the appropriate person to do this. After all, you know, you're only teaching four or five subjects at the present time and conducting half a dozen tutorials and things of this sort. You can't be teaching more than about 16 or 17 hours a week, so it would be no trouble for you. Besides you pick up these things so quickly.'

Sawer was not the only one who was busy. Bailey looked back in 1971: 'For a long time I was giving twelve lectures a week, which nowadays would be thought a recipe for inefficiency, if not a proof of lunacy in any respectable Law School'.[44]

During Bailey's absence working for the federal government in World War II, Sawer took on much of the public law teaching, and served briefly as acting dean when Paton, too, was called away. Paton had him promoted to associate professor in 1947, without his knowledge: Paton 'said in a rather apologetic way that he hoped I didn't mind but he had put me up to the Council that day for appointment to an Associate Professorship, and they had entirely agreed, and was that O.K.?'[45] The promotion may have been partly an attempt to hang on to Sawer, as his gifts and growing profile fitted him for higher appointments. He applied unsuccessfully for the chair of public law when Bailey left for good in 1946 (Bailey himself thought he was the best of the applicants), but his lack of overseas experience and postgraduate qualifications must have been a disadvantage.

When the vice-chancellor of the new Australian National University asked him if he would be interested in a readership, Sawer used a hint from Paton that he would be in the running for a third chair at Melbourne as leverage, to lift his Canberra appointment to professor. He resigned at the end of 1949, but continued to teach at Melbourne by arrangement with ANU for some months, before packing the caravan and the trailer and heading up the highway to Canberra.[46] His position there was a novelty in Australia, a research professorship of law, in the research school of social sciences. Research-only positions remained rare and usually temporary exceptions to the usual combination with teaching, but the appointment was a confirmation of the status of law as a field of academic research and not just professional expertise.

Most of the lecturers remained part-time teachers, combining their university work with legal practice, usually at the bar. The best of them brought impressive legal skills and the authority of their rising prominence in the profession, until, as generally happened, they became too busy to keep teaching. Three future judges (Edmund Herring, Charles Gavan Duffy and Wilfred Fullagar) were among the independent lecturers when Bailey joined the staff, and several others followed:

> When you could get people of that calibre, you brought the young student into touch with not only first-rate persons and first-rate minds, but people with completely active association with some of the biggest work that was going on in the profession.[47]

'We were most impressed by the presence and dominance in our teaching staff of legal practitioners', John Cain wrote. 'The down-town teachers were very professional. They ran the lectures in an uninspiring way, but they were seen by us as more authoritative'. Their lectures were a highlight, thought Sir Laurence Muir, a student in the late 1940s; Jennifer Smithers, studying nearly a decade later, still liked their interest and stimulation, 'with a more practical view of the law'. But many of them were, in Sir Daryl Dawson's words, 'very conservative, even very pedestrian'.[48]

In the 1930s, the independent lectureships were keenly sought. The pay might not have been worth a great deal to a well-established barrister, but to those just starting out, it would have been very useful, and a lectureship was also an endorsement of their expertise. Each vacancy attracted twenty or even thirty applicants, rising barristers who later became judges prominent among them. But the university also benefited from the public spirit of the part-time teachers, particularly in the case of casual lecturers, who were paid very little. When Paton asked solicitor Raymond Dunn (a Supreme Court prize-winner, but better known to many later on as president of the Richmond Football Club) to deliver some lectures on criminal procedure in 1951, he said the pay was so low he hated to mention it. Dunn didn't mind: 'delighted to assist. The fees are immaterial.'[49]

There were drawbacks in using practitioners, as Bailey well knew:

> of course these men were simply not available for students outside their ordinary class hours, except under special circumstances and at great sacrifice to themselves. It also meant that they were not able really to do anything effective in the publication line from the point of view of the research work of the Law Faculty and Law School.

Cancelled classes were an inevitable risk of teaching by busy lawyers. P. D. Phillips would occasionally try to tell students of a cancellation by putting an advertisement in the public notices section of the *Argus* newspaper that day, but few would see the warning. George Lush left before the end of one term to go and argue a case in the Privy Council in London, but no one told his students in Mercantile Law, who turned up as usual, only to find no one there to teach them.[50]

———⤜•⤛———

The depression of the early 1930s had only indirect effects on the law school, much though it shaped the lives of its students. The Supreme Court's donation made it possible to expand the staff, in the shape of the second professor, but the financial problems of the university and the state government frustrated any hopes of further growth. The main effect on student numbers was not so much to drive them down (although they did drop), but to increase the proportion of students in the articled clerks' and managing clerks' courses. It rose from about 30 per cent in 1928 to 45 per cent in 1933, after which it continued its decline. For some with money for the fees, study would have been an alternative to scarce employment; for others whose families might have supported them in better times, working their way through the course as articled clerks became their only way into the law. Total student numbers, which had remained at around 300 since 1920, dropped to about 280, but they bounced back above the earlier level in 1934.[51] The two world wars had much more significant effects on enrolments.

In 1941, when *Farrago* asked students to write about their faculties, law students had some harsh things to say. 'Our law course is academic and dead', one wrote. Other criticisms included scanty preparation by practitioner-lecturers, and low attendance at lectures. Contracts lectures were 'a wild scramble to get them down'. Students called for more tutorials and essays, more about the sociological background to law, compulsory moots, and lectures on law reform.[52]

This bleak picture was not at all the sort of course that the law school's two professors wanted to offer, in either substance or teaching style, but improvements were almost impossible to make without better funding, especially in wartime. The sociological background to law, in a broad sense, was the very thing the reforms of 1932 were meant to embrace. Bailey's study trip to the United States in 1937, funded by a grant from the Carnegie Corporation, left him only too well aware of what was possible in legal education, and of the difficulties he faced at home. 'Even the most loyal Australian', he told the *Argus*, 'must admit that the University law schools here are not adequately equipped for the task when judged by North American standards'. *Farrago* described him returning 'full of the wonders of the U.S. Law Schools, and determined to do his best to strain the mud from our own pet muddle'.[53]

The shortcomings that particularly annoyed *Farrago*'s correspondents in 1941 were those of the part-time lecturers. Some of the variations in their teaching styles were strange, even bizarre. In the late 1930s, Harold Ford had one lecturer who read his lectures at dictation speed, and another who inexplicably stopped speaking if he saw anyone taking a note. In some subjects, the Law Students' Society complained, lectures amounted to 'no more than the mechanical process of dictation of notes … It is not too much to say that some students are, after such a lecture, quite unable to say what it was about.'[54]

Tom Smith, lecturer in contract from 1933 to 1946, dictated his lectures with so little variation that students who got an old transcript knew what he would say in any given class. If they bought or borrowed the notes, they had little reason to attend, as Jack Richardson found: 'You turned up in August because there was a joke. You heard that joke and went away again.' The presentation left something to be desired, but the substance was much better, and showed the qualities that later made Smith one of the most highly regarded Supreme Court judges, quoted with approval in the House of Lords. Lectures at dictation speed had a long history as substitutes for unavailable textbooks. It was in this way that lectures were delivered in one of the contenders for the title of first American law school, at Litchfield, Connecticut, in the late eighteenth and early nineteenth centuries. There, too, some students got copies of the notes and stayed away.[55]

The teaching styles of the two professors, on the other hand, complemented each other. Geoffrey Sawer described them:

> Bailey had a somewhat English style of talking and a measured, careful style. Paton had a very Australian way of talking, vigorous and colloquial, and he had a sort of commonsensicalness, too, which Bailey didn't have. Bailey was better at considering rules and structures and things like that; Paton was extremely good at telling you about an actual case, a specific set of events and seeing how a rule applied to it, how you worked into it. Together they formed an absolutely marvellous pair, I don't think I've ever seen

the likes of them as a pair in harness, teaching different kinds of students. Paton was very good with these doughy, large classes of undergraduates that I've mentioned, because he would discuss a thing in a pleasant, easygoing way, talking fairly rapidly at first, and if he saw somebody starting to scribble he'd say 'No, don't put anything down as yet', and then after he'd finished this fairly rapid discussion he'd say 'Well now, I think we can probably summarise this in this way'. Then he'd give the students what they wanted, he'd say 'Well, now, we can sum it up thus, this is only approximate, mind you, but here's how it goes, 1—2—3—'. This was excellent for these pass students, though mind you, I found him equally good as an inspirer of honours work, too.[56]

Their teaching was almost all in formal lectures. 'In those days, professors were rather remote figures', James Lemaire recalled. 'We only saw them when they appeared on the lecture platform.' Discussion between teachers and students in lectures was almost unknown. This suited the students who wanted a good set of notes above all, as Ted Sykes, a student from 1934 to 1937 and later professor of public law, said:

As regards our lectures, we went in for extensive note-taking and for the most part we wrote like hell. It is rather ironic in the light of my later attempts to try 'case-book' method or at least to put questions to students in class, to confess that when *I* was a student, this was the very *last* thing I wanted. All I then wanted was to be left alone to write down as much as I could!

Harold Ford witnessed a rare experiment in 1939 when, inspired by his trip to the United States, Bailey tried something new. 'Lo and behold, one day he threw out some questions to get a discussion going. This was unheard of. The only student who responded was Zelman Cowen.'[57]

Bailey and Paton were more successful in getting discussion going in the small tutorials they ran for honours students. The students would be given a topic to prepare, and then, when they arrived for the class, they would be given a task:

> perhaps to be given ten minutes to write down five points on the subject we were discussing; perhaps to state in a single sentence what was decided in a great case they'd been set to prepare, and thereafter each would read what he'd got and no quarter was either given or taken, and I would submit myself to the same discipline as they had and read for them what I had put down, and they would then take me apart and assign me sometimes very low marks indeed for my performance.

The plan for a law school staffed by full-time teachers and researchers came to fruition after World War II, but the ideas that underlay it were much older. If it had not been for the depression of the 1930s and the world war that followed, the changes might have happened nearly twenty years earlier, as David Derham reflected in 1969.[58]

———————⋙•◦•⋘———————

The value Bailey and Paton attached to research was reflected in a Law Students' Society initiative, the revival of an LSS journal. The first issue of *Res Judicatae*, as the new publication was entitled, appeared in September 1935. Described as 'the Magazine of the Law Students' Society of Victoria', it was really a scholarly journal. 'The initiative came from the Society itself', Bailey reported to the council, but *Res Judicatae* also embraced the law school's goals:

> It is the proud aim of the Law Faculty at Melbourne to foster the idea of law not merely as an examination study or as the equipment for ekeing out a doubtful living, but as a social science to be continually moulded and re-made as the needs of Society changed.

It was an LSS project, but not purely one for students. In keeping with the idea that the society was also for recent graduates, the editor, John Harper, already held degrees in law and arts.[59]

There were no other Australian university law journals at the time, and few Australian law journals of any description. The nineteenth-century magazines of the Sydney and Melbourne law students and articled clerks had not survived, and the short life of the *Commonwealth Law Review* ended in 1909. The *Australian Law Times* published short articles along with its main contents, law reports, until it was supplanted in 1927 by the *Australian Law Journal*. The journal of the Law Institute of Victoria appeared in the same year. In this small field, *Res Judicatae* rapidly distinguished itself as a forum for serious research, drawing, as its founders intended, on the law school's staff, graduates and students. Bailey highlighted the project in his annual report to the council for 1939:

> The journal is entirely scientific in character and has won for itself an honourable place in the periodical literature of the law in Australia. Recent articles have been cited lately in the Commonwealth Law Reports and in the Parliament of Victoria. The journal has this year been linked to the teaching work of the School by the inclusion of notes on recent leading cases, written by students after discussion in the honours tutorial groups.[60]

The small staff wrote and published steadily. Bailey wrote a stream of articles and chapters on jurisprudence, constitutional law, international relations and the British Commonwealth, while the independent lecturers published on more technical, doctrinal topics (P. D. Phillips' articles on international relations and public administration were an exception, reflecting his interests as the lecturer in Modern Political Institutions). Even wartime conditions did not stop the work altogether. 'Research is almost rendered impossible by present conditions in the Faculty', Paton lamented during World War II, yet somehow, in the midst of it all, he managed to finish his landmark textbook on jurisprudence, which appeared in 1946. It later earned Paton the prestigious Swiney prize, awarded in Britain every five years for the best published work on jurisprudence. If it has not proved to be 'one of the outstanding legal works of the century', in the words of Harold Hanbury's early review, it undoubtedly fulfilled, through its four editions, another reviewer's prediction of being 'to many students *the* text-book of jurisprudence'.[61]

————◆————

Opportunities for postgraduate study in law at Melbourne before World War II were almost nil: 'it is almost unheard of for post-graduate work to be done at the University in ordinary circumstances', Paton wrote in 1937, and scholarships for overseas study were rare.[62] The university had awarded the degree of Master of Laws since 1881, but it was not based on postgraduate work. Initially, imitating the automatic conferral of masters' degrees at Oxford, it was given to any LLB graduate who wanted it, five years after admission to practise. But this privilege was limited to those who had received their bachelors' degrees before the LLM first became available, and from then on the master's degree was confined to LLB honours graduates, to whom it was given after a shorter delay, without further examination. It effectively remained an undergraduate honours degree until the separate LLB (Hons) was created in 1950.

Although it was no longer a graduate degree, the LLB, too, could be awarded for research. The many students who were admitted to practise through the articled clerks' course did not have law degrees, although they completed all the purely legal subjects of the LLB course, and some found, later in their careers, that they wanted to make up this deficiency. Even very eminent lawyers could feel the want of a degree, particularly if they became involved with the university. One was Sir George Pape, a judge of the Supreme Court, who wrote to David Derham in 1963:

> When I entered the legal profession I intended to become a solicitor, and was advised to do the Articled Clerks course, which I did. Having gone to the Bar, I always intended to complete the degree course, but you know what happens when you start in

practice. I just didn't have the time to do it. I should rather like to
be able to take an interest in University affairs in a mild way, but
I'm afraid I feel somewhat out of things.[63]

To accommodate such people, in 1949 a new regulation allowed for
the award of the LLB on the basis of a thesis—but not to just anyone.
Applicants had to have practised for at least ten years, and they had to
meet a vaguely-expressed criterion of good standing.

Sir John Barry was another Supreme Court judge who lacked a
law degree until he graduated under this provision in 1963. Some sat-
isfied this hankering only after decades, at the end of a long career.
E. F. (Ted) Hill won the Supreme Court prize for the best student in
the articled clerks' course in 1937. A few years earlier, Geoffrey Sawer,
then a final-year student, had coached him:

> Ted Hill always struck me as a law student as being superior to
> others that I taught subsequently, David Derham, Zelman Cowen,
> superior to them in the capacity for seeing around large numbers
> of corners ahead. He had that kind of sharpness. He would
> have made a quite magnificent technical lawyer and technical
> legal judge, if that was the line of country which he'd chosen to
> develop.

Hill became a barrister, and tutored part-time in the law school, but it
was in left-wing politics that he was best known, as one of the leaders
of the Australian Communist Party. In 1981, he was at last awarded an
LLB, for research on workers' compensation.[64]

The main research degree, such as it was, was the doctorate of
laws, the LLD. It had a double life, as both an honorary degree for distinguished visitors to the university, and a degree awarded by examination. Initially, honorary doctorates in law, like those in other
disciplines, had to be approved by an absolute majority in a faculty
meeting. This was usually uncontentious—the faculty was unlikely to
object to the five royal visitors who received LLDs down to 1934, nor

to the war heroes Sir William Birdwood and Sir John Monash, who were honoured in 1920. A degree for the prime minister, Stanley Bruce, in 1927, also received the faculty's approval, but after six LLDs were handed out to eminent visitors in the course of 1937, it became restive.

When the university offered an LLD to another prime minister, Joseph Lyons, in 1938, some faculty members (the minutes discreetly withheld names) thought the time had come to take a stand. After an informal approach to Lyons by the vice-chancellor, and endorsement by the professorial board and the council, the proposal went to the faculty for its expected approval, but it met open opposition. The meeting adopted a stern statement of principle:

> the Faculty takes the view that the Statutes as they stand at present confer upon it a real discretion in the conferring of honorary degrees in Law. In these circumstances the Faculty regrets that in the past invitations have been extended to the proposed candidate, and that both the Professorial Board and the Council of the University have expressed their views before the matter has come before the Faculty.[65]

Faced with the ghastly prospect of the prime minister's doctorate being snatched away barely two weeks before the conferring ceremony, Bailey adjourned the debate and waited for reinforcements. Sir John Latham, chief justice of the High Court, deputy chancellor, member of faculty and (before he left parliament) Lyons' close colleague as deputy prime minister, joined the meeting, perhaps summoned by Bailey, such things being possible at a time when faculty meetings were held in the city and the itinerant High Court had not yet settled in Canberra. With his support, Lyons' degree was approved, with no dissent and one anonymous abstention. The narrow escape led the university to take precautions: the regulations were promptly amended to remove the need for the faculty's approval when honorary LLDs were conferred on people 'distinguished by eminent public service'.[66]

The LLD awarded by examination was more trouble-prone. When it first became available in 1865, it was based on a series of written examinations on prescribed topics; the first to graduate in this way was John Madden, the future Victorian chief justice and university chancellor, in 1869, but the fact that it took him two attempts was a sign of things to come for the degree. Other early graduates included Richard Hodgson, who had won the Supreme Court prize as an undergraduate and later made a name for himself as a psychical researcher, and John Wilson, headmaster of Melbourne's Presbyterian Ladies' College.

A thesis replaced examination papers as the basis for the LLD in 1890, after a candidate (Harry Wollaston, who was emerging as a leading public servant in the Victorian government, and later served as one of the first Commonwealth departmental heads) asked for the assessment to be made less stringent. Wollaston himself passed the exam before it was changed, but his request was timely. Under its new dean, Jenks, the faculty wanted to establish the degree as a recognition of the highest forms of legal research, in line with its status in England and, particularly, in Europe. Dropping the exam in favour of submission of a thesis suited its purposes.[67]

Yet the task of candidates expected to submit a doctoral thesis was just as difficult. They had no supervision, and no official guidance aside from the faculty's approval of their proposed topics. The examiners had a standard in mind, but it was not always articulated to candidates. The faculty resolved in Moore's time:

> it is not desirable that the LL.D. degree should be regarded as the completion of ordinary academic studies or that it should be associated with attainments of a distinctly professional kind … it should be conferred only in respect of work marked by conspicuous ability as well as by care and research, and containing contributions of value to the study of Law.[68]

It was all too easy to work along the wrong lines, or to lose momentum and fail to finish. One candidate took twenty-nine years to submit a thesis; another failed three times. Geoffrey Sawer's plan for a doctorate came to nothing, probably overwhelmed by his demanding workload in the late 1930s. It is hard to believe that he would have stuck to his intended topic, a punishing analysis of *occupatio* and *accessio*, concepts derived from Roman property law (he threw in *commixtio*, *confusio* and *specificatio* for good measure). He assured Bailey, rather implausibly, that these topics were 'of daily occurrence in legal practice'; Bailey kept his doubts to himself, on paper at least, but commended 'the courage with which you are facing a problem of this very obscure kind'.[69]

The problems of the LLD reached a peak between 1939 and 1952, when eight theses were submitted and only two passed. The examiners took four years to report on one of them, and after the candidate spent another eight years on revisions, he failed anyway. It could be difficult even for eminent lawyers to give the examiners what they wanted, or indeed to know what was expected. Percy Joske found that he had failed, and so did Louis Voumard, who had waited six years during the war for a result. Both were independent lecturers in the faculty, and authors of the standard texts on their subjects (the law of marriage and divorce for Joske, and the sale of land for Voumard), but the examiners criticised them for deficiencies in original discussion or criticism, while recognising the value of their works as textbooks.[70]

After 1946, when the university began offering the PhD, postgraduate students had an alternative, supervised research degree to turn to. But the first PhD in law was not awarded until 1956 (to Kenneth Sutton, later dean of law at both the University of Queensland and James Cook University), and it took another three or four decades for doctorates in law to become common among academics. A small number of experts seeking a special mark of distinction continued to apply for the unsupervised LLD, but both the number of candidates and the proportion who failed declined, until only rare scholars, with a strong assurance of success, sought the degree.

For the law school, as for the country as a whole, the full impact of World War II took time to be felt. But after Japan entered the war at the end of 1941, training lawyers took a low priority in the increasing control that the government exercised over society and economy. Staff and students were needed elsewhere, and conscription for military service could apply to most of the law school's potential students, once they had turned eighteen. Students reaching eligible age were allowed to complete the first year of the course in 1942, but as the controls came to bear on them, the armed services drained many away from the campus. 'During 1942 the Faculties of Arts, Law and Commerce were denuded of all their men students of 18 and over', Bailey wrote. 'Nevertheless we have carried on, with the remainder (in our own case about 100), a full range of teaching activities.'[71]

Student numbers dropped from 345 in 1939 to 114 in 1942. Some part-time students were in reserved occupations, exempt from military service; others were excluded on medical grounds. National controls allowed the faculty to choose a small quota (up to eight for each year of the course, although not all the places were filled) who became exempt from conscription, and of whom one-third could receive means-tested financial assistance. Academic merit was the sole criterion for selection, with the result that many of those chosen were already exempt on other grounds—somewhat to the faculty's relief. 'The operation of the quota for the first year, therefore, does not lay the Faculty open to the charge of discouraging persons from entering the Forces', its minutes noted. Enrolment itself was not restricted. Outside reserved courses such as medicine, anyone whom the state did not lay claim to for the war effort was able to study as usual.[72]

Students could accept or decline the offer of a reserved place. Richard Franklin was one who opted to turn it down. He turned eighteen during his first year at university, and was offered reservation, but with a brother in the air force and a father who had been in the Royal Australian Navy and then the naval reserve, 'it just wasn't a choice'. He joined the RAAF before Christmas 1943, and returned to study after the war.[73]

After its first year, the quota applied equally to women, who could now be directed into civilian war-work under the so-called manpower regulations. Lorna Coombs' uncle joked, 'You'll be off to the pickle factory', before she won a reserved place. Many women studied part-time, while they worked in law firms, replacing absent men, and the proportion of women among the students rose sharply, reaching levels not seen again for decades. They made up nearly a quarter of the students in 1942, and were temporarily allowed new responsibilities and opportunities in the university, much as was happening outside. Airlie Smith, who had won the Supreme Court prize before the war, became president of the Law Students' Society in 1941 and edited *Res Judicatae* in 1942–43. While working at the state parliamentary draftsman's office in 1943, she tutored in Jurisprudence, in Paton's absence. Three of the five counsel for the LSS moot in July 1942 were women.[74]

There were fewer students on campus, but they were not the only ones enrolled in the course. The faculty expanded the correspondence teaching that had been established in the aftermath of the last world war, to meet the demands of a new one. Service personnel could study wherever they were, sending exercises for correction by three tutors back in Melbourne. The number of correspondence students in the armed services rose to 114 in 1945. Campus students lent notes and books, and gave informal help, while Florence Scholes, the dean's secretary, handled ' the clerical side'. Paton complimented the students cautiously on the 'relatively high quality' of their work, but the lack of books was a serious problem. Richard Franklin, like many others, ended up doing the course partly by correspondence and partly on campus. He completed two subjects while serving in the RAAF in Darwin. It was 'all very experimental and amateurish', he remembered. He had two or three books on each subject, and would send an occasional essay or exercise to be returned with comments.[75]

Staff, too, were caught up. In 1944 four of the independent lecturers were working for the defence department, giving classes at eight in the morning to fit in their commitments elsewhere. Sawer was initially less than whole-hearted: 'I think a good many of us were a little bit suspicious about the War in its early stages', he said later. But he took on a heavy workload in army education, and then, when it looked as if he might be drafted, went to work for the radio propaganda unit run by William Macmahon Ball, also seconded from the university. Even Paton, who stayed put for most of the war and carried the largest burden in keeping the law school going, dashed to London for the army in 1943, to collect information on the government of occupied territories.[76]

The most significant absence was that of Bailey. Other demands on his time had already been heavy, to the extent that he wanted to give up the deanship at the end of 1939. His Carnegie study tour occupied most of 1937, and he had reluctantly taken over most of Raymond Priestley's duties for several months in 1938, to allow the vice-chancellor to write up an extensive survey of universities before his impending resignation took effect. This last commitment, taken on in Paton's absence on leave, provoked complaints from students and faculty members that Bailey's work in the law school would suffer. Bailey replied with statistics that showed how he had kept up his work, and how onerous his job was becoming: some 120 interviews with students in the few months since his return from overseas, and three times as many written replies to inquiries. Senior students came to his defence when news of the protest appeared in the *Herald*.[77]

As if all this was not enough, Bailey chaired the university's professorial board in 1938–40, and strongly backed Douglas Copland in the hard fighting over the choice of the new vice-chancellor in 1938. Some of his colleagues thought he should resign from the chairmanship of the professorial board when Copland was beaten by John Medley in a close council vote. But instead he chose to tell Medley all about his advocacy and then support him, and the two established a good working relationship.[78]

The faculty would not let Bailey go as dean in 1940, when the fight with the Law Institute was at a critical phase; it consoled him with a promise from Paton to take over the burdensome task of interviewing and advising students about their course plans.[79] But when the federal government asked for his help, it was no longer possible to keep him, and the invitation was too attractive for Bailey to pass up. Besides, his powerful sense of duty urged him to do more active war-work. He had been providing constitutional advice to the federal government for some years, and when the attorney-general, H.V. 'Doc' Evatt, asked him to go to Canberra as a consultant, he took leave from the university. He left Melbourne at the start of 1943, and as one task for the Commonwealth led to another, remained in Canberra until the end of the war. Although he retained his chair for the first few years, and the faculty hoped that he would return (so strongly that, for decades afterwards, it recorded that he had been dean until 1946), 1942 was his last year as dean.

The deanship fell inevitably on Paton, as the only remaining professor. He had already been dean in 1937, when Bailey was overseas, and it was he who was elected for 1943, even if, in the minds of many (not least the unassuming Paton himself), he was initially standing in for his absent colleague. His peaceable disposition remained apparently untroubled in the face of Piesse's strongest provocations. 'Possible Compromise with Piesse' was the heading of a note in his papers and the theme of his dealings with the Institute, although without giving up the law school's monopoly or the ideal of a broad-based course.[80] But the settlement of the long struggle over the curriculum became only one of the tasks confronting the dean, as a flood of students engulfed the law school after the war.

4

BUILDING THE NEW JERUSALEM

1946–66

Recovery from the dislocations of the war years took time, even in a country as relatively unscathed as Australia, and the university faced a huge task in coping with a flood of students who were released from the armed forces after the fighting ended. A few enrolled in 1945, but the real influx began the following year, when the first-year law intake increased fourfold, to 150. Lorna Coombs was one of the students who had already started the course and saw the transformation. 'We were quite a close-knit group. When we returned in 1946, there was an influx of ex-servicemen—near 100 in lectures. I for one was overwhelmed.' The influx also included some women returning to the law school from the armed services, such as aircraftwoman Betty Vroland, who graduated in 1949. A refresher course provided an early form of continuing legal education for returning lawyers who had already finished their courses.[1]

The contrasts of returning to study or teaching must have been stark for many, although most kept their thoughts to themselves. Arthur Turner was a Melbourne graduate who had gathered a bunch of prizes during his law course, and served in the army and then the navy since graduation; he had escorted ships to the Normandy beach-heads after the D–Day landings in 1944 and convoys through the Arctic Ocean to Murmansk. He joined the staff in 1946. In the last years of the war, David Derham, who resumed his course in 1946 after five years in the army, had been an air liaison officer on the front line in New Guinea and the South Pacific, rising to the rank of major and witnessing some of the bloody fighting of the long Japanese retreat. He did not like the army, he said, but it taught him a lot. Harold Ford, who finished his course in 1947, had spent more than six years in the navy, partly in administration, and largely at sea in mine-sweeping, escort work, and coastal surveying, 'constructive work in a destructive context ... It was a tremendous adventure, in a way'.[2]

A small number of refugees and other migrants escaping the turmoil in Europe also found their way to the law school in the 1930s and 1940s. Nathan Jacobson came to Melbourne via Palestine as a teenager in 1936, leaving behind the rising anti-Semitism in Poland. His parents' urging led him to the university: 'They were fanatical about me getting a tertiary education', he wrote. A native speaker of Polish and Russian, he used his experience of picking up Hebrew at the University of Haifa in Palestine to persuade the university that he could learn English just as quickly, and cope with the law course. Like many others, he had a full-time job while a student. 'I had to work to support the family, so I could only do a part-time course before and after working hours.'

The reaction to some European migrants on the overwhelmingly Anglo-Saxon campus was hostile, Jacobson knew: 'generally in the late 30s and in the 40s and 50s there was a very strong feeling against new arrivals, affectionately called the "reffos", at the University'. Personally, though, he found the law school welcoming when he began the course in 1938. 'I was the only new arrival to Australia and a bit of a novelty. Both the academic staff and the students used to seek me out and enquire about my background and life in the countries I came from.'[3]

A later arrival was Miroslav Schimana, who had studied law in Czechoslovakia, where he was born, before fleeing in 1948. In Australia, he worked as a labourer, a clerk and an insurance agent, and studied law part-time, ultimately obtaining articles and winning the Supreme Court prize for the best student in the articled clerks' course in 1960. He received a doctorate in law from the Charles University of Prague in 1991. Another was Samuel Pisar, who survived Auschwitz as a teen-ager, joined surviving members of his extended family in Melbourne, and went on from the law school to postgraduate study in the United States and an international career as a lawyer and government adviser. 'There was the strange cohabitation within me of these two disparate human beings,' he said. 'The little one—sunken eyes, shaved head, skeletal—and suddenly the scholar who is pretending to compete as if he had had a normal childhood and education.'[4]

The returned service personnel were exempt from studying Roman law and jurisprudence, as if their war experience was a good substitute. Their age and maturity, as well as their sheer numbers, trans-formed the law school. It was 'crowded to the doors', Richard Franklin found when he returned after serving in the air force; 'there was such a buzz round the place'. Many returned servicemen were 'immensely keen to get back'. For the other students, the contrast was strong. Compared with the service personnel, 'we were like little kids', said Lorna Coombs. 'These people could speak with the lecturers and tutors on an equal basis.' 'The ex-servicemen were a great leveller for us', John Cain remembered. 'They were a conduit to a more worldly life … we grew up pretty quickly.' They wanted to 'get out into the work world', and the other students envied the concessions that short-ened their courses and their time as articled clerks.[5]

The students who returned from the war brought with them the university's first large amounts of federal government funding, building on the small federal research grants that had been available since 1936 and adding substantially for the first time to the fees and state grants that had until then made up the bulk of its budget. Most were sup-ported by the Commonwealth Rehabilitation Training Scheme, which paid tuition fees and gave full-time students a generous living allow-ance. The scheme made the law course a realistic option for many who would not have been able to consider it otherwise. Leslie Fitzgerald was one. 'I was a Rehabilitation student and it gave me my chance to enter the profession. We couldn't have afforded it.' The CRTS provided funds not only for students, but also for extra staff to teach them. A new full-time senior lectureship was created, with CRTS funding for five years, and it was this position that Arthur Turner filled in 1946.[6]

The return of one war-worker was brief. Bailey, released from his duties in Canberra, came back to the university for a few weeks early in 1946, but the Commonwealth government almost immediately asked him to take on another job, this time on the international committee drafting the convention on the United Nations' privileges and immunities in its host state (the United States). He agreed, and while he was away, the Commonwealth offered him the post of solicitor-general and secretary of the Attorney-General's Department. His interests turning more and more towards public administration, he found this offer too good to refuse. After eighteen years as professor, his resignation from the university took effect in the middle of the year.[7]

——⊶◦⊷——

Paton remained dean after the war, calm and apparently imperturbable as the demands of the war effort were replaced by the problems of mushrooming enrolments. The settlement of the long struggle with the Law Institute, the smooth reception of the new students after World War II, and his textbook on jurisprudence defined his deanship. He shared many of Bailey's ideas about the long-term development of the law course, but the war and its aftermath hardly allowed them to be implemented. It was later, as vice-chancellor, that he was able to do most to build up the teaching staff, although he did take the initiative in the formation of the Australian Universities Law Schools Association, whose thirteen founding members, from six universities, convened in 1946.

The association's conferences gathered the scattered inhabitants of Australian (and later New Zealand) legal academia, sharing ideas, coordinating the production of casebooks and occasionally trying, with mixed success, to take a position on issues of common interest. Its membership grew as the post-war transformation of law teaching into a full-time occupation took hold. At the University of Sydney law school, the two professors who constituted the whole of the full-time teaching staff in 1940 were joined by four sub-professorial staff by 1950; ten years later, there were sixteen full-time academics (four professors and twelve others). By 1975, the combined Australasian membership of the association had swelled to 278.[8]

Paton enjoyed teaching, and when he was offered the position of vice-chancellor in 1950, without applying for it, he found the decision difficult. 'My feelings are very mixed', he wrote. 'I have a keen sense of personal inadequacy for such a post … However, rightly or wrongly, I have accepted the offer, with the feeling that one should not shirk a fascinating task, just because the risks of failure are great.' 'It is a great wrench to give up law teaching and I hesitated long. But now the die is cast.'[9] He resigned from his chair in the middle of 1951.

The two professors (one on leave) and the two senior lecturers (Sawer and Turner) made up the whole of the full-time academic staff immediately after World War II. They were joined in 1949 by Harold Ford, who was also appointed as a senior lecturer; other new positions took the full-time teaching staff to ten by 1955. The low pay at lecturer level made appointment direct to the level of senior lecturer the norm, even for staff like Sawer, Turner and Ford who had only first degrees in law (in Sawer's case this was an LLM, given to honours graduates in the bachelors' course). Higher degrees were too rare for the faculty to insist on more. The unsupervised LLD was the only research degree in law at Melbourne, and travelling to study overseas was difficult and expensive.

Turner was distinguished by his wide knowledge of the law, his gifts as a teacher and, for thirteen years from 1950, his help to students in the endlessly time-consuming job of sub-dean, 'onerous in the extreme', in Ford's words. In conversation at morning tea—a daily ritual that kept the teaching staff in touch with each other from the

1950s into the 1970s—he could be counted on to throw light on almost any corner of the law. To Robin Sharwood, a student and then a staff member in the 1950s, 'he seemed to be omniscient'. He became a reader in 1956, and eight years later Cowen and his colleagues encouraged him to apply for a chair. Cowen also took the unusual step of suggesting that the senior staff should write to the vice-chancellor in support of Turner's application, which they did. 'It was true that he had not written a great deal', Cowen wrote, 'but our School was large enough to have among its professors men who were distinguished as teachers and general School men as well as men who were distinguished in scholarship as evidenced by writings'.[10]

The appointment was an acid test of the university's expectations for a professor of law. Enriching the life of the law school, and furthering its work with skill in teaching and dedication to fostering its students, were not enough in themselves, and were hard to quantify. Scholarship, particularly scholarship evidenced in print, was crucial, as legal academia grew. The small number of Turner's publications told against him, and the chair committee chose a younger man distinguished above all by his scholarly achievements, Colin Howard. One of Turner's colleagues, Hans Leyser, was dismayed: 'I feel strongly that he sacrificed years on the altar of the very busy Subdeanship he held, which ought to be taken into account when scanning his writings. He is a man to whom the law school is really indebted.'[11]

Turner also had the misfortune to be caught up in one of the minor skirmishes of the Cold War, when a public controversy erupted in 1961 over supposed communist influence in the university's Department of Social Studies, where Turner's wife Cynthia Turner worked. Allegations of a communist plot were published in the *Bulletin*.[12] Arthur Turner became increasingly preoccupied with the after-effects of the controversy both within and outside the university, and after he sued the magazine's publisher for defamation in 1967 his complete absorption in it became such that he resigned as reader the following year. His university career became an indirect casualty of the social studies affair and the politics of the communist scare.

Harold Ford was another Melbourne graduate. His studies interrupted by six years in the navy, he had completed the articled clerks'
course with the Supreme Court prize for the top student, and was
working as a solicitor and finishing the extra subjects needed for the
LLB, when he applied for a senior lectureship at the end of 1948. He
had not had an academic career in mind, but he was tutoring a private
student who noticed the vacancy at the law school and (apparently
impressed by his tutor) suggested that Ford apply. However accidental
his path into legal academia, it suited his talent for precise analysis and
exacting research, and he thrived, particularly after studying for an SJD
at Harvard in 1954–55. A casebook on trusts and his Harvard thesis on
unincorporated associations became the first of his many books.

Teaching had not come naturally to him, but he found the inter-
active classes at Harvard a revelation, and in 1960 David Derham
described him as 'the most successful teacher of law at present working
in this law school'. His notorious puns were partly playful, and partly
the social lubricant of a basically serious person in the serious business
of the law. When a firecracker went off in his last lecture before leaving
for Harvard in 1954, he responded: 'That is not one of the reports
which I normally recognize'.[13]

New professors, too, arrived after the war. Bailey's replacement in
the chair of public law was a catch, but one the university did not
manage to hold for long. Born and trained initially in Germany,
Wolfgang Friedmann emigrated to England in the early years of the
Nazi regime, and took a second doctorate and a readership at the
University of London. Sir Owen Dixon thought him a bold choice
for the chair: 'so German, so continental in his learning and so little
real knowledge of English law'. His wide-ranging interests lay mainly
in jurisprudence and international law, creating 'a certain awkward-
ness' in his appointment as a professor of public law, in Geoffrey Sawer's
words. But at Melbourne he developed his expertise in administrative
law, publishing the first Australian textbook on the subject in 1950.
His recent experience in the Allied military government of occupied
Germany, where he had returned after World War II, made him even

more interesting to the students. His lectures 'opened my horizons', Peter Bailey said. 'I found them liberating.' It was difficult for Melbourne to keep someone with such transportable skills, and in 1950 he resigned, moving on via the University of Toronto to a career of great eminence at Columbia University in New York.[14]

To fill the vacant chair, the university found another star, but one who was home-grown. Zelman Cowen, 'Melbourne University's own particular prodigy', as *Farrago* called him, completed his law course in 1941 with first-class honours and the final-year exhibition, one of his thirteen prizes in arts and law. He had then joined the navy, and Bailey claimed a hand in getting him steered, reluctantly, into intelligence work. A navy report described him in February 1942: 'An attractive personality with a brilliant brain. Being temperamental, highly strung and sensitive, he requires careful handling, but his predominating desire to make good in the Service will enable him to succeed.' Postings in Darwin and Brisbane led eventually to Melbourne, where towards the end of the war he found he had less and less to do, and spent most of his time reading international politics and law.[15]

On his release from the navy in 1945, he started work at the law school as an acting lecturer, teaching public international law and taking an honours tutorial in constitutional law. As the law school's first unofficial sub-dean, he relieved Paton of some of the heavy burden of student interviews that the dean carried in the days when there was no one else to approve course plans and deal with problems and inquiries. Within six months, however, he had resigned to head off to Oxford, on a Rhodes scholarship.[16]

His success continued at Oxford, where he won one of the two Vinerian scholarships awarded in 1947 for the best students in the Bachelor of Civil Law examination, and became a fellow of Oriel College and a university lecturer in law. He visited Germany to help with preparations for a meeting of foreign ministers on the country's future constitutional arrangements, and again later to study its federal reorganisation, although as a Jew he hesitated to live, however briefly, in the state where the crimes of the Holocaust had been perpetrated.

A visiting lectureship at the University of Chicago in 1949 took him for the first time to the United States. He became known for his interest in American law and government, so much so that the University of Manchester asked him if he would be interested in becoming a professor of American studies there. But that 'would have pulled me too far away from the law', he decided, and said no.[17]

The possibility of becoming a professor back in Melbourne was more appealing. Cowen had lost out to Friedmann when he applied for Bailey's vacant chair in 1946, but when Paton asked him if he was still interested on Friedmann's departure four years later, he applied again. He was offered the chair of public law not long after his thirty-first birthday. He was another of the young, high-flying candidates who became professors in the law school relatively early in their careers, although the days of professors in their twenties were over.

Cowen's academic record and experience, at a time when over-seas travel was far less common than it later became, gave him prestige, even glamour. To John Cain, then a law student, he was 'something of a cult figure almost: colourful, entertaining; a worldly man. Here was this celebrity coming back to teach in dreary old Melbourne. It was something of a coup.' 'We couldn't believe our luck', said Harold Ford. 'We thought his career was over on the other side of the world.'[18]

Although the move seemed surprising to others, a metropolitan law school like Melbourne offered Cowen at thirty-one more opportunities for contact with the profession and involvement in law reform and public affairs than Oxford. He revelled in the new possibilities:

> I am much happier in my work here than I ever was at Oxford. I feel that I am <u>doing</u> something and building up what should be a good law school ... in every way I feel that this is a much more 'real' community than that which we knew at Oxford.[19]

When Cowen accepted the offer of the chair of public law, he thought that Paton would remain dean. Almost immediately, however, Paton wrote with the news of the vice-chancellorship: 'You will have to be <u>Dean</u>. The Law Faculty is disintegrating. Sawer to National University, Friedmann to Toronto & now I have been appointed V.C. However my room will be just above yours & we can smooth things out easily.' Cowen took on the extra responsibility of the deanship and the changes in the staff with relish. 'I think of it as a zesty time', he said, looking back. 'There was such an excitement in listening to the telephone ring, just as I couldn't wait to get the mail.' It was not merely an administrative job. With like-minded colleagues, he envisioned a new and better law school: 'We were building the new Jerusalem'.[20]

Cowen did not figure prominently in the university's central administration, as many other deans did. Unlike his predecessors Hearn, Moore, Bailey and Paton, and later dean Colin Howard, he never chaired the professorial (later academic) board. The law school, rather than the wider university, absorbed him. He was a fluent writer of books and articles on an extraordinary range of topics, covering not only his legal specialties of private international law, family law and constitutional law, but also international relations, public affairs, police, urban design and biography. He appeared frequently in newspapers, and on radio and television; 'I speak a great deal on all sorts of occasions and on all sorts of subjects', he wrote in 1963.[21]

Like Friedmann and other senior staff, he publicly opposed the constitutional referendum on the banning of the Communist Party in 1951, sparking complaints the university had heard often before: 'there was a great outburst about professors engaging in politics', he wrote to Erwin Griswold at Harvard.

> It is all rubbish of course, but it shows a rather ugly temper in certain sections of the community. I cannot imagine a more appropriate occasion for a professor of Public Law to express himself upon than one involving the merits of a change in the Constitution. The referendum proposal as drafted was a catch-all, and showed as pretty a disregard for civil liberties as any I can imagine.

Cowen's opposition was conservative, not left-wing. 'It seems to me that aggressive Communism poses a very terrible threat', he reassured a member of the public who criticised one of his radio talks, and on other issues he supported the Menzies government.[22]

For others, a career like this might have included membership of one of Melbourne's exclusive social clubs (Moore, Paton, Derham, and later Howard too, were all members of the Melbourne Club), but as a Jew Cowen was not welcome. 'So far as I know there are no Jewish members of any of the leading social clubs', he wrote in 1965.

> The hurtful thing about the club situation is that a Jew like myself—and I am one of many—finds that the community accords him recognition and honour and also asks a great deal of him, and then, at a given point, the community's leaders close the door in his face. Of course we have lived with this for a long time, and one can live with it. But it is outrageous and without a shred of justification.

Things were not as bad at the university. Cowen reassured a prospective candidate for the chair of commercial law: 'I do not believe that Melbourne would have any prejudice against another Jew'.[23]

His abilities and his profile overseas, enhanced by frequent travel, predictably led to offers from other universities. An invitation to take up a chair at Chicago in 1954 was followed by months of difficult deliberation: 'It seems to be one of the perverse things that faced with a choice as between riches all I get is unhappiness'. His good humour returned when he decided that what he really wanted was to stay in Melbourne. An offer from Duke University in 1965 was capped by a tentative approach from Harvard, but by this stage he was wondering about other possibilities: 'Even if a Vice-Chancellorship were offered I would not want it … To bank on something coming up in government, which I would like, is to bank on too much of an improbability.'[24] Yet he was ready for a change, and when an unexpected offer came to become vice-chancellor at the University of New England, he accepted, and left the law school at the end of 1966. He later moved to the University of Queensland, and 'something in government' eventuated in a grand form when he became governor-general in 1977.

One of Cowen's earliest projects was the creation of a chair of commercial law. He had returned from Oxford convinced that law was best taught by full-time academics. The creation of new chairs was a key part of achieving this at Australian law schools, where so many of the staff still worked only part-time at the university. He would not, however, make the creation of the chair a hostage to the vagaries of university funding. He decided to go and get the money himself, from outside donors; the *Herald* chair in fine arts had been created in a similar way in 1946. From the rising financier Ian Potter, he obtained both a donation of £1000 and a list of others to approach. A chance meeting with one of the men on Potter's list produced another large contribution and more names of likely donors. 'Then I started to cook with gas.' He soon had pledges and donations from twenty-one blue-ribbon companies and law firms, to fund the chair for five years.[25]

The plan for the chair was unusual in another way. It was meant to have a practical emphasis and a close connection with the world of business that had funded it. The new professor, Patrick Donovan, Rhodes scholar from Queensland and reader in law at the University of Adelaide, was to begin by spending much of his time in the city, 'where', as Cowen put it, 'he will obtain at first hand a knowledge of all the principal documents on which commercial transactions are founded'.[26] After his appointment, he accordingly spent time in the international trade section of the Melbourne office of the Commonwealth Bank. Europe ultimately had a stronger attraction for him and his family, and he resigned in 1961 to become commercial counsellor at the Australian embassy in Rome. In his subsequent European career, he was Australian ambassador to the OECD, and became vice-president of the International Court of Arbitration of the International Chamber of Commerce.

In the meantime, before the creation of the chair in commercial law, Paton's resignation to become vice-chancellor had opened another vacancy for a new professor. The successful applicant was David Derham. His appointment was in some ways the last of a series that reflected conditions in legal education that were now passing, with the rise of professional legal academics and postgraduate study. He was relatively young (thirty-one), had an excellent academic record (first-class honours at Melbourne and the Supreme Court prize), but had no higher degree, and no high profile in scholarship and publications. He had the kind of intelligence and flair that appealed to the selection committee; how much his deep family links to the Melbourne medical, legal and business worlds meant to them is hard to say, but they would have done him no harm.

He had, as Cowen put it, 'embarked on a fine career at the Victorian Bar and nothing would have prevented him from taking silk early and going to the Bench'. But he also had an academic side. He taught part-time in the law school, like several other leading barristers, and the chair of jurisprudence attracted him, albeit with thoughts of returning to the bar within a few years. Arthur Dean, Supreme Court judge and member of the university council, gave him a lofty, if kindly meant, welcome:

> It certainly is something of a departure for us to appoint to this chair a man who has had no association with the Oxford School of Law, and somewhat of a disadvantage to you as you set out on the new career. But it is a striking tribute to your ability and personality that you were appointed in preference to men with a more academic background.

Derham's two predecessors in the chair of jurisprudence (Bailey and Paton) had, it is true, been Oxford graduates, but the university's preference was not as settled as this implied. Friedmann, after all, studied elsewhere, as had the sub-professorial staff, not to mention all the deans before Bailey.[27]

Constitutional law, jurisprudence and the problems of legal education became Derham's particular interests. He shared much of the faculty's administrative work with Cowen, particularly during the dean's frequent overseas trips. Generous with his time and his knowledge of the profession, he was 'the man to see when graduation and the question of articles drew near', in the words of the students' newsletter. The annual 'At Home' of the Law Students' Society tested his commitment: 'The Law Students' Ball is on tonight—so pity me', he wrote to Cowen. In the early 1960s, he was starting to look around for new opportunities. He received a tentative approach for a job of some kind for the federal government, but when a definite offer came to take on the heavy responsibility of starting the new Monash law school in 1964, he accepted. 'I am probably mad to do it but it will have some compensating fun no doubt', he wrote to a friend.[28]

At the centre of the law school's day-to-day working was Florence Scholes, nominally the dean's secretary but in fact 'the administrative eyes, ears and hands of the law school', as Louis Waller put it. When Waller joined the staff in 1959, Scholes was 'the person of course who told me everything I really needed to know, the person who knew everything that was going on'. Many shared the experience of one external student in the 1940s, who did the course 'leaning upon Miss Scholes for advice'. Successive deans' reports to the council recorded her ubiquitous work and called for her to be paid accordingly. Unmarried and without a degree, she fell into a category of women whose role and responsibilities in the university were never fully recognised in appointments and pay, however well they were acknowledged by those around them. In 1966, Cowen was still trying (unsuccessfully) to have her appointed as an Administrative Officer. Humorous, proper, 'her usual charming and beaming self', she retired in 1970 after thirty-eight years in the law school.[29]

Difficulties of rapid growth, funding shortfalls and internal mismanagement embroiled the university in serious financial problems in the early 1960s, attracting increasingly critical attention from the state government. 'The general talk was of doom and gloom', Cowen said;

'Paton was in the wars'. But the law school 'seemed to be relatively unaffected'. Nevertheless, an uncharacteristic note of irritation appeared when Cowen wrote to Julius Stone in Sydney in 1965: 'I think you know something about the incredible financial position in this place ... It sounds mean and I am depressed at having to write this way.' Students, too, were aware that the general level of funding available to the university affected what the law school could do. As one wrote in 1965, 'many of the law school's defects can be reduced to a matter of cold, hard cash'; she had the library particularly in mind.[30]

Other big events also influenced the law school only distantly, or merely as one small part of the university. Inquiries headed by Mills (1950) and Murray (1957) provided the policy framework for greater federal funding for universities, funding that backed the expansion of the law school's academic staff in the 1950s and 1960s. Australian universities were 'feeling very happy' about the Murray report, Harold Ford wrote to a friend early in 1958, and Derham was able to tell Patrick Donovan that the increased grants would pay for more staff, but hopes for enough capital funding to cover a new law building were disappointed. The Martin report of 1964, which supported the expansion of higher education by strengthening institutions other than universities, included a long chapter on legal education drafted by Derham. Its message that lawyers should be trained in universities meant more in New South Wales, where only 56 per cent of locally-trained lawyers admitted in 1962 had university degrees (and not all of those in law). In Victoria, the figure was 95 per cent, and compulsory university training for solicitors was a century old, although the report did send a shot across the bows of the alternative admission course recently created by the Council of Legal Education.[31]

The law school's small staff generally got on well together. 'The atmosphere was argumentative but friendly', in Arthur Turner's words. 'People were happy there.' One of the few incidents that caused serious friction was prompted by disappointed hopes over promotion, always a sensitive topic and later a source of grave trouble in the 1980s. Patrick

Donovan's resignation from the chair of commercial law in 1961 created the first opportunity to appoint a new professor in the law school for nearly nine years. When the appointment went to Harold Ford, already an established expert in the field, Peter Brett, whose specialties were criminal law and jurisprudence, rather than commercial law, reacted with rage, and blamed Cowen for, as he saw it, failing to deliver promised support for his application. For Cowen, it was 'the only bad personal time in my experience in the School'. After a talk with P. D. Phillips, Brett approached Cowen to mend the relationship. Brett went on to hold successively the Hearn chair and the chair of jurisprudence until his premature death in 1975.[32]

The usually friendly relations among the staff owed much to Cowen's influence. When disagreement threatened over who should be dean in his absence overseas in 1964, he was dismayed: 'We have a very happy faculty and it is absolutely disastrous if bitterness breaks out in this way'.[33] A round of reassuring letters from him dispelled the misunderstanding that started the trouble.

The ex-service personnel, older and more experienced than any other generation of students, brought the Law Students' Society to life as never before. Its activities had flagged, hampered by lack of numbers, the shortages and other restrictions of life on the home front, and 'war blues'.[34] One of its institutions, the annual mock trial, had lapsed altogether in the middle years of the war, as had publication of its learned journal, *Res Judicatae*.

The mock trial was first held in the early 1930s. Its beginnings were modest, but it had a theatrical side that persisted and grew, and a didactic purpose that withered away. The scenario for the 1934 trial was set up when a masked man burst into a lecture and snatched Bailey's mortarboard. To provide a lesson in the weakness of eye-witness testimony, the organisers prosecuted an innocent student, while the real culprit sat in the audience, unrecognised by the witnesses. Bailey's sufferings in the stories constructed for the trials were only beginning. In subsequent years he was kidnapped and blown up, and he usually had a walk-on part to give some facetious or far-fetched testimony.[35]

The trials became theatre-pieces, leading fictitious characters through elaborate stories and carefully contrived jokes. Their success varied. A big audience enjoyed the 1939 trial, but the LSS itself recorded that the following year's effort was 'a dismal failure, due to the intoxication of the foreman of the jury, and the lengthiness of the proceedings … Few members saw this case to a conclusion.' (It began at 8 p.m. with an audience of about 300, and finished more than three hours later.) When the trial was revived in 1944, its fanciful side took over, as the defendant argued that he was a were-rabbit and took on animal form in the light of the full moon.[36]

Four years later the trial had its apotheosis as part of the Royal Melbourne Show, broadcast on ABC radio through the efforts of LSS secretary Monty Hollow. Fundraising for charity took precedence over law; the question was whether justification existed for the use of classical themes by modern composers. The ABC's variety and symphony orchestras provided musical evidence in the arena at the showgrounds, joined by the National Military Band for the *1812 Overture*. Although later productions never quite reached these heights, the trial remained a big event. Participants would prepare costumes for their parts; Peter Bailey borrowed dresses when he was to be called as a female witness.[37]

The dean testified to the 'extraordinary vitality' of the LSS in 1949, as the students of 1946 approached the end of their courses. Its busy program in these years included the regular moots that had been a feature of the society and its predecessors from the start, dances, including Petting Sessions and the annual At Home (which evolved into a full-scale ball by the end of the 1950s), frequent talks and debates, and in some years a law revue. The society produced its own news-sheet, *De Minimis*, from 1948. It had a chequered history in the next three decades, sometimes serious, sometimes nothing more than a string of disconnected *doubles entendres* and fragments of toilet humour.[38]

A cloud of tobacco smoke hung over many law school activities from the earliest 'smoke night' concerts of the Articled Clerks' Law Debating Society in the 1880s. Smoking was banned in lecture theatres, and also in the law library until a room was set aside after 1959, but elsewhere it was a social ritual. Non-smokers like Robin Sharwood were left out: 'it was a real social disadvantage'. As a student, David Derham took advantage of the special ex-service personnel ration of tobacco, still restricted after the war. To get it, he had to sign a form declaring that he was 'a genuine smoker'. After an operation to remove lumps on his vocal cords in 1963, he complained that 'these idiotic medicine men insist that I shall not smoke', but the habit took its toll; he died of emphysema in 1985. Harold Ford found it hard to get tobacco for his pipe while rationing lasted: 'I was reduced to Balkan Sobranie, and at one stage had to smoke some horrible stuff from South Africa'. The image of George Paton holding his half-finished cigarette upright, to stop the ash from falling, stayed with one graduate fifty years later. In the 1960s, the smoking room of the law library was 'the social hub of the School. A meeting place; a place to read the sports pages or do the crossword.'[39]

In the early twentieth century, when smoking was less socially acceptable for women, it was also a marker of difference between male and female students. The anonymous advocate for women in the LSS who wrote in the *Melbourne University Magazine* in 1913 reassured readers that women would not make men give up this pleasure at the society's meetings: women 'would, I am sure, be grieved to think they were making martyrs of the men'. 'Equity', replying in the next issue, was not convinced. 'The men would not expect the women to sit in a reeking atmosphere for some hours; they would in decency refrain from indulging their desires, and a great source of enjoyment would be gone.'[40]

The gradual banning of smoking forced smokers to give up or go outside. The staff library became smoke-free in 1985, and soon smoking was banned in the whole quadrangle building.[41] One or two staff continued to smoke behind closed doors until the move to the new airconditioned building made detection inevitable in 2002.

Sport, a foundation of the LSS from its earliest days, flourished to such an extent that a separate Law Students' Sports Club was established in 1949. By longstanding university tradition, classes were not timetabled on Wednesday afternoons, making way for matches. The degree of athleticism varied. The annual marbles tournament catered for the less vigorous, but the football competition was a mainstay. The women's football team gave the *Sun* the sort of story it relished in the context of the gender relations of the 1950s, when Collingwood legend Lou Richards coached them for a match against Commerce: the newspaper called them 'Lou Lou's Legal Lovelies'.[42]

Fostering a little social awareness and some rare contact with the realities of the criminal justice system was another, albeit much smaller, part of the society's work. From 1950, students wearing the LSS badge could sit immediately behind the lawyers during trials in the Supreme Court. Louis Waller used the privilege to sit in on one of the sensational cases of 1952, when William O'Meally was tried for the murder of a policeman. Henry Winneke, leading the prosecution, would come over to talk to the students before the day's hearing began, and tell them what he was going to do.[43]

Tours of Pentridge Prison, initiated by the LSS as part of its burst of activity after World War II, continued into the 1970s. In 1967, Julian Phillips, then sub-dean, had the idea of combining a visit with a football match against a team from the prison's young offenders group, known as the Tigers. He asked Brian Ward, LSS vice-president and professional footballer, and together they organised the match, assembling a team that included several league players who were studying law.

The visit left Ward with vivid memories. The Tigers defeated the lawyers. 'They were unbelievably good. They loved the physical contact, and boy did they tackle hard. It was eerie playing a game surrounded by armed guards in a prison.' As if to point out the moral that different circumstances or choices might have put the law students on the other side, Ward found that he had been at school with his opponent, a man serving a long term for manslaughter. Being acquainted with a convicted killer gave Ward new respect in the eyes of his friends, he found. Looking back, he thought the whole experience sharpened his compassion for the most vulnerable in the community, expressed later in longstanding involvement with the Red Cross.[44]

The diversity and changeability of the LSS, sometimes serious and high-minded, sometimes exploring the other end of the scale, showed in one of its innovations in the 1950s: the annual conference. The first seems to have been in 1953, when the students went to Warburton for the weekend. The following year, David Derham, Sir John Latham, and socialist historian and civil liberties activist Brian Fitzpatrick gave talks. Friends from opposite ends of the political spectrum, Latham and Fitzpatrick both spoke in defence of freedom of expression. Staff representatives attended regularly, taking part in the staff–student discussion, or the grudge session, as it was known, 'a hearty and garrulous afternoon' according to *De Minimis*. Students talked about the problems of the law library, subjects they would like to see in the course, and whatever else was on their minds. Louis Waller remembered being attacked for making students buy the casebook on criminal law that he and Peter Brett produced in 1962; it was much more expensive than the duplicated notes it replaced.[45]

At other times, the conferences 'bordered on the riotous', in the words of one former student. The chance to have a big night and cause some trouble was tempting at other LSS functions, too. Revellers turned a fire-hose on one gathering in 1954, and the annual general meeting in 1956 degenerated into a drunken flour-bomb fight. When the adjourned meeting resumed, 'Prof. Cowen said that the Law Faculty were becoming renowned as a body of irresponsible louts'. The society had to pay to clean up the room and replace a broken window. Another fine followed the annual marbles match against the engineers.[46]

The society's links with the profession changed and weakened, as the number of students in the articled clerks' course continued its long decline. By the late 1950s, the society was very different from what it had once been, when most of its members studied law while working as clerks in solicitors' offices. Now, most members were full-time students, and the society's base was the university campus. The president continued to be a recent graduate, rather than a student, but this tradition from the older LSS ended in 1958. The secretary reported the following year that the election of an undergraduate president was 'an experiment which, to everyone's delight, and to some, surprise, was highly successful'.[47] The society was now a campus student club like any other.

Like its counterparts in other faculties, it sometimes had a broad appeal, and at other times gave outsiders the appearance of a clique. Its moot court competitions gave generations of students the chance to play at something they might soon be doing for real. The connection with the realities of the courtroom may have been slight, but the experience of argument and questioning from the bench put both their law and their skills to work. Ernie Schwartz, a student in the 1980s, stood up in an LSS moot and told the judge that a particular decision was a 'travesty of justice ... We both smiled: me, thinking I was Clarence Darrow, and she knowing I was basically an idiot.'[48]

The faculty believed strongly in the benefits of mooting, and from 1958 it was compulsory, in a program that P. D. Phillips QC joined the staff to organise.[49] The Carlton courthouse provided an appropriate venue for the early faculty moots, while the voluntary LSS competition continued in parallel. Phillips hosted lunches for participants, and Quo Vadis restaurant in nearby Lygon Street advertised itself in the LSS magazine as 'the choice for all Moot Court Luncheons'.

The students of the 1950s benefited from the networks fostered by the LSS and the relatively small size of the university and the law school. The first-year law students of 1956, surveyed by the university, ranked higher than most in their friendships with other students, their involvement in clubs, and their enjoyment of university. The staff did what they could, too. Derham reported to Cowen, away in the United States in 1954: 'You will be horrified to hear that once a week we have been using your room for a little afternoon tea party. Miss Scholes has made your room look specially nice on Wednesday afternoons, and we have had four or five students in for tea and a chat.' In 1956, a mentor program assigned groups of first-year students to senior staff, but it soon disappeared. Within a few years, the ratio of students to senior staff would have made such groups as large as lectures.[50]

A few students from Malaysia, Burma and Thailand came to the law school as undergraduates in the 1950s, following the children of earlier Asian migrants who had studied law from the late nineteenth century onwards. Edward Ni Gan, whose father was Chinese, completed the articled clerks' course in the 1890s and practised as a solicitor in Bendigo; William Ah Ket, whose father also migrated from China, won the Supreme Court prize for articled clerks in 1902, and was president of the Law Students' Society in 1907. A prominent barrister, he was one of three representative former students who supported the toast to Moore at an LSS dinner in his honour in 1929 (the others were Owen Dixon and Kenneth Bailey).[51]

Women were admitted to the academic staff of the law school for the first time in the 1950s, breaking out of the administrative positions to which they had previously been confined. Airlie Smith (later Airlie Blake), former president of the Law Students' Society, tutored briefly in jurisprudence in 1943, but her application for a senior lectureship two years later was unsuccessful, despite the fact that she had won the Supreme Court prize as a student. The first woman appointed to a permanent academic position was Rosemary Norris (later Justice Rosemary Balmford), who became a part-time lecturer in conveyancing in 1957, 'quite a red letter day', according to David Derham.[52]

Mary Hiscock was the first woman appointed to a full-time academic position in the law school, at the end of 1963. When a faculty meeting came to consider the appointment, P. D. Phillips made a 'blistering attack', in Derham's words. One of his objections was that the dean had made the appointment as an emergency measure without the faculty's prior approval, in order to make sure that someone was available to teach Contracts at the start of the following term; pressure of work at the bar had forced the previous lecturer's resignation. This was a question of process, but Phillips also objected to Hiscock herself. She had not yet been admitted to practise, and despite her obvious qualifications—she had just returned with a JD from Chicago, and had already served as a tutor and senior tutor—Phillips 'criticised strongly an appointment of a junior person without practical experience to teach a subject of such professional importance as Contracts'. 'I think he believed very firmly that this was undermining the whole professional basis of the school', Hiscock said.[53]

Phillips and his supporters doubtless found it more difficult to accept that a woman rather than an equally junior man could take on the task. The law school had a long history of appointing young men with little professional or teaching experience. Moore and Paton were both examples, and Phillips himself had been a temporary lecturer in the law school less than a year after getting his LLB and being admitted to practise. His peppery temperament may also have been at work. Cowen, a strong believer in what Phillips had to offer the law school, also knew that he could be 'a terrible man in some ways. He'd say some terrible things.' Derham, presiding at the faculty meeting in Cowen's absence, steered the discussion back to the question of procedure, and Hiscock's appointment stood. Phillips later publicly recanted at a faculty dinner, 'very graciously', Hiscock thought, and the two became friendly as they occupied adjoining offices.[54]

The proportion of women among the students continued to rise gradually in the period after World War II, once the distortions of the post-war influx had worked their way through the system. Women made up about 8 per cent of law students in 1950, rising to 19 per cent in 1970 and 42 per cent in 1982. For many women, the law school in the 1950s was a place where men and women mixed on equal terms, and some resist imposing later feminist thinking on their own experience. 'It was a place where men and women met as equals', Rosemary Balmford said. 'That whole woman thing was really not the

big deal it is these days … Inside the university it didn't make any difference.' Nor was the disparity in numbers necessarily a problem.
'Being a small proportion of the students, we girls really had a good
time—I did for sure', Sylvia Spigelman recalled.[55]

Women's experiences of the law school also had a different side.
Some in the 1950s and 1960s encountered the belief that they simply
did not belong, though others never met this response. Many of the
staff were supportive, but some were not. 'One didn't seem to like
women doing Law', Pamela Sublet found. 'He rang the fathers of two
I know and said their daughters should give up because they would
never pass the course.' But, in this case at least, the discouragement did
not work: 'They passed and practised and are still alive and well at 70
and still playing tennis and partying'. Mary Hiscock witnessed one
professor walk into class, throw an essay on the table, name the student
who had written it, and proceed to criticise it, saying, 'This has made
me wonder why women ever come here'. Rosemary Howell, a student in the late 1960s, was told by a staff member, 'You're actually
stealing a man's place … Maybe you'd better think seriously about
whether law's the career for you.' She nearly gave up, but when a man
who sat in front of her in class dropped out the next day, she reasoned
that he had opened up a place for someone else, and decided to
stay.[56]

At times like these, the small number of women on the staff was
a disadvantage. 'There was really nobody appropriate to go and talk
to', Rosemary Howell found when she was wondering whether to
drop out. 'It was a very blokey environment.' This changed as the
number of women in the teaching staff grew. A student of the late
1980s had different memories. 'It was great to have female lecturers.
They were role models and they sat on the poncy male students and
made you feel like you could make it, too.'[57]

The classroom was sometimes a theatre for the attitudes of male
staff, and for the power relationship between men and women in the
law school. At least one lecturer made a point of ignoring the women
in front of him, to the resentment of many male students, in his ritual

opening to each new class: 'Gentlemen!' Others concentrated on them in lectures on sexual offences. Even the popular Geoffrey Sawer ultimately provoked a protest: 'he had a mischievous streak that led him, at times, to embarrass the few girls in the class by going into unnecessary details about particular cases of sexual assault. One day the girls got up together and walked out. He was more careful after that.'[58]

Criminal Law stood out in the memories of a number of women who studied law after World War II. Sawer was not alone in aiming discussion of sexual offences at women in the class, as a student observed of Peter Brett in the 1960s: he 'used to take particular delight in singling out the women in the group ... He'd try and embarrass them, to pick on them'. Another remembered him reducing a female student to tears. Others found the atmosphere more adventurous than malicious—Brett's 'bark was much worse than his bite', one male student thought, and outside class he would go out of his way to be helpful—while some women found the meaning of the interchanges different from what it would be today. A female student of the early 1970s described Brett's Criminal Law classes as 'so incredibly sexist in a way that would not be permitted now, but actually then we just regarded as funny and a bit naughty (treating us as adults, I guess)'.[59]

The Law Students' Society brought male and female students together, but also offered them some strikingly divergent roles. The Miss Law contest began in 1948, as part of a nationwide Miss University competition. It raised money for the international World Student Relief organisation, a major focus of LSS activity in the immediate post-war years. Contestants reached the campus finals through the amount of money they raised, and were then judged on 'general attractiveness (figure, posture, features and clothes sense) and personality (general intellect, voice, mannerisms and social sense.)' *Farrago* described Miss Law: 'Twenty-three, 5ft, 2in., brunette, and eyes—well, just wait till you've gazed into them ... Her ideal man, besides possessing certain irrelevant qualities such as being an outdoor type, intelligent, and good-humoured, must be—wait for it—yes, must be a barrister.' The story included her phone number for good measure. For some who were there, the experience was different from what later readings of power and gender relations would suggest. 'It was fun,' one female student of the early 1960s emphasised; 'it was *fun*'.[60]

Male students from various faculties appeared in their own fashion parade in 1950 to raise money for World Student Relief ('Garments to be shown will include hunting, shooting, and fishing wear, satin-lined opera cloaks, tartan dinner jackets, and satin smoking jackets'), but the experiment was short-lived. The more durable Mr Law competition was judged by different standards. 'It was pretty tawdry', Graeme Johnson, a student in the late 1960s and early 1970s remembered: 'almost a pot-pourri of animal acts'.[61]

———⟫•⟪———

Money was never far from the minds of many students, as they tried to cover tuition fees and find living expenses. Vivian Hill, who worked in the Crown law office, got one of the free university places awarded by the Victorian public service board. 'I was self-supporting while at Law School, paying 7 pounds 7 shillings per subject per term until I was awarded a free place in 1953 ... I recall looking at a two-shilling piece and wondering if I could afford to spend it on a milkshake.'[62]

On average, though, law students' families were richer than those of students in other faculties. In the 1956 first-year student survey, only 16 per cent of law respondents said their family incomes were less than £1000 a year, while the figure across all faculties was 25 per cent (average male earnings were around £900). Forty-four per cent of the law respondents reported family incomes of more than £2000 a year, against an overall figure of 24 per cent, and the survey report put Law at the top of a list of faculties ranked 'in family economic sense'. Law students were also more likely to depend on their families for financial support. Eighty-five per cent of the law respondents said their families provided their only living allowance, against the university average of 60 per cent.[63]

For those who paid full fees, they were a significant amount of money. In 1962, the total fees for a full-time four-year LLB course, including fees for taking out the degree and for subjects studied during articles, were just under £600, or around half average annual earnings for men. But the number of students paying full fees had declined. In 1937, just under one-third of the university's students received assistance with their fees in the form of free places, half-fee places, scholarships, bursaries and help from the students' loan fund. Only a few of these were law students, though; there were only fourteen free places in law, in a total enrolment of 328, although this figure did not include a small, additional number of scholarship students.[64]

Federal funding provided more assistance after World War II, and in 1956, 68 per cent of the law students who responded to the first-year student survey held Commonwealth scholarships (under which fee assistance was not means tested), above the survey average of 52 per cent. The proportion on other scholarships, which were more likely to be means tested and were sometimes restricted to other courses, was low: 14 per cent, against the overall figure of 38 per cent. 'Clearly scholarships are obtained through an orthodox educational history', the survey's authors commented. 'Once more the well to do students show a higher return of Commonwealth Scholarships'. By 1968, about 57 per cent of all Australian university students had their fees entirely paid under one scheme or another. Two years later, just over half the new law students who started at Melbourne had Commonwealth scholarships. The abolition of tuition fees by the Whitlam government in 1974 was the extension of a trend rather than a sudden revolution.[65]

The greater availability of financial help accentuated the decline of the articled clerks' course, as fewer students had to work in order to pay their fees. Only 3.5 per cent of law students were enrolled in the articled clerks' course (or other apprenticeship courses) by 1961. But many missed out on scholarships, and even those awarded by the Commonwealth brought (aside from fees) at best only a small, means-tested living allowance. Outside work was usual for students to earn spending money, and essential for some to pay fees. When Robin Sharwood was a student in the early 1950s, the registrar's office did what it could to police a limit on the number of hours students worked during term, under threat of forcing them to reduce the number of subjects they took. Most students took jobs during the vacations, especially in summer, when casual work was easy to find in department stores in the city.[66]

⸻

In broad outline, the structure of the course the students studied changed little between 1945 and 1965. An introductory subject used selected topics of substantive law as a vehicle to familiarise students with basic concepts and terminology. Drawing on Paton's first-year course from the 1930s, it emphasised 'the study of the actual practices of the courts in their use of earlier decisions and in the interpretation of statutes'.[67] Arthur Turner, in particular, developed the course in the 1950s, and David Derham, Frank Maher and Louis Waller turned the materials issued to students into their casebook on the legal process in 1966. The book began with an exhortation by Arthur Koestler for students to re-live the creative process by making discoveries for themselves, applied by the authors to 'learning law through the cases'.

Legal History, British History and the first of the course's two arts electives completed first year. Compulsory subjects on doctrinal areas made up the bulk of the course, as students worked methodically through contract, crime, property, tort, and so on. A notable innovation was the full-year subject on comparative law, which became an alternative to international law from 1948. Friedmann proudly claimed it as the first of its kind in England or Australia.[68]

Another innovation had a life of its own that eventually separated it from the law school altogether. George Paton and John Barry (one of several Supreme Court judges who maintained a long and close involvement with the university) joined together with one of the senior lecturers in law, Norval Morris, to inaugurate Australia's first department of criminology, in 1951.[69] It was affiliated with the law faculty through Morris, who eventually had a joint appointment in the two disciplines; law students were able to take his course in criminology, although it was technically an arts subject. The connection, though, was only intended to be temporary, and the new department went its own way after Morris' departure to Adelaide in 1958.

One of the law school's traditions could not survive in the post-war environment: the expectation that lawyers would know some Latin. The subject had been compulsory in the degree course until 1932, when it became an option, but Latin at school level was still a prerequisite for entry for degree students and articled clerks alike. Even Major-General Sir Charles Rosenthal, architect, soldier, musician, and probably the most distinguished candidate ever to seek entry to the law course when he applied in 1939 at the age of sixty-four, was told that he would have to pass intermediate Latin first. Jack Richardson, too, was unable to get into the law course without first passing Latin in arts, not having studied it at school leaving level.[70]

When the faculty waived the Latin requirement for ex-service personnel in 1946, the days of the old rule were numbered, and the disappearance of Roman law from the curriculum soon afterwards took away another of its justifications. As Zelman Cowen explained later, in reply to an inquiry from the Queensland Law Society, 'it became apparent that further retention of the pre-requisite would debar very competent students from the Law course for a reason which was becoming more and more artificial'.[71] He could have added that the students debarred would increasingly come from the new state high schools, which were providing an alternative path to matriculation for students who did not attend the traditional teachers of Latin, the private secondary schools.

Post-war conditions even impinged on the artificial world of the law school's exam papers. In 1947 the final honours paper in Jurisprudence asked students: '"The trial of war criminals vindicates the reality of international law, which is now a system of law in every sense of the word." Discuss'. Alternatively, they could choose to say whether law would wither away with the institution of a communist state.

Life soon became harder for a minor institution of the law school, the perpetual student. The university had allowed students to continue re-enrolling and attempting exams indefinitely, as long as they paid their fees. Some remained undergraduates while whole cohorts of students came and went around them. The faculty reviewed the records of such students in 1952, finding one old campaigner who had been enrolled for seventeen years. He, like others, was excluded.[72]

Jurisprudence, British History and Legal History were compulsory subjects that offered context and perspectives for the rest of the course, but they came under increasing pressure from a movement to give students more freedom to choose their own subjects. A new curriculum introduced by stages in 1967–69 made Jurisprudence optional and allowed students to pick more options from subject groups in the last two years of the course. As the new course came into full operation, Legal History succumbed to a renewed attack on its status as a compulsory subject. It was left in the course as an option, although a broader constitutional history subject (the descendant of British History) remained compulsory under various titles until subsumed into Legal Process and its successors from 1978. There it lingered like Tinkerbell, its vitality growing or fading as belief in it waxed or waned. Private International Law, long a compulsory part of final year, was also demoted to a mere option, in 1971. The changes established specialised options as a larger part of the course, a feature that chimed with the diverse research interests of the growing full-time staff; by 1978, only one subject, Trusts, was compulsory in the last two years of the course, and students could make their own choices for the rest.

One of the main changes in course structure, the creation of a separate honours degree, was, in one way, not much of a change at all. Since 1860, the law school had listed and ranked honours students at the end of the course.[73] This distinguished them and recognised their achievement, but it was a statement of overall results rather than the award of a different degree. Robert Craig and John Madden, the first honours students, like all their successors down to 1950, graduated plain LLB, not LLB (Hons).

The possibilities for a distinct honours course had been under discussion during the debates on the curriculum in the 1930s and

1940s. At the time, the best students were encouraged to take a separate honours exam in February on subjects they had already studied during the law course. The exam led, not to an LLB (Hons), but to an LLM, which was awarded to honours graduates in the LLB course after a year's wait.

One possibility, put forward by the chief justice and taken up by a faculty committee towards the end of the long war with the Law Institute, was to add a year to the course for honours (or rather the LLM), but to exempt graduates in the extended course from doing articles.[74] Given the Law Institute's keenness in the past to increase, rather than reduce, the time spent under articles, and the small likelihood of having students admitted to practise without any practical experience, this was at best an ambit claim. Without the attraction of direct admission to practise, the proposed honours year was unrealistic, although it was adopted for the BA, the BComm and some other degrees after World War II. In a professional discipline such as law, an honours degree did not bring enough benefits for it to be worth another year of even the best students' time. Changes to the LLM were unresolved when the new undergraduate curriculum was settled in 1946.

By the late 1940s, the faculty was increasingly unhappy with the honours system, partly because of the demands of the February exam, and partly because the LLM was better reserved for research students. In 1950, it adopted an honours exam in final-year subjects, leading for the first time to a separate honours degree, awarded on the basis of performance over the whole course. Settling on a permanent form for the exam was difficult, and the faculty returned to the issue again and again in the following years. Honours graduates needed to be distinguished by something more than just high results in the pass course, but how best to do this in the absence of an honours year remained an open question as the faculty oscillated between the various possibilities.

After the new system had operated for a few years, staff revived the idea that honours students should have to draw their whole course together in a final exam. This would allow all candidates in any one year to be ranked by the same test, and late developers could show their abilities to full advantage. The degree would now be awarded on results from three honours papers in final-year subjects, and a daunting set of three four-hour exams the following February or March that could draw on any compulsory subjects in the law course, other than Legal History.[75] Unlike the old honours exam, these papers rolled up multiple issues in questions that crossed subject boundaries. At least students would now be able to take their own books and notes in with them.

Reviewing the whole law course for the final three papers was challenging. It was 'a tough examination', in Cowen's words, and had little appeal except for the best of the students who intended to practise, and those who had an academic career in mind. One persistent problem at Melbourne as at other universities was that some students easily capable of getting honours did not choose to sit the exam, perhaps out of misplaced caution about their own abilities. Staff encouraged the students who enrolled; 'essentially they were invited', Mal Smith found. Smith, who sat the final honours exam in 1968, found it 'fairly gruelling', but it was beneficial, too: 'you had to pull all the disparate subjects together'.[76]

Notwithstanding the benefits, the faculty decided after a decade's experience that the final exam was 'over-ambitious'. The practical problems of delaying honours results until March were another shortcoming. It reverted to awarding the honours degree on the basis of performance throughout the course and completion of a research paper.[77] This remained the guiding principle for the honours degree until the last intake into the LLB course in 2007, although sporadic argument continued about the relative weight to be given to earlier and later subjects in allocating points for honours, and the form the research paper should take.

Law was always sparing, indeed stingy, with high marks. First-class final honours were particularly difficult to get; for the first century of the LLB, no first-class final honours at all were awarded in most years.

The winner of the coveted Supreme Court prize for the top-ranked graduate usually had to be content with second-class honours, and one received the faint praise of the prize with third-class honours. A remarkable, even embarrassing, number of gifted lawyers failed to reach the exacting first-class standard. Graduates who fell short or did not sit the final honours exam included six chief justices of the Supreme Court of Victoria and seven justices of the High Court. From 1963 onwards, the faculty relented and became a little more generous, awarding at least some first-class honours degrees every year.[78]

Complaints about this parsimony go back to the nineteenth century. In 1894, after an eleven-year drought in first-class honours, the *Summons* argued that the pattern had more to do with the standard set by the examiners than the quality of the students, and as evidence cited the case of one who received first-class honours in jurisprudence at Oxford before doing the Melbourne LLB course, and went on to first-class honours in the Oxford BCL afterwards, but earned only second-class honours from the law school's exacting examiners. The student was Dugald McDougall, later professor of law and modern history at the University of Tasmania.[79]

Some later staff agreed, although their influence on marking was slight. Cowen, whose teaching experience gave him good opportunities for comparison, said many pass graduates at Melbourne had qualifications equivalent to second-class honours at Oxford. The tough standard became something of a joke when Norval Morris won a prize for the best PhD thesis submitted at the University of London in the previous ten years, after being judged worthy of only second-class honours at Melbourne. Sir Daryl Dawson, a student in the 1950s and later an external member of the faculty, put the results down to 'a sort of academic cringe. They were frightened of giving first class honours lest they be said to be bestowing it on people who didn't deserve it in comparison with other universities.'[80]

Whatever the underlying reasons, the pattern remained entrenched. Between 1981 and 1986, less than 15 per cent of law graduates received honours degrees. Some law schools were even stricter; the proportion of honours results was lower at Macquarie and Sydney, and at Monash, honours went only to an exclusive 6.8 per cent of students in 1984. Law students suffered when they competed for scholarships with graduates from higher-scoring faculties. Nationally, far more students received honours degrees in arts, engineering and science than law, although commerce students did worse. Shifting expectations and the adoption of a loose form of standardisation increased the proportion of honours graduates in the 1990s, but in 2006 the university was still calling for a cultural shift in the law school to raise the share of first-class honours results, which ran at less than half the university average.[81]

The core of the law school's teaching remained the formal lecture, in which the teacher expounded the law and the students took notes. Louis Waller thought the teaching was stunning when he did fourth year, dominated by the full-time academics, in 1955. Bruce Wainwright was another who revelled in it: 'It was a great time to be a student,' he said. As Ian Sutherland, also a student in the early 1950s, put it, 'The ex-servicemen had largely gone, the numbers were down, there was no competition & the quality of the teachers was outstanding'.[82]

Some of the senior staff had a low opinion of the educational value of lectures, despite relying on them so heavily in their teaching. Paton thought the lecture method achieved little. 'But in default of a perfect tutorial system, I suppose it is better than nothing', he told the Law Students' Society. Sawer looked forward to a time when lectures would not be necessary at all: 'If and when satisfactory Australian text books are available, lectures should be abolished entirely and the course should comprise tutorials only'. Cowen agreed: 'In general—though not in every case—I believe that the formal lecture is a peculiarly unsuitable technique for legal education'.[83]

There were tutorials in some subjects, usually fortnightly, but their size and the number of subjects in which they were offered fluctuated. Paton reported proudly in 1946 that, for the first time in the faculty's history, tutorials were being given in all subjects but one, for both pass and honours students. As the post-war bulge in enrolments made its way through the course, thirty or more students squeezed into Paton's room for his Jurisprudence tutorials. Daryl Dawson, studying in the early 1950s, went to tutorials of about twelve. 'That was good; they were participatory.' They were well-attended, too. A survey of first-year students in 1956 found that almost all the respondents from Law went to tutorials, a higher participation rate than across the university overall.[84]

The growth in student numbers in the late 1950s made the tutorials too big for Cowen's liking, although they were still provided in the first two years of the course, with a few more in third year. The cohort of part-time tutors had grown to twenty-two by 1961, many of them providing the drafting tutorials that taught practical skills to the conveyancing class. Some groups became much too large for the kind of interchange they had been created to foster, and sometimes the atmosphere was hardly conducive: 'Large tutorials with little personal engagement—much sarcasm', in one graduate's words. Some chose to supplement or replace the tutorials with a private study group. One such group of friends met each Sunday night. 'It was more valuable than tutorials and resulted in all of us getting honours degrees.'[85]

Peter Carter, visiting from Oxford in 1953, held Oxford-style one-on-one tutorials with a few honours students, but the weight of student numbers made the experiment impossible to repeat. The weekly meetings to discuss an essay daunted even the most gifted. 'They were terrifying, absolutely terrifying', Robin Sharwood found. Daryl Dawson had a similar experience. 'The moment you'd open your mouth he'd come out with "That's wrong".' But Dawson came to like Carter, and learned a great deal. Mark Weinberg's later encounter with him, back at Oxford, was one of the formative experiences of his career: 'he was a terror—most impressive. One of the great, great legal scholars, I think.' At least Melbourne students were spared the mid-winter tutorial at ten o'clock on Saturday night that Weinberg had to cycle through the snow to attend.[86]

In the 1950s, for the first time since Hearn, the law school made lasting efforts to use time in the lecture room in different ways. The main inspiration, as in the shorter-lived attempts of Moore and Bailey, was contact with the United States, and experience of the case method used there. The case method took many forms in American law schools, but their common theme was that classes would include discussion or questioning in which the teacher would lead inquiry by students into the conclusions to be drawn from the raw material of cases. Students would develop the skills of finding the law for themselves, instead of being presented with an authoritative exposition of legal doctrine. Discussion in larger classes often took the form of Socratic questioning, in which professors interrogated students about cases, sometimes with intimidating ferocity.

In its original form, as conceived at Harvard law school in the 1870s, an essential counterpart of the case method was the casebook. It would provide students with the judgments on which they would practise their skills, avoiding the declaratory conclusions of textbooks. The lack of casebooks on English or Australian law, and the paucity of library materials, hindered earlier experiments with the case method at Melbourne—students could not use the case method if they were unable to get hold of the cases—but such books increasingly became available after World War II. Sawer's casebook on constitutional law led the way for Australian law in 1948.

Cowen wrote from Chicago in 1954:'I am now the sworn foe of the teaching method in which the student can come into class knowing that the worst that can be expected or desired is silent comprehension'. Like most of his Melbourne colleagues, he borrowed selectively from his American experience. 'The students may be presented with a mass of half chewed, incoherent bits of law and will be left confused, unsatisfied and very unhappy. It seems to me that a class hour in which there is debate between student and instructor <u>and also</u> a measure of analysis and co-ordination by the instructor has everything to commend it.'[87]

Patrick Donovan, who had encountered the case method as Bigelow teaching fellow at the University of Chicago before he came to Melbourne, was one of the first teachers to build class participation into his lectures. 'It interested me greatly', he said, 'because it involved the real participation of the students. They were not simply writing down something that was being lectured to them.' Louis Waller was in his Contracts class in 1953: 'he tried to do something which had never been tried on us before, and we were not, shall we say, receptive. He asked us to read cases before classes and to be ready to answer questions about them.' Melbourne students were not used to this sort of thing, although Donovan made their task easier by issuing duplicated copies of much of the material. No one wanted to answer his questions, Jennifer Smithers, another Contracts student, found, except for two future QCs, Neil McPhee and Cliff Pannam. The experience stayed in William Ormiston's memory fifty years later: 'though doubtless it was "good for me", I felt all at sea when reading cases before I knew what were the basic principles'. The Torts class cheered when their visiting lecturer in 1956, Robert Heuston, announced that he would not be using the case method.[88]

The educational advantages of getting students to talk in class were too great for this lack of popularity to prevail, and experiments with the case method had spread to three subjects by 1955, as more staff got experience of teaching in American law schools and gradual improvements in casebooks and library materials alleviated some of the problems. By 1962, current and former law school staff had produced recent casebooks on trusts (Ford), contract (McGarvie and Donovan), criminal law (Brett and Waller), constitutional and administrative law (Brett), and torts (Morris and Sharwood, with W. L. Morison of Sydney). A degree of class participation slowly became a standard feature of teaching, although it was well short of the case method in some of its American forms. Students' feelings about it remained mixed. When the seats in the upper law theatre were renumbered in 1982, so that lecturers could put questions to students by number,

Bolsheviks in the back rows simply pulled the numbers off the seats. The same happened at the University of Sydney law school, after its new building opened in 1969.[89]

———•◦•———

The task of accommodating the law school's staff and students had long been difficult. There was little space even for the small number of staff, despite the fact that the independent lecturers had no rooms of their own at the university, and from the 1880s to 1925 their main base of operations was the Supreme Court building, where they lectured. The law professors, though, had to squeeze into the quadrangle, where they competed for space with other departments, the university library and the central administration.

In the decades after World War II, accommodation became a serious and apparently insoluble problem. The law school still had no building of its own. 'We do not in any physical sense have a law school at all', Cowen wrote in 1955. As one former student put it, 'the law school consisted, or seemed to consist, of bits and pieces—nothing you could point to and say, "This is the law school."' Law's total accommodation in 1955 consisted of two professors' rooms, five lecturers' rooms, three secretarial rooms, one tutorial room, and an attic. 'We simply have no place to put our people', Cowen lamented.[90]

The lack of a building and the daily journeys across the campus to lecture theatres in other faculties weakened the law students' sense of collective identity. 'There was no Law School as such,' Jennifer Smithers found. 'There was not a cohesive organization and we were probably closer to the practising profession with external lecturers and articled clerks as students.' It was difficult for articled clerks like Vivian Hill, holding down full-time jobs, to participate in campus life. He had work in the Crown law office to return to: 'I had to get back all the time'. But he could fit in a cup of tea with other students after lectures, and he went to the Law Students' Society annual conference.[91]

The amount of time full-time students spent on the campus did much to give them a sense of belonging to the university, if not to the law school, and counteract the lack of a building of their own. John Cain's routine was one he shared with many others. 'Whether or not we had lectures or tutorials, we would attend university, work in the Library, sit in the cafeteria, or take part in other university activities, five days a week ... I left home to get to the university around 9 a.m. I got home around 6 p.m. each evening, five days a week, for nine months of the year.' Weaker identification with the law school could mean stronger integration with the rest of the university. 'You still have the feeling of belonging to a university', Wolfgang Friedmann wrote on leaving Melbourne in 1950, 'rather than of fulfilling a specialized function in a professional training school'.[92]

As so often in the law school's history, the problems of the law library were particularly severe. The law collection, amounting to about 8000 books in 1947, remained part of the university's general library, housed in the northern part of the quadrangle. There were no photocopiers and few casebooks, so the only way for students to check cases and legislation was to sit in the library and read them there. It was a social hub. The law students would take the LSS flag inside on football match days and hang it up, to the disapproval of the librarians. There were also those who managed to avoid the building. 'A lot of students got by with very little library work at all', Harold Ford found.[93]

The law library's fate was bound up with that of the university library, whose accommodation problems had preoccupied the council for years. A new library building was the ultimate aim, but more room needed to be found in the meantime. Proposals including the roofing-over of the quadrangle were abandoned in favour of a cream brick extension on the north-west corner of the library, later known as the records or Scarborough wing. Its opening in 1951 allowed a reorganisation that provided a separate space for the law collection for the first time, in the old periodicals room, upstairs in the gothic north extension to the quadrangle (the home of the university library itself before 1925). 'We became a little more noisy, territorial', one of the students, John Cain, remembered. 'We saw it as being our piece of territory, and were a bit chuffed by it.' Now there was also an assistant librarian to look after the law books, Alan Brown, a law graduate from Western Australia. After Brown's sudden death in 1953, he was replaced by Peter Brett, who, as a new senior lecturer, had responsibility for the law library as well as teaching duties.[94]

As student numbers grew, so did competition for books and seats. The upstairs law library had much appeal, with its natural light, high ceiling and tall gothic window, but by 1957 it could seat only 143 of the 800 law students. The following year, as student numbers rose towards 1000, Cowen told the university council that it was 'grotesquely overcrowded'. The lack of space was compounded by a shortage of library staff, which became a mournful refrain in the dean's annual reports to the council. Students lamented the time it took for law reports to return to the shelves, and urged each other through the Law Students' Society newsletter to put them back. One strategy students used was to gather all the books they would need early in the day, and then guard them, 'like some mad Doberman'.[95]

In these conditions, it was unsurprising that many students were rarely found in the library. Yet, in first year at least, law students made more use of it than their colleagues from other faculties, partly because so much of their reading material could be found in few other places and could not be borrowed. In 1956, 87 per cent of first-year law students used a library at least once a week, nearly double the university average.[96] Some turned to the Public Library in the city (now the State Library), or the Supreme Court library, which students could ask for permission to use, while resident or non-resident members of the university's colleges could use the law books found in their libraries.

For those who got hold of the books, the underlining left by previous generations in the library's increasingly battered law reports was a way of saving time. When new copies arrived in 1952, the Law Students' Society complained: 'New copies are unmarked. This is considered unsatisfactory.' Students at the next general meeting voted overwhelmingly for the return of the old copies, but the dean turned them down.[97]

The lack of space across the whole university was so acute after World War II that the law school's needs were only some of the many that the central administration struggled to meet. A new building was at the top of Paton's list of the faculty's priorities when he was dean, but he was unable to make much progress. Cowen soon brought all his prodigious energy to bear on the problem. In his second year as dean, he could already see 'a fine new law school building' in his mind's eye.[98] One of his strategies for turning it into reality was not to wait for the university, but to push on independently. If such a scheme produced a building, well and good, and if not, at least it kept attention on the faculty's needs.

He accordingly approached Grounds, Romberg and Boyd, perhaps Melbourne's best-known firm of architects, and asked them to produce a proposal. The arrangement was that their initial work would be unpaid, but the vice-chancellor agreed to appoint them as architects if the project went ahead. Cowen took the proposal with him to the United States on his trip as a visiting professor in 1953–54, to see if he could raise the necessary funds. He described his vision in characteristic style. 'The legal profession is too obscurantist already. Let the building be light, fresh, vigorous, vital with light, light, light. The school must not be an entity unto itself, but a part of the University and its life, to promote a liberal education by close contacts throughout the University.'[99]

'Gromboyd' came up with a slim, cylindrical glass tower that would stand on the south lawn, south of Old Arts (Brian Lewis, the university's master planner, favoured the site). Cowen kept a model of the building in his office. Its predominant white colouring 'positively asked for the appellation "ivory tower"', in Harold Ford's words. The ten floors included internal gardens at the entrance, two projecting, cantilevered lecture theatres, offices, a moot court room, a legal aid clinic, the law library, a squash court, and, on the ninth floor, a law club, 'a big sitting cum reading room', 'intended as a centre for the legal fraternity of the City of Melbourne'. Despite the elegance of the model, not everyone liked the design. Derham called it the 'Gas Works'.[100]

The difficulty of estimating the future size of the law school bedevilled the project. In the absence of an entrance quota, the only way to forecast future enrolments was to guess. While the architects were working, Cowen increased his initial estimate from 500–600 to 750 students, 90 per cent of them men. Even with this adjustment, the law school would have been bursting out of the building within a few years, if it had been built. Student numbers beat Cowen's estimate within three years, and kept growing. For the moment, though, the scheme came to nothing. He had too many other claims on his time in America, and his fundraising idea lapsed.[101]

Cowen was soon doubtful about the multi-storey plan, but he still thought a new law school would be needed in the foreseeable future. Sites for the chimerical building were proposed, now here, now there, on and off the campus. In 1957, Derham was campaigning for the area occupied by two professorial houses to the south of what is now the Baillieu Library, but the council preferred a location on the northern side of the Baillieu, then occupied by Psychology and Education. At least the council had, for the first time, actually allocated a site. When later decisions about extensions to the Baillieu and the location of Economics and Commerce overtook the council's plan, Cowen formally applied for the southern site in 1962. He now assumed a first-year intake of 330, a student population of 1350, and a teaching and administrative staff of seventy, but the site was lost to Medicine.[102]

Law enrolments were high across the country. In 1962, the visiting American professor, Willard Pedrick, noted that in Australia there were only two practitioners for every enrolled law student, whereas in the United States there were five. There were proportionately two and a half times as many law students in Australia as in the United States. Law students made up nearly 5 per cent of students enrolled at Australian universities, and just over 10 per cent of the students at the University of Melbourne. In the United States, the comparable national figure was about 1.5 per cent. Pedrick guessed some of the obvious explanations: that law was an undergraduate course in Australia, unlike the USA, and that it had 'the appearance at least of offering both general and vocational education—in a medium sized economy package'. Melbourne's enrolments were boosted by the admission rules' requirements for university study, which had no counterpart in New South Wales. The law school consistently enrolled more than 40 per cent of Australia's law students from 1954 to 1963, and in some years the proportion was nearly half. Only Sydney, drawing from a larger population, enrolled comparable numbers, though below Melbourne's from 1955 until entrance quotas stabilised the figures in the 1960s.[103]

Others knew of the accommodation problem and provided suggestions of their own. Maybe a government building could usefully be recycled to make a law school, as happened later at Victoria University in Melbourne and Victoria University of Wellington. The old customs house in Flinders Street, in the centre of the city, was facing demolition in 1957; could it be used? Derham quite liked the idea when Oswald Burt, a founder of the National Trust, put it to him, but he thought its chances of success were not good, and was embarrassed when the *Age* got hold of it. Cowen was cautious: 'I think you are right in keeping our powder dry, but I believe it would be disastrous if we left the University grounds'.[104] Having ended its long experiment with city lectures, the law school remained with the rest of the university, and never sought the city location that gave the University of Sydney law school a different atmosphere and closer links with the profession.

Another will-o'-the-wisp was a law building east of Swanston Street, off the main campus. Derham recorded a moment in 1963 when it looked 'for a day or so' as if the university would recommend the project. A discouraging response from the Universities Commission, which held the purse strings for large capital works, put an end to the idea, but it re-emerged in the 1980s. In 1965, the university did recommend additional space for Law, including a new library, in a building to be shared with Arts, but the Commission preferred to give Law more space in the quadrangle, and the building (eventually named after John Medley) became one for Arts alone.[105] In all the discussion of possible sites, no one seems to have suggested the area where the new law building was finally constructed, but then the Carlton telephone exchange, the eventual location south of the main campus, was a most unlikely spot.

What the law school did get in this welter of unrealised possibilities was an increasing share of the old quadrangle, as its co-tenants moved out. The opening of the Baillieu Library in 1959 provided a new home for the university's general library, leaving the law library to take over the lower level of the old main reading room. The north wing of the quadrangle was gutted for a second time, as two new floors were constructed inside its shell, to be occupied mainly by offices for law staff. The old law library, upstairs in the gothic extension to the quadrangle, was divided into a classroom, a lecture theatre and a staff library. The ground floor of the old general library became the new law library, with a mezzanine gallery for extra shelves and seating. Staff joined in to move the collection downstairs, putting books in boxes and sending them down a chute to their new home.[106]

'The new Law Library is still a makeshift', the university librarian wrote soon after it opened. Within a few weeks of the move, it was already crowded during the day, and by the early 1960s it shared the Baillieu's problems of severe lack of space. The foyer of Wilson Hall was tried as an overflow reading room, as an experiment. 'Overcrowding is such that it is virtually impossible to maintain acceptable library conditions for users in the reading room', Derham reported to the council in 1963. The library badly needed more staff, but no more could be appointed, even if money had been available; there was nowhere for them to work. But major improvements depended on getting a new building for the law school as a whole, a project that never climbed high enough in the priorities of the university and the Universities Commission for it to be funded in the 1960s.[107]

Why was the law school so badly housed for so long? For a start, its situation was not unique, either in the university or in comparison with other law schools. Accommodation shortages were severe across the campus after World War II, and other faculties competed for attention and finance in the university's capital works program. At least law had rooms in a permanent building. Nearly half the university's buildings were 'of a temporary, army-hut variety' in 1951.[108] Law suffered like others from the university's intractable financial problems.

The needs of Medicine and Science for buildings and equipment were more obvious than those of the lawyers, whose repeated claims that the library was their laboratory, while true in a way, never cut much ice. Law also had weaker lobbying power than the more numerous professors from far larger faculties. The weight of authority elsewhere in the university prevailed, even though, for thirty-one years, the two successive vice-chancellors were former professors of jurisprudence in the law school. In common with most other faculties, Law was outflanked by Medicine when in 1963 it brilliantly parlayed an increase in its quota (a sharp reversal of its previous policy) into a major funding boost for both its operations and the construction of its new building.[109]

When national decisions were made by the Universities Commission, other universities also had strong claims. The problems of other law schools were even worse, and funds went to new law buildings that opened at Adelaide, Western Australia, Monash and Sydney in 1967-69. An authoritative statement of minimum standards for law schools might have provided some leverage, but although the Australian Universities Law Schools Association adopted such standards in 1961, it was wary of making them public (apparently fearing that they were insufficiently ambitious), and they never gained anything like the force that the accreditation standards of the American Bar Association and the Association of American Law Schools exercised in the United States.[110]

Importantly, and perhaps fatally for the new law building for many years, the image of the old quadrangle (on the outside, at least) appealed strongly to many in the faculty. Not all agreed that a new building was a good idea, and the law school had the option of expanding in the old building as other occupants moved out. Derham wrote in 1954: 'if we had the money to do it properly we might well have a better Law School out of this original U-shaped quadrangle than we would out of a totally new modern building'. Harold Ford agreed.[111]

By funding new buildings for other tenants of the Victorian rooming-house that was the quadrangle, as happened with the construction of the Baillieu Library and again ten years later with the Raymond Priestley administration building, the university and the Commission could deal with two problems at once, accommodating others and vacating extra space for Law at the same time. Derham's idea (echoed by the Commission) of moving the university administration into a new building and making the quadrangle 'a complete Law School' became reality at the start of his term as vice-chancellor, although the groundwork was laid by others, while he was dean of Law at Monash.[112]

Cowen's postgraduate study had been in England, but it was from the large and innovative American law schools that he thought his students and staff had most to learn. 'As a teacher my Harvard classes were the great experience of my life', he wrote after his visit there in 1953–54. Declaring that the Melbourne law school looked much more to the United States than to Britain, he omitted the necessary rider that this had more to do with ideas of what a law school could be and how it could operate than with the substance of the law it taught, or with the social and economic perspectives stressed in some American courses but rarely emulated in Australia.[113] At Melbourne, English cases remained authoritative, and the predominant approach was doctrinal. Of the nine full-time academic staff in 1956, five had English degrees and none yet had American qualifications.

Immediately after World War II, restrictions on foreign exchange made it hard for Australians to get behind the 'dollar curtain' and into the United States. But as conditions improved, Cowen used his contacts to facilitate teaching visits and postgraduate study, starting with Arthur Turner's Bigelow fellowship at Chicago in 1951. Even Robin

Sharwood, a self-professed Anglophile, studied at California and Harvard with Cowen's encouragement. These opportunities were still rare, however, especially for women. Norma Ford, who shared the Supreme Court prize in 1948, had to give up a PhD candidature when she got married and went to the bar; the demands on her time were too great. Mary Hiscock was one of the first women from the law school to go to the United States for postgraduate study, in 1962. Sir Owen Dixon, chief justice of the High Court, noticed the law school's increasing Americanisation with concern: 'I have nothing to say whatever against a man who has time and money to do so spending years at Harvard', he wrote. 'But no one who has seen the influence of Oxford on men could think that it is any substitute to go to Harvard.'[114]

Staff exchanges and visits grew in frequency as travel became easier. David Derham swapped with Peter Carter of Wadham College, Oxford, in 1953, and other visiting teachers who stayed for extended periods in the 1950s included Robert Heuston from Oxford, and Sanford Kadish and Daniel Dykstra, both from the University of Utah. Erwin Griswold, dean of the Harvard law school, visited more briefly in 1951 and 1959. By the mid-1960s, as jet aircraft made travel to Australia faster, if still very expensive, Cowen could record a single remarkable week in which he welcomed Tony Honoré of Oxford, J. A. Jolowicz of Cambridge, dean Anandjee of Banaras Hindu University, L.C.B. (Jim) Gower, then dean of law at the University of Lagos, and Sir Hugh Wooding, the chief justice of Trinidad, who gave the university's Southey Lecture. Cowen's frequent travels made him a one-man law school embassy to the world. In addition to the United States, his destinations as dean included Malaya, Singapore, Hong Kong, Dominica, India and Ghana. 'At the moment I am deep in the affairs of Nigeria', he wrote in 1962, while preparing opinions on its constitution.[115]

The paths to England and North America were well beaten, but staff were beginning to look elsewhere in their work. Derham undertook consultancies in India and Papua New Guinea. In a 'private

Colombo Plan' of aid to Asian neighbours, Peter Brett drafted new land codes for Brunei and the Solomon Islands, working with a panel of law school colleagues (the initiative was a by-product of one of Cowen's trips). Johannes (Hans) Leyser, who took his doctorate at Freiburg before fleeing the Nazi regime in the 1930s, developed expertise in the law of Indonesia, with Cowen's encouragement, and made two study trips there in the 1950s. He headed the university's new Board of Indonesian Studies, in 1956. Mary Hiscock and her external collaborators David Allan and Derek Roebuck obtained outside funding for a research project on Asian contract law in 1969; she made Asian law the basis of the law school's comparative law course in the same year.[116]

Norval Morris and Arthur Turner reached out closer to home by setting up a legal aid clinic in 1951. Suggestions for such a service staffed by students were nothing new; the Public Solicitor had called for such a project in 1936. Morris and Turner initially provided legal advice by themselves at the Brotherhood of St Laurence, before being joined by Leyser and student volunteers. Robin Sharwood was one of those who staffed the clinic: 'It was, for students like myself, who I guess had been brought up in a fairly sheltered middle class environment, an absolutely eye-opening experience'. For Graeme Henry, it was the thing he most enjoyed about the law school.[117]

The burden on staff and the lack of a full-time administrator ended the scheme in 1957. A formal clinical legal education program always eluded the law school, despite repeated proposals and the example of the practical training programs at Monash and, later, La Trobe and Deakin. Students and staff continued to work as volunteers in other legal aid clinics, including a legal referral service operated in the early 1970s by students and articled clerks.[118]

If it was hard to take the law school to the community through a clinical program, it was easier to bring the community, or at least the legal profession, to the law school. The tradition of occasional public lectures started by the earliest teachers continued, but after World War II specialist classes for practitioners began to appear as well: short courses on industrial law and domestic relations (or family law, as later lawyers would call it) began the trend in 1949, and in 1961 more than two hundred practitioners and others packed out a postgraduate course on the new Matrimonial Causes Act.[119]

Other outside work linked the staff to the legal profession and the wider community. In 1949, three lecturers took leave to go to London to work on the bank nationalisation case in the Privy Council, although only one, Sawer, was a full-time teacher. Two other members of the faculty appeared in the case.[120] Derham maintained a practice at the bar, by agreement with the vice-chancellor, but it contracted as his thoughts of returning there from the university receded. Nevertheless, he continued to give opinions and occasionally appear in court, most notably with Peter Brett in the dramatic proceedings that saved Robert Tait from the gallows in 1962.

Cowen, too, worked occasionally as a barrister. His absence to appear for Victoria in the *Dennis Hotels* case in the Privy Council in 1961 drew criticism from the Law Institute, but the vice-chancellor saw it as a good thing for the university's relations with the state government. The chancellor, Sir Arthur Dean, himself a judge, took a stricter line, and reprimanded both Derham and Cowen for spending too much time on their legal practice the following year; they replied, with some justice, that he misinterpreted the amount of time involved. Nevertheless, on Cowen's departure the rules for legal practice by professors were clarified and tightened.[121] The demands of professional practice, an intermittent problem since Sewell cancelled classes in 1857, returned to vex the law school in the 1980s.

Governments drew on the law school's expertise in other ways, some predictable, others more unexpected. From 1944, successive staff were members (and later secretaries) of the Chief Justice's Law Reform Committee, the state's main law reform body until the appointment of the law reform commissioner in 1974. They gave evidence before parliamentary committees and advised government in other ways. In 1952, Cowen became a liaison officer for the recruitment scheme that drew Australian graduates into the British colonial office's overseas service, a position that Bailey had earlier held. Harold Ford continued this somewhat arcane work, which paid a fee, contributing to the law school's small discretionary income.[122]

The faculty increasingly brought outsiders into its deliberations. The part-time lecturers had been a link into the profession even in the days when the faculty had no members from outside the university and its council. They outnumbered the full-time teachers throughout Cowen's time, and although he experienced the frustrations of this, he was also aware of the benefits.

> I think that although my lot as a Dean in Faculty meetings is sometimes very difficult because of the fact that the non-full-time teachers are in a majority, I am on balance inclined to believe that it is better here than it is in the English Schools. There you have full time Faculties, but the relationship with the working profession is virtually non-existent. I found this in England a very frustrating fact, and know that it is very much better here.[123]

As the number of independent lecturers shrank in proportion to the full-time staff, the influence of practitioners in faculty meetings declined. Representation from the bar was most affected, since more independent lecturers were barristers than solicitors. The Law Institute had had a designated place on the faculty since 1942 (the first such external representative to be specified in the faculty statute), but in the aftermath of the fight over the entrance quota, one of the barristers on the faculty complained that the representation of the Bar Council had declined as full-time appointments replaced independent lectureships. The faculty responded by giving the Bar Council a seat of its own, and promised to consult with it about the appointment of two of the 'additional' members appointed by the university council on the faculty's recommendation.[124] Designated places increased in the 1960s and 1970s, with spots for the Monash law faculty and the Victoria Law Foundation.

The presidents of the Law Institute and the Bar Council tried to preserve the practitioners' numbers during another round of arguments about the composition of the faculty in the mid-1970s, but they were inevitably swamped by the rising tide of full-time academics. No realistic number of outside appointments could equal the number of new full-time staff in the faculty, and the outside membership was also an obvious target for successive attempts to keep the membership to a manageable size. But removing places always provoked a fight, and the number of full-time academics set a minimum below which the faculty meetings could not shrink. Even after some minor reductions in designated places, membership had increased to around seventy in 1987.[125]

Practitioners were ever-present and often influential, but not so the government members of the faculty. Cowen pointed out the lack of government influence to Erwin Griswold at Harvard:

> So far as our Law Faculty is concerned, it is non-existent. Technically the Government representatives on the University Council who are lawyers are ex officio members of the Faculty, but they never turn up. I think that Government influence does not add up to anything so far as influence on us is concerned.[126]

The benefit to the faculty of eminent alumni was more often in the form of lustre than lobbying power. Although successive prime ministers (Menzies and Holt) and chief justices of the High Court (Isaacs, Duffy, Latham and Dixon) were law school graduates, they were more often interested observers than active friends. The exception was Latham, whose long involvement with the faculty continued after he became chief justice in 1935 (the benefits of Menzies' brief time as chancellor, in his retirement, went to the university as a whole rather than Law). But none of these famous graduates could with propriety do more than incidental favours, even if they wanted to. Nor did the law school perceptibly suffer when chief justices from Sydney and Brisbane presided over the High Court from 1964, and the centre of political gravity settled in New South Wales.

The many alumni on the Victorian Supreme Court were in a better position to support the law school, particularly through their voting power on the Council of Legal Education. But here, too, the kind of obvious help Redmond Barry gave to his university was a thing of the past. The judges on the Council held a middle line between the Law Institute and the law school during the long fight over the curriculum in the 1930s and 1940s, and when restrictions on entry to the law course tested their backing for the faculty in 1961, they decisively declared their independence, as we will see.

In the 1950s the faculty looked further afield into the business world for members with useful connections. The number of outside members appointed by the council on the faculty's recommendation rose to four in 1946, six in 1950, and eight in 1970, before being cut back to four in 1988. One such member generous with both time and money was Leonard Dooling, a law graduate who was the Commonwealth Bank's chief manager for Victoria. His membership was a by-product of his approach to Cowen to support the new chair of commercial law. The faculty saw obvious benefits in this kind of affiliation, and in 1960 it set out to strengthen its links 'with the Industrial and Commercial world'. Norman Jones, not a law graduate but a member of the university council and managing director of BHP (the Broken Hill Proprietary Company Limited, Australia's largest company at the time), became a member as a result.[127] He remained until 1967, but was able to attend few meetings.

Links outside the university led to funding for another new academic position in 1958. P. D. Phillips, closely connected with the law school as part-time teacher and faculty member since he first became a tutor in 1924, was about to retire from the bar, and was interested in finding a new outlet for his considerable energies at the law school. Cowen had met the entrepreneur Stanley Korman at one of Dooling's Commonwealth Bank lunches, and approached him to create a position for Phillips, who duly became the Stanley Korman special lecturer in law.[128] Korman's businesses later underwent a highly publicised financial collapse, but the university continued the position, with the Korman title, until Phillips' death in 1970.

Outsiders brought a critical eye. The chief justice of the High Court, Sir John Latham, long connected with the university as a student, a lecturer, a member of the law faculty and the council, and, briefly, chancellor, noticed an unusual exam question that Geoffrey Sawer set for Constitutional Law II in 1949: 'During the argument in the *State Banking Case*, counsel observed that Dixon J. did not sit in the *Uniform Tax Case*, whereupon Starke J. interjected:—"No, worse luck." Comment on the implications of his remark.'

Sawer was asking whether the court's decisions were consistent with Dixon's interpretation of the limits of federal power, but Latham disapproved of such flippancy on the part of a law teacher—and probably on the part of the notoriously forthright Starke as well, although he could do little about a fellow judge. So, like the king in the nursery rhyme, the chief justice told the chancellor, the chancellor told the dean, and the dean told the associate professor. The outcome was an apologetic letter from Paton, in which he explained the serious purpose of the question and disavowed any intention to show disrespect. Maybe Sawer had tempted fate: giving notice of his move to Canberra, he had just thanked the university for twenty years of complete intellectual freedom as student and staff member.[129]

Later students saw a gentler side of the apparently censorious Latham. In retirement in the 1950s, he continued to use the university library, sixty years after he himself had first been a student. Not knowing who he was, many of the law students took him for one of the vexatious litigants who pursued their researches there and whose encyclopaedic knowledge they drew on for their assignments. 'There was one elderly gentleman who appeared towards the end of my first year,' Mary Hiscock recalled. 'He was extremely pleasant and helpful to everybody, and so we assumed that he was a new member of the class of vexatious litigants. He really was absolutely charming.' She later found it was the former chief justice who joined in the students' discussions, sitting at the tables of the old general library.[130]

—————————

As the extra space that became available when the general library moved out in 1959 rapidly filled, pressure of student numbers was already leading the faculty to think about ways of limiting enrolments. Cowen warned the council and the profession in 1957 that student numbers might have to be limited, if the accommodation problems were not solved.[131] An interim measure, introduced the following year, was the so-called three-subject rule, under which students had to pass three subjects before they could progress from first to second year. First year was becoming a de facto entrance test for the rest of the law course.

The failure rate in first year was high enough to give rise to some exaggerated rumours and to draw criticism to the three-subject rule in the newspapers, but even when it was running at about 25 per cent in 1959 (not unusual in the university at the time), overall enrolments would remain manageable for no more than a year or two, as first-year numbers continued to rise. A limit had to be put on the intake, or library overcrowding and class sizes would force the staff to abandon class participation and their other plans to make the students more active participants in the course. Medicine had operated a quota since 1946, extending war-time restrictions, but the decisions to impose and later reduce it had been deeply controversial. In 1957, the law faculty voted to impose a quota within two years, unless more accommodation became available. The space freed up by the Baillieu Library postponed the deadline, but methodical preparation began, including the trial of a law school admission test for all new students from 1958.[132]

The crunch came in 1960. In a long and carefully-constructed memorandum whose prevailing tone was profound regret, the full-time teaching staff set out their case. Of their various arguments, one based on staffing stood out. The average staff–student ratio for United Kingdom universities was 1:7. At Melbourne, which had the worst average in Australia, it was 1:12.6. Calculated on a comparable basis, the law school's ratio was 1:50. Just to maintain it at that level, as enrolments increased, at least ten extra academic staff would be needed within three years, but the university would not appoint them.[133] More federal government money flowed into higher education following the Murray report of 1957, but it was inadequate to support expansion on this scale, and the university was getting into financial trouble of its own, leading to a crisis in the early 1960s. The faculty endorsed the quota proposal, and from 1961 students were selected for an intake of 330. Applicants were ranked primarily by matriculation exam results, but other factors could be taken into account; the law school admission test separated those with equal rankings.

Most faculties of the university were already imposing quotas, but their effect in courses other than medicine had so far been mild.[134] The proposal to exclude some students from the state's only law school hit a nerve. Some of the strongest resistance came from the legal profession, in spite of its apparent vested interest in limiting competition from new entrants. But unlike American lawyers in the 1930s, who gave new impetus to increased barriers to entry in the form of higher educational standards, Victorian lawyers in 1960 were not competing in an overcrowded profession.

Ensuring an adequate supply of future staff may have been a concern for some lawyers, but the loudest objection was that it was unfair to shut young people out of the course, and so the profession, of their choice. The thought that practitioners' children might not be able to follow them into the law was particularly galling; this exclusion of insiders seemed even more unfair, or at least closer to home, than the blighted hopes of people without family connections. As the proportion of applicants who missed out began to rise, the president of the Law Institute lamented: 'the Solicitor-Father who from his Son's cradle days looked forward to the Son following in his footsteps and joining him in practice in years to come must be almost heart broken'.[135]

Law staff heard rumours that judges had accused them of going on strike, and it was from the judiciary that the decisive move against the quota came. Even before the formal decision to introduce it had been made, Sir Norman O'Bryan, a judge of the Supreme Court, winner of the Supreme Court prize and former part-time lecturer in the law school, attacked the high pass standard for exams and the likely effects of entry restrictions. Filling the profession with 'the brilliant academic lawyer' was a bad idea, he was reported to have said. 'The community would be better served by lawyers of high principles, common-sense and a good working knowledge of the law than by brilliant men less proficient in other qualities.' Privately, he stressed the egalitarian aspect: everyone should have the opportunity to do law, despite failures in exams and long delays in finishing the course. Cowen retorted that when O'Bryan was a lecturer, he failed far more students.[136]

As the quota cut further into the rising number of applicants in 1962, some of the judges of the Supreme Court, in particular the chief justice, Sir Edmund Herring, became increasingly uneasy. As one of them, Thomas Smith, put it, 'we found that suddenly the quota was biting so deeply that it was, in our view, a catastrophe'. The tension between the university's quotas and the widely-held ideal of open access soured relations with the state government.[137] The judges decided to break the monopoly on legal education that the university had held since 1905, and establish separate exams for articled clerks, leading to admission to practise. The representatives of the Law Institute, the bar and the law faculty on the Council of Legal Education opposed the plan, but they were outvoted by the judges (the bar had been considering its own, temporary, teaching plan, pending the opening of the Monash law school).

The Council had hoped that Monash University might provide lectures, but when discussions to that end came to nothing, the Council had to back its new exams with a law school of its own, which it operated at the Royal Melbourne Institute of Technology; Smith headed the committee that organised an immediate start to teaching. The new school fielded a full staff of part-time lecturers and tutors, including some leading lights of the bar. The faculty was 'not very well pleased' with the creation of the new course, in Cowen's words, but once the decision was taken, it cooperated willingly enough, initially sharing the work of marking. On the other hand, it tried to keep the Council's students, who could use the libraries of the Supreme Court and the Law Institute, out of the overcrowded university law library.[138]

For the supporters of full-time university education for aspiring lawyers, whose case was put by Derham in his chapter on legal education in the Martin report on higher education two years later, the new school was a retrograde step, lacking a proper library or full-time staff, and supported by the desire of some solicitors for 'inexpensive junior clerking labour' from its part-time students.[139] But it gave many an opportunity they would otherwise have lost, excluded by the quota from their only local avenue into the profession.

Until 1976, only students who had been excluded from Melbourne (or from Monash, after its law school opened in 1964) were eligible for the new course. The Council school had to impose a quota of its own in 1970. The Commonwealth Tertiary Education Commission eventually squeezed the Council school out of business. The federal government became its main source of funds when tuition fees were abolished in 1974, but three years later that support became conditional on amalgamation with a recognised tertiary education institution. Negotiations with RMIT were unsuccessful, and the Council school took its last intake in 1978.[140]

Pressure on the quota came not only from outside, but also from within the university. In 1963, a state government inquiry into tertiary education in Victoria, headed by Sir Alan Ramsay, recommended an expansion of student numbers at Melbourne by nearly 40 per cent. When the full-time staff met to discuss the proposals, P. D. Phillips 'attacked at root and branch in the most vigorous way', in Derham's words. Derham (standing in for Cowen, who was overseas) initially tried to back his support for the Ramsay report in the professorial board by putting to the faculty a recommendation for expansion. 'The argument wouldn't write however', he reported to Cowen. 'There is simply no money for us in this triennium and the Library is at break-down point.'The quota remained at 330 until the alternatives provided by the Council course and the opening of the Monash law school allowed it to be reduced to 250 in 1965. It fluctuated around this figure for the next twenty years.[141]

The working of the quota imposed new administrative burdens, and spurred the appointment of a full-time administrator. Peter Nickolls, a law graduate from Adelaide who had been working in industry, filled the post, serving for twenty-six years as the law school's senior administrative officer. The number of applicants more than doubled in two years after the quota began, and exceeded 1000 in 1963.[142] Entry to the degree course had always been selective, in the sense that only some could pay the fees or get a scholarship, and matriculation itself could be out of reach. From 1961 onwards, applicants had to meet a rising standard in their earlier exam results. A new element of selection and exclusivity was added to the law school.

5

VILLAGE DEMOCRACY

1967–88

Cowen's influence persisted long after he moved on. 'The great Zelman aura permeated the law school', Mark Weinberg found when he arrived as a lecturer in 1975. 'Everybody spoke about Zelman.' Harold Ford, the longest-serving professor, and dean during Cowen's absence in 1964, was elected as his successor at the end of 1966, as Cowen had predicted (although he did not take part in the selection process).[1] Ford had been appointed to a chair at what became the law school of the Australian National University in 1960, but he found Melbourne more congenial, and Donovan's resignation allowed him to return to the law school two years later as the new professor of commercial law. His profile grew as an expert on trusts and, most of all, on company law, and even as dean, he somehow found the time to continue his prodigious flow of authoritative publications.

Aside from the seemingly endless search for a permanent solution to the faculty's accommodation problems, the main strategic initiative of Ford's first few years as dean was a serious attempt to turn Law into a graduate school. The idea was not new. Medley advocated at least two years' preparatory study before entry to professional courses as early as 1943, and for decades, successive deans had recognised the value of teaching law as a graduate course. Paton thought it would be better if the LLB was postgraduate, while Cowen supported the idea, but thought it utopian.[2] Practical difficulties had always made this little more than a distant hope, ever since falling enrolments forced the faculty to abandon the graduate LLB in the 1890s.

When he became dean, Ford had predicted that it would be at least twenty years before the law degree became a postgraduate qualification, but in 1969 the support of David Derham, now vice-chancellor, gave the idea a boost. Derham advocated a graduate LLB in a speech to the Australian Legal Convention. Increasing social complexity and regulation placed new demands on lawyers. 'How can it be supposed that lawyers can be equipped for such large undertakings', he asked, 'if their education after the age of 17 or 18 is merely designed to satisfy the immediate and technical work requirements of busy solicitors' offices?' Added to this was the familiar pedagogical argument that students would be better prepared and better able to study law after completing a generalist undergraduate degree.[3]

The example of the United States was a powerful one for staff who had studied at American law schools. There, graduate entry had become established as the norm for university law courses, backed by a campaign by the American Bar Association that was strengthened by the economic incentive to raise barriers to entry to the growing profession in the depression of the 1930s, but at Melbourne the initiative came from the university rather than the profession. It was the contrast with his experience of Harvard that led Ford to set out to turn the LLB into a graduate degree. Pedagogical reasons were among the most important. 'Many left the law school with a desultory kind of education', he recalled; a graduate course seemed to promise the possibility of different teaching methods that might reduce the likelihood of students getting through with little more than a good set of notes.[4]

Colin Howard, too, had taught at Harvard. He presented to the faculty a report on the graduate entry proposal, prepared by a committee chaired by Ford. Some 42 per cent of the 1969 intake already combined the LLB with another undergraduate course (either arts or commerce, for most). Interdisciplinary study through graduate entry, the committee argued, would prepare lawyers better for leadership roles, for creative planning of their clients' affairs, and for framing solutions to social problems through law reform. Students would be more mature and better suited to independent work and critical study, opening the way for more creative teaching methods.[5]

The faculty endorsed the plan in principle, as did the Council of Legal Education, but it met some strong opposition. Edward Woodward, then a barrister and member of faculty, and later the university's chancellor, recalled his resistance to it with pride. Graeme Johnson was one of the student representatives who argued against it in a faculty meeting: 'We said the feeling among students was that if you turn the law degree into a graduate degree it'll become elitist'. One parent, writing anonymously to the dean, said the proposal to make the course longer and more difficult was 'so vicious as to require to be resisted to the last gasp'.[6]

The committee's strategy was pedagogical, not financial (there was no mention of charging different fees for the new degree) and funding difficulties eventually proved fatal. From the start, the proposal was conditional on the availability of Commonwealth scholarships, which paid the fees of nearly 36 per cent of the university's students; the proportion was probably higher in Law, where better matriculation results attracted more of the merit-based scholarships.[7] Without them, a much larger proportion of students would have had to pay fees in the new course. After protracted negotiations, it became clear that the Commonwealth Scholarships Board would not provide scholarships for the proposed three-year graduate LLB.

A two-year graduate course remained a possibility, but investigation showed that the additional staff needed to teach it on an intensive basis made it impracticable. Even when tuition fees were abolished in 1974, the problem of funding remained, albeit in a different form: now extended Commonwealth grants would be needed for the graduate course. The faculty formally rescinded its resolution supporting graduate entry, but it had already moved on, and was exploring other, less drastic, possibilities for curriculum reform. A proposal to extend the basic course from four years to five, with only five compulsory subjects and expanded non-law studies, was rejected by the faculty in 1974; it, too, would need extra Commonwealth funding, and the Law Institute opposed it.[8]

So the four-year course remained the basis of the LLB, although a growing proportion of law students chose the combined degree courses that added one year or two to the basic four. Successive curriculum reviews in the years that followed debated the familiar problems of how best to incorporate history and legal theory, and recommended variations in subject titles, themes and course sequences, but the substance of the compulsory course remained much the same, until a new plan for first year was adopted at the end of 1988, in the aftermath of a university review of the faculty. Optional subjects, on the other hand, grew and mutated with the interests of staff and students, and the LLM by coursework created in 1974, although plagued by low completion rates, was the forerunner of the vastly expanded graduate program of the 1990s.[9]

The idea of later-year entry was revived in 1984, in a plan for Melbourne to emulate the universities of Western Australia and Tasmania by taking students into the law course only after a year's study for another degree.[10] The purpose was similar to that behind the graduate school proposal: better preparation of students, and broader studies, beyond the confines of law. Discussions dragged on for several years, but agreement with the Monash law school, which was a prerequisite, proved difficult to reach, and the scheme was overtaken by the higher education reforms of the late 1980s.

———◦———

In 1967, for the first time, the law school's full-time academic staff outnumbered its part-time teachers, including the many part-time tutors. Midway through the year, Ford put together the faculty's hopes and needs in a document about its future development. The Monash law school now had a student–staff ratio so much better than

Melbourne's that there was 'an alarming and critical disparity' between the two law schools. Melbourne made its first priority the appointment of new staff to halve its student–staff ratio of 38:1. The overall Australian university average was 11:1, and the worst ratio at any United Kingdom law school the previous year was under 21:1. Failing the appointment of more staff, the document spoke of a reduction of the entry quota by 40 per cent, although the likely political consequences of such a move made the threat a weak one.[11]

Where would the money for staff come from? Theoretically, the university could reallocate some of its funds. The way the faculty saw it (just as Paton had argued long ago, in 1944), only a fraction of the fees and government grants brought to the university by law students was spent on the law school. The law school calculated that its students attracted to the university a recurrent grant in 1969 of over $1.4 million, while their cost to the university was only about $350 000. The assumptions on which the calculation was based were only partly true (predicted enrolments were only one determinant of recurrent grants), but the figures nevertheless made a point, particularly when the fees paid by law students (another $323 000) were added in. But challenging funding allocations across the university was a battle that the small law faculty hardly had sufficient political weight to fight, and a case based on the amount of fees and grants brought in by the law students got nowhere. 'You were thought to be something of a cad for raising it', Ford found. Instead, the faculty urged the university to ask the Universities Commission for additional grants.[12]

Whatever the prospects for additional government funding in the long term, the university's budget problems meant that its immediate need was to reduce law school staff, not to appoint more. Sweeping reforms to the university's accounting system under the new vice-chancellor gave the law school a separate budget for the first time. No longer could the dean say, as Paton had in 1950, 'as Dean I spend no money and merely make recommendations to the Council'. Having presented a plan to improve the student–staff ratio, Ford instead had the gloomy task of cutting expenditure for the 1967–69 triennium by

7 per cent. Projected salary increases of about 15 per cent for 1968 only tightened the squeeze.[13]

When the Universities Commission eventually decided on grants for the next triennium, the news was bad. No extra resources had been provided, and the outlook was 'decidedly dismal', Ford wrote to a friend. In the absence of additional funding, the faculty tried to carry out its threat of cutting student numbers. When it proposed to reduce the basic first-year entrance quota from 250 to 150, the vice-chancellor came to the meeting in his capacity as an ex-officio member, and effectively vetoed the reduction by saying he would oppose it elsewhere. The faculty tried to make a gesture by formally recommending an intake of 250, while at the same time resolving that it ought to be 150, but the point was lost. Looking back, Ford thought the submission on the law school's future development had only served to make him *persona non grata* in the university administration.[14]

Outside funding allowed the first significant increase in staff numbers in the 1970s. The Victoria Law Foundation, established in 1967, supported legal research and education using the surplus from the guarantee fund for solicitors' trust accounts. In 1970, it offered the law school funding for three lectureships for a fixed term of three years. A year later, the university converted the positions to continuing ones. The Foundation also subsidised the publication of the *Melbourne University Law Review* and acquisitions for the law library, but further support became impossible when its income dried up in 1975. A major defalcation from a solicitor's trust account left the guarantee fund with little money and no surplus to pass on to the Foundation. After its income was restored, four years later, the Foundation funded many acquisitions by the law library in the 1980s, and it provided the money for the pilot study that led to the establishment of the Asian Law Centre in 1986.[15]

The extra staff significantly improved the student–staff ratio, which reached its best level for decades, helped by a stability in student numbers that had not been experienced since the 1930s. Numbers had doubled between 1945 and 1954, and doubled again between

1954 and 1961, well ahead of even the university's nearly threefold growth in the same period. This was unsustainable, and after 1961, when the entrance quota was introduced, student numbers remained between 1200 and 1400 for more than twenty-five years.[16]

The student–staff ratio fell to 24:1 in 1975, but even this was more than twice the national average. The national economic problems of the 1970s and the funding restrictions on higher education that began with the Whitlam government's last budget in August 1975 made this the limit of staffing improvements for more than a decade. Through the 1980s, the law school employed between thirty-five and forty full-time academic staff, and around twenty administrative staff. To use the phrase so often applied to Australian higher education in the late 1970s and early 1980s, the law school was in a steady state.[17]

———⋙◦⋘———

At least there was some good news about accommodation. Completion of the Raymond Priestley building allowed the university's central administration to move out, leaving the law school in possession of most of the old quadrangle in 1970. It was some consolation for the failure of the plans for a new law building, which had seemed tantalisingly close. 'This University now has a building on which appear the words "Law School"', Ford was able to say for the first time.[18] For those like Derham, who thought the quadrangle was a good home for the law school, it was a fitting solution. The completion in the same year of the law theatres adjoining the quadrangle provided two new teaching rooms, but this made a total of only three lecture theatres under the law school's control. Venues for most classes had to be found elsewhere.

The greatest flaw of the quadrangle plan was the law library. True, its capacity almost doubled when it took over space vacated by the university administration.[19] The cream brick north wing had been extended upwards with an extra floor three years earlier, for the first stage of its occupation by the law library. But more space could be created within the shell of the old building only by resorting to increasingly desperate architectural measures. A steel framework like an overgrown toy construction set supported mezzanine galleries in the area once occupied by the general library. Airconditioning ducts ran down the middle of the main reading room, closing in the ground floor between the galleries and intensifying the semi-industrial atmosphere. Books and readers spread through a cramped network of oddly shaped spaces over nine intersecting levels; the staff locker room was a large stairwell, abandoned when student records moved out. But the old building had some pleasures to offer its users. A few readers could still look out through a mullioned window into a leafy courtyard.

Even after 1970, the law school was not the only occupant of the quadrangle. In the north wing, it shared an uneasy frontier with the university bookroom. Skirmishes in the 1970s pushed the border this way and that, as one side or the other gained control of small spaces. Distant moves elsewhere on the campus had aftershocks in the quadrangle. Completion of the new physics building opened up space in Old Physics, allowing the National Bank to vacate its office in the bookroom wing and setting off a chain of moves, as the law library and the bookroom rearranged themselves with a little more floor space.[20] The faculty's long-held hope of getting the whole of the bookroom for itself went unrealised. In the end, it was Law that moved out of the quadrangle first.

In the south wing, the council chamber, finished in 1970, was outside the faculty's jurisdiction, a little Vatican City in the midst of the law school. The university administration controlled its use. Most of the time, this mattered little to the lawyers, who occasionally raided the room and took its more comfortable chairs to their own offices, but it became a source of serious disruption when demonstrators targeted the council. Staff and students found themselves unable to move around the building, or sometimes even to get into it, when demonstrators tried to occupy the council chamber. Security precautions could be nearly as disruptive as the demonstrations themselves. The dean tried to get advance warning before guards closed the building, but it could happen at short notice, as when someone made a bomb threat by phone during a council meeting in 1974.[21]

The demonstrations were aimed at the university administration rather than the law school, and they centred on university-wide issues. The faculty was usually only a bystander, but the central administration did call on law staff to serve on discipline committees hearing charges against students. Peter Brett and Colin Howard refused to join one such committee to hear charges against students who took part in the occupation of the university council chamber in May 1971. Brett considered himself involved in the events, since he had addressed the crowd. Howard disapproved of the blockade, but thought that bringing the charges after a delay of three months was provocative, and criticised the university for charging only four of the dozens of students who took part. Another fifty students petitioned the university administration, saying that they were equally involved.[22]

The incident turned into a public quarrel between Howard and Derham after Howard's refusal to take part in the proceedings was reported in the *Age*. Derham, already struggling to maintain his authority against the demonstrators, must have been even more annoyed when Howard was quoted as saying that the student blockade 'was sparked off by the desire of the great body of students for consultation on the future of the university and its government'. He and Derham exchanged letters that became increasingly bad-tempered. Derham told Howard it was improper for him to speak to journalists about the disciplinary proceedings. Howard replied that Derham's letter was offensively expressed, and added to the *Age* that the vice-chancellor had no right to reprove him for interviews given to the press. For the time being, the charges against the students proceeded nevertheless. After the university severely reprimanded one of the demonstrators, staff and students donated funds to pay for the damage to the council chamber, and the remaining charges were dropped.[23]

———

The faculty paid Ford the compliment of re-electing him dean for a block period of three years to the end of 1973 (the first time the dean of Law was formally appointed for a term of more than twelve months).

The appointment was also testimony to the importance of continuity in the growing managerial functions of the post, as the university went through a round of devolution of responsibilities to faculties. But when Ford became dean, he did not see it as a lifetime appointment, and nine years later he was ready to relinquish it. The burden was heavy. He was still teaching two undergraduate courses, fitting them in with university and faculty committees, the other work of the dean, and his research, and he was conscious that in the prevailing thinking in the university a 'permanent dean' was, as he put it, no longer fashionable.[24] In other faculties, deans held office for shorter periods, and some were not even professors. He told his colleagues that he would not accept reappointment.

Finding a professor to take over as dean was difficult. To Robin Sharwood, who continued to lecture while serving as warden of Trinity College, it was an unhappy time in the law school, as factional struggles produced a cleavage of opinion over the deanship. When Michael Crommelin, studying at the University of British Columbia, was offered a job at Melbourne in 1974, he was advised not to take it, because the law school was 'notoriously riven by factions' (the opportunities he saw at Melbourne, particularly in his field of natural resources law, led him to ignore the advice).[25]

For the first time in its history, the faculty now had, if not a fight, then at least a period of uneasy tension over who the next dean would be. The brief dispute over the deanship for 1964 was only a disagreement about whether Cowen should be reappointed as titular dean while he was on leave overseas. Before that time, the appointment of successive deans had effectively been automatic, because of the small number of professors. But from 1973, the choice became more open and contentious. In the fifteen years that followed, staff control of the choice of dean reached its peak, and divisions over the deanship were sometimes deep and bitter. At the same time, scepticism about the merits of staff election of deans grew among some key figures outside the faculty, preparing the way for a new selection process in 1988 that took the decision out of the hands of the faculty.

At the end of Ford's term as dean, the next most senior professor was Peter Brett, who had been acting dean during Ford's absence on study leave in 1972. In a letter circulated among the staff, Brett set out a list of 'essential "terms" or conditions' on which he would be willing to undertake the job. He had opposed the plan for graduate entry to the law course, and although growing difficulties made its implementation unlikely by 1973, it remained the faculty's official policy until the following year. Brett refused to take the deanship while the faculty was still committed to the plan. He equally opposed later-year entry into the course. Nor would he accept appointment from year to year; it would need to be an appointment for three years at least, and he would want to be assisted by an associate dean.

Brett wanted support for other policies. The teaching staff alone, he thought, were not entitled to decide important questions; the non-teaching members of the faculty also had to be involved. He called for cooperation with the university council and the professorial board, which he had been chairing. As for teaching, he said: 'I do not wish to conceal my belief that in the past we have laid too much stress on what is described as "teacher autonomy", regardless of the interests of students'. Staff should be prepared to teach large classes even when they preferred small groups. Marking should be more consistent between different subjects. Students had been overloaded with work. Many staff disagreed with these opinions, as Brett knew. Without a change of heart by many colleagues, he would be unacceptable to them as dean.[26]

These statements of policy and philosophy were not what the supporters of academic autonomy and small-group teaching among the staff would want to hear. Brett's personality, too, made his selection as dean less likely. Although held in great affection, he had strong opinions and a 'very lacerating tongue', in Mary Hiscock's words.[27] Besides, he was becoming heavily involved in university administration, and soon chaired the powerful academic committee of the professorial board.

After Brett, the professors in order of seniority were Colin Howard and Ted Sykes. Howard was not yet a candidate for the deanship. He was occupied elsewhere, becoming general counsel to the federal attorney-general, Lionel Murphy, and his public quarrel with the vice-chancellor over the student discipline committee in 1971 was still recent history. Sykes had come to Melbourne from the University of Queensland partly to escape being dean there, so he was hardly likely to take on new administrative burdens. He, too, had tangled with Derham over freedom of expression. The vice-chancellor had rebuked him for writing to the *Age* to oppose a plan for the university to expand northwards into the Melbourne General Cemetery.[28]

The faculty turned instead to one of the readers, Sandy Clark. It was not the first time someone other than a professor had become dean. Hearn, after all, had resigned from his chair on taking up the post. But Hearn remained a professor in all but name, and on his departure, only a professor could be dean (a rule that persisted until the end of 1973, when readers and senior lecturers became eligible). Clark was automatically appointed an acting professor, but even with a loading for that and for being dean, he still received less than a professor's salary. He wrote to Derham that 'the position of a non-professorial dean is such an invidious one, particularly in professional faculties, that it is unlikely that such appointees would be other than reluctant'.[29]

As Clark saw it, the system for choosing the dean required compromises between hard-liners and candidates who would do nothing. If Brett was the hard-liner in 1973, Clark was far from being a dean who did nothing. 'People had to be accountable', Ann Graham, his secretary, remembered. 'That was good—they had to produce.' Clark put the law school's case so forcefully in university committees that at times one of his milder-mannered colleagues almost wanted to crawl under the table. His diplomatic skills were directed more outwards, towards the legal profession, than towards the university administration. He had an old coal cellar in the quadrangle basement renovated as a venue for town-and-gown lunches, and persuaded the professors to use the end-of-year balances in their entertainment allowances to buy wine for the visitors. To Ann Graham, the lunches were useful for 'bridging that gap between them and us'.[30]

⎯⎯⎯➤•◄⎯⎯⎯

The law school did little, if anything, to mark the centenary in 1957 of the start of teaching, but planning for the 1973 centenary of the creation of the Faculty of Law began early. Ideas for commemorative events were easy enough to agree on—a lecture, a garden party—and work began on the first extended history of the law school. A proposed fundraising appeal presented more difficulties. The chancellor and the vice-chancellor sounded out their contacts in business and the legal profession about the prospects for donations. All agreed that an appeal might raise anything from $50 000 to $100 000, but what should the money be used for? Visiting fellowships? Refurbishment of the law library? Or would a chair of taxation law attract more support from business and the profession, and perhaps even repeat Zelman Cowen's famous success in raising money for the chair of commercial law? The faculty rejected the idea of an appeal for a chair of taxation law, in favour of visiting lectureships named in honour of Sir Owen Dixon, but the university council finally blocked the proposal. Harder heads there doubted the ability of the faculty to muster a large enough number of volunteers to approach potential donors.[31]

There would be no centenary lecturers, but a program of commemorative events gave the anniversary a suitable profile. The guests of honour were Gerald Gardiner, British law reformer and lord chancellor from 1964–70, and his wife Muriel Gardiner, film director, publisher and Academy award-winning screenwriter. His Southey Memorial Lecture was the intellectual centrepiece of the celebrations. Lord and Lady Gardiner's reformist achievements appealed to the left wing of the law school, while their titles were irresistible to some on the right. The columnist Claudia Wright saw them in action during the festivities: 'He is Jesus Christ Superstar to most of the law students who find the general absence of elasticity and reality in their course something to stir about'.[32]

The faculty staged a banquet in Wilson Hall, and a degree-conferring ceremony followed a few days later. An undergraduate centenary committee, which had an uneasy relationship with the Law Students' Society, hosted a commemorative dinner at Trinity College, and a garden party in the old quadrangle. The organiser of the garden party, Justin Judd, dressed up to and beyond the dress code in a grey suit with a pink carnation in the buttonhole, a detachable collar and a silk tie; other students complied by wearing tail-coats or dinner jackets with shorts. The bare walls of the quadrangle and construction work on the south lawn lacked a suitably festive appearance, but Harold Ford found the solution in his memories of dressing ship on special occasions in the navy. At his suggestion, hired flags were hung around the walls. Julian Phillips muttered, 'I think it looks like a Kevin Dennis used car yard', but the disparate elements, social and decorative, came together, and the party went well.[33]

Newer law schools were a source of increasing competition. They were innovative, better funded, and able to make attractive job offers to people who might otherwise have been recruited by the older law schools. From 1971 to 1977, new law schools opened at the University of New South Wales, Macquarie University, the Queensland Institute of Technology (which became the Queensland University of Technology) and the New South Wales Institute of Technology (the future University of Technology, Sydney). La Trobe University established a legal studies department in 1971, although it did not yet train students for admission to practise.

Recruiting staff became a serious problem when candidates got better offers elsewhere. In January 1975, Clark wrote that a law school selection committee for lectureships had made six offers, all of which were declined.

This Faculty finds itself in fierce competition from developing Universities, particularly the University of New South Wales,

which is in a position to offer junior members of staff appointment at levels which can only be regarded as extraordinary.[34]

Comparisons with Monash were frequent, and on questions of
funding and student–staff ratios they were clearly unfavourable to
Melbourne. Peter Brett warned against adopting 'a permanent attitude
of envy' and 'constantly crying about our supposed inferiority'. But the
comparisons naturally influenced current and potential staff and students. Nor were disparities in funding the only differences. 'In the 1970s,
Monash law school seemed to be a very progressive place', one
Melbourne graduate said. 'I remember the occasional trip out to Clayton
just to soak in the atmosphere of a more experimental place'.[35]

––––––>•<––––––

The student and staff activism of the 1970s was weaker at Melbourne
than on some other campuses, and the law school escaped most of its
direct effects. Law was a bystander as demonstrators concentrated their
attention on the council chamber with which it shared its building.
But some of the reform agendas of the period had lasting implications.
Changes in university administration during the 1970s left the law
school with a new framework for decision-making which emphasised
participation by staff, and eventually by students as well. A round of
decentralisation at the same time increased some of the faculty's
responsibilities. To David Penington, who was instrumental in disman-
tling some of its key features when he became vice-chancellor in 1988,
it was 'village democracy'.[36]

The law faculty had long opposed the inclusion of students in its
membership. The occasional presence of students on suitable occasions
could be welcomed (Moore invited a deputation from the Law
Students' Society to attend to discuss tutorials in 1925) but membership was a different matter. When the professorial board raised the
question in 1944, prompted by the Students' Representative Council,
the faculty said it was opposed to general student representation in its
membership.[37]

By 1970, the university was changing its mind. While a council committee headed by Sir James Darling was considering the question, the faculty made its own move by sending the president of the Law Students' Society the agenda for its meetings, with an invitation to speak to the faculty if he chose. Soon an amendment to the university statutes to provide for student representation was making its way towards adoption, and in the meantime the LSS president attended faculty meetings by invitation.[38] Full membership for student representatives followed in 1971, and law students had the chance to elect two faculty representatives from the following year (the president of the LSS became the third student member).

In such a small minority, the students were usually unable to have much influence on the faculty's decisions. The atmosphere was daunting, too. 'I remember it being terribly intimidating when you first walked in', Graeme Johnson, one of the earliest student members, recalled. The students naturally tended to act as representatives of the LSS and to vote together. This troubled some members of faculty, who believed the students should vote independently, according to their own judgement. They should not, Robin Sharwood warned, be treated as 'a separate group which makes its decisions outside Faculty'.[39] These Burkean arguments for independent representation had little effect.

It took unusually energetic student representatives to make an impact in faculty meetings. The first to have a proposal adopted by the faculty seems to have been Simon Whelan, who successfully moved that faculty meetings should be open to the public, although the initiative was short-lived. Other student representatives, Tim McCoy and Brendan Kissane, initiated a restructuring of the combined LLB/BComm course to deal with problems of uneven workload.[40] McCoy in particular continued to be an active member of the faculty, but it was in the staff committee that students had their greatest influence, even if the end results still depended on support from the staff.

The law school was largely impervious to one of the main institutional innovations of the 1970s, the creation of the university assembly. The assembly's attempts to bring about changes in law teaching had little effect. The faculty brushed off its proposal for teaching on sexuality, including a compulsory 'sex-related course'.[41] The lawyers were more sympathetic to the assembly's inquiry into clinical legal education in 1979 (a service of this kind had been an unrealised hope since the experiment of the 1950s), but practical and financial constraints remained insuperable, and the difficult relationship between the assembly on the one hand and the faculty and the council on the other weakened its advocacy.

Within the law school, however, the reforms formalised and promoted staff participation in decision-making. In the 1920s, when faculty meetings were small and frequent, they served as staff meetings, and dealt with many details of the law school's operations, although this had not always been the case. Thirty years later, they no longer had this function, thanks to the increased size and formality of the meetings, and the greater number of full-time academic staff, who now made up a group of their own, distinct from the outside members of the faculty. The full-time teachers met over lunch, which they usually ate together, and by the mid-1950s formal meetings of the full-time teaching staff, often complete with agenda and minutes, allowed them to discuss matters of common concern that did not, or did not yet, require action by the faculty itself. By the early 1960s, the full-time staff meetings were discussing all sorts of things: curriculum revision, use of the law school's meagre research funds, the Council of Legal Education course for articled clerks, special consideration, teaching, the library, problems raised by the Law Students' Society education committee, and so on.[42]

In its early years, this participatory style had its limits. In Harold Ford's words, 'professors made decisions that people down below never heard about'. As the trend towards more open and inclusive decision-making grew in the early 1970s, the framework for staff and student participation gained a new permanence and standing. 'It was an open and democratic institution', Mark Weinberg found. 'We decided major and contentious issues by a vote of the staff.'[43] But if it was a democracy, it had an ancient Athenian flavour: only part of the population could participate fully. Even at its most democratic, the process disenfranchised many people. Most administrative staff had little say, part-time staff were often excluded, and the role of students was very limited. The university and, beyond it, the government, remained powerful outside forces.

Departmental meetings were a forum for this participation, but their status in a single-department faculty such as law was ambiguous. The faculty provided for such meetings in 1973, but when the dean asked the university solicitor for advice amid growing doubts the following year, the response was not reassuring: 'I think that what it all boils down to is that the departmental meeting is not necessarily a meeting of the department but rather a meeting authorised by the department which in this instance is the faculty. Does this make any sense?' To resolve these difficulties, a staff committee was established instead. Its initial membership was the full-time teaching staff, the senior administrative officer, and the student members of the faculty, and its function was to advise the faculty on matters of academic policy and to consider anything the faculty referred to it. In practice, it also served to limit the influence of the external members of the faculty, as Michael Crommelin recalled: 'it took upon itself the task of determining things internally before they were presented to faculty, and this was seen as a way of dealing with what otherwise could have been excessive external interference in the day-to-day workings. So you had this uneasy relationship between the staff committee and the faculty'.[44]

The definition of the committee's functions could encompass almost anything, and the way it operated varied greatly over its fourteen-year existence. At the outset, it was a point of reference and a source of recommendations on policy questions, such as entry criteria, criteria for academic appointments, the composition of the faculty, and budget cuts. Over time, the scope of its business grew. Depending on the preferences of the dean and the interest of the staff, the committee met as often as once a fortnight during term. Its discussions ranged from major questions about the way the law school would be run, to administrative trivia. One meeting in 1975 debated selection procedures for academic staff, recommending that all full-time teachers with at least three years' experience should be members of selection committees, and then moved on to tea-room arrangements and the problem of periodicals disappearing from the staff library.[45]

The recommendation for selection committees echoed the old practice by which faculty meetings (which included most of the teaching staff) made recommendations to the university council for appointments to positions below professor. Selection committees reported to the faculty, which received summaries of the applications and was not bound to follow the committees' advice, although in practice it always did. By 1969, the faculty no longer had the power to recommend appointments to the council—that function now belonged to the selection committees themselves—and circulation of the applicants' details to the growing number of faculty members was compromising the confidentiality of the process. Despite the objections of some faculty members, reports on unsuccessful applicants ceased, and information about the committees' recommendations was circulated merely for information. The faculty's role in appointments was reduced to the nomination of selection committee members for appointment by the council, and even then it merely advised the dean, who submitted the list of names.[46]

The staff committee's recommendation to include all full-time staff would have restored wider involvement in the making of appointments, but it was hardly practicable in view of the number of people concerned, even if the prevailing management style of the university had permitted it. The faculty did not adopt the proposal, but the size of selection committees grew, in a gesture towards the broad participation that the staff committee had advocated. From 1977, they had thirteen members, sometimes more, including nine representatives of the teaching staff (four of them lecturers), while the external, non-teaching members of the faculty provided two representatives of the outside world. Similar thinking influenced the university council when it increased staff representation on committees for appointments to chairs in 1975. The law staff committee decided that the five staff representatives on chair committees would be elected, if there were more nominations than places.[47]

Staff representation on selection committees was one thing, but student representation was quite another. Student members of the faculty made a determined attempt to introduce it in 1979, but the vice-chancellor spotted the proposal in the faculty meeting papers, and successfully counterattacked in the committee of deans. Armed with the deans' disapproval and the support of senior members of the law school staff, including its own dean, the faculty squashed the proposal when it eventually came up for debate. Howard's tentative support for student participation back in 1971 had been left behind. Now he thought that, beyond a certain point, 'it becomes a manifest hindrance to the performance by the university of its educational and scholarly functions'.[48] There was no outright contradiction, but the sentiment had changed.

The academic staff also adopted a formal process for their involvement in the selection of the dean. Although it was the faculty meeting that appointed the dean (if the term of office was to be just one year) or recommended the appointment to the council (if the term was to be longer), decisions about who the dean would be had long been made before the faculty met to consider the matter. In 1973, when the choice of the next dean was so uncertain, informal consultation among the candidates and the other staff led to the selection of Sandy Clark. As always, just one name was put to the faculty meeting for its endorsement.

In 1978, academic staff control of the appointment was entrenched by an elaborate procedure for nominations and ballots, ahead of the consideration of the deanship by the faculty. It began with an informal meeting at which the full-time academic staff would vote on the question of reappointment of the current dean, if he or she was willing to continue in office. If the dean was defeated or unwilling to continue, the meeting would elect a committee to conduct a poll of staff. The poll merely provided information; a second staff meeting would be held at which candidates would be nominated and voted on in a secret ballot.[49]

This procedure took no legal power away from the faculty and the university council. Its only force came from the decision of the staff to follow it, backed by the majority they commanded in faculty meetings (although the faculty itself never endorsed the procedure). Nor were its convoluted steps always followed in detail. Nevertheless, power to choose the dean served as a mainstay of academic staff participation in the management of the law school.

⸺⸺

By the middle of the 1980s, these decision-making processes laboured under a burden of antagonism and division that produced the worst period of internal conflict in the law school's history. One symptom of trouble was a series of resignations, amounting to over a fifth of the teaching staff between 1985 and 1987. It was not only the number of the resignations, but their seniority that was significant. There was an almost complete turnover among the ranks of the readers, as staff moved to more senior positions at other universities, or left to go into full-time practice. Those who resigned in the late 1980s included three future judges (Susan Morgan, Richard Tracey and Mark Weinberg).

Conditions at the time, both in the university and in higher education more generally, exacerbated some of the tensions. Undergraduate courses and the small graduate program (seventy equivalent full-time students in 1980) were funded almost entirely from government grants. There were no full fee-paying places in degree courses, although students paid the university an amenities and services fee. There was little discretionary funding for the law school, independent of university allocations. Payments to successive deans for their work in the British colonial appointments scheme went into the dean's fund, and a special fund received the income from a few fee-paying courses for which degrees were not awarded, such as the professional admission summer school. Much of the money from these funds paid for additions to the library collection.[50] The law school, like the university as a whole, was therefore highly exposed to cuts in government funding. One such round of cuts occurred in 1981–82; the number of equivalent full-time staff in the law school fell between 1980 and 1984.

Disparities in funding between newer and older law schools explained some, though not all, of the painful comparisons that had been made with Melbourne since the early 1970s. In 1984, funding per student at the University of New South Wales law school, Australia's best-funded, was 38 per cent higher than at Melbourne, while the Monash law school's funding advantage over its local rival was about 5 per cent. There were particular disparities in research funding. The basic research grant to the law school for 1977 was $8821, while History got $21 865, and the comparable figure for the Monash law school was $45 563.[51]

Compared with the University of Sydney law school, however, Melbourne had little to complain about. At Sydney, funding per law student in 1984 was less than half that at UNSW, and less than a fifth of the average funding for an Australian university student across all disciplines in the previous year. Sydney's was the worst funded of Australia's ten university law schools. Like Melbourne, it suffered from a large number of resignations in the 1980s.[52]

Funding directly affected the student–staff ratio, which shadowed it in a predictable inverse relationship. Among the law schools in 1984, the student–staff ratio was best at UNSW (13:1), and worst at Sydney (nearly 33:1, although high non-law enrolments in a first-year subject inflated this figure). Melbourne (23:1) and Monash (18:1) fell in between. All these figures underscored the low funding of legal education, when they were compared with the average Australian student–staff ratio of 11.6 in 1983.[53]

Money was a recurring problem. Ann Graham saw its consequences for the administrative staff: 'It was *always* an issue. Sometimes you'd worry, "Maybe there won't be enough for my salary next year."' Nevertheless, funding and staffing had been worse in the past. Staffing in 1984 was almost lavish compared with the student–staff ratio of 50:1 just before the introduction of the entrance quota in 1961.[54] The law school had a budget surplus in 1986, and staffing continued to improve marginally. Funding was a source of tension, and the choices to be made about where to expand or cut spending could cause conflict, but the law school's problems were more widespread.

The working of the staff committee reflected the difficulties. Sometimes it operated well as a forum for consultation about big issues, and a place to raise small ones, but occasionally, at least, it was barely able to function. One meeting was held in 1980 to discuss the number of credit points for an optional subject, Labour Law 1. There was a long debate; the meeting adjourned; it resumed a couple of weeks later; more debate followed; one motion was defeated, while another lapsed; and the end result, after what must have been hours of argument, was that the issue was merely referred back to another committee.[55]

Ideological differences played a part in a disagreement such as this, but they were less significant at Melbourne than they were at some other law schools. Friction did occur over the role of doctrinal or black-letter law, the importance of teaching compared with research, the weight to be given to theory and criticism, and teaching in small groups. Some staff were antipathetic to approaches such as critical legal studies and feminist legal studies, while others championed them. But these issues were not as divisive as they were in the 1970s and 1980s at Macquarie University and, to a lesser extent, the University of New South Wales.[56]

Disputes over promotions and appointments left deep and lasting bitterness at Melbourne. Some of these disappointments were the routine frustrations of life as an academic at a time when senior positions were relatively rare. The high resignation rate among the law school's readers was partly the result of the scarcity of professorial chairs (there were five in the mid-1980s) and the long wait for a spot to become vacant; promotion to professor, as distinct from appointment to a vacant chair, was not possible until the 1990s. But junior staff also felt the pressure, as those without tenure competed for continuing positions. Much was at stake when the outcomes affected careers and livelihoods, and some staff distrusted the way in which decisions were made and the grounds on which they were based. Here, too, as in debates about the curriculum, differences of opinion about the relative values of doctrinal and critical approaches, and teaching as against research, figured in the positions selection committee members took on individual appointments, but caustic personal and factional disagreements were even more damaging.

The processes for making decisions about appointments and promotions did little to mitigate these problems, and some ways made them worse. Choosing the representatives of the teaching staff on a selection committee could either create an impression that one group within the law school dominated the process, or could reproduce wider divisions of opinion, leading to sharp disagreements within the committee about whom it should recommend for a new appointment. Although the final decision was made by a central, university committee, all readers and professors were consulted about promotions. Many academics believed, rightly or wrongly, that the personal support of all senior members of staff was a prerequisite for promotion. Some thought that particular individuals had tried unfairly to veto their appointments or promotions.

'The reality is—no-one gets promoted over the opposition of the readers and professors, and no-one gets rejected who has the support of senior colleagues', Susan Morgan told a faculty meeting in 1988. 'Lack of openness regarding promotion decisions within the faculty serves only to enhance widely held impressions that promotion or lack of it is decided upon unsubstantiated gossip, innuendo or perhaps according to the camp to which one is seen to belong. There is also a perception that to oppose the views of one's senior colleagues is to risk one's chance of confirmation or promotion.'[57] A university review of the law school in the same year said that the situation was 'clearly a source of much fear, suspicion and distrust'.[58] Morgan also called for urgent action to address the downgrading of teaching in promotion and confirmation.

Personal frictions made matters worse, and many things might have been smoothed over if relations between some of the staff had been better. Accidents of personalities turned trivial events into material for lasting grievances.[59] Some of the quarrels could have been funny in the pages of a campus novel (there was a long and acrimonious dispute over unauthorised photocopying), but their cumulative effect was insidious. They exacerbated differences over more important decisions, setting the scene for wounding disagreements and resentments.

Staff spoke of factions, sometimes on doctrinal lines (public law against private law, or black-letter law against critical approaches), but often based on personal allegiances or antagonisms. They recall the caucusing that went on over contentious issues, and the round of phone calls that would follow each new incident. The university review found a situation 'acutely distressing to many members of staff', complaints of intimidation, and talk of a crisis. 'The law school was really riven,' Andrew Neeson, who arrived as the new assistant registrar (law) in 1987, recalled. In Mary Hiscock's words, 'it just became a very unhappy place to be'. The dean's advice to one new staff member was succinct: 'Don't join a faction, and publish three articles a year'.[60]

The level of outside work by some of the staff caused disapproval and resentment. The problem was as old as the law school itself: practising lawyers on the staff brought the benefit of their experience and their links with the profession, and outside work made academic salaries more attractive (comparing poorly, as they did, with the rewards of practice), but full-time staff with commitments elsewhere could find themselves stretched thin. A Commonwealth Tertiary Education Commission discipline review panel heard complaints when it visited in 1986: 'some stringent criticisms were voiced by individual staff members who spoke to us on our visits about the commitment or lack thereof on the part of a number of members of staff who were said to be more interested in non-law school activities, particularly private practice'. 'Whether the complaints made to us were justified we cannot say', they cautioned, but their conclusion was not encouraging: 'It seemed to us that research or outside activities are given a higher priority by a significant number of the staff than teaching'.[61]

At their worst, the sheer antagonism and unhappiness of relations between some of the staff still stand out, as does the amount of time and effort that went into the fighting. Issues became 'intensely personal and very bitter', as Hiscock recalled. Carefully crafted memoranda were used as missiles, as in this exchange between professors: 'Your memorandum ... is probably the most breathtakingly offensive document that even I have ever received, although I must say that its not being anonymous made a pleasant change'.[62] In this case, the memoranda were circulated among the staff, and extracts appeared in *Farrago*.

Some of this bickering inevitably appeared in faculty meetings. Disagreements in debate and divided votes were nothing new there; they had always been characteristic of the faculty. But on some occasions, at least, the divisions became noticeably deeper. One sign of this was the tactical use of procedural points. Mark Weinberg, who became a Federal Court judge, remembered his experience of chairing faculty meetings while he was dean: 'Being a judge is easy, by comparison with the kind of formalities that people would sometimes come up with'. Similar tactics could be used from the chair. At the first question time during a faculty meeting, in 1983, the dean ruled all the questions out of order and would not answer any of them.[63]

<hr>

In this environment of conflict and distrust, choosing the dean became particularly difficult. The problems developed gradually, and the transition was smooth enough when Sandy Clark's three-year term expired at the end of 1977. 'The onset of Spring holds the promise of Summer and of better things to come', he wrote to the academic staff. 'I find the prospect of an idyllic and carefree Summer most appealing. It would accelerate my perceptible slide into irresponsibility if we could discuss the Deanship and Deputy Deanship for 1978.'[64]

Clark would have liked to continue, but he was planning to take study leave, and Colin Howard was now interested and available, having returned from his temporary Canberra job. At a time when many in the university, like Harold Ford, did not see the office of dean as permanent, the implication was that it would rotate among senior staff. As deputy dean and the senior professor after Brett's death, Howard had the backing of staff who saw him, at that time, as a supporter of the kinds of democratic decision-making that reformers of the 1970s had championed in the university's administration. The meeting of full-time teachers convened by Clark endorsed Howard as the next dean, and the faculty duly elected him.

Observers of Howard had long agreed on his great gifts, his high standards, and his clear opinions about people who did not measure up. Glanville Williams' description of him in 1964 remained true: 'an exceptionally able, interesting and active person who has kept up a constant volume of writing of high quality ... He imposes standards on himself and does not suffer slackness or incompetence in others gladly.' Who did not meet these standards, and what should be done about them, were contentious questions, and bonds to institutions or individuals would not deter Howard from expressing his opinion and acting on it. As a student who interviewed him for the Law Students' Society magazine in 1971 saw, he had a 'persistent determination to remain independent—to avoid the restrictions which are entailed by ties to people and their organizations'.[65]

A minor incident showed the new dean's style. The university's Students' Representative Council produced an orientation handbook each year for new students. The 1979 edition was more than usually irreverent. Articles such as 'Screwing your way through', 'Drugs, and why they're good for you', 'How to roll a joint', 'Drinking yourself stupid' and 'Smash all landlords!' distilled some of the campus' late-seventies counter-culture. The entry on the law school caught Howard's eye. It told freshers that exams served merely to allow students to 'regurgitate the collected wisdom', that tutorials were useless, and that the law school office was 'run like a parody of a South American government department'. To the dean, the handbook was 'an infamous document' and the section on Law 'a catalogue of vicious falsehoods'. The sub-dean circulated a rejoinder, but the jousting continued, leading Howard to warn the teaching staff that the editor was 'an ego-tripping pest' whose emotional balance was in doubt. He attempted, unsuccessfully, to veto the editor's membership of the Melbourne University Law Review Association.[66]

Over time, Howard became increasingly involved in the university's central administration. He and David Penington, then dean of the Faculty of Medicine, shook up the traditional line of succession when they combined to secure Howard's election as chairman of the academic board in 1981. 'We disturbed the central perceptions as to how the university should run to a significant extent', Penington recalled. 'He and I were both rebels in that.' Penington had clashed with the heir-apparent to the chairmanship over the way the board should prescribe content for a new master's degree in medicine. He and Howard aimed to devolve such responsibilities to faculties and reduce the amount of course-detail prescribed by the board and its academic committee. At that time they were allies, too, in the university council, chaired by the chancellor, R. D. 'Pansy' Wright. Howard 'could run rings around Pansy', or so Penington, no friend of the chancellor, saw it; 'I used to sit back and enjoy it'.[67]

Howard brought his interest in governance to bear on the law school. His review of administrative arrangements led to a reorganisation of the committee structure, creating a combined executive and budgets committee that took a key role in the running of the law school for many years. Despite the dissent of the president of the Law Students' Society, the faculty agreed with Howard's recommendation that the new committee should have no student members. The creation of a computerisation policy committee was another of his proposals.[68]

Relations between staff in the law school were deteriorating, however. 'People thought that there were favourites being played', Mark Weinberg remembered. 'It just seemed to people as though you had to be on side with the dean ideologically, socially, call it what you will, if you were to receive promotion and recognition, and that merit wasn't necessarily being rewarded, or rewarded as it ought to have been.'[69] Even minor matters became irritants, because of the way staff thought decisions had been made.

A review of the university's departmental statute in 1983 was a touchstone for these divisions. Meetings of the teaching staff discussed the law school's attitude to the report, but the atmosphere was acrimonious. The elegantly-written memos to staff that had been a feature of Howard's deanship took on a darker tone. He argued that the recommendations of the review were not in the least undemocratic: 'What is undemocratic is the effort by some of you, without even bothering to master the relevant material or find out the facts, to hog the floor with protracted and aggressive irrelevancy ... our self-appointed guardians of democracy seem to me in practice to be about as democratic as a Richmond numbers man'.[70]

Bad feeling had reached such a level that there was open criticism in the staff meeting to discuss the deanship for 1983, although Howard was re-elected. He wrote to the teaching staff: 'Disgusted I certainly am, by the sheer hypocrisy of it all, but I shall not allow that sentiment to affect the deanship'.[71] But the divisions only continued. 'Doors were closed for a year', Robert Evans recalled, as discussions went on about who the dean should be. Finally Howard's deputy, Mark Weinberg, decided to be a candidate, and a majority of the teaching staff supported him. He became dean at the start of 1984.

It was a painful process that left many wounds. Although Howard's term as chairman of the academic board had ended, he withdrew from many activities in the law school. Some staff believed that he had been badly treated and that his deputy had been disloyal, as Weinberg was aware: 'if one looks at a deputy as being somebody who is always going to be unblinkingly loyal then the last thing you expect your deputy to do is to stand against you when there's an election'. But he added: 'I've no doubt that it was the right thing to do. A clear majority of people on the faculty wanted a change'.[72]

In these circumstances, the new dean's job was a particularly difficult one. 'They were hard years', Weinberg said.[73] His work as a barrister specialising in criminal appeals was growing rapidly, and he reached a point at which it was no longer possible to combine the two careers. He resigned from the university at the end of January 1986.

———◆◆◆———

Students were largely unaware of these ructions, although they experienced their indirect effects. Their numbers changed little in the 1980s, in line with the trend across the country; enrolments in university law courses actually declined slightly between 1980 and 1989, after rapid increases for thirty years. There was an anxious moment in 1983 when first-preference applications for law at Melbourne dropped 6 per cent, while applications at Monash went up by a corresponding amount, hinting that Melbourne's problems and Monash's growing reputation might be having an effect, but the numbers soon resumed the upward trend they maintained for the rest of the decade and beyond.[74]

The growing demand for the static number of places made law more and more difficult to get into, with the result that the cut-off score for entry to the LLB course at Melbourne rose steadily, from 327 in 1980 to 362 in 1988, limiting entry to the top 3 per cent of year 12 students. After the last intake of new students into the Council of Legal Education course in 1978, Melbourne and Monash had the only law schools in Victoria, until law courses qualifying students for admission to practise began at Deakin and La Trobe in 1992. The new courses relieved some of the demand that threatened to reach a crisis-point when Monash, facing funding problems, cut its law intake drastically in 1991–92.[75]

The rising cut-off score highlighted the operation of the quota, and gave new force to the continuing debate about the best way for the law school to select its students. In the early 1970s, only about 20 per cent of first-year law students at Melbourne came from Victorian government schools. The figure was grossly disproportionate; some 66 per cent of senior secondary students in Victoria attended such schools. Twenty-eight per cent of the first-year law students came from Victorian Catholic schools, 11 per cent qualified in other ways or came from outside Victoria, and the largest single group, nearly 35 per cent, came from non-Catholic Victorian independent schools. The areas with the highest totals of school-leaver applicants for the law school were the prosperous eastern suburbs of Kew, North Balwyn, Toorak and Camberwell. The weighting towards private schools was higher in law than in most other faculties. Across the whole university, about 38 per cent of first-year students came from state schools in 1972.[76]

The old arguments about access that had reached their height when the entry quota was imposed in 1961 took on new forms, centring on the disadvantaged backgrounds of some students unable to study law. A law school committee proposed broadening the social mix of the student intake by selecting only one-third of the first-year students on the basis of their exam scores alone. The other two-thirds would be chosen by ballot, from students who had reached a minimum score in their Higher School Certificate results. Random selection was too much for the faculty, which opted instead to provide fifteen places for disadvantaged students who had passed the HSC exam. Another ten places would be open to students who had not completed their HSC. University approval was conditional on a review of the scheme once it had commenced operation.[77]

How best to run the disadvantaged entry scheme proved difficult to decide, and its merits were debated repeatedly as advocates of a more representative social mix argued with proponents of selection by exam results. Few students applied, and the scheme was expensive to administer. 'We discriminate against those who may have transcended such difficulties in favour of those who demonstrably have not done so', Ian Elliott argued in an unsuccessful attempt at abolition in 1978. The scheme's supporters continued to stress the first-year quota's 'overwhelming bias in favour of students from independent schools, whose parents are in the highest socio-economic categories', but they noted that even some students from these backgrounds could qualify as disadvantaged on grounds of illness or family circumstances.[78] The scheme continued until 1988, when a university scheme replaced it.

Helped to some extent by these special entry schemes, the proportion of first-year students from government schools rose in the 1980s, reaching about a third in 1986. Yet the figure declined over the next ten years, and by 1996 only 23 per cent of respondents to a comprehensive survey of the first-year intake came from government schools. Fifty-eight per cent came from non-Catholic independent schools, the highest proportion for any law school in Victoria, New South Wales or the Australian Capital Territory.[79] A slightly higher proportion of New South Wales secondary students attended government schools (68 per cent in 1996, as against 63 per cent in Victoria), probably accounting for a little of the difference, but selection on the basis of VCE results, despite the special entry programs, was swinging the law school's intake even further away from the government schools that educated the bulk of secondary students.

Most of the students came from Victoria; unlike American law students, few Australians travelled outside their home states to go to law school. In the 1956 first-year survey, only 3 per cent of the law students came from schools outside Victoria. Thirty years later, the figure was even lower. Erwin Griswold, dean of the Harvard law school, noted 'the lack in Australia of a really *national* law school' when he visited in 1951. One reason, as Cowen explained, was that each course was closely connected with admission to practise in a particular state, and that students rarely looked to practise elsewhere. But it was also a wider social and cultural difference, since the pattern was repeated across the university. Hardly any law undergraduates came from overseas: the LLB course took in just five overseas students in 1980, and the annual intake had been two for several years before that. It remained at five until the faculty agreed to admit fee-paying overseas students in 1988.[80]

There were almost as many different experiences of the law school as there were students, but their greater numbers compared with earlier decades, and the changing culture within the faculty and among the students, made it more likely that some would feel alienated from their teachers and fellow students. Cowen saw this coming as early as 1960, as student numbers in Law exceeded 1100 for the first time: 'I think that it has been one of the more unfortunate developments of our growth as a University that we have become a service institution to which students come in droves; to which they come and from which they go in faceless anonymity'.[81]

Being confronted with the sometimes strange culture of the law could be difficult in itself. 'I thought I had landed on the planet Serious', one student who arrived in 1982 remembered. The competitive atmosphere and the lack of direct support could be hard for law students, as for others elsewhere on the campus. 'It never seemed the friendliest environment despite having student friends', wrote a student who began the course at the same time; 'more a "sink or swim and either way it's up to you and not us" sort of approach'. 'There was a dog-eat-dog competitiveness that was not necessarily healthy.' 'It was a very solitary and impersonal experience'. Another student who finished the course in 1983 remembered 'a sense of alienation', and particularly wanted this history to be 'fleshed out by what I believe a very large, but silently-suffering, cohort felt'.[82]

Others flourished in this academic and social setting. A student who started in 1981 remembered enjoying 'the teachers who led us to fit the pieces together *ourselves* while guiding us in the right direction'. Another liked 'the fact that law lecturers were trying to teach, and not just lecture'. For some, the law school broadened their horizons: 'It was the first time I'd met gay people, Jewish people, indigenous people, so it was very enlightening for me'.[83]

School and social backgrounds contributed to fitting in or feeling isolated. Self-selection by school students who believed they could or should do law was one reason for the high representation of private schools. Kerry Greenwood, a law student from 1973 to 1978, wrote: 'As a wharfie's daughter from Maribyrnong High School, I especially disliked being patronized by snotty-nosed and ignorant public school boys of which my classes were largely composed ... It took me six months to find a peer group of state school boys with whom I found I had something in common.' Others remembered 'feeling that it was a private school boys and girls club', or encountering 'an academic world of private school behaviour and standards'. Some students who arrived through the disadvantaged entry scheme without a Higher School Certificate were embarrassed by the common question first-year students asked each other: 'What was your HSC score?'[84]

Large classes made it more difficult for students to get to know each other and the staff. Small teaching groups were used from time to time—they were used in many subjects in 1970—but the stubborn student–staff ratio made them difficult to sustain. Tutorials were abolished altogether in 1983, but were reinstated in two subjects in 1984, and in a few more in the following year. It was also in 1984 that the law school appointed a part-time learning skills adviser to help students who were having difficulties in their courses.[85]

The student–staff ratio directly affected teaching methods, but other policies were also at work, including the importance the law school placed on maintaining its excellent research record. In 1981, the dean asked staff to reduce all forms of interim assessment, because of its effect on the workloads of staff and students. Six years later, a national review of law schools questioned Melbourne's commitment to teaching, and drew attention to the relatively light teaching load of the staff, although the dean later questioned whether Melbourne's level of six class hours per week was as much below the average as the report suggested. The university's review of the law school in 1988 agreed with many of the criticisms: there were too many lectures to large groups without seminars or tutorials, and too many subjects in which end-of-year exams were the only form of assessment.[86]

A survey of all students who graduated from nine Australian law schools from 1979 to 1983 ranked Melbourne third lowest on the quality of teaching (above Adelaide and the University of Western Australia), and lowest of all on the availability and approachability of teachers. Nearly two-thirds of the Melbourne graduates thought the quality of teaching was generally good, but only one-third thought teachers were available and approachable. A dismal 16 per cent thought the law school took a genuine interest in their educational needs, but this was a weak point of all the law schools; the national average was only 28 per cent.[87]

—————

In the mid-1980s, these problems drew increasingly critical attention, both in the university and beyond. The Commonwealth Tertiary Education Commission began what was projected as a series of national reviews of disciplines or subject-areas in tertiary education; one of the first disciplines for review was law. The five-volume report of the review committee, chaired by Dennis Pearce, was published in 1987, and Melbourne's was one of several law schools singled out for particular criticism. The building and the law library were obvious grounds for concern. Most importantly, the review saw deficiencies in teaching that were more within the law school's control. It commented adversely on the reliance on examinations and large classes, called for a much greater effort to be put into teaching, and recommended a joint law school–university review of the undergraduate program.[88] The number of full-time staff with significant commitments in legal practice also attracted criticism.

The fact that the members of the review panel all came from newer law schools—the Australian National University, the University of New South Wales and Monash University—made some suspicious of their findings. 'I think people felt fairly wounded by it—that it was unfairly critical of Melbourne', Mal Smith, who had rejoined the staff not long before, recalled. But differences in funding and the resources devoted to undergraduate teaching made it likely that any review of the different law schools would rate Melbourne poorly on some measures, even without considering the law school's other problems. Even a bad report had its uses. Mary Hiscock was among those who 'actually wanted the Pearce report to give us a bit of a bagging, because we felt we needed some leverage with the University'. Nor did the report overlook Melbourne's strengths. In a foretaste of the quantitative rankings that took on great importance in later times, it ranked the law school's research record as one of the best in the country.[89]

After Mark Weinberg's departure, it was a new dean who led the faculty's involvement in the review and the response to its report. He was Harold Luntz, the George Paton Professor since 1976. He saw the deanship as a position that rotated among the professors, and believed he had an obligation to take it on in his turn. It was a difficult time. Partly as a result of the Pearce report, and partly because of the faculty's more general problems, a university committee headed by Margaret Manion, chairman of the academic board, reviewed the law school in 1988. Its report was largely written by Justice Murray Wilcox of the Federal Court.

Like the Pearce report, the university review noted the law school's obvious strengths, in its students, its research record and its graduates. As if to make the point, Melbourne students won the Jessup international law moot court competition in Washington DC around the time the report was being written. But most attention centred on the faculty's problems, and possible solutions. Manion saw the committee's role as facilitating change rather than dictating to the staff. 'Our contribution was listening and then defining what we had heard and making some suggestions to them', she said. 'They took the necessary steps once the opportunity was there.'[90]

Accommodation headed the list of recommendations. They also covered staffing, the LLB course, teaching loads and research development. The committee concluded that 'the present management structures are simply not working'. The McCaughey review of departmental structures (Howard was a member) had recommended abolition of the law school staff committee in 1983, saying it duplicated the work of other committees and confused consultation with responsibility. The committee fell into abeyance after the McCaughey report, but occasional informal meetings continued. When the national review panel visited the law school, junior staff complained strongly of lack of involvement in decision-making, but the committee was revived towards the end of 1985.[91] Now the university review recommended disbanding the committee, ending the election of deans, and changing selection and promotion procedures.

Twenty-one mainly junior academics objected to the proposal to abolish the staff committee and end election of the dean, but they could not prevail against the impetus behind the report. The university and the wider world of higher education were changing rapidly. The Tertiary Education Commission's review of efficiency and effectiveness in higher education had recommended abolishing the election of deans in 1986, warning that it might be incompatible with personnel decisions such as the assessment of staff performance. Commonwealth proposals released in December of the following year, driven by the aggressively reformist education minister, John Dawkins, outlined a new, unified higher education system, funded according to performance against priorities.[92]

David Penington, vice-chancellor from the start of 1988, wanted both to devolve more responsibility to faculties and, as a counterpart, to ensure that the increased responsibility would be well used.

> If in fact we were going to get away from central control of everything in the university, we needed to devolve responsibility to faculties to manage their affairs against general guidelines that would be set down in a strategic plan for the university ... That could only happen if there was good leadership and good management in faculties. It was absolutely central to my view of how the university needed to change.

Election of the dean was incompatible with this vision. 'They were preparing to vote on who should be the next dean ... they just assumed the university would bow down and accept this, and in my view there was no way they were going to.'[93]

One of Penington's early actions as vice-chancellor was to initiate a rapid review of the Department of Electrical Engineering, leading to its restructuring. 'That sent shockwaves through lots of parts of the university', he recalled. It added to an atmosphere of radical change: 'the fact that Dawkins was banging at the doors was something that again made people realise that change was coming'.[94] Penington supported the recommendations of the university review, and they were duly implemented. The law school's new leadership trimmed its sails to the wind of higher education reform, and hoped to leave the troubles of its recent past behind.

6

PERFORMANCE AGAINST PLAN

1989–2007

As the law school recovered from the conflicts of the 1980s, its future was shaped more and more directly by the federal government. The abolition of the Commonwealth Tertiary Education Commission in 1987 removed a mediator between universities and the new Department of Employment, Education and Training; Dawkins and his department used their augmented powers to inaugurate (as their policy statement put it) 'a new era' for higher education. The unified national system not only treated universities and colleges and institutes of education alike, but drew them under closer central control, serving a national agenda for the development of skills and competitiveness. The university, too, followed an increasingly ambitious agenda for reform. Penington adopted the government model's strategic planning, and its drive towards efficient and effective management, at the same time as he led the opposition to the unified national system.[1]

In this setting, the dean became more than ever a chief executive on corporate lines, with greater autonomy in spending the law school's budget and creating staff positions. While the university increasingly aimed to set goals for its faculties and let them find their own ways of achieving them, the goal-setting, in the form of targets, performance indicators, penalties and incentives, was a new form of central pre-scription. One of the constraints was on student numbers, as the university was bound to comply with the profiles for numbers of subsidised students agreed with the federal government each year. Although the law school had long since lost the final say over its entrance quota (at least since its attempt to reduce numbers was vetoed by the university in 1969), the university, too, had its student numbers controlled by a higher power, as the educational profiles set enrolments discipline by discipline.

Money was the instrument of much of the structural change. A new scheme of federal funding for universities, the relative funding model, abolished the detailed triennial budgeting that had been used by the Universities Commission and its successor the Tertiary Education Commission, replacing it with a single operating budget allocated according to the educational profiles that set out institutions' student loads. And some of the government's money would come direct from the students, through the Higher Education Contribution Scheme, HECS, that began in 1989: in addition to the small administration and services fee that students had paid the university since tuition fees were abolished, they would pay the government a standard contribution to the cost of their education, beginning at $1800 a year. Payment would either be delayed (made through the tax system once the student's income reached $22 000) or immediate. Cash on the nail at the time of enrolment attracted a discount of 15 per cent.[2]

These new policies (including some fee-paying courses and new arrangements for research funding) affected the law school not so much by coercing dramatic change, as by reshaping the landscape so that opportunities, incentives and penalties encouraged movement in directions favoured by the government. Such were the dynamics of the reformed higher education, in theory at least: the setting of goals, and the assessment, to use the language of the university's performance reviews, of performance against plan.

The introduction of this culture of reform both in Canberra and in the university administration coincided with the selection of a new dean. When, early in 1988, the Manion committee reported on the law school's problems, and Penington took over as vice-chancellor, Luntz was in the final year of his term. In a personal response to the university review, he defended the law school's record, but he did not oppose its recommendations.

The Manion committee's recommendation to end staff election of the dean, while prompted by the factionalism that had surrounded the elections in recent times, was consistent with Penington's aim to give the central administration the real, and not just formal, power to choose deans throughout the university. The power remained with the council, but now the effective choice would be the vice-chancellor's, though the members of the faculty would be consulted. He began by sending them a questionnaire, asking for their views about who the next dean should be. The four staff who were nominated most often in the responses as first or second preference were then put to a faculty meeting, in the form of a panel of names in alphabetical order from which it would be appropriate to make the choice. Some staff would have preferred an external appointment, but the delay involved in creating and filling an academic position for the purpose would have been too long. With the faculty's endorsement of the panel (but not of any one candidate), Penington chose a name to recommend to the council.[3]

The four names were two professors and two readers: Michael Crommelin, Mary Hiscock, Cheryl Saunders and Mal Smith. Of these, one stood out for Penington. 'I was very nervous as to who they were going to come forward with to nominate for appointment as dean, but once Michael's name came forward, I reckoned we were home and hosed.' Penington's management model devolved responsibility (including greater financial autonomy) from the centre to the faculties, but coupled it with accountability through the planning process, so that the increased powers would be used in a way that was consistent with the university's aims; he felt he had found someone who could do the job he had in mind. As Crommelin put it, 'David's basic proposition to me was that he wanted the law school fixed'.[4]

Crommelin continued the run of deans who had not studied at Melbourne as undergraduates, a partial corrective to the inwardness of a staff that included a high proportion of Melbourne graduates. (Harold Ford had been the last former student to become dean, although some of his successors had taken postgraduate degrees at the law school.) Probably a large number of local appointments to the staff was inevitable; even as travel became cheaper, Australia remained remote from the common-law jurisdictions of the northern hemisphere that were the main overseas recruiting-ground, and its salaries and conditions could not compare with those on offer in the United States. But Melbourne had been noted for employing a higher proportion of its own graduates than other law schools in the mid-1980s, and the first international review of the law school warned of the dangers of in-breeding when it found that, in 1994, about two-thirds of the academic staff with first law degrees from an Australian university got them at Melbourne. Rosemary Hunter, herself a Melbourne graduate appointed as a lecturer in 1990, found the new staff were 'mostly alumni, so it did get a bit incestuous for a while, but they were good alumni'.[5]

Crommelin was a graduate of the University of Queensland, and from there he went to the University of British Columbia, where he graduated with an LLM and then a PhD on the law of oil and gas resources. His first permanent academic appointment was at Melbourne, in 1975, and there he stayed, becoming a professor ten years later, coupling his interest in resources law with constitutional and administrative law. He kept up the academic side of his work, but it was the deanship that increasingly demanded his time. From the start, he encountered the force of Penington's energy for reform. The vice-chancellor was 'almost driven to change, to achieving major change', Crommelin found, but the culture of constant change and continuous improvement suited him. 'I wouldn't be happy if things just went along', Crommelin said. 'I think the whole university system in

Australia is so precarious that unless you're restlessly active—and in some constructive way: you can make all the wrong decisions—I just don't think you can survive.'[6]

Crommelin had good relations with Colin Howard, and his own appointment as Zelman Cowen professor, like many other decisions at the time about appointments and promotions, was regarded by some staff as a victory for one faction over another. Yet the factions faded away after he became dean. To some of the more Latinate staff, the long period of relative peace was the *Pax Crommeliana*. As the name implied, it owed something to the style of the new dean, who avoided prolonging old hostilities, gave few causes for new ones, and used the growing power of his office in ways most staff were content with.

The internal politics of the law school had changed under the new dispensation in the university. After the abolition of the staff committee, there were fewer issues to form factions over, and the end of election of the dean 'removed a whole area of political activity that probably had occupied the minds of the faculty, particularly when the deans were an annual appointment', as Mal Smith observed.[7] Most staff no longer regarded the law school, as Mark Weinberg once had, as a democratic institution, but this was rarely a cause of much regret.

The single-department structure of the faculty concentrated power, as Richard Mitchell found when he moved from the multi-department Faculty of Economics and Commerce. Usually, working groups, committee meetings and discussions with key people ahead of faculty meetings ensured a smooth ride for important proposals, and discussion was brief, unlike the hard-fought debates of some earlier times. The pattern showed a degree of consensus, but also the willingness of staff to leave the running of the law school to others. One staff member was blunt about both the centralisation of decision-making and the advantages of being shielded from the burden of administration: 'It's bliss'. It was difficult, too, to develop alternative policies from outside the law school's administration, as decisions became more complex and technical, and each faculty's responsibility for its own budget made financial demands more imperative.[8]

New appointments to the teaching staff were eclectic, ranging from technical black-letter lawyers to exponents of theory and criticism, and although some felt their talents were not recognised and left unhappily, the law school built up concentrations of expertise in diverse areas from corporate law to legal theory. A distinctive pattern emerged of advertising an unspecified number of positions on several levels and making appointments according to the applications received. Academic staff numbers grew steadily, rising from 38 equivalent full-time staff in 1984 to almost 90 in 2006. But growing student numbers kept the student–staff ratio stubbornly high. Even when it fell to approximately 22:1 in 2006, it was still above leading North American law schools, and well over Melbourne's university-wide average of about 16:1. Law kept its unwanted place alongside other professional faculties—Architecture, Economics and Commerce, and Education—with the university's highest student–staff ratios.[9]

The proportion of women on the staff continued to rise, but, as in many workplaces, they were better represented in lower-paid jobs. By 2006, just over half the law school's academics were women, but only 34 per cent of the professors; women held 72 per cent of professional (or administrative) positions. The staffing profile also changed thanks to a longstanding aim of lifting the number of senior teaching positions. By 2006, nearly 20 per cent of the full-time (or fractional full-time) teaching and research staff were professors, bringing Law closer to the level of the Faculty of Medicine, Dentistry and Health Sciences.[10]

Administrative positions multiplied even faster than teaching posts. The number rose from 17 in 1984 to 86 in 2006; in proportion to teaching staff, the figure was considerably higher than in most North American law schools.[11] Program managers took charge of the administrative side of undergraduate and postgraduate courses; for a time, successive general managers (Julie Anne Quinn and Penny Swain) acted as general faculty administrators, though their functions were later redistributed through the administrative structure. Information technology, marketing and communications, research support and research centres added new branches to the administrative staff, beside the older, and continuing, work of student administration.

Teaching staff took on a growing range of administrative responsibilities, which threatened to swallow up much of the time of the most heavily burdened. A central and demanding position, under various titles, was held by an academic in charge of teaching staff (in 2007, the deputy dean), as work on staff appraisal, contract terms, confirmation criteria, promotions and the other multiplying tasks under the umbrella of human resources required a dedicated manager to handle them.

Academics became equal opportunity liaison officers for minority groups of students, and associate deans with an expanding suite of designated responsibilities: undergraduate and postgraduate studies, international matters, information, and research. Like the chairs of the faculty's committees, the associate deans were sometimes influential, sometimes not. Professors were often reluctant to take on these additional demands, but the positions had less clout when filled from lower in the academic hierarchy. Cheryl Saunders added graduate studies to her many other responsibilities and drove much of that program's expansion; Ian Ramsay's influence as committee chair shaped information technology and the library. But Richard Mitchell's experience as associate dean (research) was different: 'your ability to actually exercise a lot of discretion in that position was quite slight, I felt … You don't really have a lot of discretion even in quite senior positions in the law faculty, because of the concentration of power.' Mitchell enjoyed the opportunities he found in the law school to pursue his own work, but his ideas for a redirection of resources away from teaching and into research made little headway.[12]

One of the law school's problems, though minor by comparison with the poor reputation of its undergraduate teaching and the divisions among the staff, had been its small postgraduate coursework program. The LLM by coursework had been approved in 1971, but initially there were not enough staff available to teach the necessary subjects. When it began operation three years later, sharing some subjects with Monash, it allowed students to earn the degree by passing four subjects, which suited practitioners and others who wanted to develop their expertise without undertaking the major research project required for an LLM by thesis. By 1977, though, four subjects, even at the high pass mark of 70 per cent, were judged an inadequate test for a master's degree, and a minor thesis was added. Students were not deterred: there were 79 studying for the LLM by coursework by 1981 (compared with six doing the LLM by thesis, and four, two of them staff members, studying for PhDs).[13] All the places, like those for LLB students, were subsidised by the federal government, free of fees, and there were routinely more applicants than places.

The minor thesis became the LLM's greatest weakness. Although students got through the coursework subjects in respectable numbers, only a disturbingly small proportion managed to finish the degree. The faculty considered winding up the program altogether in 1988, but gave it a reprieve. Yet when it was reviewed in 1989, the completion rate was found to be a mere 12 per cent.[14]

If the students could not get themselves through the thesis, maybe the program could be rehabilitated by allowing students to do coursework alone and giving them something less than a master's degree—a graduate diploma. The faculty adopted this solution as early as 1980, but was unable to implement it: the increased subsidised student numbers in three new specialist diplomas (in commercial law, public law and taxation law) would disrupt the quota for the LLB, so the diplomas were shelved.[15] But the changed conditions of the late 1980s gave the idea new life.

The federal government's higher education reforms of 1988 not only introduced the contribution to be paid by undergraduates, but also allowed universities to charge fees for some postgraduate courses. Here the law school found an opening for extra revenue, beyond the limited funding brought in by the rigid quota of subsidised places. As Crommelin put it, 'the only way we could acquire a little bit of space, a little bit of an opportunity to do anything else, was by introducing a fee-paying program'. As he saw it, the poor level of funding to law as a discipline drove the law school to find money elsewhere.[16]

The faculty approved a new scheme of graduate diplomas in 1988, but with a difference: now, fees would be charged both for the diplomas and for the coursework LLM. A key aim was that the new program would be profitable, allowing resources to be reallocated to under-graduate teaching and research. Critics in the faculty argued that the diplomas would divert teaching time from undergraduate subjects, where it was badly needed. This argument prevailed at Monash, which chose, until the 1990s, to concentrate on the quality of its undergrad-uate teaching, rather than develop a fee-paying postgraduate program; as a result, it drew much less of its overall revenue from fees.[17]

Melbourne's strategy took advantage of the trend towards increasing specialisation in the profession, demonstrated by the Law Institute's plans to recognise specialist status with a scheme of accredi-tation, and backed by requests from practitioners at 'town and gown' meetings about the program. The trend went with the increasing size of some law firms, as corporate practices merged and their work moved far beyond the 'traditional staples' of conveyancing, probate and personal injuries.[18]

Others had already seen the opportunity to meet the demand for specialisation with fee-paying courses. Independent conference and seminar organisers were running conferences for the profession for profit, sometimes engaging law school staff as presenters. Practitioners were paying high fees for them, Cheryl Saunders found as she led the design of the new program. 'So it occurred to us that if they were putting pots of money there, they might be able to put slightly smaller pots in our direction, as long as the product was a high quality one.'[19]

It was more than just a return to charging tuition fees, something the university had done throughout its history until 1974. Much as the fees had affected the social composition of the student body, there had never been a problem finding more than enough students willing to enrol and pay them. Since the introduction of the quota, the problem had been keeping students away rather than attracting them. 'The Law School lacks experience in being enterprising, market-responsive and competitive', the consultant engaged to write a marketing plan for the program said; the comment was as much about the law school as about the vocabulary of the new culture into which the fee-paying courses were taking it. Now, it would offer new courses that were relatively expensive to run (with small class sizes), but with no assurance that enough students would turn up to make them pay. It was a different kind of operation, to which students had constantly to be attracted in order for it to be viable. 'You had to provide what they wanted', as Kaye Nankervis, who managed the program, put it.[20]

Penington's backing for Crommelin now came in handy, since the fee-paying program needed university approval and was still, at the time, relatively unusual. The vice-chancellor not only supported its introduction, but ensured that the law school got a generous 80–20 split in the distribution of the fees between the central administration and the faculty. The allocation of fee revenue was a recurring tug-of-war for years, but Penington continued to defend Law's share against erosion, and it survived until 2004, bringing significant extra revenue.[21]

The law school tussled with the central administration to fit the flexible graduate timetable into the academic year and the federal government's reporting requirements, and won exemptions from the standard definitions of masters' degrees and graduate diplomas. Cheryl Saunders, as associate dean (graduate studies), took part: 'Year after year we fought this somewhat grisly battle'. For the central administration, Law's departure from familiar models was challenging and its use of consultants' market research innovative, although the Melbourne Business School had already applied some of the same techniques.[22]

The bet that fee-paying students would come to a new postgraduate program turned out to be a good one. After a small beginning with one graduate diploma, in Asian law (making the most of the strength and distinctiveness of the Asian Law Centre), there were thirteen in 1995, and twenty in 2007, with a corresponding expansion in the subjects that students could credit either towards a diploma or an

LLM. Unsupported by a quota of subsidised but inflexible places, unconstrained by course prescriptions for admission to practise, and constantly adjusting itself to suit its market, the diploma program had a different culture from that of the LLB. In contrast with the slow adoption of student evaluation questionnaires in undergraduate subjects, extensive student questionnaires were used in all the new graduate subjects from the start, and class sizes were capped at twenty-five. Over time, most of the subjects came to be taught intensively, giving students the chance to take a block of time away from their jobs for a week of classes and work on their research papers or exams. From 1994, a coursework doctorate, the SJD, supplemented the research master's and PhD degrees, based on four subjects and a thesis, plus an advanced legal theory and research course.[23]

The teachers, too, were different. While practitioners and other part-time teachers had virtually disappeared from undergraduate subjects, apart from a few staff in active practice as barristers, they returned to graduate teaching in strength, reviving the connections that the law school had once maintained with the profession through teaching. Of the 157 teachers in the 2007 graduate program, only one-third were members of the law school's staff; practitioners (now largely solicitors, taking the place of the barristers who dominated part-time teaching in previous decades) and academics from other universities made up most of the rest, along with a significant group of consultants, public servants and officials of non-government organisations. Many came from overseas. While the graduate teachers' involvement in presenting mainly week-long courses was less than that of the practitioners of previous decades (who generally taught all year), they formed a network of associates and friends of the law school.[24]

It was an unexpected solution to the disengagement between the law school and the profession, which had grown with the number of full-time academics. 'When I was a young academic in the faculty, we agonised endlessly about our relationship with the profession', Cheryl Saunders remembered. 'We used to have these terribly stilted lunches here or down at Owen Dixon, and nothing ever happened. There was no meeting of the minds at all. And once we started doing this with the graduate program we never worried about it again, at least in the same way … It made a connection that works for us both.'[25]

As the courses drew in an ever-larger number of students, they ranged more widely across the legal landscape and drilled deeper into specialist topics. In 2007, the 123 subjects on offer included everything from A, if not to Z, then at least to W, from Accounting for Commercial Lawyers to WTO: Dumping, Subsidies and Safeguards. The constant response to demand did not merely take the program in the predictable direction of subjects with a commercial bent, but also drove the development of a substantial specialisation in human rights studies.

Nor were lawyers the only audience. An undergraduate degree in law was a prerequisite only for the LLM; graduates in other disciplines could study for the diplomas and specialist masters' degrees, as long as they could show relevant professional experience. The whole operation was on a scale found in few other law schools. Enrolments reached 700 in 1997, still overwhelmingly from Australia (only forty overseas students enrolled), and when an international panel reviewed the law school in 2006, it described the graduate coursework program in glowing terms:'To our knowledge, no faculty of law in North America comes close to replicating the rich array of offerings, and the scope and diversity of teachers'. As they pointed out, the program effectively served as a 'targeted part-time qualification upgrade curriculum', as well as offering full-time coursework.[26] Therein lay much of the reason for its success, riding a wave of specialisation, not only among lawyers, but among other professionals as well.

———◆———

The market for postgraduate coursework produced a boom, but the rise of research higher degrees in law was much slower. Doctorates were far from the norm among academic lawyers, and the demand for them outside academia was small. Only twelve of the law school's thirty-nine full-time academic staff had doctorates in 1989. The pattern was not unique to Melbourne, or indeed to Australia: only 13 per cent of common-law legal academics in Canada had doctorates in 1981, although the proportion among those who worked in the French-based civil law system was much higher. At Melbourne, even in 2007, the law school described a PhD as merely desirable, not essential, when it advertised vacancies at the level of lecturer and above, although the best applicants generally had one close to completion or already behind them.[27]

Many staff had research masters' degrees, some of which, like Greg Craven's thesis on secession, published in 1986, were awarded for substantial work on an almost doctoral scale. As the university strove to improve its performance, the pressure on the law school for more postgraduate research enrolments and completions grew. But in 1997, the law school still had disproportionately low numbers of postgraduate research students, enrolling 5.2 per cent of the university's equivalent full-time students, but carrying only 1.3 per cent of its load for higher research degrees.[28]

The drive for more higher degree enrolments was part of a wider movement to assimilate law to the research culture of the humanities and social sciences, with their reliance on the doctorate as a basic qualification for an academic career and their growing use of competitive research grants. External funding had only occasionally played much of a role in the law school's research. A grant from the Australian National University helped get Hans Leyser to Indonesia on his research trip in 1952–53, and there were also special projects undertaken for other organisations, like the drafting of the land codes for Brunei and the Solomon Islands. In 1967, Sandy Clark won funding for research on water law from the Australian Research Grants Committee, whose creation two years earlier showed the growing federal interest in allocating funds for centrally selected research projects to supplement research funding through general university operating grants.[29] Its larger and better-funded descendant, the Australian Research Council, was created as part of the Dawkins reforms, and took an increasingly important role in the research of the law school.

In the decade to 1977, staff received outside funding for ten research projects, including two more ARGC grants and others from government agencies. Mary Hiscock's collaborative project on Asian contract law received major funding ($65 000) from the Ford Foundation and the Asian Development Bank. When the Victorian government provided $30 000 a year, starting in 1981, for work on intergovernmental relations, it was the largest external research grant the law school had yet received.[30]

Targeted rather than general research funding was an element of the Dawkins reforms in the white paper of 1988, and increasing amounts of federal money were reallocated from operating grants to competitive research grants. The law school reacted with its first national competitive grant applications for many years, submitting seventeen of the twenty-six Australian applications for legal projects in the 1989 ARC round. Only three grants resulted, two of which went to Melbourne, but the success rate was higher for small grants, where the university chose eight of the law school's eleven applications for funding.[31]

Legal research often fitted awkwardly into templates derived from other disciplines, and even describing it as research could bemuse those more familiar with the physical sciences. The white paper's emphasis on research as 'the discovery of previously unknown phenomena' and 'the development of explanatory theory' seemed to leave out researchers who investigated what the law was or should be, although at least a catch-all covering 'the construction of original works of significant intellectual merit' gave them some hope. The format of ARC applications, too, drew (or forced) legal research into an unfamiliar model of competitively-judged significance and innovation, methodology, outcomes and benefits that applied more naturally to the sciences.[32]

The faculty's expanding research reports recorded the flow of books, articles and conference papers expected from any university department, and also the submissions and reports through which government drew on legal academics' expertise, continuing the practice begun by Hearn with his work on the civil service in the 1850s. When the law school argued (unsuccessfully) for a greater share of the university's internal research funding in 1977, its submission listed thirty-seven government inquiries of all kinds for which staff had provided submissions, comments, memoranda, opinions and other research in the previous twelve months; 'law reform and government research has become a major obligation of the faculty', the submission said.[33]

That Law was not a mere trade school, the point so often reiterated by deans from Bailey onwards, had uncomfortable consequences for the appraisal of its research performance. Assimilation to the social sciences meant judgement by their standards, as research output was recorded with increasing precision by the university in the 1990s, under direction from the federal government, and publication data began to feed into funding formulae. Comparisons of performance became increasingly important. Melbourne ranked well against other law schools, but indifferently against other faculties in the university. Some of the work of legal academics, in textbooks, casebooks and submissions, registered poorly in the recognised categories of research, and a culture of seeking competitive research grants was slow to take hold. Other factors were a drag on the measures: Law's student–staff ratio of 22:1 in 2006, though better than in previous years, was still above Arts' 17:1.[34] But official scores, however calculated, were weighty, and Law like other faculties strove to lift them.

The many different approaches taken in the research of staff and graduate students reflected a pluralism also found in English law schools.[35] The methodologies were new, but the diversity, ranging far beyond black-letter legal doctrine, was not; since Hearn, the full-time staff had written on wider topics, and so had some of their part-time colleagues (P. D. Phillips was an example). Among the work highlighted in the faculty's research reports were applications of post-colonial and feminist theory, studies of economic and social roles of law, empirical perspectives on a range of topics, commercial and otherwise, and less eclectic projects to articulate and analyse both obscure corners and broad sweeps of the law, saying what it was and what it ought to be. International scope received increasing emphasis, both in topics and in intended audience.

The influence of this research was diffuse, but most easily documented in two forums, courts and classrooms. In the High Court, Harold Luntz's *Assessment of Damages for Personal Injury and Death* ranked high in a survey of legal texts cited by the judges in 1996, one of whom later described it as 'one of the most outstanding treatises ever written on Australian law'. It was joined in the list by books from earlier generations: Moore's apparently inexhaustible *Constitution of the Commonwealth* and a book of essays by Cowen. Texts that were widely prescribed for courses in other universities included Luntz's co-authored casebook on torts, the long-lived textbook on corporations law by Ford and Ramsay (joined, for some of its many editions, by Robert Austin), and Jenny Morgan's innovative *Hidden Gender of Law*, written with Regina Graycar of the University of Sydney law school.[36]

Research centres proliferated across the university from the 1980s onwards, focusing and directing research effort and providing structures for external funding. They sprang up also in the law school. Its first was the pioneering Asian Law Centre, established at the start of 1986 as the result of discussions between Crommelin and Mal Smith, a Melbourne graduate who had been at the University of British Columbia and became the centre's inaugural director. Backed by the federal Attorney-General's Department, it attracted funding from the Victoria Law Foundation and the Law School Foundation, with support from law firms. By 2003, headed now by Indonesian law expert Tim Lindsey, the centre claimed the largest teaching program, covering the broadest range of Asian legal subjects, in the world. Its Asian links were a counterweight to the law school's older Anglophone affiliations.

The Asian Law Centre was followed only a few months later in 1986 by the Centre for Natural Resources Law, established after a sixteen-year gestation that began with an unsuccessful proposal for a natural resources planning unit in 1970. In 1988, the Centre for

Comparative Constitutional Studies grew out of the intergovern-mental relations research that had been funded by the Victorian government since 1981, led by Cheryl Saunders.[37]

The winning of research grants and the creation of centres fostered connections between staff and students, drawing later-year stu-dents into the work of the law school as research assistants, in ways common in many other departments but previously rare in Law. In 2007, the law school had eight centres and two research institutes (some of them established in collaboration with other organisations). They hosted visitors and conferences, and provided a framework for publica-tions, research projects, outreach to the community and the media, postgraduate research, and journal editing. The scale of their operations depended partly on the number of interested staff, but most of all on external funding. Some were so active that the university's central administration feared they were behaving like mini-departments, while others appeared to be under-performing.[38]

The way the centres worked varied so much that the analogy with departments was hard to sustain. Their operations ranged from closely coordinated work for externally funded research projects, sup-ported by specially appointed administrative and research staff, to loose associations of people with similar research interests who were linked by their shared teaching of large subjects and their collaboration in organising conferences and seminars. The way a single centre worked could change dramatically, as the Centre for Comparative Constitutional Studies did at the end of its funding from the Constitutional Centenary Foundation, when it lost its two main staff positions and a significant part of its day-to-day work.[39]

The fees from the new graduate program raised hopes of significant new income for the law school, but for several years growth was gradual, costs of the program were high, and the main game for funding remained the budget allocated by the university. Under Penington, the basis for these allocations was largely historical, the result of years of jostling by faculties for a better share, but under the strategic planning process some could now be gained or lost depending on the university's appraisal of each faculty's performance.

Good performance judged against the university's priorities exempted the law school (along with the Faculty of Economics and Commerce, though its reprieve was temporary) from a 1.25 per cent funding cut for 1990. And in the budget for 1991, when all faculties suffered a 0.75 per cent cut (following a clawback by the federal government of funds that were redirected to research), the law faculty received extra funding of $100 000. As Penington saw it, 'Law in fact showed that it was really performing very, very much better within two years of Michael taking over, and Cheryl as deputy, and we gave them an extra bonus to their budget, at the same time as we reduced the budget of Economics and Commerce, because it was just failing to deal with the issues of quality of undergraduate education. So Law was the first faculty to get an actual increase in its ongoing budget because of performance on the basis of quality.'[40]

Law was the only faculty to score increased funding in the 1993 planning cycle, but it was all of 1 per cent.[41] The amounts were small (though still welcome), but the benefits were not only monetary; approval from the central administration was worth something too, and had already brought significant benefits, outside the budget allocations, in the preferential split of graduate fees. Measured against the performance standards of the new regime, Law was in favour.

Even with these marginal bonuses, what the law school was doing began to run ahead of its capacity to pay. Salary costs (always by far the biggest expense) rose as more staff were appointed, particularly to teach the small classes of a new first-year program; numbers increased from 38.88 equivalent full-time teaching and research staff in 1990, to 44.59 in 1991. The fee-paying graduate program, which was also expensive to run, was still having difficulty covering its costs. In 1992, the faculty ran up an accumulated deficit of $500 000, and lamented its 'serious, and deteriorating financial plight' in its submission to the university's planning group, but responsibility for fixing it now devolved largely on the law school itself.[42]

Having contributed to the problem, the graduate program came to the rescue by boosting the law school's budget with its fee income. The recession of the early 1990s probably held back its early growth, but within a few years the program was bringing in more and more revenue. Revenue outside the operating grant from the university made up about 20 per cent of the law school's revenue in 1993, but the following year the figure had risen to 35 per cent, most of the increase coming from the graduate program. With this boost, and some careful management, the deficit was effectively removed by the end of 1994.[43]

Another source of money to make up the deficit came from one of the university's few departmental reorganisations that affected Law. While some of its counterparts elsewhere became part of larger faculties—Business, Economics and Law at Queensland, a Faculty of the Professions at Adelaide—Law at Melbourne remained one of the university's minority of smaller, single-department faculties, never subdivided and never merged. This was partly the result of the relative stability of Melbourne's faculties, which did not undergo the transformations seen at some other universities. It also reflected the law school's sense of specialisation and uniqueness (enhanced by the distinct professional culture and the requirements of admission to practise), and its resistance to occasional ideas for amalgamation in pursuit of economies of scale.

A merger with Economics and Commerce, as at Queensland, was one possibility. The two faculties had long been connected through the teaching of business law—or, more accurately, they worked in some of the same areas, but usually operated independently. Economics and Commerce had taught law of various kinds for decades (Frank Maher taught elementary jurisprudence and constitutional law in Economics and Commerce before resuming his long career in the law school in 1958), and the overlap of its teaching on company law and taxation was obvious.[44] But the law school's sense of its separate identity was strong, and the idea of a merger never reached the stage of a concrete proposal for the faculty; if it had, opposition to being swallowed by a much larger faculty would have been intense.

The two mergers that did occur in the 1990s were on a smaller scale, and offered advantages for Law. Though Economics and Commerce remained separate, its most legal department, Business Law, moved across, having been hived off from a combined department with Accounting in 1991. Business Law was smaller than the law school (it had about 300 equivalent full-time students as against Law's 1000), and most of its staff wanted to move to Law rather than have to continue defending their patch in a multidisciplinary faculty. From the law school's point of view, there were other advantages. Like the university amalgamations of the late 1980s, the merger was partly a real-estate deal, since Business Law brought with it much-needed space in another university building, Baldwin Spencer. It also brought a significant slice of income. The 'takeover called an amalgamation', in Crommelin's words, was financially attractive.[45]

Most importantly, the merger brought within the faculty a law program that had been operating independently of it, though inevitably associated with it in public perception as undifferentiated Law at Melbourne University. As Crommelin saw it, particularly after Business Law established its own graduate program, 'in terms of reputation, the outside world didn't distinguish between the law school and the Department of Business Law in the commerce faculty'.[46]

In a faculty meeting, the dean added another reason for the merger, adapting for his own purpose what he called 'the myth widely held in the University that the Law School is isolationist and self interested'. The Manion review of 1988 had backed the criticism. 'As an institution the Faculty of Law seems to have cut itself off from general university life', it reported. 'It has ignored and, in turn, been ignored.' This exasperated Luntz, who had himself spent so much time on central committees, and had seen colleagues do the same and more. 'To imply that the University was ignorant of the deplorable conditions under which we have had to work because we have not made it aware of them is a travesty', he retorted. Nor did the criticism make sense to someone like Paul Morgan, associate registrar in the central administration in the 1980s, who found the lawyers 'enormously valuable and very even-handed'. Their involvement continued in later years, headed by Sally Walker as senior deputy vice-chancellor and Loane Skene as president of the academic board.[47]

Rejecting the merger proposal would consolidate the myth of isolationism, Crommelin argued. The law school could make a cooperative gesture by going along, although the additional income hardly refuted the accusation of self-interest. But some in the law faculty resisted, former dean Harold Luntz in particular. Commerce students' needs were different, he told the faculty meeting (Law would take on the teaching of a significant number of them in the business law subjects that came with the department). There could be problems with staffing if expiring appointments in Business Law were not renewed, and Commerce might still teach law even after Business Law had gone. But he was in a minority, and the merger took effect in 1994, at the same time as a smaller amalgamation with the legal studies section of the former Melbourne College of Advanced Education, which the university had taken over. The law school continued to teach business law for Economics and Commerce, but it shed the legal studies courses, which disappeared from the university's offerings.

———————— ⇒≽•◦◦⊱⇐ ————————

Clawing back the accumulated deficit gave only brief breathing space, as government funding per student continued its inexorable downward trend. The new conservative federal government elected in 1996, led by John Howard, announced university funding cuts of 6 per cent over four years, and the end of additional funding to cover salary increases (which represented an even deeper cut in real terms). The combined effect led the law school to forecast a drop in its public funding of more than 10 per cent in 1998 alone, while the university expected an effective reduction in 'publicly funded operating capacity' of around 25 per cent over five years. Growing ambitions to be 'one of the finest universities in the world', as Melbourne's strategic plan expressed its mission, clashed with declining public funding.[48]

The law school's response, aside from its usual strategy of expanding the graduate program whenever more money was needed, was to take advantage of another key element of the federal government's higher education plans: the introduction of fee-paying undergraduate places for domestic students. International students had had to pay fees since the Dawkins reforms of the late 1980s, and the law school enrolled its first three full-fee paying overseas undergraduate students in 1989. The fee revenue was irresistible, the benefits of international links were obvious, and numbers had risen despite the headwind of limited portability of the qualification, compared with Commerce or Medicine. By 1996, Melbourne had ninety-six fee-paying undergraduate overseas students in Law; only Bond University had more. Now fee-paying places would be opened to domestic as well as overseas undergraduates. From 1998, the government allowed enrolment of up to 25 per cent of the domestic student load in any course on a fee-paying basis (the ceiling rose to 35 per cent from 2005). Fees for the new places in the LLB began at $15 000 a year, nearly three times the HECS charge paid by subsidised students.[49]

Fees were controversial, and not only because of their implications for access to education. They made a difference, albeit small, to entrance standards: the minimum entrance score for school-leavers seeking fee-paying places was several points lower than that for subsidised places. On the other hand, the university's policy of coupling the introduction of fee-paying places with a scholarship scheme gave most of the new places in the LLB to scholarship-holders, who had among the highest entrance scores in the university. Of the target of fifty fee-paying places in 1998, thirty-one were for scholarship holders; their fees were paid from the scholarship endowment, rather than the students' own resources. But while argument about fees for degrees swirled in the university and the wider community, it had little traction in Law. Student members of the faculty reiterated the primacy of selection on merit, regardless of fee status, and urged the establishment of scholarships for all fee-paying places, but otherwise the proposal went without significant opposition.[50]

Another potential source of income, donations and bequests, included some notable contributions but never amounted to a significant part of the law school's budget. The Law School Foundation, established in 1984, raised $1.3 million in its first sixteen years, and supported the early phases of several of the law school's research centres, particularly the Asian Law Centre. Other donations funded named chairs, but without the strings attached that had made the CCH chair of taxation law so controversial when it was created in Economics and Commerce on the condition that Bernard Marks was appointed to it. The Davies Collison Cave chair of intellectual property, the Australian Red Cross chair of international humanitarian law, and the Harold Ford chair of commercial law (established in his honour by donations from seven law firms) were among them. But even with these successes, the amounts raised were small when measured against the law school's overall expenses, despite continued prodding from the central administration. The university's 2006 operational performance review commented critically on the modest returns of the faculty's fundraising efforts.[51]

The creation of full-time teaching positions in law after World War II (like the expansion of Australian universities) had been underwritten by the increases in federal funding that culminated in the abolition of tuition fees in 1974, but from the late 1980s onwards students were again paying an increasing share of the cost of their education. As a proportion of the university's income, student fees accounted for about half in 1891, rose to 63 per cent in the depression year of 1933, and fell almost to nothing in 1974. By 2005, the law school again drew something over half its revenue from student fees (more still, if HECS was included), though this was above the overall university figure. Government funding had gone full circle, though the staffing of the law school had been transformed in the process.[52]

The way the law school's staff worked changed more after 1980 than it had in the previous 120 years. In the 1970s, the main task of the administrative staff, bigger by far than any other, was typing. If any academics had typewriters, they were so rare as to have disappeared from memory, and all their written work—correspondence, publications, course materials, and so on—was typed by others, or left in manuscript. Each professor had a secretary ('they were always the elite', one administrative staff member remembered), and other academics brought their typing to the General Office, where documents would also be proof-read, one staff member reading aloud to another. The social rituals of the office staff sometimes intersected those of the academics, and sometimes ran in parallel. Each group would often eat lunch together, the office staff sometimes sitting on the grass in the quadrangle (before chains around the perimeter discouraged trespassers), the academics at the staff club. Morning tea was a joint effort, but the academics would sit together in the centre of the common room, and the office staff separately, by the window, to the bemusement of one of the secretaries.[53]

In the 1980s, this pattern began to change. Word-processing machines supplanted typewriters, and a rudimentary network linked the typing pool with a research assistant's office, though not with any academics. Work was backed up nightly on disks the size of dinnerplates. In the late 1980s, computers began appearing on academics' desks, and the typing work of the General Office slowly declined. A basic computer network was installed in 1991, and in the same year a small computer laboratory for students (with eighteen computers) opened in part of the law library. A computer-assisted tutorial for first-year students followed two years later. The law school appeared on the World Wide Web after the university's first home page went live in 1994, and staff and students were increasingly linked to the explosion of legal information on the Internet. By the time the law school moved to its new building in 2002, getting cases and legislation electronically was the norm, remarkable only when compared with the paper-based communication that it had so recently replaced.[54]

The other main prospect for new funds, as the law school tried to protect its budget from the cuts of the late 1990s, was the graduate program. Expansion of the existing coursework subjects was all very well, and they continued to grow, but there was an opportunity for something more. One of the graduate program's distinguishing features had been that it did not qualify students for admission to practise; only the LLB did that. Postgraduate students could deepen their knowledge or develop their specialisations, but those who came from other disciplines, without law degrees, could turn themselves into practising lawyers only by going back to the undergraduate LLB course. Maybe such people could be attracted to a course of their own, and maybe they would pay.

'There was a demand for what you might call a career-change program', as Crommelin put it. 'Every year we had a few medical practitioners and various others who decided they wanted to do law', people who had already worked after graduation but came back to study and enrolled in the LLB. 'In one sense it was a natural evolution from the graduate program, because we got the graduate program to a certain point, and the next question was, well, what further opportunities were there, again that were consistent with the sort of law school we wanted to be, but for which there was a market.' The new course was one of the favoured options from a consultants' review of the law school's deteriorating financial prospects in 1997, along with more fee-paying undergraduates, an expanded graduate program, and profit-making seminars and conferences.[55]

The concept, new to Australian law schools at the time, was a separate course for graduates in other disciplines that would meet the requirements for admission to practise and bring in fee revenue. Crommelin told the faculty: 'the proposal aimed to *assist* all areas within the Faculty of Law by providing a much needed source of revenue'. The plan aimed high, in quality and in small class sizes, both to support the law school's ambitions for its national and international profile, and to justify the heavy charges the new students would pay ($72 000 for the whole course, when it eventually began operation).[56]

For a special course, there would be a special title: a graduate would not be a mere Master of Laws, but a Doctor of Law, a *Juris Doctor*, like the alumni of graduate law courses in the United States, although (like them) unable to use the title 'doctor'.

The prospect of bringing the course on-stream for the difficult budget year of 1998 was enticing, and at first things moved with great speed. The first many staff heard of the new course was when the proposal appeared in meeting papers for the endorsement of the faculty in September 1997. Rosemary Hunter was one of them: 'it was dropped upon us … the faculty board was pretty much treated as a rubber stamp, except that I would get the papers and read through them, and then run around the corridors saying, "Have you seen this?"'. Hunter and other opponents quickly organised themselves for the faculty meeting. 'It was possible to do the odd ambush, because nobody would ever see it coming. Nobody would have any idea that there was any dissent, because no space had been allowed in which dissent could be aired or offered.' This time, the haste, the surprise, and the reaction were all much greater than usual. As Hunter put it: 'so here's this proposal for a whole new degree program without any consultation … some people got quite cross about that'.[57]

There was a rare divided vote. Even the ever-reticent faculty minutes caught some of the mood of resistance:

> A concern was expressed at the apparent lack of consultation amongst academic staff within the Faculty of Law regarding the proposal for a JD degree. It was suggested that the proposed JD degree could be characterised as 'law for the rich' because it did not contain subjects such as family and labour law. It was suggested that a Departmental Meeting should be held to discuss the content of the proposed JD degree … A concern was expressed that the proposed JD degree was motivated by financial, rather than academic, concerns.[58]

'There was a feeling that this was a case of buying degrees', Michael Bryan, later deputy dean, said.[59] The faculty rejected the proposal. It was one of the few occasions when any motion was defeated in a faculty meeting during Crommelin's deanship.

Too much depended on the JD plan for it to drop, and the suggestion for a departmental meeting, bringing the academic staff together without the other members of the faculty, was an obvious way through the roadblock. One was promptly convened, some changes were made, and a massaged proposal returned to the faculty within a month. Legal theory and labour law would now be included, selection would expressly be based on high academic merit, and the demanding standards of the new course were reiterated. Concerns about the title (would it devalue doctorates?) and the curriculum (not enough optional subjects?) remained, but the proposal was adopted. Crommelin left no doubt about the need for the new course: 'The Dean advised Faculty that, following a decrease in public funding to the University, the Faculty of Law was obliged either to cut back the existing curriculum choices, or pursue initiatives such as the proposed JD program in an effort to diversify the funding base'.[60]

The JD faced two more tests. The university's central committees were even more unhappy with the doctoral title than the faculty members had been, and for a time they forced a relegation to a master's degree, an SJM, as the proposal worked its way through the system. The American title was restored by turning some of the central administration's favourite weapons back on it: the law school used a marketing and benchmarking study to show its widespread use by leading overseas universities. These arguments persuaded the university, but getting agreement from Canberra was more difficult, and it was only after considerable efforts that the course was recognised by the federal government as equivalent to a fee-paying master's.[61] After the protracted approval process, and unexpected delays in course planning and marketing, the JD program enrolled its first students in 2000.

The law school's undergraduate teaching, target of some of the harshest criticisms of the external reviews of the mid-1980s, responded to different imperatives. Unlike the new graduate program, which depended on the ultimate test of fee-paying student demand, the LLB course continued to be dominated by a rigid quota of subsidised places, for which demand always far outran the number available. But the outside scrutiny, the growing demands from the university's central administration for improved performance, and the teachers' own ideas of how things could be done better, drove the framing of a different kind of course, in which students' experiences would hopefully be more positive.

A laborious curriculum review in 1988 examined the optional program, grouping, deleting and renaming subjects. Melbourne retained a relatively low proportion of compulsory subjects: 54 per cent of the course was compulsory in 1992, one of the lowest figures for Australian law schools at the time. The review then turned to first year, replacing Legal Process (the name of the introductory subject since 1971) with a new subject that took torts as the vehicle for an introduction to legal methods and research. Torts and the Process of Law, as the subject became when teaching began in 1990, was complemented in first year by a new introduction to history, theory and critical approaches to law, under the title History and Philosophy of Law. The compulsory study of legal theory was supplemented by a requirement to take one of a list of theory and context subjects later in the course, part of a wider revival in Australian law schools of the compulsory study of jurisprudence and other forms of legal theory.[62] The two new subjects were known, thanks to their initials, as Hipple and Tipple.

The curriculum changes cemented a different approach to first-year teaching that one student in the rare position to make the comparison had already noticed. Belinda Fehlberg began the law course in 1982, but lasted only six weeks. A student from a state high school, she found few of her classmates at the university, and none in law: 'So I felt quite isolated at university, and I felt particularly isolated in the law school'. The first Legal Process assignment, based on a hypothetical problem, was such a traumatic experience that she dropped out when it was due. 'There were no hints given as to where to start with solving this problem. You were basically just told to go to the law library and do your best.' But after spending a year in a full-time job, and then doing an arts degree and working as a research assistant, she applied to do law as a mature-age student. In 1988, both she and the course were different. Even the Legal Process assignment was less intimidating: 'It was guided, it was structured, it was comprehensible. I felt we were much more supported.' This time round, she flourished; she later studied overseas, and became a professor in the law school in 2005.[63]

Not everyone found the course so supportive (the students' counter-handbook called pointedly for more guidance with legal research and writing), and once the new first-year subjects began, History and Philosophy of Law proved difficult to settle into a durable and workable shape. The rapid movement between separate sections on history, philosophy and sociology, taught by different teachers from challenging course materials, left the student reviewer of the course's first year (quoting Oscar Wilde) with an overall impression of 'chaos, illumined by flashes of lightning'.[64]

The reaction to one innovation was particularly strong. The history component of the course began, not just with the English law of colonisation (long a standard part of legal history courses), but with Aboriginal law. As Rosemary Hunter, who prepared much of the material for the course, put it, 'if you were going to talk about the history of law in Australia, you had to start with the law that was in Australia first, which was Aboriginal law ... The students were hotly resistant to the whole Aboriginal law and Aboriginal rights issues, and they generated some really heated debates.'[65]

The large number of staff allocated to the weekly seminars in small groups also drew critical comment. The Pearce report had recommended cutting first-year class sizes, and the new curriculum was designed accordingly, at the expense of class sizes in later years. The new subjects inverted a pattern, found in some other faculties, of large lectures in first year and small groups for later-year students. Assessment was spread across several different tasks, taking some of the intimidating weight off the final exam.

Both the content and the teaching format of the new subjects tested Penington's system of performance review. Under the strategic planning system, the vice-chancellor and his senior staff made an annual visitation to the faculty—'the inquisition', Crommelin called it—to review its performance against its plans, on the basis of extensive reports. 'David was tremendously interventionist, in the sense that he had extremely detailed knowledge of what was going on right across the university, in a way that was quite extraordinary … He conducted the whole thing like a cross-examination, personally. We were always amused by the fact that no one else in his team ever got to speak.'[66]

The questioning about the new first-year subjects was intense. The vice-chancellor had detailed information about class sizes, course content, and the scores from student evaluation questionnaires (which became compulsory in 1992). 'How could the law school possibly be short of resources, and yet be teaching in this way in first year?', Crommelin remembered him asking. 'How come so-and-so's got 2.8 and it should be 4.2?' Despite appearances, the model was not dictatorship, but management by ordeal. When the law school's representatives, the dean and senior staff, withstood the onslaught, they were allowed to carry out their own plans. 'I'm not sure that we ever convinced David', Crommelin said, 'but he at no stage said, "Well, look, I think you're wrong, and you might have to do it some other way or you'll be punished in resource terms". He accepted ultimately that that's a matter that we had to decide. And he was prepared to be persuaded, even when it was perfectly clear that he didn't agree.'[67] The first-year subjects, with their small (or at least smaller) groups, continued, although History and Philosophy of Law went through several revisions before being replaced in a revised curriculum in 2006.

DEANS

William Hearn

Edward Jenks

William Harrison Moore

Kenneth Bailey

George Paton

Zelman Cowen

Harold Ford

Sandy Clark

Colin Howard

Mark Weinberg

Harold Luntz

Michael Crommelin

Ian Ramsay

Student numbers resumed their old pattern of growth at the end of the 1980s, after two decades of relative stability, and re-confirmed an enduring characteristic: compared with many of its counterparts in Australia and overseas, Melbourne's was a big law school. The growth came not only from the mushrooming graduate program, but from creeping increases in the undergraduate intake as well, as declining federal funding per student encouraged universities to lift enrolments in order to maintain revenue.

The number of subsidised places in Law edged upwards, hitting 280 equivalent full-time students in the 2003 intake, but the greatest increase came in fee-paying places. By 2004, these were adding another 205 to the subsidised enrolment, giving a record first-year target of 484. Most of the 205 fee-paying places went to local students, while just under half were filled from overseas. Women had outnumbered men in the first-year intake for the first time in 1989, and accounted for the majority of law school enrolments overall from 1995. Melbourne's 1900 equivalent full-time law students represented around 5.5 per cent of the university's 33 600 equivalent full-time students in 2004.[68]

Despite the university's good intentions about expanding its intake beyond Victorian school-leavers, they continued to dominate; there were many more law students from overseas than from other states of Australia. In 2004, international students made up 18 per cent of the undergraduate intake, while only 4–5 per cent came from other parts of Australia. Seventy-seven per cent of the new students were school leavers, 10 per cent came through the access program for disadvantaged applicants (soon to increase under a university initiative), and the remainder were graduates, or transferred from other courses. Only 12 per cent enrolled in a pure LLB course; most combined law with other degrees.[69]

In the expanding enrolment, Indigenous students appeared in significant numbers for the first time. Under-represented in secondary and higher education across the country, they faced particularly high barriers to entry in law, with its daunting selection requirements and intimidating culture. The university had slowly developed, over decades, an institutional framework for redressing what was once the complete absence of Indigenous students from the campus, and the law school eventually adopted measures of its own.

The National Union of Australian University Students gave the university £1300 in 1955 to establish scholarships for Aboriginal students, tenable at any Australian university, but candidates had to meet the ordinary requirements for entry to their courses, and the subsequent spread of quotas across the faculties raised barriers even higher. The university created a special admission scheme for Aboriginal and Torres Strait Islander students, initiated by Peter Brett, in 1968, allowing the enrolment of Indigenous students who had not matriculated. He was prompted by the creation of a new scholarship for Aboriginal students, and by his experience at the University of Texas, where the indirect exclusion of African–American students through the operation of admission requirements had stirred controversy while he was a visiting professor. A place in law at Melbourne was offered to an Aboriginal student in 1972, but he chose another course, and another enrolled in 1976, but discontinued after a year; by 1990, only one Indigenous student had graduated (one of twenty-one Indigenous law graduates across the country).[70]

In the 1990s, the number of Indigenous students rose, and the law school provided more support and encouragement, including the designation of a staff member as Koori liaison officer in 1993. Tom Cannon was one of the students who started in 1991. Like many Indigenous students, he felt divided loyalties: 'You wondered when you were doing it whether you were selling out'. Parts of the course that confirmed Indigenous dispossession were confronting, and Property, before the *Mabo* case, was 'a bit of an affront', but as a mature-age student he found his wider experience made it easier to cope with the sometimes forbidding atmosphere that he knew many other students, Indigenous and non-Indigenous, also felt. They all had a go, he remembered; 'we had fun doing it'. But others had harsher memories. A more recent graduate warmly thanked lecturers and the

Undergraduate Office staff for their support, but found 'every day was a struggle', and ultimately regretted choosing law.[71]

There were fourteen Indigenous law graduates at Melbourne between 1991 and 2000; in 1997, thirty-one of the university's 199 Indigenous students were enrolled in Law. But attrition rates remained high, at Melbourne as at other law schools, and many more students started the course than were able to finish it. Over the next ten years, Indigenous student numbers in Law declined, but completion rates increased, gradually building up a critical mass of Indigenous graduates.[72]

———⟫•⟪———

The decades-long quest for accommodation became an ever more time-consuming preoccupation for the law school's senior staff, although the two new law theatres, the space made available when the central administration moved out of the quadrangle, and relatively stable student numbers reduced the pressure for a time after 1970. Outwardly, the quadrangle kept its charm and remained inseparable from the public image of the law school. 'The camellias were out; I was entranced by the architecture', wrote one graduate who was a student in the 1970s. 'To me, the cloisters breathed learning and justice.' 'One would look up at the gothic offices and imagine staff doing their secret, magical "academic business" up there', wrote another. The quadrangle became a popular, even congested, venue for wedding photographs, as Andrew Neeson found when he worked in his ground-floor office during the weekend: 'This bloody confetti would come flooding in through my window'.[73]

Inside, it was a different story. 'You had to jam people in somewhere', remembered Neeson, who was responsible for room allocations in the late 1980s. By 1991, the law school had 65 academic and research staff requiring accommodation, and 46 rooms. It had the worst space allocation of any faculty.[74] A few rooms in the east and west wings kept their spacious nineteenth-century proportions intact and matched the image of the outside of the building, but other staff were slotted into a hierarchy of offices, some built in 1959 inside the shell of the north wing with views of the quadrangle and its surrounds, others with views of the underside of the library airconditioning plant, and a few with no windows at all. Tiny, carrel-like offices for academic staff were created inside the roof-space of the east and west wings in 1992–94, envied in summer for their airconditioning. The faculty's one large lecture theatre, in the north wing, was a museum piece, unchanged since its creation in the rebuilding of 1959; after its airconditioning broke down, never to be repaired, it was almost uninhabitable on hot days.

The imperative to use every corner of the old building and keep its ageing rooms in repair forced a series of rolling renovations, as new offices were created and old ones refurbished. The General Office, the law school's administrative centre, point of contact for its students and base for many non-academic staff, was particularly difficult to fit into a workable layout in its wing of the ground floor, and it went through protracted building work. 'The office always seemed to be being renovated', said Ann Graham. 'I used to sit in the corner in a pile of dust.' Cables had to be installed for a computer network in 1991, a task complicated by heritage controls and the building's strange internal layout, the result of successive reconstructions.[75] As if the internal renovations were not enough, the quadrangle's stonework had decayed to such an extent that scaffolding was needed, first to protect passers-by as sections threatened to fall off, and then to provide access for a painstaking restoration project. The dust from the work on the outside walls became so thick inside the building that holes were cut in office doors and fitted with large fans to exclude it, by forcing air outwards through the gaps around the windows. Strongly though many staff and students were attached to it, the difficulties of the old building mounted.

The search for accommodation led to the establishment of outposts elsewhere on the campus, and beyond. The merger with Business Law brought space in the Baldwin Spencer building, not far from the quadrangle. The Asian Law Centre, the Centre for Comparative

Constitutional Studies and the Australian Institute for Judicial Administration (affiliated to the law school) operated from terrace houses in Barry Street, south of the campus, at various times from the mid-1980s on; later, the Centre for Comparative Constitutional Studies and the JD program occupied space in an office building in Swanston Street, near the university. This dispersal of staff was matched by the scattering of classes across the campus in the annual competition for teaching space, as law subjects, like those of other faculties with few teaching rooms under their own control, were taught at the four corners of the university.

A series of events quickened the pace in the mid-1980s, restoring building plans to the central place they had had in the 1950s and 1960s, but initially with just as little success. The Pearce report's criticism of the library was one spur to action, given added weight by the Manion inquiry's description of the library accommodation as 'appalling'; another was the need to respond to unwelcome solutions that originated elsewhere in the university.

In June 1988, the university's buildings committee supported the idea of finding space for the law library somewhere else on the campus, by putting it in an expanded Baillieu Library. The dean, Harold Luntz, protested that the proposal had been adopted without consultation, and that moving the library away to a separate location was not acceptable. Alternative ideas were needed, and the law school appointed its own architects to draw up an accommodation master plan. Its original version set out four options: the expanded Baillieu was included as a matter of form, although the faculty still refused to have anything to do with it, and even as a concept labelled it temporary; the phantom law building in the university's eastern precinct, across Swanston Street from the main campus, put in an appearance as option B; tinkering with the old building and gaining a few rooms by building above the law theatres made up option A, which would have provided a little temporary relief; and the main option, into which the faculty put its efforts over the next ten years, was a northward extension of the old quadrangle, in the shape of a new library.[76]

Taking over as dean in 1989, Crommelin pursued the same strategy, strongly opposing the separation of the law school from a new library above the Baillieu, despite Penington's support for it. 'The iconic quality of the quadrangle was important,' he said, 'and if there was a way that we could satisfy our requirements and retain that, that was seen as being a big plus'. He was also nervous about the sort of building that might be offered for relocation in the eastern precinct. He knew the Earth Sciences building that had been built there in the 1970s, and was not impressed.[77]

The first plan for the new library had little chance of success, involving as it did the demolition of the gothic northern extension of the quadrangle, completed in 1875. The attraction of demolition, such as it was, was that it would provide more space for a new building to replace the old, but the north wing was far too historic a part of the university's fabric for such drastic measures. Besides, the new building's three above-ground levels (with two below) would take up much of the area between the quadrangle and the union building to its north, crowding the busy courtyard at the centre of the campus.

These drawbacks gave the plan a chilly reception from the university's buildings committee, but it left open the possibility of leaving the gothic north extension intact, shifting the new library to one side, and putting most of it underground. This would require demolition of the unsightly bookroom (attached to the north wing in 1955–56) and the old records or Scarborough wing of 1949–51, also stuck onto the quadrangle at a time when cream brick was considered, if not an ideal extension to Tudor gothic freestone, then at least economical. Crommelin suggested going underground after visiting the subterranean library extension at the University of Michigan. Modifications of the plan sought to cope with the limitations of the site and provide the necessary floor space, and it evolved to comprise a building above ground on the Scarborough site, linked to an underground library. A bait for the central administration was a new council chamber, with a secure walkway to the Raymond Priestley building, shielded from the demonstrations that disrupted access to the council chamber in the quadrangle.[78]

The scheme had a sceptical reception in the buildings committee, which was wary of the chaos that a huge excavation followed by major construction work could cause in the heavily populated heart of the campus. The constraints of the small site implied, too, that even the new building would struggle to meet the library's projected needs. But one member, Peter McIntyre, head of the Department of Architecture and Building, particularly liked the idea, and produced his own concept plan for an underground library north of the quadrangle. The committee still had reservations, but in 1991 it supported the underground library concept in principle.[79]

The law school bolstered the proposal with more planning work and a feasibility report from a consulting engineer. By 1997, the result of this persistence was that the university budget, the capital projects committee and the planning and budget committee all listed the underground redevelopment as a potential project for 1999 onwards, but on a smaller scale than originally conceived, and without providing full funding. The faculty itself would have to find a substantial part of the cost: $6 million from a revised and lower estimate of $17 million (earlier figures had been $24 or $25 million). But there was a sign that was both ominous and cryptic. The new vice-chancellor, Alan Gilbert, opposed the scheme because of the disruption it would cause, but also because it might unnecessarily limit another, much newer project. The underground library was being left behind by a far grander plan, for Melbourne University Private.[80]

<hr />

The fate of the law school's building plans suddenly became bound up with a bold idea for a new source of revenue for the university, revenue that was needed to match the university's income to its growing ambitions. Throughout its earlier history, Melbourne had been proud to count itself as a respectable member of the wider community of British universities, recognised overseas in the interchange of graduates and staff, and contributing, where it could, to the international corpus of academic research. But this was a matter of the maintenance of standards and the encouragement of achievement, rather than the ranking of Melbourne against more famous universities elsewhere. When Fink's royal commission in 1904 and Priestley in the 1930s talked about the university and its future, they wanted it to be better, and to do as well as it could (Priestley took British and American universities as his guide), but their aims were necessarily modest, and framed as a recovery from long neglect rather than a leap for international stardom. Such a thing was hardly conceivable in the context of the time.

Even the university's first strategic plan, in 1988, stated its mission (as it was now called) in a way that politely avoided comparison with anyone or anywhere else. The university had 'a special place in the Australian higher education system and in the Victorian community', it said. Its aims were 'to preserve, refine and advance knowledge'; to 'provide undergraduate, graduate and continuing education'; and to 'contribute to the intellectual, cultural, social and economic development of the community'.[81]

Despite this mild language, the idea was spreading that the university could aspire to more, and that its achievements could be measured against those of others, who were increasingly to be seen not just as counterparts but as competitors. Like strategic planning, the higher goals were not unique or distinctive to Melbourne, but echoed in other universities, and linked with the wider changes in organisation and entrepreneurial spirit that Simon Marginson and Mark Considine called the emergence of the enterprise university.[82]

As vice-chancellor, Alan Gilbert took the university's aspirations to new levels. Its mission was now not only to secure its position as 'the premier research and teaching university in Australia', but to make itself 'one of the finest universities in the world'.[83] In what became a trademark of Gilbert's style, the new strategic plan swept the horizon, in a conspectus of the university's external environment, internationalisation, the decline of public funding, deregulation, competition, access, information technology, and Melbourne's internal characteristics. One of its seven goals was to make the university much less dependent on public funding.

One source of that new funding was a radical experiment, a private offshoot of the public university, which would offer fee-paying, commercially-oriented courses, free from the regulatory restrictions that came with subsidised undergraduate students. Melbourne University Private, as it was named, grew out of a recognition of two things, so the university's strategic audit (an expanded bird's-eye view of the strategic map) said after its establishment:

> Firstly, that a viable long-term solution to over-dependence on public funding demanded a new, more entrepreneurial operating environment within the University of Melbourne. Secondly, as international benchmarking confirms, a high proportion of the world's most renowned, scholarly, and progressive universities, are private institutions, able to operate with a degree of institutional autonomy rarely matched in the public sector.[84]

Behind the diplomatic language lay a hope that the private university would be able to make money in ways closed to its parent. Revenue would flow back to the public university through royalty and licence fees paid for accreditation of the new courses, and through agreements under which the public university would provide teaching and other services.

The private university needed a home, and after an initial flirtation with a campus in Melbourne's redeveloped docklands, its public parent planned to establish it across the road, around the park known as University Square. The university already occupied many of the nineteenth-century terrace houses that fronted the square (some of them used by the law school), and its co-owned Melbourne Business School was based there. In keeping with the scale of the private university concept (projections of up to 10 000 students appeared in the press), this would be no refurbishment of old buildings, but a major construction project, one of the biggest in the university's history.[85]

From an early stage, though, the private university was not intended to be the only occupant of the new buildings that would rise around the square. Indeed, the private university plan became partly a means to finance more accommodation for the public university, which was more and more crowded on the main campus. Suddenly, the shadowy option of relocating the law school became a real possibility, one that took on more definite shape as the fast-moving University Square development evolved. As the proposal was first formally put to the dean in May 1998, the law school was offered a tall, thin tower, twenty-two storeys high, at the southern end of the square, as part of 'new facilities under the aegis of Melbourne University Private'.[86]

After decades of thwarted plans, it was startling that a new building on such a grand scale would drop from the sky, or at least from the vice-chancellor's office, and it signified the speed and magnitude of the Square project. For the law school, the offer had obvious advantages. It would bring everything—staff, library, teaching rooms and everything else—under one roof, something that could not have happened on the main campus. Even in an expanded quadrangle, the law school would have needed to keep its space in the Baldwin Spencer building and elsewhere, and use the lecture theatres of other faculties.

Gilbert offered a building designed with the law school's participation and paid for entirely by the university, without any of the fundraising obligations that had weighed down the redevelopment plans and that dogged other faculties (such as Engineering) in need of new accommodation. No price was mentioned to Crommelin. 'I thought it was an extraordinarily good proposal, an enormously generous proposal on the part of the university, because it didn't involve any fundraising on our part.'[87]

For all that, abandoning the quadrangle, the law school's symbol and its dominant image, stirred strong feelings, and the move had significant drawbacks. Some staff were either wary or firmly opposed, and the Law Students' Society organised a campaign against the move. A building off the main campus would cause problems for combined-course students moving between classes, some staff and students argued, and the twenty-two storey tower block mentioned in the university's initial approach to the faculty would not work as a law school. Staff with experience of high-rise university buildings at Melbourne and elsewhere (including Sydney's multi-storey law building, with its inadequate and idiosyncratic lifts) doubted that such a design could cope with large numbers of students, and feared the effects on collegiality.[88]

The LSS, like other opponents of the move, stressed the shortcomings of distance and isolation from the main campus, and argued that the quadrangle project was not being presented fairly as an option for the faculty, because of the lack of financial support from the university. 'The whole process of involvement of law faculty members has been redundant', it argued. 'In financial terms, there appears to be no choice. The failure of the university to provide all the funds necessary for the on-campus expansion, and the resultant need of the faculty to borrow $6 million amounts to a gun to the head for the faculty.'[89]

Ron Castan QC, alerted by the LSS, voiced this argument in a trenchant letter to the vice-chancellor:

> If the University is prepared to provide $17M for a new Law School, it has no business blackmailing the Law Faculty, who are not business people, and should not be expected to fund their own operations.
>
> There is some fakery going on here. You either have the money available or you don't. If you do have the money available, it is iniquitous for you to force the Law School off-campus, thereby depriving the faculty and students of the benefit of being at the heart of the University … The kind of 'bribe' being offered to the faculty to move off-campus is offensive.[90]

Melbourne University Private's connection with University Square fuelled more criticism. Law was a faculty of the public university, and would remain so, but a graduate law school was a key element of early ideas for the private university, and was identified as one of its projected future schools in 1997. A link between the law school and

MU Private grew stronger in public perception, as the plan for the new building emerged. At the function held to launch the private university, Crommelin saw the conflating of MU Private, University Square and the new law building as a serious problem: 'the muddying of the waters between Melbourne University Private and the University Square project was very, very worrying to me, because the inference was that the two were the same thing, and if the law school was here in University Square, then it was part of the private university'.[91]

The university's own diagram of the University Square development identified the whole area, including the law building, as Melbourne University Private. Many students, graduates and journalists jumped to the natural conclusion that the law school would not only be near the private university, but would be part of it. 'The University of Melbourne wants to move its prestigious law faculty to the new Melbourne University Private', said the *Age*, under the headline 'Uni law faculty may go private'.[92]

The accusation stirred strong feelings about the elitism of the law school, its role as a public institution, and access for students unable to pay high fees. Crommelin found himself being taken to task for privatising the law school. A judge he met at a social function was typical: 'He knew. We'd been privatised. We were part of Melbourne University Private.' When Crommelin tried to disagree, he got nowhere. 'Of course you are, you're moving to University Square', the judge replied. 'He absolutely gave me heaps', Crommelin said. 'He wasn't alone.'[93]

Despite appearances, any potential connection with the private university was withering away. Putting aside the proximity of the new building, the law school's involvement with MU Private was intended to be like that of other faculties, through agreements for provision of courses and teaching. But the plan for a graduate law school in the private university threatened the existing graduate program, an essential part of the law school's operations and a source of vital revenue, as Barry Sheehan, president and chief executive officer of MU Private, found:

Michael Crommelin went various shades of pale at the thought
of it. Didn't absolutely resist it; was prepared to talk about it; but
again, to take the law school, which was a prize of the university,
and hand it as a prize to something that wasn't the university, was
a bit too much to contemplate, I think, and there was a lot of
resistance to that.[94]

Law told the central administration that it was willing to discuss providing postgraduate coursework programs through MU Private, but
nothing eventuated. The law school had a favourable arrangement for
the split of its graduate fees with the central administration, and its
financial advantage lay in running the programs for itself. As Sheehan
himself put it, from the dean's point of view 'there was no reason to
sell his courses off to someone else and have them take a margin'.[95]

The arguments for and against the move were aired at staff and
faculty meetings in August 1998, in the weeks following the launch of
MU Private. The LSS lobbied faculty members and graduates, and its
representatives voted against relocation in the faculty meeting, but
they and their allies among the staff were heavily outnumbered: the
vote in favour of moving was thirty-six to nine. The problems of the
quadrangle and the benefits of the new facilities were overwhelming.
But acceptance of the offer of a new building was on three carefully-
framed conditions. The building would be designed to meet the current and planned requirements of the faculty, the university would
meet the costs of construction, fit-out and relocation, and the building
would be provided on a rent-free basis.[96]

———→•◦←———

It might have seemed, more than forty years after Cowen had begun
concerted lobbying for a new building, that once the university had
made a commitment to construct it the worst was over. But, in the
nature of such projects, turning the concept into reality was, in some
ways, even more difficult. The university did not engage architects for
the University Square project, but signed a development agreement

with a large construction and development group, covering both design and construction. This arrangement had the great advantage for the university of controlling its costs by specifying an overall price. But under the agreement, the developer undertook to design and build a 'base building', without fit-out or the special features (such as lecture theatres) that the law school would need. Fit-out would be covered by a separate agreement, and variations to the base building would be at the university's expense.[97]

This framework had obvious benefits for the university, by helping it manage the cost and duration of the project, but the realities of what would be available gradually squeezed the functional specifications (the lists of necessary spaces and facilities) that were prepared with great effort by the law school. For a start, the site for the law building was a difficult one, partly occupied by the Carlton telephone exchange. Once it became clear that the exchange would not be moved, the building had to be constructed around it, without impinging on the prime space it occupied at the front of the ground floor. The exchange became invisible to most of the building's users, its presence felt only through the windowless section of the ground and mezzanine levels that was effectively cut out of the law school's floor-plan. Its red-brick front wall remained intact, concealed behind the façade of the new building.

University Square, with its streetscape of nineteenth-century terrace houses, was a contentious location for a development on the scale the university proposed. The complete demolition of two terrace houses for other buildings in the square, the partial demolition of many more (leaving their front sections to a depth of two rooms), and the project's association with Melbourne University Private sparked strong opposition, although the development had the backing of the state government, which took control of planning approval. The National Trust, the Carlton Residents Association and the Melbourne City Council joined a chorus of objectors, leading to design changes.[98] The other buildings in the square project were the focus of these objections, but the concept for the law building, too, altered. The acquisition of more land allowed the original twenty-two storeys to be halved, as the building became lower and wider, though still tall.

Beyond all this, the open-handed offer of the vice-chancellor's first approach to the dean had to be qualified, as the project became a reality. 'The blank-cheque nature of it gave rise to a lot of problems,' Crommelin said, 'because at some point the university realised that this was going to cost a heap of money, miles more than originally intended … The university became increasingly concerned about the cost of our specifications, and there were endless, and understandable, efforts, to pare back here, and cut back that, and save money there.'[99]

Crommelin wrote to Gilbert:

You will recall that, immediately prior to the execution of the development agreement, I met with you to express my concern about the process of modification of the base building to achieve a purpose-built law school. I have to say that process has turned out to be seriously flawed.[100]

From the vice-chancellor's point of view, though, Law was getting an outstanding building, a vast improvement on its existing accommodation and better than anything that could have been done with the quadrangle:

Law must fit its current plans to the space available—which is massive in comparison to current usage—and recognise that the building is sited to provide major potential for future expansion southwards in due course.

I would not say that if the space were not so generous—by international as well as national standards. The university is providing a wonderful facility here, in comparison with which what would eventuate on the main campus would be quite sub-standard![101]

Decisions were made at speed and under pressure, as construction proceeded. Penny Swain, Ruth Bird (previously manager of information services at a large law firm, and head of the law library from 1996 to 2000), Bird's successor Nicki McLaurin Smith, information technology manager Peter Jones, the dean and other staff spent much of their working (even waking) time meeting the demands of the design process. The entrance to the Legal Resource Centre, as the library was now called, moved up a level from the preferred location on the second floor. The lecture theatres changed in size and configuration, and lost the windows that were going to provide natural light; they were installed in the outer walls, but were covered by internal panelling, to cut out traffic noise. Despite repeated reassurances about acoustics, academics in the new building found themselves unwilling eavesdroppers on their neighbours' conversations. For all the successes of the project, Crommelin felt the contrast with what might have been: 'Now, frankly, I don't think it's worked out all that badly at all. But it wasn't what we ordered.'[102]

But what the new building provided was so much better than the quadrangle, and so good by any standards, that there could be few complaints about the facilities. One common fear was assuaged as the lifts coped with the large numbers of students. Distance from the main campus turned out not to be a serious difficulty, and more academic departments arrived in the other buildings of University Square. Proximity to Melbourne University Private came to nothing, as the private university failed to meet its creators' expectations and changes in federal higher education policy overtook it. It ultimately occupied only token space in the development built to house it, and in 2005 it merged with the public university from which it arose, after accumulating operating losses of $20 million. The buildings were paid for largely from a bank loan, itself a sign of a new willingness and ability of Australian universities to take on debt.[103]

The accommodation was among the best in the university (and most of the teaching spaces were under Law's direct control, wrested from the central timetabling system), but there was less agreement about the style and atmosphere. On the one hand, the building was certainly impressive. Its polish and sheer size alone counted for something, and there were views in every direction from the upper floors, from Port Phillip Bay to the hills in the distance. But the high finish of the entrance, which looked like a city office building, and the colour scheme in ubiquitous grey were not to everyone's liking. 'It's a bit anonymous, it's a bit cold, it's a bit corporate', one staff member said.[104] The many levels isolated staff offices from most of the students, although the upper floors of the quadrangle, too, had been inaccessible.

Students who experienced both commonly missed the old-world charm of the quadrangle, but enthused about the new facilities and the outlook to the park in University Square. For a few, the move represented wider changes that made them both sad and angry: 'The transition from the old building to the new building seemed to symbolise the changes in the ethos and spirit of the law school: it went from comfortable to cold, from communal to individualistic, from sharing to "getting ahead"'. 'The new building makes you feel like you're in a corporate lawyer factory, which I think is very unfortunate', wrote another. For many others who made the move, the culture of the new building was simpler and more appealing: 'The new building is fantastic—best in the uni', was one graduate's response. And from another: 'We always used to say that there must be a pool on the top deck—it had everything else'.[105]

⸺◈⸺

By 2004, it had been fifteen years since the last comprehensive review of the LLB curriculum. A few year-long compulsory subjects had so far escaped the university-wide shift towards teaching in single semesters, but they, too, would now have to be 'semesterised'. The result was a curriculum review, but one that turned out to be the speediest and least contentious of the LLB's history. Within four months, the curriculum outline was complete and had been approved by the faculty, although details remained to be filled in and piloted through the university's committees. A review committee carefully consulted with the groups of teachers whose subjects would be affected, and its recommendations were mild enough to rouse little opposition. As the law school grew in size, what happened to other people's subjects was less of a general concern than it had once been.

The new course maintained a relatively low proportion of compulsory subjects, which made up about 58 per cent of the law subjects students studied through the course (not including two subjects that were required for admission to practise, although not for the degree). The titles of many of the eight compulsory subjects recalled the long-standing doctrinal core of the law course: Torts, Contracts, Constitutional Law, Trusts, Criminal Law and Procedure, Administrative Law, and Property. They were joined by other compulsory subjects that would not have been familiar to teachers in earlier times, though they implemented in a new form the old intention that students should see law in its social and theoretical context: Dispute Resolution, Legal Theory, and Legal Ethics (which included professional conduct and trust accounts). Public law again became an introductory subject, under the title Principles of Public Law, as it had been when Harrison Moore introduced students to the sources and history of law in Constitutional History and Law I and II in the early years of the twentieth century. The small proportion of students (about 12 per cent) who enrolled for the LLB alone spent half of their first two years on subjects from other faculties, unless they already had university degrees. Most undergraduates enrolled in combined-degree courses.[106]

The life of the new LLB course was unexpectedly cut short by another phase of the university's grand strategy. Under a new vice-chancellor, Glyn Davis, the strategic plan of 2006 set out sweeping aims for research, teaching and interaction with the wider community. One, in particular, fundamentally affected the law school: professional training would overwhelmingly be offered at graduate level. The number of different courses leading to undergraduate degrees would be greatly reduced, and students seeking professional qualifications would study postgraduate courses. The plan referred to alignment with the Bologna Declaration of 1999, which promoted a common framework for European higher education degrees, but its fee-based graduate schools also owed much to American models.[107]

The professional disciplines that would switch to graduate training were not identified in the plan itself, but the law school became an early adopter of the model. Graduate legal education on North American lines had been a favoured idea for many in the faculty at least since the graduate LLB plan of 1969, although it had usually been little more than a faint hope. Now, as the result of a university-wide initiative rather than a law school proposal, it would become a reality. While the existing JD provided a model of a kind, and gave its name to the new course, the curriculum adopted for commencement in 2008 was based on the revised LLB course.[108] Unlike the existing JD, it would be a three-year, semester-based course, and its enrolments would include subsidised students (who would pay the HECS contribution) amongst an increased number of fee-paying places.

The prospect of lower student numbers and higher fee income held out the hope of inroads into the law school's stubborn student–staff ratio, along with the other pedagogical advantages that earlier proponents of graduate training had advocated. Other law schools had graduate courses leading to admission to practise, under varying titles, but the abolition of the LLB was unique in Australia. Like the strategic plan for the university, with its graduate schools and new undergraduate degrees, it showed the intensity of Melbourne's effort not just to do well, but to climb in world rankings.

Crommelin's appointment as dean was regularly renewed, although corporate law specialist Ian Ramsay took on the job in 2002–03, while Crommelin was a visiting professor at Georgetown University. After nearly eighteen years, Crommelin decided to retire as dean at the end of 2007. 'You never know when is the right time, but I think this is as good a time as any', he said.[109] It was yet another of the transitions that closed the law school's first 150 years with a neatness unusual in significant anniversaries. Within the space of a few years, the law school moved for the first time since it opened, took the last intake into its

Bachelor of Laws course, adopted a plan to turn itself into a fully graduate school, and awaited the appointment of a successor to its long-serving dean.

CONCLUSION

In 1857, Richard Sewell told the university's first law students that 'those, whose anxious care has been devoted to the moral and intellectual training of our youth, have proposed to establish that, which, if it be successfully carried out, will, I trust, be, in its highest sense, a School of Law'.[1] His successors have been working out the meanings of a school of law ever since. At the University of Melbourne, it was, above all, a school for lawyers—a training-ground for practitioners, not just the place to gain an understanding of law for its own sake. What was so important in 1857 remained true 150 years later, despite experiments with separate admission exams along the way: the university's successful students entered practice without further examination of their legal knowledge, and the law school was not just an educator, but one of the gatekeepers of the profession.

This characteristic, shared with other Australian universities, was both an advantage and a limitation. It drew students to the law school, especially when, for nearly ninety years until the independent Council of Legal Education course opened in 1962, anyone wanting to become a lawyer in Victoria had to do some or all of the university's course. But it was also a constraint, in that it tied teaching to the admission requirements. The law school always guarded the admission certification that gave it its first success and ensured its survival, and never cut itself loose to teach whatever it thought students should learn, or whatever students themselves wanted to be taught. Its courses were designed primarily for the majority who would go on to legal practice. Even when optional subjects were at their height in the 1970s, the core of the course was the set of doctrinal subjects needed to keep the LLB's endorsement under the admission rules.

Yet, like most other university law schools, Melbourne aimed to be something different from a professional training college—from a trade school, to use the pejorative language of the battles with the Law Institute in the 1930s and 1940s. Partly, the wider aim was ethical (although the Institute, too, had its ideals and professional standards). Sewell included moral training among the concerns of the law school's founders, and for some students, they succeeded. 'Most importantly I learned ethics and moral principles', said one former student from the 1950s. But the distinction from a trade school was made most of all through things that the law school hoped to have in common with the Faculty of Arts (with which it was linked, for much of its history, by shared subjects): exploring elements or foundations, putting ideas in their social and intellectual context, and, as Bailey put it in 1938, 'the development of the law by research'. This was what distinguished a university law course, Bailey said: it 'aimed to develop the intellectual capacity so as to enable graduates to get to the heart of things', not just to give them some knowledge of law.[2]

The result was a course that aimed to teach legal principles rather than legal practice, in the belief that principles would be of most lasting value. Paton explained with typical modesty: 'The most impractical way of teaching is to make a course too practical and technical. All that a law course aims at is to teach the student some background and how to use the legal tools.'[3] Besides, the law school taught an increasing number of students who would not work as legal practitioners. The destinations of its graduates have always been diverse, ever since some of the earliest went on to work in government, in teaching, and in business. Among those who followed were journalists, novelists, historians, actors and even the occasional criminal. By 1965, fully 45 per cent of first-year law students said they did not intend to practise law.[4]

The students took away with them some knowledge of legal doctrine and an analytic habit of thought that would help them to find and apply the law, if that was where their work lay, or would give them abilities that could be used elsewhere. Asked how well the law school prepared them for their working lives, former students answered in many ways. Many were painfully aware of the gulf between academic study and legal practice. 'The Law School was a simply dreadful preparation for working life', said one student from the early 1980s. 'If I had seen an indemnity on the footpath I would not have recognised it', said another, from the 1960s; 'the relationship between what we studied and what real life was about was non-existent'. A more recent graduate was pragmatic: 'it's the name of the place that has helped the most'. Nor did all expect such practical training from the university. Some, echoing Bailey and Paton, said it was not the law school's job.[5]

Later students tended to be less critical, and reactions from all periods varied. For a few, the more theoretical subjects were, as Bailey might have hoped, the ones that prepared them best. 'I found in my fifteen year practice in Legal Aid that philosophy and history are the best guides to understanding criminal law and Magistrates' Court practice', one wrote. Others credited the law school with teaching them a wide range of things they put to use in later life: hard work, self-reliance, organisation, efficiency, motivation, creativity, attention to detail, time-management. 'The Law School gave me tools and some knowledge of the law. A sort of mind training', one said. 'Learned where to look for the answers. How to think through a problem', wrote another.[6]

As numbers grew, fewer mentioned the friendliness and sense of belonging that came to mind for many graduates of the 1940s and 1950s. The entrance quota became a barrier, entrance scores rose, and more described the law school as serious and competitive. Fewer remembered such things as playing cricket in the aisles of the law library, as one student of the early 1960s did—and more thought of the law school as prestigious or elite, like those who were 'challenged and inspired by studying law at a prestigious law school', and who 'valued being around people/part of an elite group with time to think'.[7]

The students' strongest memories were of people and places: the quadrangle and the law library; friends; lecturers who impressed them or whose enthusiasm was infectious. Some remembered their pride or surprise at getting a place in the quota, their enjoyment of university life, or the difficulty of meeting people like themselves in a student body dominated by other backgrounds. Together, the lives of the students and their teachers give the fullest meaning to the idea of a school of law.

ACKNOWLEDGEMENTS

Work on this book was greatly assisted by many people. I owe a particular debt to the staff of the University of Melbourne Archives and the special collections reading room of the Baillieu Library, where much of the research was carried out. My thanks go, too, to the ever-helpful staff of the law school's Legal Resource Centre, the manuscripts and oral history sections of the National Library, James Butler at the Supreme Court Library, Anne Ferguson, for Council of Legal Education minutes, Pauline Reid at the Law Institute of Victoria, and Leanne Dyson at the university's Minutes Office. Michael Crommelin provided that rare thing in the writing of institutional histories, support and assistance without any attempt at editorial control. Others helped in varied ways: Sir Zelman Cowen; Peter Bailey; Mark Derham and Katharine Derham Moore; Samantha Kimpton; Jason White; Vivian Hill; Sylvia Spigelman; Susan Morgan; Rosalind Robson; Harold Ford; Robert Evans; Robin Sharwood; Ruth Campbell; Dick Selleck and Don Garden, who provided information about Edward Jenks and Rosalie Hearn; Bill Rosenberg, and Ann and Wolfgang Rosenberg; Wes Pue; Jenny Morgan; Kaye Nankervis; Cally Martin; Mardi Richardson; Lillian Wong; and Ian Malkin.

The histories of the university by Dick Selleck and by John Poynter and Carolyn Rasmussen have been invaluable guides, without which my work would have been far more difficult. Stuart Macintyre was involved with the project from its inception, commenting in detail and giving expert and unstinting advice throughout. Finally, I particularly thank the many former students and staff who generously provided their recollections of the law school through questionnaires and interviews, giving eloquent testimony of its life and theirs.

ABBREVIATIONS

ADB	*Australian Dictionary of Biography*
CM	Council Minutes, UMA
DP	David Derham Papers, UMA
FLC	Faculty of Law Correspondence 1932–77, UMA
HCP	Law School Historical and Centenary Papers, UMA
LFM	Law Faculty Minutes
LIV	Law Institute of Victoria
LRC	Legal Resource Centre, University of Melbourne
MLS	Melbourne Law School Historical Collection
NAA	National Archives of Australia
NLA	National Library of Australia
PFS	Melbourne Law School Policy Filing System
PROV	Public Record Office Victoria
QR	Questionnaire response(s)
RC	Registrar's Correspondence, UMA
RMC	Registrar's Miscellaneous Correspondence, UMA
SLV	State Library of Victoria
UMA	University of Melbourne Archives
VPLA	*Votes and Proceedings of the Legislative Assembly*
VPLC	*Votes and Proceedings of the Legislative Council*

NOTES

Preface

1 Dean's Report, 1935, RC, 1935/152, p. 2.

2 Bailey, 'Legal Education in the United States', and 'Legal Education. Memorandum of Observations made in the United Kingdom and in North America', DP, box 'Fac. Law 1954–63', file 'Curriculum Committee'.

1   A school of law: 1857–88

1 Levack, 'Law', pp. 565, 568; Holdsworth, *History of English Law*, vol. 12, pp. 83–4; Nicholas, 'Jurisprudence', p. 385.

2 Blackstone, *Commentaries*, vol. 1, pp. 5–6, 33. No degrees: Select Committee on Legal Education, *Report*, p. iv.

3 Lawson, *The Oxford Law School*, pp. 20, 31. 'Anything less': ibid., p. 37. Nicholas, 'Jurisprudence', pp. 394–5.

4 Searby, *History of the University of Cambridge*, vol. 3, pp. 189–90, 193; Brooke, *History of the University of Cambridge*, vol. 4, p. 210. 'These reforms': Brooks and Lobban, 'Apprenticeship or Academy?', pp. 374–5.

5 Baker, 'University College and Legal Education', pp. 2–5; Girvin, 'Nineteenth-Century Reforms', p. 131. 'No Legal Education': Select Committee on Legal Education, *Report*, p. lvi.

6 Holdsworth, *History of English Law*, vol. 12, pp. 26, 54–5, 79; Brooks, *Lawyers, Litigation and English Society*, pp. 149–54, 177.

7 Brooks and Lobban, 'Apprenticeship or Academy?', pp. 360–2, 369–70.

8 Hogan, *The Legal Profession in Ireland*, pp. 104–11.

9 Baker, 'Legal Education in Upper Canada', pp. 50–1.

10 Johnson, *Schooled Lawyers*, p. 24; Stevens, *Law School*, pp. 74–80; Burrage, *Revolution and the Making of the Contemporary Legal Profession*, pp. 284–91; Abel, *American Lawyers*, p. 42.

11 Martin, 'From Apprenticeship to Law School', pp. 113–20; Bennett, *A History of the New South Wales Bar*, pp. 220–1; Bennett, *A History of Solicitors in New South Wales*, pp. 56, 108–12.

12 Mackinolty and Mackinolty (eds), *A Century Down Town*, pp. 19–26, 211, 256; Turney, Bygott and Chippendale, *Australia's First*, pp. 115, 236–8.

13 Mackinolty and Mackinolty (eds), *A Century Down Town*, p. 14; Turney, Bygott and Chippendale, *Australia's First*, p. 123; Martin, 'From Apprenticeship to Law School', p. 127.

14 Bennett, *A History of the New South Wales Bar*, p. 230; Committee of Inquiry into Legal Education, *Legal Education in New South Wales*, p. 13; Act 20 Vict. No. 14 (1857, NSW).

15 Selleck, *The Shop*, pp. 58–65.

16 Selleck, *The Shop*, p. 61; Supreme Court Rules, 15 February 1857, *VPLA*, 1856–57, vol. 1, no. A51.

17 Statistics of the Colony of Victoria, 1866, pt VII, *VPLA*, 2nd sess. 1867, vol. 2, no. 6, p. 6; *Victorian Year Book*, 1973, p. 1104.

18 CM, 5 January 1857; Selleck, *The Shop*, p. 63.

19 CM, 26 January 1857; Barry to Billing, 2 June 1870, and undated reply, RMC, Law School, loose item 1; Professorial Board Minutes, 9 November 1957, item 4.

20 Sewell, *The Speech of R.C. Sewell, Esq.* n.p.; Sewell in court: 'Supreme Court', *Herald*, 20 November 1856; 'Supreme Court', *Herald*, Supplement, 26 November 1856; 'Supreme Court', *Herald*, 22 April 1857; ibid., 23 April 1857.

21 'Election Qualifications Committee', *Herald*, 8 January 1857; ibid., 9 January 1857.

22 Sewell, *Legal Education*, p. 25.

23 Leading article, *Victoria Law Times*, 24 May 1856.

24 Sewell, *Legal Education*, pp. 3–4.

25 Middleton, *Dr Routh*, p. 178.

26 'Supreme Court', *Herald*, 24 August 1857.

27 Sewell, *Legal Education*, ch. 2.

28 'The Law Lectures at the University', *Herald*, 20 June 1857; CM, 15 and 25 May 1857; Sewell to Registrar, 19 May 1857, RMC, Law School, 403.

29 Petition to Chancellor, 17 June 1857, RMC, Law School, 432a; 'Irregularity of the Law Lectures at the University', *Herald*, 1 June 1857; 'The Law Lectures at the University', *Herald*, 13 June 1857. Sewell's resignation and death: Selleck, *The Shop*, p. 62; *Argus*, 9 November 1864, p. 5.

30 CM, 12 March 1857.

31 Chapman lectures, 12 April 1861, 7 March 1864, and 9–11 March 1864, MLS.

32 Irving to Chairman of Council, 29 October 1860, RMC, Law School, loose item 1; CM, 26 November 1860.

33 LFM, 31 July 1882, p. 63; CM, 25 September 1882, p. 260; Senate Minutes, 6 December 1882, p. 307.

34 Supreme Court Rules, 1852, *VPLC*, 1852–53, vol. 1, pp. 611–14; *In re Spensley* (1864) 1 WW&a'B(L) 173, 183.

35 Supreme Court Rules, 1852, *VPLC*, 1852–53, vol. 1, pp. 611–14; 'Domestic Intelligence', *Argus*, 29 October 1853, p. 5; Banco Court Minute Book, PROV, VPRS 5364/P0/1. Henry Lawes, who was admitted in 1859, has previously been identified as the first locally trained barrister.

36 Dean, *A Multitude of Counsellors*, pp. 25–6.

37 Supreme Court Rules, December 1853, *Victoria Government Gazette*, 14 February 1854, pp. 329–32; *In re Spensley* (1864) 1 WW&a'B(L) 173, 184; Holdsworth, *History of English Law*, vol. 12, p. 19.

38 Victoria, *Parliamentary Debates*, Legislative Assembly, 1 November 1861, p. 255; *In re Goslett* (1864) 1 WW&a'B(L) 161; *Ex parte Duffy* (1876) 2 VLR(L) 142; *In re Embling* (1903) 29 VLR 1.

39 Victoria, *Parliamentary Debates*, Legislative Assembly, 1 November 1861, p. 255.

40 ibid., Legislative Assembly, 1 November 1861, p. 255, and 19 December 1861, p. 375; ibid., Legislative Council, 4 February 1862, p. 546.

41 Supreme Court Rules, 23 December 1865, *Victoria Government Gazette*, 19 January 1866, pp. 137–40.

42 'Their own exertions': Royal Commission on Law Reform, *Report*, p. xxxviii. John Rickard, 'Higgins, Henry Bournes', *ADB*, vol. 9, pp. 285–9; 'Amalgamation and the Law Commission', *Summons*, vol. 7, no. 4, June 1898, p. 4; Victoria, *Parliamentary Debates*, Legislative Council, 11 December 1894, p. 894.

43 Forbes, *The Divided Legal Profession*, pp. 79, 83, 118–21.

44 Supreme Court Rules, 23 December 1865, *Victoria Government Gazette*, 19 January 1866, p. 137; Geoffrey Serle, 'Mackey, Sir John Emanuel', *ADB*, vol. 10, pp. 309–11.

45 *Law List* (Melbourne), 1863; *Law List of Australasia*, 1891–92; *Sands & McDougall's Melbourne and Suburban Directory*, 1863 and 1891; Dean, *A Multitude of Counsellors*, pp. 48–9.

46 Supreme Court Rules, 15 February 1857, *VPLA*, 1856–57, vol. 1, no. A51; Supreme Court Rules, October 1863, *VPLA*, 1864, vol. 1, no. A7.

47 Supreme Court Rules, 23 December 1865, *Victoria Government Gazette*, 19 January 1866, pp. 137–40.

48 Supreme Court Rules, 3 December 1872, *Victoria Government Gazette*, 24 January 1873, pp. 129–33; Admission of Barristers Files, PROV, VPRS 1356/P0/2, no. 153.

49 Committee of Inquiry into Legal Education, *Legal Education in New South Wales*, p. 11; Stevens, *Law School*, p. 174; Committee on Legal Education, *Report*, pp. 5–28; Law Society of England and Wales, Ways to Qualify as a Solicitor; College of Law, History of the College.

50 Castles, Ligertwood and Kelly (eds), *Law on North Terrace*, p. 11.

51 Brooks and Lobban, 'Apprenticeship or Academy?', pp. 360–2; Lawson, *The Oxford Law School*, pp. 21–2.

52 Barry's initiative: Selleck, *The Shop*, p. 62. This account of Chapman's career is based on Spiller, *The Chapman Legal Family*.

53 'Mr. Chapman', *Herald*, 7 January 1858.

54 Spiller, *The Chapman Legal Family*, p. 241.

55 University of Melbourne, *Calendar*, 1861–62, p. cliv; *Milirrpum v. Nabalco Pty Ltd* (1971) 17 FLR 141.

56 CM, 28 December 1857.

57 Forde, *The Story of the Bar of Victoria*, p. 227; Gibbney and Smith, *A Biographical Register*, vol. 1, p. 58; 'Death of Judge Billing', *Australasian*, supplement, 24 June 1882, p. 7. Bar tradition: Forde, *The Story of the Bar of Victoria*, pp. 231–2. De Serville, *Pounds and Pedigrees*, p. 275; Golding, *Sylliott-Hill*; presentation cup with lid, silver, Powerhouse Museum, Sydney, 85/450.

58 A. Thomson Zain'uddin, 'Stephen, James Wilberforce', *ADB*, vol. 6, pp. 188–90; Brownless to Chancellor, 24 February 1860, RMC, Law School, loose item 1. Student protest: *Argus*, 20 March 1860, p. 5.

59 Webb to Council, 21 February 1862, RMC, Law School, loose item 1; CM, 3 February and 19 February 1862.

60 Leading article, *Argus*, 18 February 1862; Serle, *The Golden Age*, p. 312; 'The Law Lectureship at the University', *Argus*, 27 February 1862; Robert Miller, 'Webb, George Henry Frederick', *ADB*, vol. 6, p. 372.

61 Selleck, *The Shop*, pp. 62–3.

62 Crozier, 'Political Legacies', pp. 9–10.

63 Brogue: Robertson, 'The University of Melbourne', p. 145. J. A. La Nauze, 'Hearn, William Edward', *ADB*, vol. 4, pp. 370–2.

64 Hearn on Ireland: Selleck, *The Shop*, p. 38. Classes: RC, 1875/21.

65 Hearn as examiner and lecturer for Chapman: Selleck, *The Shop*, p. 63; Chapman lectures, MLS. Wig and lectures: Selleck, *The Shop*, pp. 111, 245. Higgins, Draft autobiography, NLA, MS 1057/3, p. 59. 'Green oases': 'Legal Echoes', *Melbourne University Review*, vol. 4, no. 1, May 1888, p. 30.

66 Arts student's recollection: Robertson, 'The University of Melbourne', pp. 144–5. Still remembered: 'LLB', 'The Inadequacy of the Law School', p. 32.

67 Moore, 'Selling Plutology', p. 63; Dicey, *Introduction to the Study of the Law of the Constitution*, p. vi. 'Considerable respect': La Nauze, *Political Economy in Australia*, p. 47. Moore, 'A Biographical Sketch of William Edward Hearn', pp. 27–8.

68 'Our mission': Hearn, *National Loyalty*, quoted in Selleck, *The Shop*, p. 303. 'Unwritten traditions': Hearn, *The Government of England*, p. 1.

69 Hearn, *The Government of England*, p. 17.

70 Selleck, *The Shop*, pp. 114–15, 226–37; 'Banking Institutions', *Herald*, 26 September 1885, p. 1; F. M. Dunn, 'Clarke, William', *ADB*, vol. 3, pp. 419–20.

71 Goodman, *The Church in Victoria*, p. 188.

72 Alexander Sutherland, 'William Edward Hearn', *Argus*, 28 April 1888, p. 5.

73 J. A. La Nauze, 'Hearn, William Edward', *ADB*, vol. 4, p. 371; Serle, 'The Victorian Legislative Council', p. 137; Hearn, *The Government of England*, pp. 582–93.

74 Hearn as barrister: Hearn Papers, UMA, group 4; 'Elections Qualifications Committee', *Herald*, 1 November 1861; 'Topics of the Day', *Herald*, 2 September 1873 and 29 November 1873. The Land Act: Selleck, *The Shop*, pp. 84–5; Ireland, 'The Victorian Land Act of 1862 Revisited', pp. 138–9.

75 Consolidation: 'The Legislative Council and Consolidation of Laws', *Herald*, 23 October 1879, p. 2. General substantive law: Hearn, *The Theory of Legal Rights and Duties*, p. 379, quoted in Clayton, 'The Hearn Code', p. 40.

76 This account is based on Clayton, 'The Hearn Code'.

77 Selleck, *The Shop*, p. 85; Inquest on Rosalie Hearn, 13 June 1877, PROV, VPRS 24/P0/367, 1877/183. A hard life: Alexander Sutherland, 'William Edward Hearn', *Argus*, 28 April 1888, p. 5.

78 Selleck, *The Shop*, p. 84.

79 Selleck, *The Shop*, pp. 63, 124–5.

80 CM, 25 May 1857; Selleck, *The Shop*, p. 124; University of Melbourne, *Calendar*, 1859–60, p. 73.

81 Mackay to Council, 26 May 1873, RMC, Law School, 403.

82 Hearn to Barry, 14 March 1873, RMC, Law, 200a.

83 ibid.

84 CM, 28 July 1873, p. 78, and 25 August 1873, p. 80.

85 Selleck, *The Shop*, p. 128; Registrar to professors, 2 December 1876, RC, 1876/35.

86 Castieau: Finnane (ed.), *The Difficulties of My Position*, p. 238. Brownless to Agent-General, 15 October 1888, CM, 15 October 1888, p. 188.

87 Statute: CM, 30 June 1873, p. 66. Selleck, *The Shop*, p. 125.

88 Bartrop: Admission of Barristers Files, PROV, VPRS 1356/P0/2, no. 121; Gibbney and Smith, *A Biographical Register*, vol. 1, p. 38. Bernard Barrett, 'FitzGibbon, Edmund Gerald', *ADB*, vol. 4, pp. 181–2.

89 Enrolment figures are derived from *Statistics of the Colony of Victoria* and *Statistical Register of Victoria*, VPLA. Queensland: Thomis, *A Place of Light and Learning*, pp. 130–2.

90 Rosemary Howard Gill, 'Byrnes, Thomas Joseph', *ADB*, vol. 7, pp. 517–19; W. Ross Johnston and D. J. Murphy, 'Ryan, Thomas Joseph', *ADB*, vol. 11, pp. 496–500.

91 Lecture times: CM, 12 March 1857. 'More central location': CM, 15 May 1857.

92 Lectures in chambers: Dobson to Registrar, 6 October 1875, RC, 1875/21; Dobson to Registrar, 21 March 1876, 19 June 1876 and 26 August 1876, RC, 1876/26. CM, 5 May 1884, p. 48; Hearn to Council, 31 March 1885, RC, 1885/25.

93 'Unity of the University': CM, 9 April 1884, p. 35. 'Disastrous effect': Elkington and Hansford to Council, 5 March 1894, RC, 1894/21.

94 'Our sympathy': *Melbourne University Review*, vol. 1, no. 1, July 1884, p. 3.
'Disgraceful condition': Gregory to Registrar, 9 May 1889, RC, 1889/27, part 1.
Gregory to Registrar, 16 December 1889, RC, 1889/27, part 6; CM, 3 February
1890, p. 5.

95 'The atmosphere': petition of property students, 7 April 1893, RC, 1893/14.
'The University buildings': Pearson to Gillies, 3 July 1886, PROV, VPRS 1163/
P0/176, file 89/283.

96 'Students to be informed': CM, 6 May 1889, p. 284. Davis and others to
Registrar, April 1889, RC, 1889/26; CM, 14 May 1888, p. 80, and 16 July 1888,
p. 143; Robertson and others to Council, 4 May 1888, RC, 1888/27.

97 CM, 1 May 1893, p. 39; petition of law students, January 1894, RC, 1894/21;
Moore to Council, 27 February 1894, RC, 1894/21.

98 'Small and ill-ventilated': Harrison Moore, Memorandum for Attorney-General,
7 November 1919, RC, 1924/304. 'Clippings from the Courts', *Alma Mater*,
vol. 3, no. 1, April 1898, p. 24; Dean's Report, 1913, RC, 1913/72. 'Unsatisfactory
character': Estimates re Numbers of Students and Needs of Various Departments:
Law, RC, 1919/369.

99 Harrison Moore to Attorney-General, 7 November 1919, RC, 1924/304.

100 Foster to Registrar, 31 July 1924, RC, 1924/304.

101 Registrar to Foster, 12 August 1924, RC, 1924/304.

2   Cinderella: 1889–1927

1   CM, 15 October 1888, p. 190.

2   F. C. Hutley, 'Cobbett, William Pitt', *ADB*, vol. 8, pp. 40–1; Edgeloe, 'The Adelaide
Law School', p. 8; Michael Roe, 'Brown, William Jethro', *ADB*, vol. 7, pp. 447–8.

3   Edgeloe, 'The Adelaide Law School', pp. 4, 7.

4   Wolfgang Friedmann had just turned forty when he was appointed in 1947, and
David Derham, appointed in 1951, had degrees from Melbourne. Hearn had
Irish, not English, degrees, but he was never a professor of law.

5   Selleck, *The Shop*, pp. 197, 285.

6   Tony Honoré, 'Jenks, Edward', *Oxford Dictionary of National Biography*, <www.
oxforddnb.com/view/article/34179> (viewed 25 May 2007); Campbell,
A History of the Melbourne Law School, pp. 75–6; CM, 11 March 1889, p. 250.

7   Selleck, *The Shop*, pp. 331–4.

8   Jenks, *Legal Fore-Words*, p. 1.

9   Jenks, *Legal Fore-Words*, p. 4.

10 Jenks, *The Government of Victoria*, p. v.

11 Selleck, 'Empires and Empiricism', p. 17.

12 Selleck, *The Shop*, pp. 334–42; à Beckett to Council, 22 July 1889, RC, 1892/19.

13 Jenks to Registrar, 16 July 1889, RC, 1892/19. 'Superior knowledge': à Beckett to Jenks, 17 July 1889, and draft, 16 July 1889, RC, 1892/19.

14 Selleck, *The Shop*, pp. 432–5; CM, 22 July 1889, p. 366.

15 Selleck, *The Shop*, p. 340.

16 'Misled': 'International Law and the University Senate', *Argus*, 20 May 1890, p. 9. Jenks, *Legal Fore-Words*, p. 8; LFM, 22 August 1889, p. 101; Jenks to Warden of the Senate, 5 May 1890, RC, 1890/25.

17 *Argus*, 9 May 1890, p. 5.

18 'University of Melbourne', *Argus*, 21 May 1890, p. 9.

19 Shearer, 'The Teaching of International Law', pp. 62–9; Zines, 'The Growth of Australian Nationhood', pp. 7–8.

20 CM, 20 November 1890, p. 177. Correspondence between Jenks, McInerney and the Registrar is in RC, 1891/28, parts 1 and 2, and University of Melbourne, Council Papers, Appointment of Professors, vol. 3: Jenks, Moore, pp. 311–71.

21 'Arts standpoint': Jenks to Warden of the Senate, 5 May 1890, RC, 1890/25. LFM, 22 August 1889, p. 101; Jenks to Council, 24 May 1890, RC, 1890/25.

22 LFM, 22 October 1889, p. 105; CM, 17 December 1890, p. 188.

23 CM, 17 December 1890, p. 189; Jenks to Chancellor, 30 March 1891, RC, 1891/28, part 1.

24 Selleck, *The Shop*, pp. 306, 339–40, 347, 351; Jenks to Registrar, 25 September 1891, and CM, 5 October 1891, both in RC, 1891/28, part 1. 'All-round capacity': Jenks to Oscar Browning, 5 February 1890, Browning papers, Cambridge University Library.

25 Selleck, *The Shop*, pp. 347, 744.

26 Tony Honoré, 'Jenks, Edward', *Oxford Dictionary of National Biography*, <www.oxforddnb.com/view/article/34179> (viewed 25 May 2007).

27 'The Melbourne Law Professorship', *Argus*, 25 April 1892; Clarke to Premier, telegram, 9 March 1892; Brownless to Premier, 15 March 1892; Munro to Premier, telegram, 21 April 1892 (all in PROV, VPRS 1163/P0/293, file 92/1068). Dossier: Council Papers, Appointment of Professors, vol. 3: Jenks, Moore, pp. 311–71.

28 Council Papers, Appointment of Professors, vol. 3: Jenks, Moore.

29 Agent-General: Munro to Chancellor, 27 May 1892, RC, 1892/21. 'Of all the men': application from Moore, Council Papers, Appointment of Professors, vol. 3: Jenks, Moore. Change Jenks' mind: 'Anecdotal Photographs', *Table Talk*, 5 February 1892, p. 5.

30 Interview with Sir Kenneth Bailey, 1971–72, NLA, 1:1/33.

31 Interview with Sir Kenneth Bailey, 1971–72, NLA, 1:1/30–1.

32 Elizabeth Barrow, 'Dobson, Frank Stanley', *ADB*, vol. 4, pp. 77–8.

33 H. A. Finlay, 'Rogers, John Warrington', *ADB*, vol. 6, pp. 53–4; Selleck, *The Shop*, p. 155.

34 Jenny Cook and B. Keon-Cohen, 'Cussen, Sir Leo Finn Bernard', *ADB*, vol. 8, pp. 184–5.

35 Gregory to Registrar, 9 October 1873, RC, 1873/14. 'Eagle eye': Dobson to Madden, 17 January 1893, RC, 1893/14.

36 'This conduct': 'Topics of the Month', *Melbourne University Review*, vol. 1, no. 3, September 1884, p. 35. Minutes of Professorial Board, 8, 17 and 26 September 1884, vol. 4, pp. 317–21.

37 Alice Gregory to Chancellor, 23 April 1888, and doctor's certificate from James Teague, both in RC, 1888/45.

38 Kew Asylum, Nominal Register of Patients, PROV, VPRS 7425/P1; Kew Asylum, Case Books of Male Patients, PROV, VPRS 7398/P1/14, pp. 581–2.

39 'I am not mad', *Herald*, 31 August 1899, p. 3.

40 Kew Asylum, Case Books of Male Patients, PROV, VPRS 7398/P1/15, p. 498; *In re Gregory* (1899) 25 VLR 539; 'I am not mad', *Herald*, 4 September 1899, p. 4, 5 September 1899, pp. 3–4, and 11 September 1899, p. 2.

41 Shepherd and others to Registrar, 21 January 1889, RC, 1889/26; CM, 4 February 1889, p. 243.

42 Royal Commission on the University of Melbourne, *Minutes of Evidence*, p. 8.

43 Selleck, *The Shop*, p. 596.

44 University of Melbourne, *Calendar*, 1904, p. 118; University of Melbourne, *Calendar*, 1921, p. 68.

45 LFM, 22 November 1920, p. 469.

46 Lawson, *The Oxford Law School*, p. 119. 'Prodigy': Nicholas, 'Jurisprudence', p. 389.

47 LFM, 1 September 1922, p. 512, and 30 November 1922, p. 524.

48 RC, 1931/248; A. G. L. Shaw, 'Behan, Sir John Clifford Valentine', *ADB*, vol. 7, pp. 247–8.

49 Selleck, *The Shop*, pp. 443–4; Anderson and Vervoorn, *Access to Privilege*, p. 67.

50 Information supplied by Faculty of Law to United States Commissioner of Education, 3 June 1891, RC, 1891/28, part 1; Vamplew, *Australians: Historical Statistics*, p. 160; Selleck, *The Shop*, pp. 241, 547; Martin, *Robert Menzies*, vol. 1, p. 19.

51 Susan Blackburn Abeyasekere, 'Blackburn, Maurice McCrae', *ADB*, vol. 7, pp. 310–12.

52 Statement Prepared by the Council of the University for the Information of Members of Parliament, October 1919, RC, 1919/241, pp. 9–11.

53 Robertson and others to Council, 4 May 1888, RC, 1888/27.

54 Ruth Campbell and J. Barton Hack, 'Greig, Grata Flos Matilda', *ADB*, vol. 9, pp. 101–2; Ruth Campbell and Margaret Morgen, 'Brennan, Anna Teresa', *ADB*, vol. 7, p. 395.

55 'Alarming feature': 1892 law student quoted in Campbell, *The Melbourne Law School*, p. 25. Notice of meeting and minutes, 22 April 1897, Law Students' Society Minute Book, vol. 1, Supreme Court Library.

56 Mossman, *The First Women Lawyers*, pp. 40–54; Legal Profession Practice Act 1891 (Vic.), s. 11; Rules for Admission of Barristers and Solicitors, *Victoria Government Gazette*, 16 December 1892, p. 4808; Acts Interpretation Act 1890 (Vic.), s. 5.

57 Joan M. O'Brien, 'Evans, Ada Emily', *ADB*, vol. 8, pp. 443–4.

58 Wright, *A People's Counsel*, p. 134.

59 Greig, 'Law as a Profession for Women'; Geoffrey Serle, 'Mackey, Sir John Emanuel', *ADB*, vol. 10, pp. 309–11; Victoria, *Parliamentary Debates*, Legislative Council, 20 December 1894, p. 1252, and Legislative Assembly, 5 March 1903, pp. 2820–2; Mossman, *The First Women Lawyers*, pp. 13–14.

60 'Equity', 'Women and the Law Students' Society', p. 144.

61 'Quo Vadit', 'Women of the World', pp. 94–5; Mossman, *The First Women Lawyers*, pp. 10–13, 54–65.

62 'Quo Vadit', 'Women of the World', p. 95; Campbell, *The Melbourne Law School*, p. 30; Mathews, 'The Changing Profile of Women in the Law', p. 635.

63 Greig to John Latham, 4 November 1918, NLA, MS 1009/1/542–3.

64 Greig, Brennan, Smith, Rosanove, Hain, Harford and Hoy: *ADB*, vols 7, 9, 14, 16.

65 Norma Marshall, 'Maxwell, George Arnot', *ADB*, vol. 10, p. 459.

66 Jason White, email to author, 23 November 2006; LFM, 2 May 1889, p. 94; Charles Lloyd Purvis Chase, student record card, Student Administration Records, UMA.

67 Blackshield, Coper and Williams (eds), *Oxford Companion to the High Court of Australia*, pp. 2, 687–8; Tregent, Dudley Ackerley, First AIF Personnel Dossiers, 1914–1920, NAA, B2455.

68 Derham to N. Penn, 14 September 1962, DP, General Correspondence 1951–64, box 3, file 'P'.

69 LFM, 16 May 1941, p. 459; Ford to von Bibra, 15 April 1971, Harold Ford Papers; Lawrence McCredie, telephone interview, 23 March 2007.

70 Sewell, *Legal Education*, p. 31; 'The Law Lectures at the University', *Herald*, 13 June 1857; 'Sir Redmond Barry's Address to the Forensic Debating Society', *Argus*, 16 October 1860, p. 5.

71 *Argus*, 2 September 1863, p. 5, 26 September 1863, p. 5, 30 June 1864, p. 5, 21 July 1871, p. 5, and 1 March 1873, p. 5.

72 *Argus*, 28 September 1878, p. 7; 'Cricket', *Herald*, 17 March 1880; 'Meetings', *Herald*, 23 May 1884; 'Prima Facie', 'Victorian Law Clerks', *Herald*, 12 August 1889; 'Victorian United Law Clerks' Society', *Herald*, 25 November 1889, p. 4.

73 Minutes of meeting 25 May 1893, Law Students' Society Minute Book, vol. 1, Supreme Court Library.

74 Articled Clerks' Law Debating Society, Third Annual Report, 1889–90, LRC.

75 *Summons*, vol. 2, no. 1, September 1892, p. 3; Report of the Committee, 1894, Law Students' Society Minute Book, vol. 1, Supreme Court Library.

76 'Junior Members': notice of meeting 24 April 1901, Law Students' Society Minute Book, vol. 1, Supreme Court Library. 'Swamped out': 'Law Students' Society', *Summons*, vol. 10, no. 4, June 1901, p. 7.

77 Minutes of meeting 18 July 1901, Law Students' Society Minute Book, vol. 1, Supreme Court Library; 'Law Students' Society', *Alma Mater*, vol. 6, no. 7, July 1901, p. 222.

78 CM, 25 May 1857; Sewell, *Legal Education*, pp. 30–1; Dean's Report, 1890, RC, 1890/3.

79 Chorley, 'Edward Jenks', p. 114.

80 Brown, 'The American Law School', pp. 69, 78.

81 'Learn from America': Royal Commission on the University of Melbourne, *Minutes of Evidence*, p. 5. Moore, 'Legal Education in the United States', pp. 207–8.

82 Moore, 'Legal Education in the United States', pp. 208–9.

83 Maturity and contract: Moore, 'Legal Education in the United States', pp. 209–10. Castles and Harris, *Lawmakers and Wayward Whigs*, pp. 339–40.

84 Moore, 'Legal Education in the United States', pp. 210–11.

85 Dean's Report, 1911–12, RC, 1912/27.

86 Dean's Report, 1913, RC, 1913/72.

87 'Law School—Present Requirements', LFM, 15 May 1919, p. 430.

88 Moore to Registrar, 25 November 1919, RC, 1919/151; LFM, 24 November 1919, p. 441.

89 'Ballarat Law Students and the University', *Argus*, 20 July 1861; Hill, 'Henry Isaac Crawcour'.

90 CM, 1 March 1920, p. 404; Dean's Report 1928, RC, 1928/209, p. 4; LFM, 27 February 1920, pp. 450–1; Paton to Stewart F. Brown, 10 May 1948, HCP, box 3, UM 420/43.

91 LFM, 2 November 1922, pp. 519–22, and 4 December 1962, pp. 178–82.

92 Jenks, *Outline of a Suggested Course*.

93 'Can not teach it': C.J.Z. Woinarski to Dean, 7 September 1906, RC, 1905/30. Moore to Registrar, 14 September 1906, RC, 1905/30. 'No scope': Royal Commission on the University of Melbourne, *Minutes of Evidence*, p. 321.

94 Dean's Report, 1907, RC, 1907/11; Moore to Registrar, 23 May 1919, RC, 1919/196; Moore to Registrar, 25 November 1919, RC, 1919/151; Appointment of Miss E. May, RC, 1924/305.

95 LFM, 26 April 1922, p. 501; *In re Gellatly* [1923] VLR 248.

96 LFM, 27 October 1927, p. 109; Dean's Report, 1929, RC, 1929/195, p. 3.

97 'Law Students and University Prizes', *Summons*, vol. 4, no. 4, June 1895, p. 1.

98 Forbes, *The Divided Legal Profession*, p. 112.

99 'Topics of the Month', *Melbourne University Review*, vol. 2, no. 3, October 1885, p. 102.

100 'Degeneration and confusion': 'Amalgamation of the Legal Profession', *Summons*, vol. 1, no. 1, September 1891, p. 2. CM, 10 August 1891, p. 303; Articled Law Clerks' Society, Fourth Annual Report, 1890–91, p. 8, LRC; Articled Law Clerks' Society, Report and Balance Sheet, 1891, p. 5, LRC.

101 LFM, 18 July 1895, p. 195.

102 CM, 13 August 1894, p. 206; Legal Profession Practice Act 1895 (Vic.).

103 LFM, 18 July 1895, pp. 199–200. The minute-taker (who was not Moore) wrongly substituted 'BA' for 'LLB', and entered the wrong date in places.

104 LFM, 18 July 1895, pp. 193–4, 200.

105 LFM, 18 July 1895, pp. 196, 199–200, 12 September 1895, pp. 202–3, and 19 September 1895, pp. 204–5; CM, 28 October 1895, pp. 403–6.

106 'Final Examinations', *Summons*, vol. 1, no. 3, March 1892, p. 1.

107 'Articled Law Clerks' Society', *Quadrangle*, vol. 1, no. 1, May 1892, p. 10.

108 'The August "Final"', *Summons*, vol. 10, no. 2, December 1900, pp. 6–7; extracts from minutes of Council of Judges, 1892 and 1900, DP, box 'Law School Expansion' etc., file 'Legal Education'. Latham's comment: Latham to Derham, 19 August 1957, DP, General Correspondence 1951–64, box 2, file 'L'.

109 *In re Kerin* (1892) 18 VLR 215.

110 Legal Profession Practice Act 1895 (Vic.), s. 2; Legal Practitioners Reciprocity Act 1903 (Vic.), ss. 2, 6; Victoria, *Parliamentary Debates*, Legislative Assembly, 18 December 1903, pp. 2120–1 (Fink); Royal Commission on the University of Melbourne, *Final Report*, p. 60.

111 Rules of the Council of Legal Education, 16 February 1905, *Victorian Statutes of Utility*, 1904–05; Royal Commission on the University of Melbourne, *Final Report*, p. 60. Moore's comment: Dean's Report, 1905, RC, 1906/17.

112 Weisbrot, *Australian Lawyers*, pp. 63, 141–2.

113 'Three celebrated works': Winterton, 'Introduction', p. v. *Commonwealth Law Reports* database search, and Smyth, 'Other Than "Accepted Sources of Law"', p. 48.

114 LFM, 3 May 1900, pp. 277–9.

115 Dean's Report, 1907, RC, 1907/11.

116 LFM, 30 August 1917, pp. 408–9.

117 'Principles involved': Modern Political Institutions printed notes, Moore Papers, UMA, 4/2/40. Moore's comments: Report by Professor Moore, March 1925, RC, 1927/368.

118 Dean's Report, 1907, RC, 1907/11.

119 Dean's Report, 1904, and Moore to Registrar, 4 November 1904, both in RC, 1904/31.

120 Dean's Report, 1946, RC, 1946/288, p. 16; Dean's Report, 1917, RC, 1917/63; Dean's Report, 1915, RC, 1915/56.

121 'Join together': 'Enlist in the Sportsmen's Thousand', poster, Troedel collection, State Library of Victoria, H2001.34/1. Greig to Latham, 6 November 1918, NLA, MS 1009/1/544.

122 Moore to Vice-Chancellor, 1 July 1919, RC, 1919/199. CM, 1 September 1919, p. 322.

123 Priestley, *Diary of a Vice-Chancellor*, pp. 412–13.

124 'Brushing up': Moore to Registrar, 23 May 1919, RC, 1919/196. CM, 16 June 1919, p. 301; Dean's Report, 1919, RC, 1919/82.

125 Dean's Report 1919, RC, 1919/82; Martin, *Robert Menzies*, vol. 1, pp. 27–8.

126 Dean's Report, 1946, RC, 1946/288, p. 16; University deputation to the Premier, 19 September 1922, PROV, VPRS 1163/P0/540, file 23/3224.

127 Hearn to Chancellor, 20 July 1878, RC, 1878/9.

128 CM, 1 July 1912, and Summary of Request for Assistance, 1919, both in RC, 1919/369; Moore to Registrar, 14 April 1927, RC, 1927/194A.

129 Jenks to Acting Registrar, 26 March 1890, RC, 1890/39, part 2; University Library Committee Minutes, 4 October 1892, p. 26A. Librarian's comments: Bromby, 'The University Library', p. 65. Dean's Report, 1947, RC, 1947/264, p. 19.

130 1919 allotment: 'Law School—Present Requirements', LFM, 15 May 1919, p. 430. History books: University Library Committee Minutes, 7 May 1914, p. 156C. Fees: University of Melbourne, *Calendar*, 1919, pp. 95, 98. Dean's Report, 1913, RC, 1913/72; Ulrich to Registrar, 10 September 1919, RC, 1919/152; 'University's Fight against Money Shortage', *Herald*, 28 October 1926, p. 6; information from Dr Caitlin Stone, LRC.

131 Information from Dr Caitlin Stone, LRC; Dean's Report, 1929, RC, 1929/195, pp. 1–2. Paton: Dean's Report, 1946, RC, 1946/288, p. 18.

132 University Library Committee Minutes, 25 November 1898, p. 45, and 26 September 1905, p. 82. 'Much inconvenience': Dean's Report, 1913, RC, 1913/72.

133 LFM, 6 December 1918, p. 421. 'Impossible to provide': LFM, 8 April 1920, p. 455. Dean's Report, 1930, RC, 1930/179, p. 2.

134 'Law School—Present Requirements', LFM, 15 May 1919, p. 430.

135 Ulrich to Barrett, 26 April 1919, RC, 1919/369.

136 Acting Dean's Report, 1922–23, RC, 1923/119.

137 Dean's Report, 1921–22, RC, 1922/115.

138 LFM, 24 June 1927, p. 104; CM, 25 July 1927, p. 262; Annual Report, 1925–26, University of Melbourne, *Calendar*, 1927, p. 949; Summary of the Reasons urged by Professor Moore, RC, 1919/369.

139 Interview with Professor Geoffrey Sawer, 1971–72, NLA, 1:1/28–9.

140 Mary Hiscock, interview, 5 September 2006.

141 Jenks to Registrar, 18 July 1889, RC, 1889/27, part 3; Jenks to Acting Registrar, 26 March 1890, RC, 1890/39, part 2.

142 Royal Commission on the University of Melbourne, *Final Report*, pp. 104, 165–6; Bailey to Registrar, 10 December 1935, RC, 1935/268.

143 Accountant to Russell Grimwade, 15 February 1940, RC, 1940/385.

144 'LLB', 'The Inadequacy of the Law School', p. 43.

145 Cowen to John R. Bishop, 5 March 1957, FLC, box 1, file 'Law School: Future Developments'.

146 Jenks, *The History of the Doctrine of Consideration*, dedication.

147 Dean's Report, 1915, RC, 1915/56; Fitzhardinge, *The Little Digger*, p. 54; Winterton, 'Introduction', pp. xxv–vi, xxix.

148 Fitzhardinge, *The Little Digger*, p. 304; Winterton, 'Introduction', p. xxv; opinion on reservation of bills, 28 March 1921, VPRS 7571/P1/15.

149 Interview with Sir Kenneth Bailey, 1971–72, NLA, 2:1/2.

150 Selleck, *The Shop*, p. 621.

3 Liberal and cultured: 1928–45

1 'Law School—Present Requirements', LFM, 15 May 1919, p. 430.

2 Cussen Committee Report, RC, 1927/368; Dean's Report, 1946, RC, 1946/288, p. 16.

3 Cussen Committee Report, RC, 1927/368; 'Law School—Present Requirements', LFM, 15 May 1919, p. 431.

4 Interview with Sir Kenneth Bailey, 1971–72, NLA, 1:1/3–6.

5 Interview with Sir Kenneth Bailey, 1971–72, NLA, 1:1/6; Parnaby, *Queen's College*, p. 155. Told to enrol downstairs: Interview with Yseult Bailey, 1973, NLA, 1:1/5. 'Sound': Report of Chair of Jurisprudence Committee, CM, 5 December 1927, p. 349.

6 Jack Richardson (1938–42), QR; Interview with Professor Geoffrey Sawer, 1971–72, NLA, 1:1/22; James Lemaire (1937–40), QR.

7 Geoffrey Lindell, conversation with author; Bailey to Priestley, 20 April 1938, RC, 1938/358.

8   'Law was best studied': Interview with Sir Kenneth Bailey, 1971–72, NLA,
     1:1/9. 'Most burdensome': notice of meeting and minutes, 2 December 1897,
     Law Students' Society Minute Book, vol. 1, Supreme Court Library. Victoria,
     Parliamentary Debates, Legislative Council, 11 December 1894, pp. 894, 899–901;
     Legal Profession Practice Act 1895 (Vic.), s. 7.

9   Supreme Court Library Committee Minutes, 8 May 1930, Supreme Court
     Library.

10   'My first Chair': Interview with Sir Kenneth Bailey, 1971–72, NLA, 1:1/8. Bailey
     to Chancellor, 6 June 1930, RC, 1930/329; Chancellor to Bailey, 26 June 1930,
     RC, 1931/248; Cowen to Vice-Chancellor, 25 October 1954, RC, 1955/655.

11   Chair of Jurisprudence Committee Report, 18 December 1930, RC, 1931/248.

12   Cowen, 'Professor Sir George Whitecross Paton', p. 1.

13   LFM, 18 September 1931, p. 194, and 20 May 1932, pp. 211–12; Minute of
     Informal Discussions, 15 October 1931, FLC, box 1, file 'Legal Education'.

14   'Teach the technical rules': University Curriculum in Law: Draft Report, LFM,
     21 April 1939, p. 358. 'We systematized': Interview with Sir Kenneth Bailey,
     1971–72, NLA, 1:1/9. 'Medium of education': Some Explanatory Notes on
     Proposed Changes in the Law Course, September 1932, FLC, box 1, file 'Legal
     Education'. LFM, 7 June 1940, p. 420.

15   'Professor Bailey on Legal Education', *Farrago*, 8 May 1928, p. 1.

16   'More into line': 'The University Law Course', p. 73. Dean's Report, 1928, RC,
     1928/209, p. 3. Anonymous student: 'LLB', 'The Inadequacy of the Law School',
     p. 32.

17   LFM, 4 November 1932, p. 225, 25 May 1934, p. 247, and 16 May 1941, p. 460.

18   LFM, 16 September 1932, pp. 220–1; Minute of Informal Discussions, 15
     October 1931, FLC, box 1, file 'Legal Education'.

19   LFM, 25 May 1934, pp. 250–1, and 22 July 1935, p. 271.

20   'Articles were reduced': 'Service in Articles', *Law Institute Journal*, vol. 10, no. 11,
     November 1936, p. 171. 'Four-fifths': 'Service in Articles', *Law Institute Journal*,
     vol. 10, no. 6, June 1936, p. 83.

21   McQueen, 'Together We Fall', p. 324.

22   'Right education': Memorandum from Council of Law Institute to Council
     of Legal Education, September 1936, FLC, box 1, file 'Legal Education'.
     Eggleston: LFM, 21 April 1939, p. 364. Latham to Lowe, 31 July 1944, NLA, MS
     1009/12/947.

23   'Candidates are entering', and Institute's figures: Gubbins to G. Forrest Davies,
     February 1938, draft, LIV records, UMA, first accession, 10/3/1. Dean's Report,
     1935, RC, 1935/152, p. 1; McQueen, 'Together We Fall', p. 322; Stevens, *Law
     School*, pp. 177–80; Abel, *American Lawyers*, pp. 48–62.

24 Ford: Maclean, 'And All the Time He was Learning from Us', p. 76. Russell
    Boughton to Cally Martin, 13 April 2006, MLS; Interview with Professor
    Geoffrey Sawer, 1971–72, NLA, 1:1/32. Wages: 'The Prospect Before Us', *De
    Minimis*, April 1953, p. 2; Vamplew, *Australians: Historical Statistics*, p. 155.

25 'Use is eagerly made': Law Students' Society, 'Report on Legal Education', p. 103.
    Derham, Report on Visit to New Zealand, 1955, DP, box 'Law School Expansion'
    etc., file 'Legal Education', pp. 4–5; Hardie Boys, 'Reflections on the Last Fifty
    Years', pp. 39–40.

26 Bailey: Legal Education: Memorandum of Observations, 1938, DP, box 'Fac. Law
    1954–63', file 'Curriculum Committee', p. 3. Paton: University Survey: Faculty of
    Law, 1937, RC, 1938/748, p. 25.

27 LFM, 7 June 1940, pp. 408–19; Bailey, 'The University Law Course', p. 169.

28 Bailey to Mann, 28 August 1940, RC, 1949/565; Financing the Activities of the
    Law School, LFM, 24 August 1989, pp. 184–5.

29 Moir: Minutes of Meeting of Council of Institute with Members of Faculty,
    3 August 1939, LIV records, UMA, first accession, 10/3/1, p. 12. LFM, 9 August
    1940, pp. 426, 429–30, and 25 October 1940, pp. 433–4.

30 'No control whatever': Piesse to Paton, 12 September 1944, FLC, box 1, file 'Legal
    Education'. 'Mutilated': memorandum by Piesse, LFM, 4 August 1944, p. 84.

31 Townsley, 'The Electoral System and the Constituencies', pp. 74, 79; N. K.
    Meaney, 'Piesse, Edmund Leolin', *ADB*, vol. 11, pp. 227–9.

32 Megarry, 'Elements of Drafting'; Taxation lecturer's notes and exercises, LIV
    records, UMA, first accession, 10/3/3.

33 'Deep debt': LFM, 1 August 1947, p. 212. Paton to Piesse, 14 December 1944,
    FLC, box 1, file 'Legal Education'. 'Wallows in antiquities': memorandum by
    Piesse, LFM, 4 August 1944, p. 86. 'Not interested': Piesse to Paton, 21 July 1944,
    FLC, box 1, file 'Legal Education'.

34 Memorandum by Piesse, LFM, 4 August 1944, p. 86.

35 Medley: Serle, *Sir John Medley*, p. 129. Latham: Latham to Lowe, 31 July 1944,
    NLA, MS 1009/12/947.

36 Paton: 'Possible Compromise with Piesse', FLC, box 1, file 'Legal Education'.
    LFM, 22 March 1946, p. 172.

37 Bailey: LFM, 21 September 1945, pp. 146, 148. Course changes: ibid., pp. 137–45.

38 Mann to Paton, 11 February 1944, and note of interview with Chief Justice,
    6 September 1944, FLC, box 1, file 'Legal Education'; Paton to Bailey, 28
    October 1944, NAA, M1504/6. Latham: Latham to Lowe, 31 July 1944, NLA,
    MS 1009/12/947–8.

39 'Piesse's Coaching College': Coppel to Paton, 22 June 1944, FLC, box 1, file
    'Legal Education'. LFM, 22 March 1946, pp. 173–5, and 17 May 1946, pp. 182–7.

40 Law Institute Council draft minutes, 14 December 1939, UMA, first accession, 3/1/180–1, p. 12; ibid., 17 October 1940, 3/1/191, p. 8.

41 Memorandum by the Vice-Chancellor on University Needs, 5 July 1939, Finance Committee Minutes, 17 August 1939, in CM, vol. 26, p. 380.

42 Interview with Professor Geoffrey Sawer, 1971–72, NLA, 1:1/14, 21.

43 Round Table: Interview with Professor Geoffrey Sawer, 1971–72, NLA, 1:1/43. 'Professed Marxist': Interview with Sir Kenneth Bailey, 1971–72, NLA, 1:1/37. 'Born teacher': Interview with Sir Kenneth Bailey, 1971–72, NLA, 1:1/10.

44 Interview with Professor Geoffrey Sawer, 1971–72, NLA, 2:1/9–10; Interview with Sir Kenneth Bailey, 1971–72, NLA, 1:1/36.

45 Interview with Professor Geoffrey Sawer, 1971–72, NLA, 2:1/2.

46 Interview with Professor Geoffrey Sawer, 1971–72, NLA, 2:1/45; Foster and Varghese, *The Making of the Australian National University*, p. 100.

47 Interview with Sir Kenneth Bailey, 1971–72, NLA, 1:1/7–8.

48 'Most impressed': John Cain (1949–52), QR. 'Down-town teachers': John Cain, telephone interview, 27 March 2006. Laurence Muir (1947–49) and Jennifer Smithers (1954–58), QR; Daryl Dawson, interview, 16 January 2006.

49 Dunn to Paton, 18 January 1951, HCP, box 2, UM 420/19.

50 'Simply not available': Interview with Sir Kenneth Bailey, 1971–72, NLA, 1:1/8. Phillips: information from Peter Wickens, July 2005, MLS. Louis Waller, interview, 19 December 2005.

51 Dean's Report, 1928, RC, 1928/209, p. 1; Dean's Report, 1934, RC, 1934/110, p. 1; Dean's Report, 1946, RC, 1946/288, p. 16.

52 'Faculty for Trial. Law Course Indicted', *Farrago*, 8 July 1941, p. 1.

53 'Even the most loyal': 'Lessons for Australia: Law Schools in U.S.A.', *Argus*, 15 February 1938, p. 11. 'Full of the wonders': 'Why?', *Farrago*, 26 April 1938, p. 2.

54 Harold Ford, interview, 7 November 2005. 'Mechanical process': Law Students' Society, 'Report on Legal Education', pp. 99–100.

55 'Turned up in August': Interview with Professor Jack Richardson, 1995–97, NLA, 1:1. *Ebrahimi v. Westbourne Galleries Ltd* [1973] AC 360, 378; Sheppard, 'Casebooks, Commentaries, and Curmudgeons', pp. 566–7.

56 Interview with Professor Geoffrey Sawer, 1971–72, NLA, 1:1/23.

57 James Lemaire, telephone interview, 27 March 2006; Sykes, 'Sykes on Sykes', p. 45; Harold Ford, interview, 7 November 2005.

58 Tutorials: Interview with Sir Kenneth Bailey, 1971–72, NLA, 1:1/10–11. Derham, 'Legal Education: A Challenge to the Profession', p. 530.

59 'Initiative came': Dean's Report, 1936, RC, 1936/116, p. 1. 'The proud aim': 'Res Judicatae', p. v.

60 Dean's Report, 1939, RC, 1939/188, p. 2.

61 'Almost rendered impossible': Dean's Report, 1944, RC, 1944/181, p. 17. Hanbury, '*A Text-Book of Jurisprudence*', p. 121; Graveson, '*A Text-Book of Jurisprudence*', p. 80.
62 University Survey: Faculty of Law, 1937, RC, 1938/748, p. 27.
63 Pape to Derham, 27 September 1963, DP, General Correspondence 1951–64, box 3, file 'P'.
64 Interview with Professor Geoffrey Sawer, 1971–72, NLA, 1:1/31; LFM, 17 September 1981, p. 190.
65 LFM, 24 March 1938, p. 324. Informal approach: Priestley, *Diary of a Vice-Chancellor*, p. 429.
66 University of Melbourne, *Calendar*, 1939, p. 101.
67 LFM, 18 July 1889, p. 97, and 5 September 1889, p. 102; CM, 8 July 1889, pp. 345–6.
68 LFM, 16 July 1915, p. 393.
69 Sawer to Bailey, 24 October 1936, and Bailey to Sawer, 7 November 1936, FLC, box 1, file 'Doctoral Theses'.
70 FLC, box 1, file 'Doctoral Theses'.
71 Dean's Report, 1942, RC, 1942/176, pp. 14–15. 'During 1942': Bailey to Sir William Holdsworth, 6 January 1943, FLC, box 1, file 'Doctoral Theses'.
72 Dean's Report, 1946, RC, 1946/288, p. 16; Butlin and Schedvin, *War Economy*, pp. 36–7. 'Operation of the quota': LFM, 5 March 1943, pp. 39–40.
73 Richard Franklin, telephone interview, 15 February 2006.
74 Lorna Coombs, telephone interview, 3 July 2006; Butlin and Schedvin, *War Economy*, p. 367; Dean's Report, 1942, RC, 1942/176, p. 15. Smith: Paton to Johnston, 5 July 1943, and Smith to Paton, 3 June 1943, HCP, box 3, UM 420/38. Notice of LSS meeting, 6 July 1942, HCP, box 1, UM 420/16.
75 Dean's Report, 1945, RC, 1945/222, pp. 12–13; Richard Franklin, telephone interview, 15 February 2006.
76 Dean's Report, 1944, RC, 1944/181, p. 16; Interview with Professor Geoffrey Sawer, 1971–72, NLA, 1:2/3 and 1:2/5, 8; Paton to H. Norman Tucker, 16 December 1943, HCP, box 3, UM 420/38.
77 LFM, 22 December 1939, p. 401; 'Why?', *Farrago*, 26 April 1938, p. 2; Bailey to Vice-Chancellor, 11 April 1938, RC, 1938/358; 'What Really Happened. Law Students' Meeting', *Farrago*, 3 May 1938, p. 2; 'Law Students' Dispute', *Herald*, 28 April 1938, p. 10.
78 Interview with Sir Kenneth Bailey, 1971–72, NLA, 1:1/22.
79 LFM, 22 December 1939, p. 401.
80 FLC, box 1, file 'Legal Education'.

4 Building the new Jerusalem: 1946–66

1 Lorna Coombs (1945–50), QR; Dean's Report, October 1946, RC, 1946/288, pp. 16–18.

2 Arthur Turner, interview, 19 December 2005; Wilken, 'Conversation with Sir David Derham', p. 1029; Harold Ford, interview, 31 May 2006.

3 Nathan Jacobson, letter to author, 28 November 2005.

4 Hill, 'Biography of Miroslav Schimana'; Perkins, 'Blood and Hope', p. 40.

5 Richard Franklin, telephone interview, 15 February 2006; Lorna Coombs, telephone interview, 3 July 2006; John Cain, telephone interview, 27 March 2006.

6 Leslie Fitzgerald (1946–50), QR; LFM, 21 September 1945, p. 135.

7 Interview with Sir Kenneth Bailey, 1971–72, NLA, 1:2/20.

8 Interview with Professor Geoffrey Sawer, 1971–72, NLA, 2:1/5; Connell et al., *Australia's First*, p. 460; Tarlo, 'Law Schools and Law Teachers in Australia', pp. 33–6.

9 'My feelings': Paton to John Barry, 6 December 1950, NLA, MS 2505/1/1575–6. 'A great wrench': Paton to Cowen, undated (December 1950), NLA, MS 6736/1/1.

10 Harold Ford, interview, 7 November 2005; Robin Sharwood, interview, 25 January 2006; Cowen to Leyser, 11 November 1964, NLA, MS 6736/2/14.

11 Leyser to Cowen, 24 November 1964, NLA, MS 6736/2/15.

12 Anderson, *An Historian's Life*, pp. 326–45.

13 Derham to T. M. Owen, 5 April 1960, DP, General Correspondence 1951–64, box 2, file 'F'. Firecracker: Derham to Cowen, 10 August 1954, NLA, MS 6736/2/12.

14 Ayres, *Owen Dixon*, p. 182; Interview with Professor Geoffrey Sawer, 1971–72, NLA, 2:1/2; Peter Bailey, interview, 24 May 2006.

15 'Boy Wonder Does it Again!', *Farrago*, 26 March 1941, p. 1; Interview with Sir Kenneth Bailey, 1971–72, NLA, 1:2/2; Cowen, Zelman, Confidential Report, NAA, A3978; Cowen to H.W.G. Nobbs, 5 October 1960, NLA, MS 6736/3/23; Cowen, *A Public Life*, pp. 97–112.

16 Dean's Report, 1945, RC, 1945/222, p. 14.

17 Cowen, *A Public Life*, pp. 145, 157–9. 'Pulled me too far away': Cowen to Paton, draft, 26 May 1950, NLA, MS 6736/1/2.

18 John Cain, telephone interview, 27 March 2006; Harold Ford, interview, 31 May 2006.

19 Cowen to S. H. Frankel, 12 November 1952, NLA, MS 6736/2/10.

20 Paton to Cowen, undated, December 1950, NLA, MS 6736/1/1; Zelman Cowen, interviews, 2 February and 12 October 2006.

21 Cowen to Stephen Gilbert, 29 March 1963, NLA, MS 6736/2/13.

22 Cowen to Griswold, 17 October 1951, NLA, MS 6736/3/17. 'Terrible threat': Cowen to Mrs D. J. Clayton, 29 May 1958, NLA, MS 6736/3/20.

23 'Hurtful thing': Cowen to Archbishop of Melbourne, 7 October 1965, NLA, MS 6736/5/42. 'Any prejudice': Cowen to Raphael Powell, 26 May 1952, NLA, MS 6736/2/10.

24 'Perverse things': Cowen to Erwin Griswold, 28 January 1955, NLA, MS 6736/3/19. 'Bank on something': Cowen to Pedrick, 12 July 1965, NLA, MS 6736/5/41.

25 Cowen, *A Public Life*, p. 139. 'Cook with gas': Zelman Cowen, interview, 2 February 2006. Donors: RC, 1957/294.

26 Dean's Report, 1952, RC, 1952/271, p. 24.

27 Cowen to H. J. Davis, 24 July 1952, NLA, MS 6736/2/10; Wilken, 'Conversation with Sir David Derham', p. 1026; Arthur Dean to Derham, 6 June 1951, DP, box 'Private 1/6', file 'Private letters 1951/52'.

28 'The man to see': 'I'm Nearly Finished', *De Minimis*, undated (July 1955), p. 1. 'Pity me': Derham to Cowen, 7–9 July 1954, NLA, MS 6736/2/12. 'Probably mad': Derham to Charles O. Gregory, 20 January 1964, DP, General Correspondence 1951–64, box 2, file 'G'.

29 'Administrative eyes': Interview with Professor Louis Waller, 1995–97, NLA, p. 355. 'Told me everything': Louis Waller, interview, 16 January 2006. 'Leaning upon Miss Scholes': anonymous student (1942–1950), QR. Appointment: RC, 1966/356. 'Charming and beaming': Interview with Professor Louis Waller, 1995–97, NLA, p. 306.

30 'Doom and gloom': Zelman Cowen, interview, 12 October 2006. 'Financial position': Cowen to Stone, 19 July 1965, FLC, box 4, file 'Faculty of Law 1965'. 'Cold, hard cash': McIvor, 'The Law Course Revivified', p. 28.

31 'Feeling very happy': Harold Ford to Sanford Kadish, 16 January 1958, Harold Ford Papers, folder 'Miscellaneous'. Derham to F. P. Donovan, 23 December 1957, DP, General Correspondence 1951–64, box 1, file 'D'; Committee on the Future of Tertiary Education, *Tertiary Education in Australia*, pp. 54, 62, 70.

32 'People were happy': Arthur Turner, interview, 19 December 2005. Cowen to Derham, 28 June 1961, NLA, MS 6736/4/26. 'Bad personal time': Cowen to Derham, 8 January 1962, DP, box 'Colleges 1959–1962', file 'Prof. Cowen'. Cowen to Griswold, 20 July 1961, NLA, MS 6736/4/26; Interview with Professor Louis Waller, 1995–97, NLA, p. 378.

33 Cowen to Derham, 11 December 1963, DP, box 'Colleges 1959–1962' etc., file 'Prof. Cowen'.

34 Law Students' Society Minute Book, 1939–59, p. 134, LRC.

35 'Mock Trial at University', *Herald*, 21 June 1934, p. 20; 'Law Professor "Kidnapped"', *Argus*, 17 June 1936, p. 8; Law Students' Society Minute Book, 1939–59, p. 1, LRC.

36   'Dismal failure': Law Students' Society Minute Book, 1939–59, p. 49, LRC. Were-
      rabbit: ibid., p. 146.

37   Law Students' Society Minute Book, 1939–59, p. 245, LRC; Peter Bailey,
      interview, 24 May 2006.

38   Dean's Report, 1949, RC, 1949/264, p. 17; Mason, 'A History of De Minimis'.

39   'Social disadvantage': Robin Sharwood, interview, 26 April 2006. Ration
      declaration, DP, box 'Private, 1/2', file 'Military & Demobilisation Papers'.
      'Medicine men': Derham to Willard Pedrick, 21 May 1963, DP, General
      Correspondence 1951–64, box 3, file 'P'. Harold Ford, interview, 18 July 2006.
      'Social hub': Graeme Johnson (1967–72), QR.

40   'Grieved': 'Quo Vadit', 'Women of the World', p. 94. 'Equity', 'Women and the
      Law Students' Society', p. 144.

41   LFM, 10 December 1985, p. 127–8.

42   Keith Dunstan, 'Misses Miss Out On "Murder"', Sun, 20 July 1959, p. 6.

43   Louis Waller, interview, 19 December 2005.

44   Brian Ward, email to author, March 2006.

45   'Conference', De Minimis, undated (June 1954), p. 4. 'Hearty': 'I'm Nearly
      Finished', De Minimis, undated (July 1955), p. 1. Louis Waller, interview, 19
      December 2005.

46   'Riotous': Michael Kelly (1953–56), QR. 'Louts': 'Just Nattering', Herald, 10 April
      1954, p. 20. Law Students' Society Minute Book, 1939–59, pp. 522–3, 529, 539,
      LRC.

47   Secretary's Report 1958–59, De Minimis, July 1959, p. 12.

48   Ernie Schwartz (1982–86), QR.

49   Dean's Report, 1958, RC, 1958/373, p. 1.

50   First Year Student Survey 1956, Centre for the Study of Higher Education
      Records, UMA, pp. 97, 104, 121. 'Horrified': Derham to Cowen, 16 June 1954,
      NLA, MS 6736/2/12. Staff meeting, 29 June 1956, DP, box 'Fac. Law 1954–63',
      file 'Faculty of Law. Full-Time Meetings'.

51   Bendigo Advertiser, 20 April 1897; John Lack, 'Ah Ket, William', ADB, vol. 7,
      pp. 19–20; Melbourne University Magazine, vol. 1, no. 1, June 1907, p. 20; 'Law
      Students' Society. Dinner to Sir Harrison Moore', Farrago, 23 April 1929, p. 2.

52   Smith: Paton to Johnston, 5 July 1943, HCP, box 3, UM 420/38. 'Red letter day':
      Derham to F. P. Donovan, 23 December 1957, DP, General Correspondence
      1951–64, box 1, file 'D'.

53   'Criticised strongly': Derham to Cowen, 2 December 1963, DP, box 'Colleges
      1959–1962' etc., file 'Prof. Cowen'. Mary Hiscock, interview, 5 September 2006.

54   Zelman Cowen, interview, 2 February 2006; Mary Hiscock, interview,
      5 September 2006.

55 Mathews, 'The Changing Profile of Women in the Law', p. 635; Rosemary Balmford, video interview, 20 April 2006, MLS; Sylvia Spigelman (1957–61), QR.

56 Pamela Sublet (1953–59), QR; Mary Hiscock, interview, 5 September 2006; Rosemary Howell, telephone interview, 20 February 2006.

57 Rosemary Howell, telephone interview, 20 February 2006; anonymous student (1986–94), QR.

58 'Gentlemen': Robin Sharwood, video interview, MLS. Sawer: Woodward, *One Brief Interval*, p. 21.

59 'Singling out': Samantha Kimpton, interview with anonymous student, 1962–66. 'Worse than his bite': Mick O'Brien (1969–72), QR. 'Sexist': anonymous student (1972–80), QR.

60 'General attractiveness': '"Miss University" Appeal', *Farrago*, 22 June 1948, p. 1. Description of Miss Law: 'Law Candidate for Miss University', *Farrago*, 13 July 1949, p. 1. 'Fun': anonymous student, 1959–63, interview, 2006.

61 'Male mannequins', *Argus*, 16 May 1950, p. 10; Graeme Johnson, telephone interview, 10 February 2006.

62 Vivian Hill (1949–55), QR.

63 First Year Student Survey 1956, Centre for the Study of Higher Education Records, UMA, pp. 43–4, 61–3.

64 Derham to E. O. C. Cameron, 3 October 1962, DP, General Correspondence 1951–64, box 1, file 'C'; Vamplew, *Australians: Historical Statistics*, p. 157; University of Melbourne, *Calendar*, 1939, pp. 639–40.

65 First Year Student Survey 1956, Centre for the Study of Higher Education Records, UMA, pp. 49–51; Anderson et al., *Students in Australian Higher Education*, p. 163; Dow et al., 'The Social Composition of Students', p. 89.

66 Robin Sharwood, interview, 26 April 2006.

67 Derham, Maher and Waller, *Cases and Materials on the Legal Process*, p. vii.

68 Friedmann, 'A Comparative Law Course', p. 274.

69 Finnane, 'The ABC of Criminology', pp. 408–9.

70 LFM, 24 March 1939, p. 353; Interview with Professor Jack Richardson, 1995–97, NLA, 1:1.

71 Dean's Report, 1946, RC, 1946/288, p. 16; Cowen to N. V. Henderson, draft, January 1952, HCP, box 2, UM 420/19.

72 HCP, box 2, UM 420/19.

73 Annual Report, CM, 28 May 1860.

74 Note of interview with Chief Justice, 6 September 1944, FLC, box 1, file 'Legal Education'; LFM, 21 September 1945, p. 137.

75 LFM, 4 March 1957, pp. 426–35.

76 'Tough examination': Cowen to S. H. Sheffield, 3 July 1962, FLC, box 4, file 'Faculty of Law '62'. LFM, 19 March 1948, p. 229; Mal Smith, interview, 29 May 2006.

77 LFM, 27 November 1967, pp. 58–63.

78 Law Final Honour Examination Results, 1864–1964, HCP, box 1, UM 420/9; Balmford, 'The Pursuit of Excellence', p. 231. Chief Justices of the Supreme Court: Madden, Irvine, Mann, Lowe, Young and Phillips. Justices of the High Court: Higgins, Duffy, Latham, Dixon, Menzies, Stephen and Dawson.

79 'The LLB Final Honour Examination', *Summons*, vol. 4, no. 2, December 1894, p. 1; Elliott, *Balliol College Register*, p. 181.

80 Cowen to S. H. Sheffield, 3 July 1962, FLC, box 4, file 'Faculty of Law '62'; Wilken, 'Goodbye Mr Chips', p. 352; Daryl Dawson, interview, 16 January 2006.

81 LFM, 6 December 1988, pp. 401, 409; Pearce, Campbell and Harding, *Australian Law Schools*, vol. 2, p. 503; Faculty of Law, International Review, August 2005, p. 15, PFS; University of Melbourne, Planning and Budget Committee, Operational Performance Review 2006, Faculty of Law, PFS.

82 Louis Waller, interview, 19 December 2005; Bruce Wainwright (1953–57) and Ian Sutherland (1951–55), QR.

83 Sawer: Report of Melbourne Faculty Bureau of Law, 1948, pp. 9, 10, MLS. Report on Leave by Professor Zelman Cowen, 1955, RC, 1955/279, p. 3.

84 Dean's Report, 1946, RC, 1946/288, p. 17; Robert Houghton (1944–49), QR; Daryl Dawson, interview, 16 January 2006; First Year Student Survey 1956, Centre for the Study of Higher Education Records, UMA, p. 112.

85 Dean's Report, 1957, RC, 1957/359, p. 25; Cowen to Registrar, 13 June 1961, RC, 1961/761. 'Large tutorials': anonymous student (1960–65), QR. 'More valuable': anonymous student (1957–62), QR.

86 Robin Sharwood, interview, 25 January 2006; Daryl Dawson, interview, 16 January 2006; Interview with Mark Weinberg, 1996–97, NLA, pp. 24–5.

87 'Sworn foe': Cowen to Derham, 21 June 1954, NLA, MS 6736/2/12. 'Incoherent bits': Report on Leave by Professor Zelman Cowen, 19 April 1955, RC, 1955/279, p. 3.

88 Patrick Donovan, letter to author, 2 December 2006; Interview with Professor Louis Waller, 1995–97, NLA, p. 145; Jennifer Smithers (1954–58), QR; William Ormiston (1954–57), QR. Torts class: Derham to Morris, 21 March 1956, DP, box 'Norval Morris' etc., file 'Morris, Norval'.

89 Dean's Report, October 1955, RC, 1955/314, p. 24; Howard to teaching staff, 8 March 1982, Robert Evans Papers; Mackinolty and Mackinolty (eds), *A Century Down Town*, p. 134.

90 'Any physical sense': Report on Leave by Professor Zelman Cowen, 1955, RC, 1955/279, p. 6. Former student: anonymous graduate (1946–48), QR. Buildings Committee: Memorandum from the Faculty of Law, 22 June 1955, RC, 1958/804, p. 2. 'No place': Cowen to Rogers, 19 May 1955, RC, 1958/804.

91 Jennifer Smithers (1954–58), QR; Vivian Hill, telephone interview, 16 February 2006.

92 John Cain (1949–52), QR; Friedmann, 'On Leaving Melbourne', p. 63.

93 Dean's Report, 1947, RC, 1947/264, p. 19; John Cain, telephone interview, 27 March 2006; Harold Ford, interview, 23 March 2006.

94 'Action On Library At Last', Farrago, 15 June 1948, p. 1; Annual Report, 1951, University of Melbourne, Calendar, 1952, p. 494; Dean's Report, 1951, RC, 1951/282, p. 24; John Cain, telephone interview, 27 March 2006; LFM, 7 May 1954, p. 377.

95 Cowen to Vice-Chancellor, 3 October 1957, RC, 1959/905. 'Grotesquely overcrowded': Dean's Report, 1958, RC, 1958/373, p. 3. Dean's Report, 1957, RC, 1957/359, p. 25. 'Mad Doberman': Mary Hiscock, interview, 5 September 2006.

96 First Year Student Survey 1956, Centre for the Study of Higher Education Records, UMA, p. 114.

97 Law Students' Society Minute Book, 1939–59, pp. 412, 422, 424, LRC.

98 'Needs of Faculty of Law', HCP, box 3, file 'Faculty of Law 1944–48'; Cowen to Griswold, 1 September 1952, NLA, MS 6736/3/17.

99 Cowen to Grounds, Romberg and Boyd, 27 March 1953, FLC, box 1, file 'Law School: Future Developments'. 'Legal profession': Interview with Professor Zelman Cowen, 9 April 1953, SLV, MS 13363, box 26/1.

100 Harold Ford, interview, 30 August 2006; A Proposal for a New Law School at the University of Melbourne, NLA, MS 6736/9/73; Interview with Professor Zelman Cowen, 9 April 1953, SLV, MS 13363, box 26/1; Derham to Morris, 30 November 1955, DP, box 'Norval Morris' etc., file 'Morris, Norval'.

101 Interview with Professor Zelman Cowen, 9 April 1953, SLV, MS 13363, box 26/1; Cowen to Derham, 4 May 1954, NLA, MS 6736/2/12.

102 Note of telephone conversation, Cowen and Romberg, 10 June 1955, SLV, MS 13363, box 26/1; Derham to Cowen, 23 December 1957, DP, box 'Colleges 1959–1962' etc., file 'Prof. Cowen'; LFM, 17 December 1957, p. 465; Cowen to Vice-Chancellor, 8 August 1962, and Cowen to Featherstone, 10 May 1962, FLC, box 1, file 'Law School: Future Developments'.

103 Pedrick, 'A Learned Profession?', pp. 167–9; Committee on the Future of Tertiary Education, Tertiary Education in Australia, vol. 2, p. 81; Connell et al., Australia's First, p. 460; University of Melbourne, Statistics, 1973, p. 25.

104 Derham to Cowen, 30 October 1957, and Cowen to Derham, 6 November 1957, DP, box 'Colleges 1959–1962' etc., file 'Prof. Cowen'.

105 Derham to Cowen, 2 December 1963, DP, box 'Colleges 1959–1962' etc., file 'Prof. Cowen'; CM, 20 March 1965, p. 131, and 3 May 1965, p. 247; Poynter and Rasmussen, *A Place Apart*, p. 504.

106 Information for Students on Building Developments, March 1959, FLC, box 1, file 'Law School: Future Developments'; Harold Ford, interview, 7 November 2005.

107 'Makeshift': K. A. Lodewycks, letter to the editor, *De Minimis*, undated (May 1959), p. 2. Harold Ford to Donald J. MacDougall, 17 April 1959, Harold Ford Papers, file 'Tutors'; meeting of full-time staff, 9 May 1962, DP, box 'Fac. Law 1954–63', file 'Faculty—Full-Time'. 'Over-crowding': Acting Dean's Report, 1963, RC, 1963/352, p. 3. Derham to Vice-Chancellor, 10 September 1963, DP, box 'Admission tests—Law School c. 1954–58' etc., file 'Law Library'.

108 Annual Report, 1951, University of Melbourne, *Calendar*, 1952, p. 494.

109 Poynter and Rasmussen, *A Place Apart*, pp. 247–53.

110 Committee on the Future of Tertiary Education, *Tertiary Education in Australia*, vol. 2, pp. 77–81; Tarlo, 'Law Schools and Law Teachers in Australia', pp. 33–4.

111 Derham to Cowen, 23 April 1954, NLA, MS 6736/2/12; Harold Ford to Sanford Kadish, 16 January 1958, Harold Ford Papers, folder 'Miscellaneous'.

112 Derham to Cowen, 23 April 1954, NLA, MS 6736/2/12; Poynter and Rasmussen, *A Place Apart*, p. 504.

113 'Report on Leave by Professor Zelman Cowen', 19 April 1955, RC, 1955/279, p. 3; Cowen to Aidan Crawley, 28 September 1959, NLA, MS 6736/3/21.

114 'Dollar curtain': Sawer, 'Legal Education in the United States', p. 398. Norma Ford, telephone interview, 17 July 2006; Dixon to John Young, 14 February 1959, in Ayres, *Owen Dixon*, p. 270.

115 Cowen to Griswold, 17 September 1965, NLA, MS 6736/5/43. Nigeria: Cowen to Robert M. Hutchins, 14 May 1962, NLA, MS 6736/4/28.

116 Brett, 'North Borneo', p. 565; 'Law Reform at Home and Abroad', pp. 90–2; Report on Study Trip to Indonesia, 1953, DP, box 'Papers pre-1968', file 'Leyser, Dr H.'; Dean's Report, 1956, RC, 1956/325, p. 21.

117 'Benefit to Poor Litigants', *Herald*, 7 August 1936, p. 16; 'The Legal Aid Service', *De Minimis*, undated (June 1953), p. 2; LFM, 4 May 1951, p. 309; Robin Sharwood, interview, 25 January 2006; Graeme Henry (1952–55), QR.

118 Dean's Report, 1957, RC, 1957/359, p. 25; Harold Ford Papers, file 'Student Agitation'; Strong, 'Melbourne University Legal Referral Service'.

119 Dean's Report, 1949, RC, 1949/264, p. 18; Dean's Report, 1961, p. 2, RC, 1961/366.

120 Dean's Report, 1949, RC, 1949/264, p. 17.

121 Paton to Greening, 22 May 1961, RC, 1961/761; Arthur Dean to Derham, 8
November 1962, and Derham to Arthur Dean, 9 November 1962, DP, General
Correspondence 1951–64, box 1, file 'D'; Cowen to Arthur Dean, 9 November
1962, NLA, MS 6736/4/30; Johnston to Ford, Brett and Howard, 7 July 1966,
RC, 1966/350.

122 O'Brien, 'The Victorian Chief Justice's Law Reform Committee', p. 457; Cowen
to Provost, Oriel College, 13 June 1952, NLA, MS 6736/2/10; 'Notes by H. A. J.
Ford', Harold Ford Papers, pp. 48–51.

123 Cowen to Griswold, 13 May 1952, NLA, MS 6736/3/17.

124 University of Melbourne, *Calendar*, 1942, p. 28; LFM, 5 April 1962, p. 142, and
1 May 1962, p. 146.

125 LFM, 16 September 1975, pp. 691–2, and 9 April 1987, p. 29.

126 Cowen to Griswold, 13 May 1952, NLA, MS 6736/3/17.

127 LFM, 1 July 1960, p. 63, and 19 July 1960, p. 84.

128 LFM, 13 February 1958, pp. 1–2.

129 Paton to Lowe, 7 December 1949, HCP, box 2, UM 420/30; Sawer to Medley, 20
September 1949, RC, 1950/910.

130 Mary Hiscock, interview, 5 September 2006.

131 Dean's Report, 1957, RC, 1957/359, p. 25; Cowen, 'Legal Education at the
Cross-Roads', p. 213.

132 'The Law School and its Examinations', DP, box 'Law School Expansion',
etc., file 'Limitation of Numbers 1961'; Poynter and Rasmussen, *A Place Apart*,
pp. 153–61; LFM, 9 August 1957, p. 455, and 15 October 1958, pp. 26–9.

133 LFM, 1 July 1960, pp. 66–8.

134 Poynter and Rasmussen, *A Place Apart*, p. 196.

135 Greening, 'Presidential Address', p. 148.

136 'Notes by H. A. J. Ford', Harold Ford Papers, p. 52; 'Judge Criticises Law Exam
Level', *Age*, 2 May 1960, p. 3; O'Bryan to Derham, 2 June 1960, DP, box 'Law
School Expansion' etc., file 'Limitation of Numbers 1961'; 'Law Pass Standards at
the University of Melbourne', *Age*, 3 May 1960, p. 2.

137 Wilken, 'The Honourable T. W. Smith', pp. 814–15; Poynter and Rasmussen,
A Place Apart, pp. 242–7.

138 'Legal Education', *Law Institute Journal*, vol. 36, no. 5, May 1962, p. 178; Wilken,
'The Honourable T. W. Smith', pp. 814–15; Cowen to W. Prest, 6 April 1962, FLC,
box 4, file 'Faculty of Law '62'; LFM, 26 February 1963, pp. 194–5; Meeting of
Full-Time Staff, 21 June 1962, DP, box 'Fac. Law 1954–63', file 'Faculty—Full-
Time'.

139 Committee on the Future of Tertiary Education, *Tertiary Education in Australia*, vol. 2, pp. 49, 62–3.

140 Sharwood, 'The Training of Lawyers Outside Universities', p. 311; 'RMIT Course to be Phased Out', p. 365.

141 Derham to Cowen, 6 November 1963, DP, box 'Colleges 1959–1962' etc., file 'Prof. Cowen'; LFM, 31 October 1963, pp. 240–9, and 19 May 1965, pp. 347–53; Poynter and Rasmussen, *A Place Apart*, pp. 244–5.

142 LFM, 24 April 1963, pp. 199–200.

5   Village democracy: 1967–88

1   Mark Weinberg, interview, 24 January 2006; Cowen to Griswold, 7 July 1966, NLA, MS 6736/6/44.

2   Poynter and Rasmussen, *A Place Apart*, p. 75; Paton to W. F. Connell, 23 April 1952, HCP, box 2, UM 420/19; Report on Leave by Professor Zelman Cowen, 1955, RC, 1955/279, p. 4.

3   Burdekin, 'Profile: H. A. J. Ford', p. 8; Derham, 'Legal Education: A Challenge to the Profession', p. 532.

4   Stevens, *Law School*, pp. 177–80; Abel, *American Lawyers*, pp. 48–9; Harold Ford, interview, 23 March 2006.

5   Proposal that the Course for LLB (Melb.) become a Graduate Course, LFM, 3 July 1969, pp. 149–52.

6   Graeme Johnson, telephone interview, 10 February 2006; anonymous parent to Dean, 19 July 1974, FLC, box 2, file 'Faculty Correspondence June–Sept 1974'

7   University of Melbourne, *Calendar*, 1970–71, p. 850.

8   LFM, 6 December 1972, pp. 274–5, 28 February 1974, pp. 389–90, and 9 April 1974, p. 393.

9   LFM, 6 July 1988, pp. 186, 227–46.

10   LFM, 30 April 1984, pp. 59–76; Dixon, *Looking Back*, pp. 47–9; Payne, 'University Education for Lawyers', pp. 23, 38.

11   LFM, 14 September 1967, pp. 24–36.

12   LFM, 14 September 1967, p. 33, and 17 September 1969, p. 175; Dean's Report, 1944, RC, 1944/181, p. 16. The figure for 1969 was the law school's total budget of $258 034 plus thirty-five per cent for estimated overhead costs. 'Something of a cad': Harold Ford, interview, 17 July 2006.

13   Paton to F. R. Gubbins, 18 October 1950, HCP, box 2, UM 420/19; Ford to Vice-Principal, 15 December 1966, Vice-Chancellor's Working Papers 1951–68, UMA, VC 408; Ford to Vice-Principal, 30 November 1967, RC, 1966/356.

14   'Dismal': Ford to Sidney Picker, 18 September 1969, Harold Ford Papers, file 'Visitors to Law School (2)'. LFM, 20 October 1969, pp. 214–16. *Persona non grata*: Harold Ford, interview, 7 November 2006.

15 LFM, 9 December 1970, p. 316, 8 December 1971, p. 129, 13 September 1982, p. 48, and 11 December 1984, p. 142; Victoria Law Foundation, *Sixth Annual Report: 1975*, p. 3; ibid., *Tenth Annual Report: 1979*, p. 3.

16 University of Melbourne, *Statistics*, 1979, p. 36; ibid., 1989, p. 47.

17 Review of Allocations Formula, LFM, 13 April 1981, p. 175; Commonwealth Tertiary Education Commission, *Review of Efficiency and Effectiveness*, pp. 56–7; Connell, *Reshaping Australian Education*, p. 411.

18 Ford to John Feltham, 18 March 1970, Harold Ford Papers, file 'J. Feltham'.

19 CM, 6 March 1967, p. 207, and 2 June 1969, p. 975.

20 Clark to Peter Ryan, 26 July 1974, and Clark to M. R. Pawsey, 26 July 1974, FLC, box 1, file 'Faculty Correspondence June–Sept 1974'.

21 A.T.J. Bell to Clark, 6 September 1974, FLC, box 1, file 'Faculty Correspondence June–Sept 1974'.

22 Iola Hack, 'Professor won't sit at "trial"', *Age*, 11 August 1971, p. 3; Poynter and Rasmussen, *A Place Apart*, p. 404.

23 Gary Dean, 'Varsity Chief Accused of Gag', *Age*, 28 August 1971, p. 3; 'University Row "Now a Matter of Rights"', *Age*, 30 August 1971, p. 3; 'University Drops Lock-In Charges', *Age*, 29 September 1971, p. 5.

24 Harold Ford, interview, 17 July 2006; Burdekin, 'Profile: H. A. J. Ford', p. 8.

25 Robin Sharwood, interview, 25 January 2006; Michael Crommelin, interview, 10 October 2006.

26 Brett to Howard, 16 August 1973, Harold Ford Papers, file 'Brett, Professor Peter'.

27 Mary Hiscock, interview, 5 September 2006.

28 Sykes to Cowen, 5 September 1966, NLA, MS 6736/6/51; Sykes, 'The Sad, Frustrating Facts of a Professor's Life', *Australian*, 31 May 1967, p. 9; Sykes, 'Academics Have Right to Speak', *Age*, 3 September 1971, p. 9.

29 Clark to Derham, 23 August 1974, FLC, box 2, file 'June–September 1974'.

30 Ann Graham, interview, 27 April 2006; Clark to law professors, 5 November 1974, FLC, box 2, file 'October–December 1974'.

31 DP, box 'General University', file 'Law School Centenary'; LFM, 17 April 1973, p. 280.

32 Claudia Wright, 'The Law's a Gentleman', *Herald*, 14 April 1973, p. 41.

33 ibid.; information from Harold Ford.

34 Clark to Caro, 17 January 1975, FLC, box 2, file 'October–December 1974'.

35 Brett to Howard, 16 August 1973, Harold Ford Papers; anonymous student (1973–79), QR.

36 David Penington, interview, 21 March 2006.

37 LFM, 14 July 1925, p. 52, and 6 October 1944, p. 99.

38 Ford to Julian Phillips, 18 March 1970, Harold Ford Papers, file 'Julian Phillips'; LFM, 17 September 1970, p. 287.

39 Graeme Johnson, telephone interview, 10 February 2006; Sharwood to Clark, 28 May 1974, FLC, box 2, file 'Faculty Correspondence January–May 1974'.
40 LFM, 23 July 1975, p. 633, and 27 July 1977, p. 70.
41 LFM, 13 April 1977, pp. 3, 30–1.
42 DP, box 'Fac. Law 1954–63', files 'Faculty—Full Time', and 'Faculty of Law. Full-Time Meetings'.
43 Harold Ford, interview, 7 November 2005; Mark Weinberg, interview, 24 January 2006.
44 University solicitor: Patricia Wood to Clark, 13 June 1974, LFM, 17 July 1974, pp. 493–4. LFM, 17 July 1974, pp. 483, 490; Michael Crommelin, interview, 10 October 2006.
45 LFM, 21 April 1976, pp. 765–8.
46 LFM, 22 March 1969, p. 115, 24 June 1969, p. 119, and 16 September 1971, p. 72.
47 LFM, 23 July 1975, p. 663, and 7 December 1976, pp. 932, 943; Dean to teaching staff, 10 May 1982, Robert Evans Papers.
48 LFM, 5 December 1979, p. 191.
49 Procedure for Choosing Dean, July 1978, Robert Evans Papers.
50 Clark to Castles, 19 November 1974, FLC, box 2, file 'Faculty Correspondence October–December 1974'.
51 Pearce, Campbell and Harding, *Australian Law Schools*, vol. 2, p. 655; Commonwealth Tertiary Education Commission, *Review of Efficiency and Effectiveness*, pp. 56–7; Australasian Universities Law Schools Association, *Report No. 2*, pp. 37–8.
52 Mackinolty and Mackinolty (eds), *A Century Down Town*, pp. 185, 200.
53 Pearce, Campbell and Harding, *Australian Law Schools*, vol. 2, p. 550 (rounded figures); Commonwealth Tertiary Education Commission, *Review of Efficiency and Effectiveness*, pp. 56–7.
54 Ann Graham, interview, 27 April 2006; LFM, 1 July 1960, p. 66.
55 LFM, 3 December 1980, pp. 127–8.
56 'Historical Documents', pp. 53–132; Dixon, *Thirty Up*, pp. 21–2, 40, 72–3; Blackshield, 'Lang, Diogenes and Macquarie Law School', pp. 45–50.
57 Susan Morgan, statement to faculty meeting, 1988, MLS.
58 Review of the Faculty of Law, LFM, 23 May 1988, p. 17.
59 ibid., p. 2.
60 ibid.; Andrew Neeson, interview, 8 June 2006; Mary Hiscock, interview, 5 September 2006; Jenny Morgan, conversation with author.
61 Pearce, Campbell and Harding, *Australian Law Schools*, vol. 1, pp. 216–17, and vol. 2, p. 573.
62 Mary Hiscock, interview, 5 September 2006; Howard to Luntz, 2 March 1987, Robert Evans Papers.

63 Mark Weinberg, interview, 24 January 2006; LFM, 12 April 1983, p. 163.

64 Clark to academic staff, 7 September 1977, FLC, box 3, file '1977 Sept–Dec'.

65 Williams to Registrar, 4 April 1964, RC, 1964/757; Erika Feller, 'Prof. Colin Howard', *Summons*, 1971, p. 45.

66 Howard to President, SRC, 6 March 1979, R.R.S. Tracey to Editor, Orientation Handbook, 2 March 1979, and Howard to teaching staff, 29 March 1979, Robert Evans Papers; de Jong, 'A History of the Melbourne University Law Review', MLS, p. 30.

67 David Penington, interview, 21 March 2006.

68 LFM, 13 September 1982, pp. 45–6, 58–73, and 7 December 1982, p. 87.

69 Interview with Mark Weinberg, 1996–97, NLA, p. 45; Mark Weinberg, interview, 24 January 2006.

70 Howard to staff, 14 March 1983, Robert Evans Papers.

71 Howard to teaching staff, 5 July 1982, Robert Evans Papers.

72 Interview with Mark Weinberg, 1996–97, NLA, pp. 45–6.

73 Mark Weinberg, interview, 24 January 2006.

74 Weisbrot, 'Recent Statistical Trends', p. 222; LFM, 12 April 1983, p. 185.

75 LFM, 30 April 1980, p. 28, and 12 April 1988, p. 83; Marginson, *Monash*, p. 237.

76 Commonwealth Schools Commission, *Australian Students*, p. 40; LFM, 17 September 1974, p. 527, and 25 July 1979, p. 153 (suburb data for 1976–78); Anderson and Vervoorn, *Access to Privilege*, p. 69. The schooling of the remaining six per cent of law entrants was unknown.

77 LFM, 17 September 1974, pp. 499, 521.

78 'We discriminate': LFM, 19 April 1978, p. 25. LFM, 25 July 1979, pp. 138, 143.

79 Goldring, 'An Updated Social Profile', p. 5; Goldring and Vignaendra, *A Social Profile of New Law Students*, p. 140.

80 First Year Student Survey 1956, Centre for the Study of Higher Education Records, UMA, p. 20; LFM, 8 April 1986, p. 50; Griswold, 'Observations on Legal Education in Australia', p. 140; Cowen to Griswold, 13 May 1952, NLA, MS 6736/3/17; LFM, 5 December 1979, p. 209.

81 Dean's Report, 1960, RC, 1961/366, p. 2.

82 'Planet Serious': Ernie Schwartz (1982–86), QR. 'Sink or swim': Mark Worsnop (1982–86), QR. Anonymous students (commenced 1983, 1983–88, and 1979–83), QR.

83 'Fit the pieces together': anonymous student (1981–86), QR. 'Not just lecture': Philip Ryan (1983–89), QR. 'The first time': Amanda Gorely (1984–90), QR.

84 Kerry Greenwood (1972–78), QR; anonymous students (1979–83 and 1985–89), QR; LFM, 25 July 1979, p. 137.

85 McTaggart, Smith and Wortley, 'Small Group Teaching'; LFM, 7 December 1982, p. 107, 13 December 1983, p. 343, 30 April 1984, p. 16, and 11 December 1984, p. 141.

86 Dean to teaching staff, 23 March 1981, Robert Evans Papers; Pearce, Campbell and Harding, *Australian Law Schools*, vol. 1, pp. 216–17; Review of the Law School: Submission by Harold Luntz, February 1988, p. 5, MLS; Review of the Faculty of Law, LFM, 23 May 1988, p. 11.

87 Pearce, Campbell and Harding, *Australian Law Schools*, vol. 4, p. 166.

88 Pearce, Campbell and Harding, *Australian Law Schools*, vol. 1, pp. 216–17.

89 Mal Smith, interview, 29 May 2006; Mary Hiscock, interview, 5 September 2006; Pearce, Campbell and Harding, *Australian Law Schools*, vol. 2, pp. 357–9.

90 Margaret Manion, interview, 7 March 2006.

91 Review of the Faculty of Law, LFM, 23 May 1988, p. 17; LFM, 12 April 1983, p. 255.

92 LFM, 8 June 1988, pp. 181–2; Commonwealth Tertiary Education Commission, *Review of Efficiency and Effectiveness*, p. 255.

93 David Penington, interview, 21 March 2006.

94 ibid.

6   Performance against plan: 1989–2007

1   McPhee, *Pansy*, p. 188.

2   Marginson, *Monash*, pp. 62–3; John Dawkins, letter to university students, 31 October 1988, MLS.

3   LFM, 6 July 1988, pp. 190–1, 330.

4   David Penington, interview, 21 March 2006; Michael Crommelin, interview, 10 January 2007.

5   Pearce, Campbell and Harding, *Australian Law Schools*, vol. 2, p. 559; Review of the Law School, April 1995, LFM, 9 August 1995, p. 14; Rosemary Hunter, interview, 16 January 2007.

6   Michael Crommelin, interview, 10 January 2007.

7   Mal Smith, interview, 29 May 2006.

8   Richard Mitchell, interview, 16 March 2007; interview with anonymous staff member, 2007.

9   Pearce, Campbell and Harding, *Australian Law Schools*, vol. 2, p. 669; University Statistics Book 2006, preliminary, table 4.15, <www.upo.unimelb.edu.au> (viewed 25 May 2007); Faculty of Law, International Review, August 2005, p. 24.

10 University Statistics Book 2006, tables 4.10, 4.12(a), 4.12(c), <www.upo.unimelb. edu.au> (viewed 25 May 2007).

11 Pearce, Campbell and Harding, *Australian Law Schools*, vol. 2, p. 669; University Statistics Book 2006, table 4.10, <www.upo.unimelb.edu.au> (viewed 25 May 2007); Faculty of Law, International Review, August 2005, p. 24.

12 Richard Mitchell, interview, 16 March 2007.

13 Minor thesis: LFM, 17 April 1973, p. 280, and 13 April 1977, pp. 2, 21. 1981 figures: LFM, 14 April 1982, p. 12.

14 LFM, 6 July 1988, p. 187; Graduate Studies Program Marketing Plan, LFM, 11 April 1989, p. 58; Future Directions for the Graduate Studies Programme: Issues Paper, LFM, 3 April 1990, p. 50.

15 LFM, 3 December 1980, pp. 120–5, and 17 September 1981, p. 190.

16 Michael Crommelin, interview, 10 January 2007; Higher Education Funding Act 1988 (Cth) s. 13.

17 LFM, 6 July 1988, p. 186, and 11 April 1989, pp. 52, 58; Marginson, *Monash*, pp. 176, 237–8.

18 Weisbrot, *Australian Lawyers*, p. 272.

19 Cheryl Saunders, interview, 7 February 2007.

20 Graduate Studies Program Marketing Plan, LFM, 11 April 1989, p. 61; Kaye Nankervis, conversation with author.

21 Michael Crommelin, interview, 10 January 2007. Later, a 65–35 or 70–30 split was more common.

22 Cheryl Saunders, interview, 7 February 2007; Ian Marshman, interview, 28 March 2007.

23 Graduate Studies Advisory Board Report, LFM, 26 July 1993, p. 113.

24 Postgraduate Studies in Law 2007, Staff Profiles, <http://graduate.law.unimelb. edu.au> (viewed 25 May 2007).

25 Cheryl Saunders, interview, 7 February 2007.

26 Graduate Studies Advisory Board Report, LFM, 26 March 1997, item 15; Faculty of Law, International Review, August 2005, p. 5.

27 Consultative Group on Research and Education in Law, *Law and Learning*, p. 89; Pearce, Campbell and Harding, *Australian Law Schools*, vol. 2, p. 557.

28 Dean's Report, LFM, 4 June 1998, 4.1.

29 LFM, 31 October 1952, p. 351; Ford to Brett, 2 November 1967, Harold Ford Papers, file 'Peter Brett'; Poynter and Rasmussen, *A Place Apart*, pp. 222–3.

30 Research Activities in the Faculty of Law (submission to University of Melbourne Research and Graduate Studies Committee, November 1977), University Central Records, p. 29; LFM, 23 July 1980, p. 34.

31 *Higher Education: A Policy Statement*, p. 94; Research Committee Report, LFM, 12 December 1989, p. 260.

32 *Higher Education: A Policy Statement*, p. 92.

33 Research Activities in the Faculty of Law (submission to University of Melbourne Research and Graduate Studies Committee, November 1977), University Central Records, pp. 5–8.

34 University Statistics Book 2006, preliminary, table 4.15, <www.upo.unimelb.edu.au> (viewed 25 May 2007).

35 Cownie, *Legal Academics*, p. 58.

36 Heydon, '*Assessment of Damages*', p. 411; Academic Profile, LFM, 23 November 1994, p. 362.

37 Mal Smith, interview, 29 May 2006; Asian Law Centre, Annual Report, 2002, LFM, 5 November 2003, 4.12; Centre for Natural Resources Law Report, 1989, LFM, 3 April 1990, p. 81; LFM, 30 July 1970, p. 268; Report of Review Committee on Centre for Comparative Constitutional Studies, August 1996, LFM, 26 March 1997, item 16.

38 Research Committee Report, LFM, 3 April 1990, p. 30; University of Melbourne Planning and Budget Committee, Operational Performance Review 2003, LFM, 6 August 2003, 5.4, p. 9.

39 Centre for Comparative Constitutional Studies, Annual Report, 2000, LFM, 24 April 2002, 5.12.

40 LFM, 12 December 1989, p. 202, and 20 September 1990, p. 200; David Penington, interview, 21 March 2006.

41 LFM, 22 September 1993, p. 253.

42 Report to Planning Group, LFM, 29 July 1992, pp. 180–2; LFM, 25 November 1992, p. 7.

43 Annual Report, 1994, LFM, 22 March 1995, p. 85; Executive and Budgets Committee Report, LFM, 22 March 1995, p. 27.

44 LFM, 13 February 1958, p. 2.

45 Joint Committee on Policy, Report of Working Group on Business Law, LFM, 25 November 1992, item 15; University of Melbourne, *Statistics*, 1992, p. 110; Richard Mitchell, interview, 16 March 2007; Michael Crommelin, interview, 10 January 2007.

46 Michael Crommelin, interview, 10 January 2007.

47 'Myth widely held': LFM, 25 November 1992, p. 12. Review of the Faculty of Law, LFM, 23 May 1988, p. 2; A Personal Response from the Dean to the Report of the Committee of Review, 1988, p. 6; Paul Morgan, email to author, 5 February 2007.

48 Draft Operational Plan 1998, LFM, 27 August 1997, item 4; Draft University of Melbourne Strategic Plan 1998, LFM, 31 March 1998, 6.1A, p. 5.

49 Report on Selection of the Entry Quota for Legal Process 1989, LFM, 11 April 1989, p. 45; *Australasian Legal Education Yearbook*, 1996, pp. 44–5; Melbourne Law School Admission Information 1998, <www.law.unimelb.edu.au> (viewed 2 December 1998, copy on file with author).

50 Undergraduate Selection Committee Report, 1998, LFM, 31 March 1998, 5.10; LFM, 27 May 1997, 6.2.

51 Melbourne University Law School Foundation, Annual Report, 1992, LFM, 26 July 1993, p. 191; Melbourne University Law School Foundation, Annual Report, 2000, LFM, 31 July 2001, 5.10, p. 7; Operational Performance Review, 2006, LFM, 9 August 2006, 6.2.

52 Royal Commission on the University of Melbourne, *Final Report*, p. 104; Poynter and Rasmussen, *A Place Apart*, p. 13; LFM, 9 August 2006, item 6.1, attachment D.

53 Former General Office staff member, interview, 22 February 2007.

54 Maria Luzza, conversation with author; Executive and Budgets Committee Report, LFM, 11 December 1990, pp. 256–7; Dean's Report, LFM, 10 April 1991, p. 25; Executive and Budgets Committee Report, LFM, 10 April 1991, p. 33; Report to Planning Group, 1993, LFM, 26 July 1993, pp. 64–5.

55 Michael Crommelin, interview, 10 January 2007; Submission to Lindenderry Conference 1997, LFM, 27 August 1997, item 4.

56 'Aimed to assist': LFM, 27 August 1997, p. 10. Fees: LFM, 18 August 1999, item 5.

57 Rosemary Hunter, interview, 16 January 2007.

58 LFM, 27 August 1997, p. 10.

59 Michael Bryan, interview, 14 March 2007.

60 LFM, 22 September 1997, pp. 2–3. 'Dean advised': LFM, 22 September 1997, p. 3.

61 Michael Crommelin, interview, 10 January 2007; Ian Marshman, interview, 28 March 2007.

62 Centre for Legal Education, *The Cost of Legal Education*, p. 59; LFM, 6 July 1988, pp. 250–94, and 6 December 1988, pp. 465–528; Keyes and Johnstone, 'Changing Legal Education', p. 550.

63 Belinda Fehlberg, interview, 1 February 2007.

64 *Law Students' Society Counter Handbook*, 1991, p. 61, MLS.

65 Rosemary Hunter, interview, 16 January 2007.

66 Michael Crommelin, interview, 10 January 2007.

67 ibid.

68 LLB Selection 2004, LFM, 17 March 2004, 5.3.2; University of Melbourne, *Statistics*, 1996, p. 1.22; University of Melbourne, Historical and Summary Data, Load and Enrolments by Faculty, 2004 <www.upo.unimelb.edu.au> (viewed 25 May 2007).

69 Review of the LLB, LFM, 8 December 2004, 5.3, p. 3.

70 Professorial Board Minutes, 16 July 1968, p. 268; University of Melbourne, *Calendar*, 1958, p. 469; LFM, 20 April 1972, p. 153, and 10 December 1975, p. 724; Lavery, 'The Participation of Indigenous Australians', p. 179.

71 Tom Cannon, telephone interview, 9 March 2007; anonymous student (1999–2006), QR.

72 Draft submission to June budget conference, LFM, 27 May 1997, 6.3, p. 7; Douglas, 'The Participation of Indigenous Australians', pp. 489, 492; information from Miranda Stewart, Law School Koori Liaison Officer.

73 'Camellias': Kerry Greenwood (1972–78), QR. Anonymous graduate (commenced 1983), QR; Andrew Neeson, interview, 8 June 2006.

74 Report to Planning Group, LFM, 27 November 1991, p. 333; Report to Planning Group, LFM, 29 July 1992, p. 172.

75 Ann Graham, interview, 27 April 2006; Executive and Budgets Committee report, LFM, 11 December 1990, pp. 256–7; Dean's Report, LFM, 10 April 1991, p. 25; Executive and Budgets Committee Report, LFM, 10 April 1991, p. 33.

76 Law Building Project Chronology, LFM, 25 August 1998, item 2, p. 1; Law School Master Plan, LFM, 13 December 1988, pp. 572–7.

77 Michael Crommelin, interview, 10 January 2007.

78 Dean's Report, LFM, 12 December 1989, p. 217; Michael Crommelin, interview, 10 January 2007; Law School Master Plan, LFM, 10 April 1991, p. 85; LFM, 31 March 1998, p. 5.

79 Dean's Report, LFM, 12 December 1989, p. 217; LFM, 23 July 1991, p. 105; Minutes of University Buildings Committee, LFM, 23 July 1991, p. 205.

80 Law Building Project Chronology, LFM, 25 August 1998, item 2, p. 5; Executive and Budgets Committee report, LFM, 24 November 1997, 12.1.

81 University of Melbourne, *Looking to the Future*, p. 7.

82 Marginson and Considine, *The Enterprise University*, p. 4.

83 University of Melbourne, *Earning Esteem*, p. 1.

84 University of Melbourne, Strategic Audit 2000, 2.4.2, <www.unimelb.edu.au/vc/stratplan> (viewed 18 October 2000, copy on file with author).

85 Guy Healy, 'Backers Drop High-Tech Park', *Australian*, 25 February 1998, p. 4; Alex Messina, 'Uni Unveils Private Campus', *Age*, 9 July 1997, p. 3.

86 Sheehan to Crommelin, 21 May 1998, LFM, 4 June 1998, 5.1.1.

87 Michael Crommelin, interview, 10 January 2007; Rasmussen, *Increasing Momentum*, p. 216.

88 LFM, 4 June 1998, pp. 5–6.

89 Emily Russell and Renate Krelle to faculty members, 25 August 1998, Building Project File, PFS.

90 Ron Castan QC to Gilbert, 21 August 1998, Building Project File, PFS.

91 Alex Messina, 'Uni Unveils Private Campus', *Age*, 9 July 1997, p. 3; Barry Sheehan, interview, 3 March 2007; Michael Crommelin, interview, 10 January 2007.

92 Christopher Richards, 'Uni Law Faculty May Go Private', *Age*, 11 August 1998, p. 5.

93 Michael Crommelin, interview, 10 January 2007.

94 Barry Sheehan, interview, 9 March 2007.

95 1998 Operational Performance Review, LFM, 4 June 1998, p. 5; Barry Sheehan, interview, 9 March 2007.

96 LFM, 25 August 1998, p. 2.

97 Building Project File, PFS.

98 Ian Munro, 'Building Blocks', *Age*, 13 June 1999, p. 4; Kerry Taylor, 'Designers Try Again in University Square Wrangle', *Age*, 24 November 1999, p. 13.

99 Michael Crommelin, interview, 10 January 2007.

100 Crommelin to Gilbert, 9 July 1999, Building Project File, PFS.

101 Gilbert to Potter and Crommelin, email, 29 April 1999, Building Project File, PFS.

102 Michael Crommelin, interview, 10 January 2007.

103 Christina Buckridge, 'Private Uni Will Merge With UoM', *UniNews*, vol. 14, no. 10, 13–27 June 2005; University of Melbourne, *Annual Budget*, 2002, p. 76.

104 Martin Vranken, interview, 10 January 2007.

105 'The transition': Matthew McKenna (2000–05), QR. 'Corporate lawyer factory': Nicholas Aberle (1997–2002), QR. 'Fantastic': anonymous student (1998–2003), QR. 'Pool on the top deck': Fiona Rose Rotstein (1999–2003), QR.

106 Review of the LLB, LFM, 8 December 2004, 5.3.

107 University of Melbourne, *Growing Esteem*.

108 Curriculum Architecture for the JD, LFM, 25 May 2006, 6.2.

109 Michael Crommelin, interview, 10 October 2006.

Conclusion

1 Sewell, *Legal Education*, p. 26.

2 John Date (1952–56), QR; Bailey, 'Legal Education in the United States', p. 299; 'Professor Bailey on Legal Education', *Farrago*, 8 May 1928, p. 1.

3 Report of Melbourne Faculty Bureau of Law, 1948, MLS, p. 9.

4 LFM, 3 July 1969, p. 150.

5 Anonymous students (1979–83 and 1963–67) and James Williams (1997–2002), QR.

6 Kerry Greenwood (1972–78), Leigh Mackay (1970–73) and anonymous student (1964–68), QR.

7 Anonymous students (1983–88 and 1996–2000), QR.

SELECT BIBLIOGRAPHY

Archives

The early records of the law school are found in the University of Melbourne Archives in three main series: Faculty of Law Correspondence 1932–77; Historical and Centenary Papers (UM 420); and Faculty of Law Minutes 1873–1981 (UM 76). Later faculty minutes are held by the University Secretary's Department and by the law school. Minute-books of the Law Students' Society are held by the Supreme Court Library (1893–1902) and the University of Melbourne Legal Resource Centre (1939–78). The Legal Resource Centre also holds early reports of the Articled Law Clerks' Society.

The other main archival sources for the law school's history are the records of the university's central administration, notably: Registrar's Correspondence (UM 312); the separate, smaller series, Registrar's Miscellaneous Correspondence (UM 447); Council Minutes (UM 174); and Professorial Board Minutes (UM 410).

Records of the law school building project have been drawn from the working files of the Policy Filing System in the office of the dean. The law school's small collection of historical records currently include papers donated by Harold Ford and Robert Evans, copies of lecture notes by Henry Chapman (from originals in the National Library of New Zealand), and some issues of *De Minimis*, the newsletter of the Law Students' Society.

Other significant archival sources include the papers of Sir Zelman Cowen (NLA), Sir David Derham (UMA), Sir Kenneth Bailey (NLA and NAA), Sir John Latham (NLA), Sir John Barry (NLA), the Law Institute of Victoria (UMA), William Hearn (UMA) and Sir William Harrison Moore (UMA). Minute-books of the Supreme Court judges' meetings, consulted by David Derham in the 1950s, have since been lost; if found, they may be an important source for the judges' decisions about admission to the profession.

Interviews

Peter Bailey

Michael Bryan

Zelman Cowen

Michael Crommelin

Daryl Dawson

Belinda Fehlberg

Harold Ford

Ann Graham

Mary Hiscock

Rosemary Hunter

Margaret Manion

Ian Marshman

Richard Mitchell

Susan Morgan

Kaye Nankervis

Andrew Neeson

David Penington

Julie Anne Quinn

Cheryl Saunders

Robin Sharwood

Barry Sheehan

Mal Smith

Arthur Turner

Martin Vranken

Louis Waller

Mark Weinberg

Oral history transcripts and recordings

Interview with Sir Kenneth Bailey, 1971–72, NLA

Interview with Yseult Bailey, 1973, NLA

Rosemary Balmford, video interview, MLS

Harold Luntz, video interview, MLS

Interview with Professor Jack Richardson, 1995–97, NLA

Interview with Professor Geoffrey Sawer, 1971–72, NLA

Robin Sharwood, video interview, MLS

Interview with Mark Weinberg, 1996–97, NLA

Interviews with four women law graduates by Samantha Kimpton, Oral History Workshop, University of Melbourne, 2000

Law student publications

De Minimis

Law Alternative Handbook

Law Counter-Handbook

Melbourne University Law Review

Purely Dicta

Res Judicatae

Summons

Other sources cited

A comprehensive bibliography of the history of the University of Melbourne by Juliet Flesch is found in the research links of the History of the University Unit at <www.history.unimelb.edu.au/huu>.

Abel, Richard L., *American Lawyers*, Oxford University Press, New York, 1989.

Anderson, D. S. and Vervoorn, A. E., *Access to Privilege: Patterns of Participation in Australian Post-Secondary Education*, Australian National University Press, Canberra, 1983.

Anderson, D. S. et al., *Students in Australian Higher Education: A Study of their Social Composition since the Abolition of Fees*, Australian Government Publishing Service, Canberra, 1980.

Anderson, Fay, *An Historian's Life: Max Crawford and the Politics of Academic Freedom*, Melbourne University Press, Melbourne, 2005.

Australasian Universities Law Schools Association, *Report No. 2: Legal Education in Australian Universities*, Butterworths, Sydney, 1977.

Australian Dictionary of Biography, Melbourne University Press, Melbourne, vols 1–16 and Supplement.

Australian Legal Education Yearbook, Centre for Legal Education, Sydney, 1996.

Ayres, Philip, *Owen Dixon*, Miegunyah Press, Melbourne, 2003.

Bailey, Kenneth, 'The University Law Course', *Law Institute Journal*, vol. 3, 1929, pp. 168–9.

Baker, G. Blaine, 'Legal Education in Upper Canada 1785–1889: The Law Society as Educator', in David H. Flaherty (ed.), *Essays in the History of Canadian Law*, vol. 2, University of Toronto Press, Toronto, 1983, pp. 49–142.

Baker, J. H., 'University College and Legal Education 1826–1976', *Current Legal Problems 1977*, pp. 1–13.

Balmford, Peter, 'The Pursuit of Excellence: Supreme Court Prizewinners', *Law Institute Journal*, vol. 58, 1984, pp. 226–55.

Bennett, J. M. (ed.), *A History of the New South Wales Bar*, Law Book Co., Sydney, 1969.

Blackshield, Tony, 'Lang, Diogenes and Macquarie Law School', *Law Society Journal*, vol. 27, 1989, pp. 45–50.

Blackshield, Tony, Coper, Michael and Williams, George (eds), *The Oxford Companion to the High Court of Australia*, Oxford University Press, Melbourne, 2001.

Blackstone, William, *Commentaries on the Laws of England*, 9th edn, 1783 (Garland Publishing, New York, 1978).

Bradshaw, F. Maxwell, 'The First Fifty Years', *Res Judicatae*, vol. 1, 1937, pp. 268–75.

Brett, Peter, 'North Borneo: Redrafting the Land Legislation of Brunei', *American Journal of Comparative Law*, vol. 6, 1957, pp. 565–77.

Bromby, E. H., 'The University Library', *University Review*, vol. 1, 1915, pp. 63–7.

Brooke, Christopher N. L., *A History of the University of Cambridge*, vol. 4, Cambridge University Press, Cambridge, 1992.

Brooks, Christopher W. and Lobban, Michael, 'Apprenticeship or Academy? The Idea of a Law University, 1830–1860', in Jonathan A. Bush and Alain Wijffels (eds), *Learning the Law: Teaching and the Transformation of Law in England 1150–1900*, Hambledon Press, London, 1999, p. 353.

Brooks, Christopher W., *Lawyers, Litigation, and English Society since 1450*, Hambledon Press, London, 1998.

Brown, W. Jethro, 'The American Law School', *Law Quarterly Review*, vol. 21, 1905, pp. 69–78.

Burdekin, Brian, 'Profile: H.A.J. Ford', *Summons*, 1967, pp. 7–8.

Burrage, Michael, *Revolution and the Making of the Contemporary Legal Profession: England, France, and the United States*, Oxford University Press, Oxford, 2006.

Butlin, S. J. and Schedvin, C. B., *War Economy 1942–1945 (Australia in the War of 1939–1945*, ser. 4, vol. IV), Australian War Memorial, Canberra, 1977.

Campbell, Ruth, *A History of the Melbourne Law School 1857 to 1973*, Faculty of Law, University of Melbourne, 1977.

Castles, Alex and Harris, Michael C., *Lawmakers and Wayward Whigs: Government and Law in South Australia 1836–1986*, Wakefield Press, Adelaide, 1987.

Castles, Alex, Ligertwood, Andrew and Kelly, Peter (eds), *Law on North Terrace, 1883–1983*, Faculty of Law, University of Adelaide, 1983.

Centre for Legal Education and Committee of Australian Law Deans, *The Cost of Legal Education in Australia: The Achievement of Quality Legal Education*, Centre for Legal Education, Sydney, 1994.

Chorley, Robert, 1st Baron Chorley, 'Edward Jenks, 1861–1939', *Journal of the Society of Public Teachers of Law*, new series, vol. 1, 1947, pp. 114–17.

Clayton, Alan, 'The Hearn Code: Its Place in the Nineteenth Century Codification Movement', LLB Research Project, University of Melbourne, 1987.

College of Law of England and Wales, History of the College, <www.college-of-law. co.uk> (viewed 25 May 2007).

Committee of Inquiry into Legal Education in New South Wales, *Legal Education in New South Wales* (Bowen Report), Government Printer, Sydney, 1979.

Committee on Legal Education, *Report* (Ormrod Report), Cmnd 4595, HMSO, London, 1971.

Committee on the Future of Tertiary Education in Australia, *Tertiary Education in Australia* (Martin Report), Government Printer, Canberra, 1964.

Commonwealth Schools Commission, *Australian Students and their Schools*, Schools Commission, Canberra, 1979.

Commonwealth Tertiary Education Commission, *Review of Efficiency and Effectiveness in Higher Education*, Australian Government Publishing Service, Canberra, 1986.

Connell, W. F. et al., *Australia's First: A History of the University of Sydney*, vol. 2, University of Sydney and Hale & Iremonger, Sydney, 1995.

Connell, W. F., *Reshaping Australian Education 1960–1985*, Australian Council for Educational Research, Melbourne, 1993.

Consultative Group on Research and Education in Law, *Law and Learning: Report to the Social Sciences and Humanities Research Council of Canada* (Arthurs Report), Social Sciences and Humanities Research Council of Canada, Ottawa, 1983.

Cowen, Zelman, 'Legal Education at the Cross-Roads', *Law Institute Journal*, vol. 31, 1957, pp. 213–16.

——, 'Professor Sir George Whitecross Paton', *University of Melbourne Gazette*, vol. 24, no. 2, April 1968, pp. 1–2.

——, *A Public Life: The Memoirs of Sir Zelman Cowen*, Miegunyah Press, Melbourne, 2006.

Cownie, Fiona, *Legal Academics: Culture and Identities*, Hart Publishing, Oxford, 2004.

Crozier, Michael, 'Political Legacies: Australian Political Studies and the University of Melbourne', *Melbourne Journal of Politics*, vol. 29, 2003, pp. 8–23.

De Serville, Paul, *Pounds and Pedigrees: The Upper Class in Victoria 1850–80*, Oxford University Press, Melbourne, 1991.

Dean, Arthur, *A Multitude of Counsellors: A History of the Bar of Victoria*, Cheshire, Melbourne, 1968.

Derham, David, 'Legal Education: A Challenge to the Profession', *Australian Law Journal*, vol. 43, 1969, pp. 530–49.

Derham, David P., Maher, F.K.H. and Waller, Louis, *Cases and Materials on the Legal Process*, Law Book Co., Sydney, 1966.

Dicey, A.V., *Introduction to the Study of the Law of the Constitution*, 4th edn, Macmillan, London, 1893.

Dixon, Marion, *Looking Back: A Short History of the UWA Law School, 1927–1992*, University of Western Australia, Perth, 1992.

——, *Thirty Up: The Story of the UNSW Law School, 1971–2001*, UNSW Law School, Sydney, 2001.

Douglas, Heather, 'The Participation of Indigenous Australians in Legal Education 1991–2001', *University of New South Wales Law Journal*, vol. 24, 2001, pp. 485–514.

Dow, Kwong Lee, Jones, Lorraine D. and Osman, Liesl M., 'The Social Composition of Students Entering the University of Melbourne in 1969 and 1970', *Melbourne Studies in Education 1972*, pp. 77–95.

Edgeloe, Victor, 'The Adelaide Law School 1883–1983', *Adelaide Law Review*, vol. 9, 1983, pp. 1–42.

Elliott, Ivo, *The Balliol College Register, 1833–1933*, 2nd edn, Oxford University Press, Oxford, 1934.

'Equity', 'Women and The Law Students' Society', *Melbourne University Magazine*, vol. 7, 1913, pp. 143–5.

Finnane, Mark (ed.), *The Difficulties of My Position: The Diaries of Prison Governor John Buckley Castieau 1855–1884*, National Library of Australia, Canberra, 2004.

Finnane, Mark, 'The ABC of Criminology: Anita Muhl, J.V. Barry, Norval Morris and the Making of a Discipline in Australia', *British Journal of Criminology*, vol. 46, 2006, pp. 399–422.

Fitzhardinge, L. F., *The Little Digger, 1914–1952 (William Morris Hughes: A Political Biography*, vol. 2), Angus & Robertson, Sydney, 1979.

Forbes, J.R.S., *The Divided Legal Profession in Australia: History, Rationalisation and Rationale*, Law Book Co., Sydney, 1979.

Ford, H.A.J., Austin, R. P. and Ramsay, I. M., *Ford's Principles of Corporations Law*, 8th edn, Butterworths, Sydney, 1997.

Forde, John Leonard, *The Story of the Bar of Victoria*, Whitcombe and Tombs, Melbourne, n.d.

Foster, Stephen and Varghese, Margaret, *The Making of the Australian National University 1946–96*, Allen & Unwin, Sydney, 1996.

Friedmann, Wolfgang, 'A Comparative Law Course at Melbourne University', *Journal of the Society of Public Teachers of Law*, new series, vol. 1, 1949, pp. 274–82.

——, 'On Leaving Melbourne', *Melbourne Graduate*, vol. 1, 1950, pp. 63–6.

Gibbney, H. J. and Smith, Ann G., *A Biographical Register 1788–1939: Notes from the Name Index of the Australian Dictionary of Biography*, Australian Dictionary of Biography, Canberra, 1987.

Girvin, Stephen D., 'Nineteenth-Century Reforms in Scottish Legal Education: The Universities and the Bar', *Journal of Legal History*, vol. 14, 1993, pp. 127–41.

Golding, Elizabeth, *Sylliott-Hill and Richard Annesley Billing, Victorian Barrister, Q.C. and Judge, His Home in Melbourne*, The Author, Melbourne, 1997–2000.

Goldring, John and Vignaendra, Sumitra, *A Social Profile of New Law Students in the Australian Capital Territory, New South Wales and Victoria*, Law Foundation of New South Wales, Sydney, 1997.

Goldring, John, 'An Updated Social Profile of Students Entering Law Courses', in Dennis Pearce, Enid Campbell and Don Harding, *Australian Law Schools: A Discipline Assessment for the Commonwealth Tertiary Education Commission*, Australian Government Publishing Service, Canberra, 1987, vol. 3, app. 4.

Goodman, George, *The Church in Victoria during the Episcopate of the Right Reverend Charles Perry*, Seeley, London, 1892.

Graveson, R. H., 'A Text-Book of Jurisprudence', Modern Law Review, vol. 10, 1947, pp. 80–3.

Graycar, Regina and Morgan, Jenny, The Hidden Gender of Law, 1st edn, Federation Press, Sydney, 1990.

Greening, Hulbert, 'Presidential Address', Law Institute Journal, vol. 36, 1962, pp. 145–9.

Greig, G. Flos, 'The Law as a Profession for Women', Commonwealth Law Review, vol. 6, 1909, pp. 145–54.

Griswold, E. N., 'Observations on Legal Education in Australia', Journal of Legal Education, vol. 5, 1952, pp. 139–54.

Hanbury, H. G., 'A Text-Book of Jurisprudence', Law Quarterly Review, vol. 63, 1947, pp. 115–21.

Hardie Boys, Michael, 'Reflections on the Last Fifty Years of the Law and Law School', Victoria University of Wellington Law Review, vol. 31, 2000, pp. 37–45.

Hearn, William, The Government of England: Its Structure and its Development, 2nd edn, Robertson, Melbourne, 1886.

Heydon, Dyson, 'Assessment of Damages for Personal Injury and Death', Sydney Law Review, vol. 25, 2003, pp. 409–12.

Higher Education: A Policy Statement, Australian Government Publishing Service, Canberra, 1988.

Hill, Vivian, 'Biography of Miroslav Schimana', Geelong Lawyers' Collection, Deakin University Library, <www.deakin.edu.au/library/geelonglawyers> (viewed 25 May 2007).

Hill, Vivian, 'Henry Isaac Crawcour', Geelong Lawyers' Collection, Deakin University Library, <www.deakin.edu.au/library/geelonglawyers> (viewed 25 May 2007).

'Historical Documents', Australian Journal of Law and Society, vol. 5, 1988–89, pp. 53–132.

Hogan, Daire, The Legal Profession in Ireland 1789–1922, Incorporated Law Society of Ireland, Dublin, 1986.

Holdsworth, William, A History of English Law, Methuen: Sweet and Maxwell, London, 1964–72.

Ireland, John, 'The Victorian Land Act of 1862 Revisited', Victorian Historical Journal, vol. 65, 1994, pp. 130–44.

Jenks, Edward, Legal Fore-Words: A Lecture Introductory to the Session of 1890, Delivered before the Law School of the University of Melbourne, Ford & Son, Melbourne, 1890.

——, Outline of a Suggested Course of Reading on the Public Law of Victoria, Edgerton and Moore, Melbourne, 1889.

——, The Government of Victoria (Australia), new issue, Robertson, Melbourne, 1897.

——, The History of the Doctrine of Consideration in English Law, Clay, London, 1892.

Keyes, Mary and Johnstone, Richard, 'Changing Legal Education: Rhetoric, Reality, and Prospects for the Future', *Sydney Law Review*, vol. 26, 2004, pp. 537–64.

La Nauze, J. A., *Political Economy in Australia: Historical Studies*, Melbourne University Press, Melbourne, 1949.

Lavery, Daniel, 'The Participation of Indigenous Australians in Legal Education', *Legal Education Review*, vol. 4, 1993, pp. 177–200.

'Law Reform at Home and Abroad', *Discovery: University of Melbourne*, no. 2, 1957, pp. 88–92.

Law Society of England and Wales, Ways to Qualify as a Solicitor, <www.lawsociety. org.uk> (viewed 25 May 2007).

'The Law Students' Society in the Nineties', *Law Institute Journal*, vol. 2, 1928, p. 166.

Law Students' Society of Victoria, 'Report on Legal Education', *Res Judicatae*, vol. 2, 1940, pp. 99–108.

Lawson, F. H., *The Oxford Law School 1850–1965*, Oxford University Press, Oxford, 1968.

Levack, Brian P., 'Law', in Nicholas Tyacke (ed.), *The History of the University of Oxford*, vol. 4, Oxford University Press, Oxford, 1997, pp. 559–68.

'LLB', 'The Inadequacy of the Law School', *Law Institute Journal*, vol. 2, 1928, pp. 32, 43.

Luntz, Harold, *Assessment of Damages for Personal Injury and Death*, 1st edn, Butterworths, Sydney, 1974.

Luntz, Harold, Hambly, David and Hayes, Robert, *Torts: Cases and Commentary*, 1st edn, Butterworths, Sydney, 1980.

McInnis, Craig and Marginson, Simon, *Australian Law Schools after the 1987 Pearce Report*, Australian Government Publishing Service, Canberra, 1994.

Mackinolty, John and Mackinolty, Judy (eds), *A Century Down Town: Sydney University Law School's First Hundred Years*, University of Sydney Law School, Sydney, 1991.

Maclean, Chris, 'And All the Time He was Learning from Us', *Law Institute Journal*, vol. 59, 1985, pp. 76–7.

McPhee, Peter, *Pansy: A Life of Roy Douglas Wright*, Melbourne University Press, Melbourne, 1999.

McQueen, Rob, 'Together We Fall, Divided We Stand: The Victorian Legal Profession in Crisis 1890–1940', in W. Wesley Pue and David Sugarman (eds), *Lawyers and Vampires: Cultural Histories of Legal Professions*, Hart Publishing, Oxford 2003, pp. 293–328.

McTaggart, B. B., Smith, M.D.H. and Wortley, R. E., 'Small Group Teaching', *Summons*, 1971, pp. 8–9.

Marginson, Simon and Considine, Mark, *The Enterprise University: Power, Governance and Reinvention in Australia*, Cambridge University Press, Melbourne, 2000.

Marginson, Simon, *Monash: Remaking the University*, Allen & Unwin, Sydney, 2000.

Martin, Linda, 'From Apprenticeship to Law School: A Social History of Legal Education in Nineteenth Century New South Wales', *University of New South Wales Law Journal*, vol. 9, no. 2, 1986, pp. 111–43.

Martin, A. W., *Robert Menzies: A Life*, Melbourne University Press, Melbourne, 1993–99.

Mason, Tim, 'A History of De Minimis, Published by Melbourne University Law Students Society 1948–1976', Legal History essay, Melbourne Law School, 1981.

Mathews, Jane H., 'The Changing Profile of Women in the Law', *Australian Law Journal*, vol. 56, 1982, pp. 634–42.

Megarry, R. E., '*Elements of Drafting*', *Law Quarterly Review*, vol. 68, 1947, pp. 380–1.

Middleton, R. D., *Dr Routh*, Oxford University Press, Oxford, 1938.

Moore, Gregory C. G., 'A Biographical Sketch of William Edward Hearn (1826–1888): A Slightly "Irish" Perspective', paper presented to the Australian Conference of Economists, Melbourne, September 2005.

——, 'Selling Plutology: Correspondence relating to the Failure of Australia's First Economics Text', *History of Economics Review*, no. 35, Winter 2002, pp. 63–77.

Moore, W. Harrison, *The Constitution of the Commonwealth of Australia*, 2nd edn, 1910 (Legal Books, Sydney, 1997).

——, 'Legal Education in the United States', *Journal of the Society of Comparative Legislation*, 2nd series, vol. 13, 1913, pp. 207–12.

Mossman, Mary Jane, *The First Women Lawyers*, Hart Publishing, Oxford, 2006.

Nicholas, Barry, 'Jurisprudence', in M. G. Brock and M. C. Curthoys (eds), *The History of the University of Oxford*, vol. 7, Oxford University Press, Oxford, 2000, pp. 385–96.

O'Brien, F. C., 'The Victorian Chief Justice's Law Reform Committee', *Melbourne University Law Review*, vol. 8, 1972, pp. 440–83.

Parnaby, Owen, *Queen's College, University of Melbourne: A Centenary History*, Melbourne University Press, Melbourne, 1990.

Payne, Douglas, 'University Education for Lawyers: The Case for a Prerequisite Year of Non-Legal Studies before Entry to Law School', in Australian Law Council Foundation, *Legal Education in Australia: Proceedings of National Conference, Sydney, August 15–20, 1976*, Australian Law Council Foundation, Melbourne, 1978, vol. 1, pp. 22–44.

Pearce, Dennis, Campbell, Enid and Harding, Don, *Australian Law Schools: A Discipline Assessment for the Commonwealth Tertiary Education Commission*, Australian Government Publishing Service, Canberra, 1987.

Pedrick, Willard H., 'A Learned Profession?', *Melbourne University Law Review*, vol. 4, 1963, pp. 167–79.

Perkins, Christine, 'Blood and Hope: Samuel Pisar's Triumph of the Spirit', *Harvard Law Bulletin*, Fall 2005, p. 40.

Poynter, John and Rasmussen, Carolyn, *A Place Apart: The University of Melbourne: Decades of Challenge*, Melbourne University Press, Melbourne, 1996.

Priestley, Raymond E., *The Diary of a Vice-Chancellor: University of Melbourne 1935– 1938*, Melbourne University Press, Melbourne, 2002.

Pue, W. Wesley, *Law School: The Story of Legal Education in British Columbia*, Faculty of Law, University of British Columbia, Vancouver, 1995.

'Quo Vadit', 'Women of the World. Should they be Encouraged?', *Melbourne University Magazine*, vol. 7, 1913, pp. 93–5.

Rasmussen, Carolyn, *Increasing Momentum: Engineering at the University of Melbourne 1861–2004*, Melbourne University Press, Melbourne, 2004.

'Res Judicatae', *Res Judicatae*, vol. 1, 1935, p. v.

Ricketson, Sam, 'The Lawyers', in Stuart Macintyre (ed.), *Ormond College Centenary Essays*, Melbourne University Press, Melbourne, 1984, pp. 136–52.

'RMIT Course to be Phased Out', *Law Institute Journal*, vol. 52, 1978, p. 365.

Robertson, J. Steele, 'The University of Melbourne', *Centennial Magazine*, vol. 1, 1888, pp. 143–54.

Royal Commission on Law Reform, *Report*, VPLA, 1899–1900, vol. 3, no. 15.

Royal Commission on the University of Melbourne, *Final Report*, VPLA, 1904, vol. 2, no. 13.

Royal Commission on the University of Melbourne, *Minutes of Evidence*, VPLA, 1903, 2nd sess., vol. 2, no. 20.

Sawer, Geoffrey, 'Legal Education in the United States', *University of Western Australia Annual Law Review*, vol. 1, 1948–50, pp. 398–403.

Searby, Peter, *A History of the University of Cambridge*, vol. 3, Cambridge University Press, Cambridge, 1997.

Select Committee on Legal Education, *Report*, House of Commons Parliamentary Papers, 1846, vol. 10, no. 686.

Selleck, Richard, 'Empires and Empiricism: The Teaching of History at the University of Melbourne, 1855–1936', in Fay Anderson and Stuart Macintyre (eds), *The Life of the Past: The Discipline of History at the University of Melbourne, 1855–2005*, Department of History, University of Melbourne, 2006, pp. 3–38.

——, *The Shop: The University of Melbourne, 1850–1939*, Melbourne University Press, Melbourne, 2003.

Serle, Geoffrey, 'The Victorian Legislative Council, 1856–1950', in J. J. Eastwood and F. B. Smith (eds), *Historical Studies Australia and New Zealand: Selected Articles*, Melbourne University Press, Melbourne, 1964, pp. 127–51.

——, *Sir John Medley: A Memoir*, Melbourne University Press, Melbourne, 1993.

——, *The Golden Age: A History of the Colony of Victoria, 1851–1861*, Melbourne University Press, Melbourne, 1977.

Sewell, Richard Clarke, *Gesta Stephani, Regis Anglorum*, English Historical Society, London, 1846.

——, *Legal Education. An Inaugural Lecture on the Study of the Law, Delivered before the Chancellor and Students of the University of Melbourne*, Robertson, Melbourne, 1857.

——, *The Speech of R. C. Sewell, Esq., LL.D., Delivered at Melbourne on 1st July, 1859, In Defence of George Chamberlain, and William Armstrong, Charged with Shooting, with Intent to Murder, William Green, Mounted Constable, at Omeo*, Anderson, Melbourne, n.d.

Sharwood, Robin, 'A Short History of the Law School', *Faculty of Law Handbook*, University of Melbourne, 1963.

——, 'The Training of Lawyers Outside Universities', in Australian Law Council Foundation, *Legal Education in Australia: Proceedings of National Conference, Sydney, August 15–20, 1976*, Australian Law Council Foundation, Melbourne, 1978, vol. 1, pp. 307–41.

Shearer, Ivan A., 'The Teaching of International Law in Australian Law Schools', *Adelaide Law Review*, vol. 9, 1983, pp. 61–78.

Sheppard, Steve, 'Casebooks, Commentaries, and Curmudgeons: An Introductory History of Law in the Lecture Hall', *Iowa Law Review*, vol. 82, 1997, pp. 547–644.

Smyth, Russell, 'Other Than "Accepted Sources of Law"? A Quantitative Study of Secondary Source Citations in the High Court', *University of New South Wales Law Journal*, vol. 22, 1999, pp. 19–59.

Spiller, Peter, *The Chapman Legal Family*, Victoria University Press, Wellington, 1992.

Stevens, Robert, *Law School: Legal Education in America from the 1850s to the 1980s*, University of North Carolina Press, Chapel Hill, 1983.

Strong, Robert, 'Melbourne University Legal Referral Service', *Summons*, 1972, p. 31.

Sykes, E. I., 'Sykes on Sykes: Reflections of a Law Teacher', *Summons*, 1975, pp. 44–8.

Tarlo, Hyman, 'Law Schools and Law Teachers in Australia: 1946–1974', *University of Queensland Law Journal*, vol. 9, 1975, pp. 26–38.

Thomis, Malcolm I., *A Place of Light and Learning: The University of Queensland's First Seventy-Five Years*, University of Queensland Press, Brisbane, 1985.

Townsley, W. A., 'The Electoral System and the Constituencies', in F. C. Green (ed.), *A Century of Responsible Government*, Government Printer, Hobart, 1956, pp. 57–112.

Turney, Clifford, Bygott, Ursula and Chippendale, Peter, *Australia's First: A History of the University of Sydney*, vol. 1, University of Sydney and Hale & Iremonger, 1991.

'The University Law Course', *Law Institute Journal*, vol. 1, 1927, p. 73.

University of Melbourne, *Earning Esteem: The University of Melbourne Strategic Plan 1997–2001*, University of Melbourne, 1996.

——, *Growing Esteem: The University of Melbourne Strategic Plan*, University of Melbourne, 2006.

——, *Looking to the Future: The Strategic Plan for the University of Melbourne*, University of Melbourne, 1988.

Vamplew, Wray, *Australians: Historical Statistics*, Fairfax, Syme & Weldon Associates, 1987.

Weisbrot, David, *Australian Lawyers*, Longman Cheshire, Melbourne, 1990.

——, 'Recent Statistical Trends in Legal Education', *Legal Education Review*, vol. 2, 1990, pp. 219–51.

Wilken, David, 'Conversation with Sir David Derham: Part I', *Law Institute Journal*, vol. 56, 1982, pp. 1024–30.

——, 'Goodbye Mr Chips: Conversation with Sir George Paton', *Law Institute Journal*, vol. 58, 1984, pp. 352–9.

——, 'The Honourable T. W. Smith, Q.C.', *Law Institute Journal*, vol. 57, 1983, pp. 654–60, 811–19.

Winterton, George, 'Introduction', in W. Harrison Moore, *The Constitution of the Commonwealth of Australia*, Legal Books, Sydney, 1997, pp. v–lvii.

Woodward, Edward, *One Brief Interval: A Memoir*, Miegunyah Press, Melbourne, 2005.

Wright, Raymond, *A People's Counsel: A History of the Parliament of Victoria 1856–1990*, Oxford University Press, Melbourne, 1992.

Zines, Leslie, 'The Growth of Australian Nationhood and its Effect on the Powers of the Commonwealth', in Leslie Zines (ed.), *Commentaries on the Australian Constitution*, Butterworths, Sydney, 1977, pp. 1–49.

INDEX